D1393721

Foreign Influences on Medieval English

STUDIES IN ENGLISH MEDIEVAL LANGUAGE AND LITERATURE

Edited by Jacek Fisiak

Vol. 28

PETER LANG

Frankfurt am Main · Berlin · Bern · Bruxelles · New York · Oxford · Wien

Jacek Fisiak / Magdalena Bator
(eds.)

Foreign Influences on Medieval English

PETER LANG
Internationaler Verlag der Wissenschaften

Bibliographic Information published by the Deutsche Nationalbibliothek
The Deutsche Nationalbibliothek lists this publication in the Deutsche Nationalbibliografie; detailed bibliographic data is available in the internet at http://dnb.d-nb.de.

Cover design:
Olaf Glöckler, Atelier Platen, Friedberg

Typesetting by motivex.

ISSN 1436-7521
ISBN 978-3-631-61424-2
© Peter Lang GmbH
Internationaler Verlag der Wissenschaften
Frankfurt am Main 2011
All rights reserved.

www.peterlang.de

Contents

Preface

The present volume is a selection of papers presented at the International Conference on Foreign Influences on Medieval English held in Warsaw on 12-13 December 2009 and organized by the School of English at the Warsaw Division of the Academy of Management in Łódź (Wyższa Szkoła Przedsiębiorczości i Zarządzania). The Conference was attended by 60 scholars from Poland, USA, UK, Germany, Austria, Japan, Finland, Italy, Ukraine and Slovenia. 41 papers were delivered. They cover a wide range of topics concerning the area of language contact in Old and Middle English from orthography, morphology and syntax to word semantics and onomastics.

Both the conference and the present volume have demonstrated the need for constant reviewing of issues which often seem to have been solved. Different views on the same topic could be heard during proceedings and can be found in contributions to this volume. Intensive research conducted in the field of language contact over the last twenty years has yielded new insights and fresh data which fully justifies revisions in established views and their dissemination.

The aim of the conference was not to look for definite solutions in the area of linguistic borrowing but to look at some old and new problems and attempt new formulations which may lead to some improvements. If this has been accomplished in some way, the goal of the conference has been reached. Whether it is the case we leave to our readers to judge.

It is our pleasure and duty to acknowledge the efficiency and dedication of the colleagues who have helped with numerous administrative problems and contributed to the success of the conference, in particular, Mrs. Ilona Banasiak-Ryba, M.A., Dr Marta Sylwanowicz, Dr Karolina Iwan and Dr Kinga Sądej-Sobolewska.

Last but not least, our words of thanks go to the Dean of the Warsaw Division of the Academy of Management Dr Zdzisław Szymański and the authorities of the Academy for providing first-class facilities and generous financial support.

Jacek Fisiak
Magdalena Bator

Warsaw, July 2010

New prepositions and subordinating conjunctions of Romance origin in Middle English

Rafał Molencki, University of Silesia, Katowice

ABSTRACT

This article is concerned with the new Romance prepositions and conjuctions that arose in late Middle English as a result of language contact situation. Bilingual Anglo-Norman and Middle English speakers often code-switched between the languages they knew, so it is not surprising that some grammatical items were used in both. The evidence from the Anglo-Norman corpus shows that some of the new function words developed only in Anglo-French, as no cognate forms are recorded in the continental dialects of medieval French. Most of the new items came into being through grammaticalization and/or loan translation, sometimes also through morphological hybridization.

KEYWORDS: bilingualism; conjunction; grammaticalization; loan translation; preposition

1. Introduction

Prepositions and conjunctions are high frequency grammatical items that belong to the closed system and as such are not prone to quick changes. However, Middle English was the time of great and comprehensive modifications in the language on all its levels so it should not be surprising that many changes affected the inventory of prepositions and conjunctions, as well. The external factors here were foreign influences often resulting in common bilingualism (cf. Short 1980) and the development of abstract and/or argumentative writing that required greater precision of expression and new devices for rendering condition, cause, concession and contrast. The intralinguistic causes were increasing hypotactic clause combining and the need for prepositions and conjunctions to obtain distinct morphological and phonetic properties, thus making them less polyfunctional and less semantically opaque (cf. Kortmann 1997, Rissanen 2007).

In this article we will pay special attention to foreign, predominantly French influences on the system of Middle English prepositions and conjunctions. The language data come from several digitalized databases such as *Middle English dictionary*, *Middle English compendium*, *Helsinki corpus*, *Oxford English dictionary* and the *Anglo-Norman hub*. The example sources are marked according to the practices used by their compilers. The availability of the Anglo-Norman digitalized corpora has given scholars new opportunities of tracing the parallel developments in Anglo-Norman and Middle English syntax. It also sheds new light on the origin and evolution of new function words in medieval English.

New prepositions and conjunctions appeared in Middle English from both native and foreign sources. The native new items may have arisen through the extension of function and/or grammaticalization of the existing words, e.g., *before, after, while, for* (cf. Traugott 1989, Molencki 2005, 2007b). Some of them were used in non-West Saxon dialects of Old English, e.g., *on, til*. Finally Old English items underwent far reaching phonetic and/or morphological transformations, e.g., *siþþan > since, ealswa > as* (cf. Molencki 2003, 2007a)

Foreign elements were borrowed first from Old Norse, e.g., *til* (also used in Anglian), *fro, þou3*), later from Romance (Anglo-Norman, Old French, Latin), e.g., *during, purveyed/provided, save, except, maugre, (a)round*. We also find some Anglo-Norse and Anglo-Romance hybrids, e.g., *until, tilinto, outtaken, although, because* and loan translations (calques), e.g., *al be it, un-less*.

As for their morphological complexity we have single morpheme words (*til, þou3*) and formations created through affixation (*unless, since*). New conjunctions were often followed by subordinating particles *þe, þat*. There were also complex phrases (e.g., *for/after þis (þat)*) functioning as prepositions and conjuctions, which later were often univerbated: *by the cause that > because, all though > although, all be it > albeit, þy læs þe > lest, on rounde > around*. Many arose as a result of grammaticalization either from nouns, e.g., *because, while* or from verbs (especially participles), e.g., *during, according to, except, outtaken*.

Some Old English forms disappeared altogether, e.g., *mid, ymb, oþ, oþþæt*, others were replaced by foreign elements, e.g., *þeah* gave way to Norse *though*[1], hybrid *because* ousted *for þi þat*. Other replacements included *siþþan* (*sithen /sithenes > since*),whose role in one of the senses was taken over by *after* and Old English conditional conjunctions *butan* equivalent to later *unless*.

The Norse influence is first of all seen in the adoption of both spatial and temporal prepositions *til* and *fro*, as in (1). These words also became conjunctions in very early Middle English (2). Another interesting development was the grammaticalization of the preposition *outaken* 'except' derived from the past participle of the phrasal verb *out-take/take-out* of Norse origin, exemplified in (3).

(1)   ?c1200 *Orm.*(Jun 1) ded.208: Hiss hall3he sawle stah **Fra** rode dun **till** helle.

(2)   a1131 *Peterb.Chron.* an.1127: **Fram þat** he þider com, eall þat lented tid on an to Eastren.

---

1   We have a very interesting example in the late annals of the *Peterborough chronicle*, where in the First Continuation the scribe still used the Old English form while later scribes came to use the Norse loanword:

a1121 *Peterb.Chron.*(LdMisc 636) an.1120: An se arcebiscop Turstein of Eoferwic wearð þurh þone papan wið þone cyng acordad 7 his biscoprices onfeng, **þeah** hit þam arcebiscop of Cantwarabyrig swyðe un gewille wære?

a1160 *Peterb.Chron.*(LdMisc 636) an.1135: Hi to gædere comen & wurðe sæhte, **þoþ** it litel for stode.

?a1160 *Peterb.Chron.* an.1137: Þe king Stephne ...nam...hise neues, 7 dide ælle in prisun **til** hi iafen up here castles.

(3)   (c1384) *WBible(1)* Mat.5.32: Euery man that shal leeue his wyf, **outaken** cause of fornicacioun, he makith hire do lecherie.

2. Anglo-French and Middle English bilingualism

The traditionally accepted opinion is that French used in England in the thirteenth, and especially the fourteenth century was a language in the state of decline (cf. Price 1984, Kibbee 1991). But more recently this view has been rejected, e.g., Trotter (2003) noted that the differences between Anglo-Norman and Central French could be compared to any differences between modern dialects. His interpretation is that Anglo-Norman simply formed a branch of the medieval French dialect continuum. Studies of pronoun syntax and word order by Ingham (2006) seem to offer support for the hypothesis. Ingham (2009) observed that "syntactically speaking, as late as the mid-C14 AN [Anglo-Norman] was quite clearly not a deviant form of French".

Besides, late medieval England and France were characterized by the enduring language contact. In that kind of linguistic situation it is very probable that there was an important and influential group of people, especially in the Chancery and the royal court in London, who were perfectly bilingual speakers (and writers!) of Anglo-Norman and Middle English. There is some evidence of common code switching at the time (cf. Rothwell 1996, Schendl 1996, 2000). It is obvious that under the circumstances the two languages influenced each other. In the fourteenth and fifteenth centuries English borrowed numerous conjunctions and prepositions from French. But what is interesting here is the fact that some of these novel grammatical words were not found outside England, in Central French, which means that they must have arisen among the English bilinguals. Parallel developments may have strengthened the processes of grammaticalizing new items in both languages.

3. Prepositions and conjunction of French origin

3.1 Deverbal

Let us now take a closer look at some of the new items. Several participles, both active and passive, of French verbs have turned into quasi-prepositions. The process may have begun in French and bilingual speakers copied the habit in their English, using exactly the same verbs. However, we cannot be certain whether this decategorialization (very characteristic of grammaticalization) occurred in both languages independently. It is more likely that the process began in French, as most of the Anglo-Norman instances are slightly older than their Middle English parallels, but at the same time the new English usage may have strengthened and accelerated the grammaticalization of the new prepositions and conjunctions in the variety of French spoken then in England.

Thus the present participle of the verb *accord(er)* developed into a complex preposition *accordant a/according to*. In (4) the participle still retains its original deverbal sense while in (5) it appears to have performed the function of a complex preposition already, similarly to its Anglo-Norman cognate in (6):

(4)   ?a1425(c1380) Chaucer *Bo* .3.pr.11.156: Every thing kepeth thilke that is **accordynge** and propre to hym.
       (a1398) Trev. *Barth* .12a/b: Material corrupcioun may in no wise be **acordinge** to him [angels].

(5)   a1400 *Lanfranc* 124.7: For in mannys bodi a medicyn schal not be preued which þat is not **acordynge** to resoun.
       (a1402) Trev. *Dial.MC* 32/3: Hit semiþ **acordyng** to þe gospel.

(6)   e pus conta **acordant** a son bref *YBB* 30-31
       lour ceyntures & lienge **accordant** a lour estat *Rot Parl*1 ii 279

The Middle English verb *duren* 'last' as in (7) was obviously derived from Anglo-Norman *durer*, exemplified in (8):

(7)   c1250 *Body & S.(4)* 30b: So longe sa it [a wind] **dures** Þe casteles sulen dun þrouen.
       c1300 Lay. *Brut* (Otho) 26708: Al þane day long, **durede** þat fiht strong
       (a1387) Trev.*Higd.* 4.115: Þe fuyre þat hadde **i-dured** þre score 3ere and ten.

(8)   Mes la peine **durra** sans fin *Jos* 360
       eit lettres de sauvegarde q'il demande au **durer** par troys aunz *Rot Parl*2

Its present participle *durant(e)* came to be used as a preposition (*during, as long as [...] lasts*), which appears to have been specifically Anglo-Norman development, as in (9). The Continental French dialects grammaticalized the present participle of a different verb *pendre* into the equivalent preposition *pendant* still used in Modern French. In late Middle English we find the departicipial preposition with both the conservative ending *-and* and the novel *-ing* reflecting the rich dialectal variation. Occasionally *during* was postpositional.

(9)   **duraunt** matrimoigne remaint la accioun de dowarie BRITT ii 264
       durante sa vie *Rot Scot* i 800

(10) (a1387) Trev.*Higd*.5.125: **Durynge** þat persecucioun Silvester...fli3 out of þe citee.

(c1410) York *MGame* 16: Þei bene heyest in grece in August alle the moneth **duryng**.

?a1425(?a1350) Castleford *Chron.* 20920: He segede it suo **durand** four woukes.

c1450(?a1400) *Wars Alex.* 1188: Neuer Persy to paire...In damaging of Darius **durand** his lyfe.

The partiples of the French verb *considerer* (active *considerant* and passive *consideree(s)*) are often found in the Anglo-Norman corpus with and without grammatical agreement in the quasi-prepositional function equivalent to *in view of (the fact that)*, *taking into account* (11). Parallel uses are found in Middle English (12):

(11) **considerant** la povertee de dit chapellein_ *Lett & Pet* 94.16

Considerantz [...] qe le dit suppliant eit la garde *Northumb* 177

s'il semble a mes executours que ce pourra estre fait **consideree** la quantitee de mes biens *Test Ebor* i 225

Considerees les grauntes courtoises et sufferances les queux ...il m'a ...monstrez *Reg Chich* ii 64

(12) (c1395) Chaucer *CT.Sq.* F.675: I preise wel thy wit...**considerynge** thy youthe.

(c1390) Chaucer *CT.Mel.* B.3039: That thynketh me muchel agayn resoun...**considered** the power that they han yeuen yow.

(a1470) Malory *Wks.* 559/24: Ye ar no valyaunte knyght to aske batayle of me, **consyderynge** my grete travayle.

The conditional connectives *provided/providing (that)* are apparently clear examples of grammaticalization down the verb-to-conjunction cline (cf. Álvarez and Cruz 2003). There are, however, certain problems with such simple explanation. The first instances of the quasi-conjunction uses appear in the 1420s and are contemporary with the first English occurrences of the verb *provide*, the more Latinate counterpart of its earlier Romance doublet *purvey*, which came into English c1300. The Central French form was *porvoir* while its Norman cognate was *porveir* (first attested c1180 in the Anglo-Norman dialect). Both in Old French and Middle English the verb developed multiple senses, one of which was 'to consider', 'to make provision'. Its French passive participial form *pourvu* came to be combined with the conjunction *que* resulting in the formation of the grammaticalized conjunction phrase in the fourteenth century that developed both temporal (=*dès lors que, du moment que*) and conditional (=*en cas que, à condition que*) uses. Below is an example of the Anglo-Norman conjunction in amalgamation with the subordinating particle *que* (*pourvehuez*) in a wider context:

(13)   Johan etc. a nostre cher et bien ame Robert de Morton nostre 1315
        receyvour en le counte d'Everwyk saluz. Come nostre bien ame F. 191 a
        Johan de Ryther soit tenuz et obligez de paier a nous vint livres a le fest de
        Penticost ore prochein avenir, et ensi d'an en an tanque il avéra paiez
        quatrevint livres, nepurquant nous ly eions grantez et ly voulons estre
        respitez de la dit paiement des vint livres susdites tanque a le fest de
        Penticost adonqes proschein avenir après le fest de Penticost susdit, c'est
        un an ; si voulons et vous mandons que de touz maneres de demandes a ly
        faire pur le paie-ment sudit, vous surseez en le mesne temps, **pourvehuez**
        toutes voies que adonqes il paie les vint livres susdites, et de illoeques
        GAUNT1 ii 181.

It is very likely that the first Middle English uses of the conjunction derived from
both doublets were calqued among bilingual Anglo-Norman speakers in the
Chancery milieu at the turn of the 15th c., e.g.:

(14)   (1398) in *Rymer's Foedera (1709-10)* 8.61: The Conservatours..sal be
        haldin to do...in the manere forsaid of bath the Partize; **purvait that**
        Heritages on bathe the Syds stand in the fourme and vertue as is compris'd
        within the Trewes.
        (1448) *Doc.*in Sundby *Dial.Wor.*(Eg Charter 608) 255: The kyng...shal
        graunte of newe by his letters patens the foreseid xxij li. vn to the seid
        Thomas and John...**prouidet** alweys that this surrendur and newe patent be
        haid wytheinne towe yere.

The Middle English verb *excepten* is another example of direct borrowing from
the Anglo-French *excepter*. First English instances are recorded at the turn of the
fifteenth century:

(15)   Jeo voile **excepter** sa dulce mere Ke li fust de assez plus chere BOZ *S
        Mad* 111

(16)   (a1393) Gower *CA* 7.2745: To the povere and to the riche Hise lawes
        myhten stonde liche, He schal **excepte** no persone.
        c1425(a1420) Lydg. *TB* 2.379: Þei wern alle, I **excepte** noon, Worþi
        kny3tes.

Both in Anglo-French and Middle English we find the new preposition *except*
grammaticalized from the past participle. Interestingly, in Middle English some
postpositional uses are also found, which means that the obligatorification of
position (cf. Lehmann 1985) was more advanced in the source language.

(17)   le roy lour ad pardonez toutz maners concelementz, **exceptz** ceux qe sount
        faitz par les officers du roy *Rot Parl*1 iv 7
        toutz lez autrez tens...**except** le pretert parfit *Liber Donati* (D) 9.74

(18)   c1425(a1420) Lydg.*TB* 2.1120: His sones wern ...present, **Ector except**.
        c1425(a1420) Lydg.*TB* 2.4895: **Excepte Ector**, þer was nat swiche anoþer

The word followed by subordinating *que/that* also became a conjunction in both
languages:

(19)   qe nulles solempnitees soient faites **except qe** je veuille qe les chapelleins
        Reg Chich ii 64
        c1425(a1420) Lydg.*TB* 5.1112: I can nat seyn what lif þat þei ladde,
        Except þat she by hym a dou3ter hadde.

3.2 Deadjectival and denominal

Except competed with another French deadjectival preposition *sauve*, adapted in
Middle English as *sauf/save* and also with the departicipial *outtaken*, ultimately of
Norse origin. Again this is a clear example of grammaticalization down the
adjective-to-preposition cline:

(20)   tot li chatel seient otrié al mort, **sauves** les reignables parties de sa feme e
        de ses enfanz *Magna Carta* 26
        totes maneres de plees **sauve** plees de terre et de la coroune *Rot Parl*2 130

(21)   c1330(?c1300) *Amis* 346: For þat he was so hende & gode, Men blisced
        him...**Saue þe** steward.
        (a1382) *WBible(1)* Num.32.12: Þei wolde not sewe me **saue** [*WB(2)*:
        outakun] caleph...& Iosue.

And like synonymous *except* the preposition *sauf/save* had the force of
conjunction when followed by the subordinating *que/that*:

(22)   Eyent bref...de aler avant...**sauve q'**il ne rendent le juggement, le roi nient
        cunseillé *Rot Parl*2 188

(23)   (a1387) Trev. *Higd.* 7.339: In his tyme þe monkes of Caunterbury...were
        nou3t onliche to seculer men, **sauf þat** [L nisi quod] þey lefte nou3t...her
        chastite.
        (a1464) Capgr. *Chron.*(Cmb Gg.4.12) 232: King Edward was...nevir
        steyned, **save that** in his age he was gretly langaged with lecchery.

The French noun *malgre* 'ill will', 'suffering' with the vocalization of the lateral consonant was also borrowed into late Middle English:

(24)   sanz avoir nulle **malgré** ou disease de vous de ma noun venue *Lett & Pet* 38.21
        De quere **maulgré** saunz nul prou Haute deverie est tenu BOZ *Prov* (S) 63.1

(25)   (1402) Hoccl. *Cupid* (Hnt HM 744) 376: Wytith the feend, and his be the **maugree**.
        (a1470) Malory *Wks.* 551/19: I have harde muche of youre **magre** ayenste me.

In both languages the noun became the source of the new grammaticalized preposition meaning *in spite of, against* as in the following Anglo-French and Middle English examples:

(26)   Un home puet atorner sa rente...**maugré** a cely ki la rente ly rend *Brev Plac* 30
        il tendra la chose duraunt le terme **maugré** les denz l'autre, saunz nul countredit *Irish Docs* 247.

(27)   a1400 *Cursor*(Trin-C)18583: **Maugrey** þe iewes, his fals foos, þus he heried helle.
        ?a1425(c1400) *Mandev.(1)* 210/26: And now I am comen hom, **mawgree** myself [F *maugre mien*], to reste.

In English we also find the word as a part of the complex conjunction introducing concessive *maugre-wh...* (=no matter-wh...)-clauses:

(28)   (a1393) Gower *CA* 1.1329: **Malgre wher** sche wole or non, Min herte is everemore in on, So that I can non other chese.
        (a1470) Malory *Wks.* 49/21: Thys custom...have I used and woll use, **magre who** seyth nay.

3.3 Direct borrowings and calques

So far we have been discussing the cases of Anglo-French verbs (participles), adjectives and nouns grammaticalized as prepositions and/or conjunctions in both Anglo-Norman and Middle English. Another interesting group of borrowings are Romance phrases directly borrowed by the Middle English writers in the French form or calqued word for word, albeit sometimes phonetically reduced and/or univerbated.

The French preposition *sans* was commonly used in Anglo-Norman texts, whence it was readily adapted by Middle English writers:

(29)   **sanz** paiaunt la custume et subside *Northumb* 214
alme ke seint A. apele pres la plus haute chose ke soit **sanz** Deu memes *Ancren2* 230.11

(30)   c1390 *Susan.*(Vrn) 181: Þer com...Þe prestes **sauns** pite And ful of Falshede.
a1500 *Rich.* 681: Go in, **sans** bydyng, And saye thus to thy lord the kyng.

Continental Old French made use of the conjuction *quanses (que)* derived from the Latin *quasi* < *quam sic* 'as if'. No instances of *quanses* are recorded in the *Anglo-Norman dictionary.* Yet the word is found in the 15th century English with a prothetic vowel *ascaunce/ascances* (often split as *as scaunce*) in the same sense (cf. Livingston 1925).

(31)   Et si feit **quanses** que il n'ot 1175 Chrétien de Troyes *Cligés* 4555

(32)   (?a1439) Lydg.*FP* 4.2554: A fals pretence of..magnificence, **As scauns** she hadde been in vertu strong.
c1460(?c1400) *Beryn* 1797: They walkid to & fro...**as skaunce** þey knewe nau3te.

A detailed account of the grammaticalization of *albeit* can be found in Molencki (1997). *Al* followed by an inverted clause was often used in a concessive function in Middle English, especially in the phrase *al be it*, which was directly calqued from Central French *tout soit il* and Norman *tout seit il,* as in:

(33)   il est mut sage, **tut seit il** de petit age *Enfances* 1202
defender son droit sur la matire **tout soit il qe** il riens cleime el patronage en cas susdit *Edw III* (1350)

In Middle English one can find numerous instances of *al* + V + NP structure (34), but *al be it,* gradually univerbated into *albe(h)it* appears to have been most common and as such was grammaticalized as a concessive conjunction (35):

(34)   a1250 *HMaid.* 39/642,653: [Pride] bihat eche wununge alle hire modres, **al beon ha** meidenes, wið hare awariede fader in inwarde helle. Ne telle þu nawt eðelich, **al beo þu** meiden, to widewen ne to iweddede.
What I have suffred sith I was a wyf With myn housbonde, **al be he** youre cosyn.

(?a1439) Lydg.*FP* (Bod 263) 7.1645: **Al wer it** so, he felte ful vnsofte.

c1450(c1370) Chaucer *ABC* (Benson-Robinson) 45: **Al have I ben** a beste in wil and deede, Yit, ladi, thou me clothe with thi grace.

a1425(?a1400) *RRose* (Htrn 409) 1754: The hokede heed...in myn herte still it stod, **Al bledde I** not a drope of blod.

(35)   (a1393) Gower *CA* (Frf 3) 4.2393: **Al be it** so the bodi deie, The name of hem schal nevere aweie.

(1418) *Let.War France* 71 it was withouten the deth of any mannes persone of oures **albehit** that our enemys with grete power assembled nigh thé saine riuer for to have let and defended us the same passage.

Another Middle English conjunction modelled on Old French is *unless* (cf. Traugott 1997). Central French phrase *à moins que* 'on a less condition than', first recorded in the 14th century, had the Norman counterpart *a meins qe*, e.g.:

(36)   La mene apoplexie est ke ne tout mie le sen ne movement de tut, mes nome'ment en partye e greve plus ke la menore **e meins ke** la grenur spiritualtes *Anglo-Norman Medicine*

hommes efluz per ferement, dount lesii ferrount chivalers **a meins qe** per nulle affinite ne touchent les prifons *Statutes*

Bilingual Anglo-French speakers translated it literally into Middle English as *of lesse than/that*, as in (37), and then the first syllable was assimilated to *un-*, probably supported by the fact that the prefix *un-* had the negative force like the new connective (38):

(37)   (1414) *RParl.*4.22b: That thar sholde no Statut no Lawe be made **oflasse than** they yaf therto their assent.

(1448) *Shillingford* 52: He woll do more; **of lesse** then they wold come when they were somned.

(38)   (1440) *Wars France* in *RS 22.2* 458: The kyng conceyveth wele that, **onlesse** that it like him so to tendre the saide duc, he renneth in perpetuell undoing.

3.4 Hybrid *because*

Finally let us take a look at the story of English *because*, a Germanic-Romance hybrid formation (for a detailed account see Molencki 2008). The Anglo-Norman corpus has numerous examples of both the preposition *par cause de* and the complex conjunction *a cause que/par cause que*, first attested in the fourteenth century. According to French etymological dictionaries the first continental occurrences are at least two centuries later. Contrary to what we find in English etymological dictionaries and reference books, the word-phrase is not a direct French loan but appears to have arisen among bilingual Anglo-Norman and Middle English speakers in the last quarter of the 14th century. Witness the following examples from the fourteenth century Anglo-Norman documents:

(39)   1345 *Foedera* si que vous ne s'en puist excuser **par cause de** ignorance.

(40)   1344 *Foedera* Et, pur ce que, avant ces heures, gentz ount este desceuz **par cause qil** n'aveit nulle eschange overte.
   1349 *Negotiations for the Ransom of David Bruce* Item coment grant empeschement est a les grosses busoignes le Roi **par cause qe** monsieur E. de B. ne voet accorder a bones voies de paiz tieles come.
   1377 *Fœdera* et **a cause que** le dit Esmond le pier morust seisi de mesme le manoir en son demesne come de fee, mesme cest Esmond le fitz adonques esteant deinz age, notre seignur le Roi, laiel notre seignur le Roi q'ore est, seisit le dit Esmond le fitz en sa garde, **par cause** que fuisit trove en mesme le livre que le dit manoir fuist tenuz par an par tieux services, et prist les profitz de mesme le manoir par quatre ans come de sa garde.
   1378 *Stonor Letters* par quey, treshonore seignour, le dit Richard et Marjorye sa femme vous prie enterement, si il soit a vostre voluntee qe le jour puet estre pro|longe tanke a le Chandelure, pur cause qe il ne at mye seme tot soun semaile de furment, et auxi pur ceste temps est pluviouse et bret jours.

The first English examples are found in the last quarter of the fourteenth century, most likely modelled according to the Anglo-Norman pattern as a hybrid with the French preposition *par* rendered by English *by* but retaining the Romance noun *cause*, both as the preposition and the conjunction. The subsequent stages of grammaticalizing the phrase into a causal preposition/conjunction in English are evidenced by the examples where the noun *cause* is preceded by the definite article (41), dropping the article (42), the preposition *by* gradually becoming a phonetically weakened prefix (43), loss of the subordinating particle *that* (44) and the final univerbation (45).

(41)   c1450 *Godstow nunnery register* 282: to the abbesse and mynchons of Godestowe, all her right that she had or might have, **by the cause of** her dowery or mariage.
   a1400 *Lanfranc* (Ashm 1396) 233: **Bi þe cause þat** cirurgians ben clepid algate to þis manere passioun, þerfore I haue studied to make a general chapitre of passiouns of ioinctis.

(42)   (CMMANDEV 30): In Egypt þere ben but fewe Forcelettes or castelles **be cause þat** the contree is so strong of himself.

(43)   a1400 *Lanfranc* (Ashm 1396) 114/19: Al þe brayn is deemed cold & moist, **bicause þat** he schulde atempren spiritual fumosite þat comen of þe herte...& þe brayn is whijt, **bicause þat** he schulde þe bettere resseyue resoun & vnderstondynge.

(44)   a1425(?a1400) Chaucer *RRose* 4518: He may not out, and that is wrong, **By cause** the tour is so strong.

(45)   1461 *Paston Letters* 2.254: And so whas I lefte stille at Cotton with xij men with me, **be-cauce** they report and we a-bode there ij dayes we schulde be pult out be the heedes.
        a1425(c1385) Chaucer *TC* 4.125 Bycause he nolde payen hem here hire, The town of Troie shal ben set on-fire.
        c1450 *Alph.Tales* (Add 25719)11/21: Hur susters þe nonnys...was passand fayn þerof, becauce sho wa so strayte vnto þaim at þai myght have a cauce to accuse hur in.

In this way the English language acquired a new distinct causal connective introducing subordinating clauses, which allowed *for* to specialize as a paratactic causal conjunction by analogy with the French distinction between paratactic *car* and hypotactic *par ce que/par cause que*.

4. Conclusion

A great many new prepositions and conjunction arose in Middle English, created by both syntactic and semantic extension, grammaticalization, but predominantly due to language contact, especially between the Anglo-Norman dialect of French and Middle English, in the bilingual environment in the fourteenth and fifteenth century. Such transfers were natural in the situation of common code-switching among bilinguals, especially among the educated literate circles of the Chancery and the royal court. In the article we have shown that some of the new Anglo-Norman forms do not have counterparts in the continental dialects of medieval French (most conspicuous examples being *durant* and *par cause que*, sources of English *during* and *because*, respectively), which is the best evidence proving their Anglo-French origin. It is very likely that parallel uses of new grammatical items may have contributed to their higher frequency in both languages.

The need for creating new grammatical words was also connected with the decrease in semantic and syntactic polyfunctionality of earlier items. The development of argumentative writing in late Middle English required more precise and distinct expression of abstract relationships such as condition, cause, concession and contrast. The more and more mature style of English writing was characterized by the increase of hypotactic clause combining, which paved the ground for creating new subordinators. In the case of causal connectives late Middle English speakers simply copied the French distinction between coordinate and subordinate conjunctions (earlier Middle English had used the conjunction *for* for both). Major word formation processes involved in the creation of new prepositions and conjunction were grammaticalization (e.g., *save, during, except, providing*), calquing (loan translation, e.g., *albeit, unless*) and also hybridization (e.g., *because*), which all often resulted in univerbation. Some grammatical words were also directly borrowed in the French form (*maugre, sans*), but – interestingly – they were lost in Early Modern English.

References

PRIMARY SOURCES

Anglo-Norman hub. Available at: www.anglo-norman.net
The Helsinki corpus of English texts. 1991. Helsinki: Department of English. Available at: http://helmer.aksis.uib.no/-icame/hc/index.htm
ICAME corpus. Available at: www.icame.uib.no
MEC *Middle English compendium*. Available at: http://ets.umdl.umich.edu/m/mec
MED *Middle English dictionary online*. Available at: http://ets.umdl.umich.edu/m/med
OED *Oxford English dictionary online*. Available at: http://www.oed.com

SECONDARY SOURCES

Álvarez, Rosa María Cougil – Ana I. González Cruz
    2003   "On the development of deverbal conjunctions. A case-study on the grammaticalisation of *provided (that)* in early Modern English", *SEDERI* 13: 33-44.
Amano, Masachiyo – Michiko Ogura – Masayuki Ohkado (eds.)
    2008   *Historical Englishes in varieties of texts and contexts*. Frankfurt/Main: Peter Lang Verlag.
Athanasiadou Angeliki – René Dirven (eds.)
    1997   *On conditionals again*. Amsterdam: John Benjamins.
Hopper, Paul – Elizabeth Closs Traugott
    2003   *Grammaticalization*. (2nd edition). Cambridge: Cambridge University Press.

Ingham, Richard
  2006   "Syntactic change in Anglo-Norman and continental French chronicles:
            was there a 'Middle' Anglo-Norman?", *Journal of French Language
            Studies* 16.1: 25-49.
  2009   "Middle English and Anglo-Norman in contact". (Paper presented at the
            English Literary Society of Japan Conference). Available at
            http://www.elsj.org/meeting/81st/81s10ingham.pdf.
Kibbee, Douglas
  1991   *For to speke Frenche trewely. The French language in England
            1000-1600: its status, description and instruction.* Amsterdam: John
            Benjamins.
Kortmann, Bernd
  1997   *Adverbial subordinators: A typology and history of adverbial
            subordinators based on European languages.* Berlin; New York: Mouton
            de Gruyter.
Lehmann, Christian
  1985   "Grammaticalization: synchronic variation and diachronic stage", *Lingua
            e Stile* 20: 303-318.
Lenker, Ursula – Anneli Meurman-Solin (eds.)
  2007   *Connectives in the history of English.* Amsterdam and Philadelphia: John
            Benjamins.
Livingston, Charles
  1925   "Middle English 'askances'", *The Modern Language Review* 20.1: 71-72.
Molencki, Rafał
  1997   "*Albeit* a conjunction, yet it is a clause: a counterexample to the
            unidirectionality hypothesis?", *Studia Anglica Posnaniensia* 3: 163-178.
  2003   "The etymology and development of the conjunction *as* in Middle
            English", *Linguistica Silesiana* 24: 25-39.
  2005   "On the syntactic and semantic development of *after* in medieval
            English", *Medieval English Mirror* 2: 47-67.
  2007a   "The evolution of *since* in medieval English", in: Lenker, Ursula –
            Anneli Meurman-Solin (eds.), 97-113.
  2007b   "On the rise of the temporal preposition/conjunction *before*", *Medieval
            English Mirror* 3: 37-54.
  2008   "The rise of *because* in Middle English", in: Amano, Masachiyo –
            Michiko Ogura – Masayuki Ohkado (eds.), 201-216.
Pasicki, Adam
  1987   *Temporal adverbials in Old and Middle English.* Lublin: Wydawnictwo
            Katolickiego Uniwersytetu Lubelskiego.
Price, Glanville
  1984   *The languages of Britain.* London: Edward Arnold.
Rissanen, Matti
  2007   "From *op* to *till*: early loss of an adverbial subordinator", in: Lenker
            Ursula – Anneli Meurman-Solin (eds.), 61-76.

Rothwell, William
  1996   "The Anglo-French element in the vulgar register of Late Middle English", *Neuphilologische Mitteilungen* 97: 423-436.
Schendl, Herbert
  1996   "Text types and code switching in medieval and Early Modern English", *Vienna English Working Papers* 5: 50-62.
  2000   "Linguistic aspects of code-switching in medieval English texts.", in: Trotter David (ed.), 77-92.
Short, Ian
  1980   "On bilingualism in Anglo-Norman England", *Romance Philology* 33: 467-479.
Traugott, Elizabeth Closs
  1989   "On the rise of epistemic meanings in English: An example of subjectification in semantic change", *Language* 57: 33-65.
  1997   "*Unless* and *but* conditionals: A historical perspective", in: Athanasiadou Angeliki – René Dirven (eds.), 145-167.
Trotter, David
  2003   "L'anglo-normand: variété insulaire ou variété isolée?", *Médiévales* 45: 43-54.
Trotter David (ed.)
  2000   *Multilingualism in later medieval Britain.* Cambridge: D.S. Brewer.

Multilingualism in Trinity College Cambridge Manuscript O.1.77.[1]

Alpo Honkapohja, University of Helsinki

ABSTRACT

England has a rich tradition of medieval medical manuscripts surviving both in the vernacular and Latin, which were for a long period of time paid fairly little attention. The last two decades have seen an increase in research into scientific and medical works in the vernacular. What is, however, seriously lacking is a comprehensive treatment of the other side of vernacularisation, the Latin and mixed-language materials that make up the vast majority of medical texts surviving from England in the Middle Ages. My PhD is intended to be the first genuinely bilingual digital edition of the manuscript Trinity College, Cambridge, O.1.77, a small late-medieval medical handbook. This article looks into multilingualism in the manuscript. It starts with a description of the manuscript, which summarises known background facts about the codex and presents a slight revision of the manuscripts date. James (1902) has dated the manuscript 1460, based on markings on the fly-leaves, which is probably not accurate. I offer a new date of 1454-1459. The main part of the article consists of looking into multilingualism in the manuscript, firstly, on which texts are in Middle English and which in Latin, and secondly, by analysing code-switching between Latin and Middle English with a discourse-functional pragmatic approach. After which, I relate the findings into the socio-historical context of fifteenth century, based on other studies. The article finishes with a discussion of the possibilities the digital edition offers for the study of multilingualism in the manuscript and related text.

KEYWORDS: discourse-functional approach to multilingualism; manuscript studies; multilingualism; medical writing; astrology; code-switching; Latin; Middle English

1. Introduction

Medieval England had a rich tradition of medical writing, both in Latin and English. Vernacular remedy books survive from the Old English period, which is rare in a European perspective, and the tradition continued into the later Middle Ages, with a slight break in the thirteenth century (see Pahta and Taavitsainen 2004: 9). The biggest wave of vernacularisation took place in the final century of the Middle English period, between 1375 and 1475, which saw the use of vernacular extended to new kinds of texts, previously the exclusive domain of Latin. By 1475, even learned university texts can be found as vernacular translations (Voigts 1996: 814).

Estimates on the number of surviving medical and scientific manuscripts vary, and certain factors complicate the issue, such as defining what counts as a

---

1   This paper describes the aspects of my PhD dissertation related to multilingualism. It is a slightly expanded version of the paper I gave in the Foreign Influences on Medieval English conference in Warsaw in 12-13 December 2009. I am grateful to Prof. Irma Taavitsainen and Dr. Matti Kilpiö for their comments, and Dr. Mark Shackleton for his very quick and efficient language check.

medical and scientific manuscript: medical manuscripts may contain material, like magical charms or astrology, which do not fit into modern conceptions of science and medical recipes can be found scribbled in all kinds of manuscripts, wherever there is an empty space. According to one definition any manuscript transmitting information, excluding literary and devotional writings, can be counted among the medieval *fachliteratur* (see Voigts 1989: 347).

What is clear from the surveys that have been carried out[2] is that:

- Latin manuscripts are more common than vernacular ones,
- manuscripts containing more than one language (Latin, and English, sometimes French) are more common than ones containing only a single language, and
- Latin manuscripts remain more numerous up to the end of the Middle English period, and even in the following decades, at least until 1500.[3]

Research into medical and scientific manuscripts was for a long time, paid very little attention, and it was very unusual for them to be published in a scholarly edition. In 1919, Waley Singer wrote: "for the period intervening from the fall of Greek science to the rise of the more modern work, roughly for the 1,000 years from 500 A.D. to 1500, printed material is extraordinarily scarce. The ideas of our mediaeval forefathers on science and medicine are at present largely hidden from us." (97). Fifty years later, Robbins described the field as a "Yukon territory crying out for exploration. So little is known, so much has to be discovered" (1970: 413), meaning that several very popular texts, "of considerable biographical, sociological and historical interest" (414) were not accessible to modern scholars at the time (see also Harley 1982: 171).

---

2   One of the most comprehensive surveys was carried out by Dorothea Waley Singer in the early 20th century (see Waley Singer 1919), though her figure of 15,000 examined MSS may be slightly exaggerated (Robbins 1970: 393) and she frequently dates manuscripts too early (Voigts 1989: 387). Her figures for 14th and 15th centuries are: 14th century: 1948 surviving Latin, and 140 surviving English manuscripts; fifteenth century: 3729 Latin, and 872 English MSS; showing a sixfold increase in English language MSS and a doubling in Latin ones.

Voigts carried out a survey of 178 manuscripts between 1375-1500 with scientific and utilitarian contents: she discovered 52 manuscripts exclusively in Latin (36 science, 10 medicine, 6 containing both science and medicine), 40 exclusively in English (10 science, 24 medicine, 6 both science and medicine), 86 containing more than one language (15 science, 37 medicine, 34 both science and medicine. 75 of these contained Latin and English and 11 Latin, English, French).

Pahta and Taavitsainen (2004: 4) use the eVk database, which lists ca. 10,000 extant items in Middle English. They emphasize the fact that less than hundred editions have appeared out of all these items.

3   According to Pahta and Taavitsainen (2004: 8-9) Latin remained more common for scientific publications until the end of the seventeenth century.

Recent decades have seen an increase in the attention given to medieval medical and scientific works, and the situation has slowly changed. The limited corpus of Old English texts has been studied in fairly good detail (Getz 1998: 39), and considerably more has been done with Middle English. Printed editions like Manzaloui 1977 and Tavormina 2006 have made available specific families of texts, such as the *Secretum Secretorum* tradition, or individual manuscripts, the massive Trinity College Cambridge MS R 14.52. Both also have very thorough introductions. There are also new electronic corpora which make linguistic enquiry into the medical materials easier. *Middle English medical texts* (MEMT), published 2005, collects all pre-2005 medical texts into a single searchable electronic database, and *A corpus of Middle English scientific prose*, currently being compiled as a collaboration between the University of Malaga and Hunter Library in Glasgow, collects in an electronic database all of the Middle English medical manuscripts in the Hunter collection.

To elaborate on Robbins' figure of speech, the field is no longer quite the unexplored Yukon territory. Major areas of it are now filled with flags staking the claims of various research projects and researchers. Much remains to be done, and it will be a long time before the data is exhausted – but at least, at this point, the Middle English versions of the most influential and popular medical works are available, and considerably more is known about medical writing in Middle English than when Robbins wrote his article.

What is, however, seriously lacking is a comprehensive treatment of the other side of vernacularisation, the Latin and mixed-language materials that make up the vast majority of medical texts surviving from England in the Middle Ages. This can be considered a serious omission, since the developments did not take place in isolation. Nearly all vernacular medical writing in the Middle Ages was translated from Latin, and was very dependent on classical models (see e.g., Getz 1998: 35, Taavitsainen 2004). The same holds true for the earliest surviving Old English texts, *Lacnunga* and *Læceboc*, which are ultimately derived from the encyclopedia of Pliny the elder with some folk remedies (Getz 1998: 47) and vernacular treatises continue to be in close relation to Latin during the most important period of medieval vernacularisation, 1375-1500.

2. Trinity College Cambridge MS O.1.77

My PhD project is intended as the first genuinely bilingual online resource of medical manuscripts in late Medieval England, and will hopefully pave the way for similar resources in the future. The edition will contain the complete manuscript, giving equal amount of detail to Latin and Middle English texts. It is designed for both historical linguists and historians, but special attention is paid to the needs of historical linguistics, and it is primarily intended for the study of multilingualism. This paper summarises the known background facts about the manuscript, and presents a preliminary analysis of multilingualism. The final section of this paper will contain an account of what the electronic edition will contain, and what are the research questions I plan to pursue when it is finished.

The text which I am editing, Trinity College Manuscript O.1.77, is a medical handbook containing texts on medicine, alchemy and astrology. Like all the manuscripts with the O-designation in the Trinity College, it was part of a collection, accumulated by Dr Thomas Gale (1635/6-1702) and his eldest son Roger (1672-1744), which was donated to the library by the latter in 1738 (see James 1902: v).

One of the most striking features of the manuscript is its small size. At only 75 x 100 mm, it can be best described as pocket-sized. It contains 202 folios, quired in eights (Voigts 1990: 50-51). The pages are frame ruled. The manuscript is mainly written on paper, but there are vellum leaves in the beginning and the end. Watermarks can be seen on folios 1r, 90v, 181v, 187r and 188v, and they are one of the factors which connect the manuscript to the so-called Sloane group (see below and Voigts 1990).

The manuscript is, for the most part, written by a single hand, responsible for both the Latin and Middle English texts in the manuscript (henceforth hand A). James (1902: 76) describes hand A as "roughly written". Voigts labels it "pointed Anglicana" (1990: 51). Items on the flyleaves in the beginning and end are not by the main hand, even though they are in Anglicana. It is quite possible that the same hand was responsible for all of the additions as well as marginal comments (see Mooney 1995: 85), but lacking certain identification I will not refer to them as hand B.

Like many other scientific and utilitarian manuscripts, Trinity O.1.77 is rather austere in appearance compared to many liturgical or literary manuscripts. It is, however, among the more decorated of the Sloane group and sibling manuscripts, and does have some decorative initials, decorations, a number *litterae notabiliores*, in red and blue, as well as many red underlinings, and highlighting strokes at the beginning of paragraphs in red. Incipits and explicits are in a slightly more formal hand, which may also belong to hand A. The rubricator not only adds red highlights, but has read the text closely, and frequently corrects mistakes made by hand A, ruling them over in red and writing between the lines in a very similar hand. It is possible that the same scribe was responsible for both, although a master–apprentice type of relationship also seems possible.

The manuscript contains 10 to 18 texts on medicine, depending on the manner of counting the texts. The exact number of texts in the collection receives somewhat conflicting information in various sources. James (1902) lists ten items, including both Latin and Middle English, not including items on the flyleaves. He treats the astrological section as a single item. Mooney (1995) lists six Middle English items, including the flyleaves. The eTK and eVK databases yield altogether eighteen items: seven in Middle English (eVK) and eleven in Latin (eTK). They include some of the items on the flyleaves, listing the astrological note which James uses as the basis of dating manuscript as a separate item, and also treating the passage on apothecaries' weights as an individual item.

2.1. The Sloane Group of Middle English Manuscripts

Voigts (1990) relates the contents of Trinity College Manuscript O.1.77 to what she calls the Sloane group of Middle English manuscripts, a group of scientific and utilitarian manuscripts now part of the collection donated to the British library by Sir Hans Sloane.

The Sloane group can be better understood as consisting of two groups of manuscripts: six codices in the British library with "striking physical similarity" (28), but no textual overlap; and six manuscripts which share a number of texts and illustrations, but are less unified in terms of their physical appearance.

The manuscripts in the first group are BL Sloane 1118, Sloane 1313, Sloane 2320, Sloane 2567, Sloane 2948 and the BL add. MS 19674. The latter group consists of five more manuscripts. Three "siblings", Trinity MS O.1.77 Boston Countway Library of Medicine MS 19 and BL Sloane MS 3566, share texts with one of the group manuscripts, Sloane 2320, but are smaller in size, Trinity MS O.1.77 being the smallest of the lot; and two luxuriously decorated post-medieval (1480s–1490s) codices, Tokyo Takamiya 33 and Gonville and Caius 336/725, which Voigts calls "a second generation that has grown prosperous" (27).[4]

Following Voigts' nomenclature, I will refer to the first group as the "core manuscripts" and to the latter as the "sibling manuscripts" (including also the "second generation of a family that has grown prosperous", since they contain the same texts as the siblings).

One manuscript, Sloane 2320, belongs to both groups, having the physical characteristics of the core manuscripts, and the set of texts of the sibling manuscripts. Indeed, it may have been the exemplar from which the sibling manuscripts derive their content, since it appears to be of an earlier date than any of the sibling manuscripts, and, unlike the others, has a different hand for the Latin and English texts. Voigts also describes "considerable wear" on the first and last leaves of each gathering, which may suggest that it saw service as an exemplar – or alternatively circulated in booklet form (Voigts 1990: 29). This, of course, does not mean that the manuscript in question has been the one to serve as the exemplar for the sibling manuscripts, such as Trinity O.1.77 and Boston MS 19.

---

4   In addition, Voigts mentions three manuscripts bearing "some family resemblance" to manuscripts in the group: London Wellcome Historical Library of Medicine MS 784 shares one plague tract with the sibling manuscripts, British Library, Add. MS 5467 has nine folios, with the physical characteristics of the core manuscripts, and Oxford, Bodleian MS Rawlinson C. 815 contains two leaves of laxative recipes and charms, with the layout of the core manuscripts (27).

Both the core and the sibling manuscripts are characterized by having texts in a variety of languages. There are no single language codices in the group (Voigts 1990: 30). Trinity College Cambridge MS O.1.77 is actually the manuscript which has most English of the core or the sibling MSS (see Taavitsainen 2004b). None of them have appeared in a modern edition, with the exception of the Middle English texts in the sibling manuscript Boston Countway Library of Medicine MS 19 (Harley 1982).

The Boston manuscript is also interesting because it has been identified as the "litill booke of pheesyk" commissioned by Sir John Paston II and copied by the freelance scribe William Ebesham. It can also be assigned a certain date because it is apparent from the letters that Ebesham undertook the work while Sir John Paston was overseas, which is known to be in the summer of 1468, for the marriage of Princess Margaret of York (see Doyle 1956-1957: 299).

The Sloane group and related manuscripts were most likely copied in London or Westminster. The identification is based on the connection of William Ebesham with Boston Countway MS 19, since he is known to have operated in the London area. The related MS 5467, in addition to containing some leaves with the Sloane core group type of layout, contains two texts translated by John Shirley, another well-known figure of fifteenth-century London (Voigts 1990: 27).

The assumption is supported by a LALME-analysis Taavitsainen (2004b) has carried out on the language of MS O.1.77. Her conclusion is that the language resembles the Rosemary type identified by Angus McIntosh (1983), with some very provincial spelling characteristics and some Central Midland forms which can be found in a number of medical, especially surgical manuscripts (McIntosh 1983: 243).

2.2. Dating the manuscript O.1.77

Rather unusually, all of the sources describing manuscript O.1.77 assign an exact date to it: 1460. The first one to suggest it is James (1902: 77), who makes the following observation: "On the last leaf are some astronomical notes in Latin and English. The first refers to 1460."

The passage he refers to reads as follows:

(1)   Notandu(m) q(uo)d *Anno d(omi)ni mill(esi)mo*
        cccc(mo).lx(mo) co(n)iu(n)ctio solis & lune h(oc)
        modo f(a)c(t)a e(st) (fol. 200r)

[(...)In the year 1460 the conjunction of the sun and the moon took place in this way(...)[5]]

_____

5   I am very grateful to Dr. Matti Kilpiö for reading through my Modern English translations of

James makes the assumption based on this piece of internal evidence, and it has carried into subsequent research. For instance both Voigts (1990) and Taavitsainen (2004) cite it as fact [emphases mine]:

> Cambridge, Trinity College MS.O.1.77, *dated 1460*, and Harvard Medical School, Countway Library of Medicine MS. 19., both contain the core of texts and illustrations found in Sloane MSS(...)
>
> (Voigts 1990: 27)

> (...)but it does not yield much material for dialectal analysis. Some forms point to the Central Midlands rather than London. Cambridge, Trinity College MS O.1.77, *dated 1460*, is another manuscript in this group(...)
>
> (Taavitsainen 2004b: 235)

There are, however, two problems with this dating. Firstly, the astrological notes on the last leaf are not in hand A. Mooney, for instance, (who only lists Middle English items in the manuscript) treats the hands as separate (1995: 85). Secondly, Folio 127b contains a crossed-out marginal comment in Latin (to a Middle English astrological text), which mentions the year 1459 [emphasis mine].

(2)   *Ista planeta mart(is) i(n)trauit i(n) ariete domo de sua kalendis septe(m)bris an(no) do(mino) millesimo cccc(mo) lix(m). et luna xvj h(oc) e(st) p(ri)ma existe(n)te i(n) num(er)o viz xvj. (fol. 127v)*

[This planet Mars entered in Aries from its home of on the first of September in the year 1459(...)]

These two observations suggest that the actual date for the copying of the manuscript may have been somewhat earlier than 1460, as suggested by James.

Concentrating on the date of production is a commonplace bias in manuscript studies. As Harris notes: "(...)research tends to be conducted in terms of a manuscript's genesis (1989: 172)". Although her point has to do with the market of second hand books in London, the observation is also valid here. Manuscript scholars sometimes make the mistake of interpreting too much based on the time when the manuscript was first made, whereas it is entirely possible, and to be expected, that the codex saw use later on.

A better interpretation would be to take the appearance of the dates 1459 and 1460 as evidence of provenance, suggesting that the manuscript was used by someone interested in astronomy in 1459-1460. They could also be taken to provide a *terminus ad quem*, concluding that the manuscript originates in the mid-

---

Latin and Middle English and for his feedback on them.

fifteenth century, before 1459. Voigts assigns the date 1454 to Sloane 2320 (1990: 27), and if that is accurate and the manuscript has served as an exemplar to the sibling manuscripts, including Trinity O.1.77, then it may have been composed between 1454 and 1459.

3. Bilingualism in Trinity MS O.1.77

The manuscript contains about 24,000 words in Latin and 5,500 in Middle English, which means that about about 82 per cent of the whole are in Latin and no more than 18 per cent in Middle English.[6] Of the related manuscripts, it is the one which contains most Middle English.

The codex includes texts on medicine, and the related fields of astrology and alchemy, including subjects such as laxative and purgative remedies, a uroscopy with coloured illustrations of urine flasks, a regimen of health attributed to Aristotle, three versions of the plague treatises by John of Burgundy, astrological medicine, a treatise on the medical properties of wines, and the book of Quintessence.

Table 1 contains the list of contents based on James (1902, texts on flyleaves added in the beginning and end).

Table 1)

[Flyleaves: a note on apothecaries' weights	mixed language]
1. Inc. manipulum medicine de digestiuis et laxatiuis.	Latin, ff.1–21
2. *It is to vnderstonde who so wil loke an vryne.*	*ME, ff.21–30*
3. Exposiciones vrinarum in ordine	Latin, 30–1
4. Tractatus nobilis de regimine sanitatis.	Latin, 31–53
5. Inc. tract. Mag. Joh. de Burgundia de epidemia	Latin, 53–73
6. *Joh. de burdegala extractus in lingua anglicana*	*ME, 73–83*
7. exortacio bona contra morbum pestilencialem	Latin, 83–92
8. *Inc. de condicionibus Vij^{tem} planetarum*	*mixed, 92–137*
9. tract. Vinorum diuersorum & vinum extractionis…	Latin, 137–173
10. quinte essentie	Latin, 173–199
[flyleaves: some astrological notes	mixed language]

The texts that contain English are one uroscopical treatise (2), one plague treatise, attributed to John of Burgundy (6), and two sections on the conditions of seven planets (8).

Texts that are exclusively in Latin without an English equivalent include laxative and purgative remedies (1), a regimen of health attributed to Aristotle (4), two texts on the medical properties of wines (9), and the book of quintessence (11).

---

6   Word count taken from MS Word. When the text is available in XML tagged form, it will be possible to give a more accurate figure.

All of the English texts appear next to Latin texts on the same subject matter (uroscopy, pestilence, astrology). In one case (a plague treatise attributed to John of Burgundy) the English text (6) is a translation of the Latin one (5) (see Harley 1982: 171–172).

There does not appear to be a clear-cut division between learned, prestigious Latin texts and more popular English ones. The English texts do not gloss the Latin ones, or otherwise facilitate understanding them, and their contents appear to be on the same level as the Latin treatises. Voigts notes the same phenomenon with the Sloane group in general: "The English texts usually either precede or follow different Latin texts on the same subject, and the texts in each language are of equal sophistication" (1996: 816, see also Pahta 2004: 75).

On the other hand, with the English texts there are always Latin texts which cover the same subject matter, whereas there are several subjects that do not have a corresponding English equivalent (laxative and purgative remedies, the regimen of health, medical properties of wines, the book of quintessence).

Of the two urine tracts, the English tract (2) is longer than the Latin one (3) and appears to be the main one. It contains the theoretical part, and pictures of urine flasks in which the urine is depicted with coloured ink.

(3)   Also it behoueth
       to co(n)sider(e) þe s(u)b
       stau(n)ce of þe vryne whe
       þ(er) it be thykke or thy(n)ne.
       & þe qualite wheþ(er) it
       be hygh(e) or lowe of colo(ur)
       & þe quantite wheþ(er) it [22r]
       be litil or mych(e).& þe co(n)
       tentys & þe cloudis þ(at)
       ben þ(er)yn . And i(n) which(e)
       r(e)giou(n) þey ben yn.& if
       þey ben ou(er)al i(n) lyche col
       lourid . or if it be more
       remisse i(n) one r(e)gione(…) (fols. 21v-22r)

The Latin tract, in contrast, is a short mnemonic piece, which simply lists the colours of each urine comparing them with what they resemble.

(4)   COlor rubeus e(st) quasi
       fla(m)ma ignis/
       (…)
       Karapos;
       albestens se(m)(per) spissa est
       ut vellus cameli (fol. 31r)

[The colour Rubeus is like a flame(...) Karapos becoming white always thick like the skin of a camel.]

Of the astrological texts, Harley notes, the Middle English one, which describes an individual's character and disposition based on the ruling planet at the time of his birth, is more popular than the Latin material it accompanies, some of it in the form of astrological charts (Harley 1982: 172). Trinity O.1.77, uniquely among the sibling MSS, includes a second Middle English astrological tract, which relates the effects of the seven planets to the twelve signs of the zodiac (fols. 122v-136v). As an interesting side observation, all of the texts related to the seven planets are in English, and those related to the twelve signs in Latin. The same is true of the short Middle English mnemonic list on the Seven planets, not in hand A, located on the last flyleaf 200(v) as the very last item of the manuscript.

3.1. How are Latin and Middle English used in texts, as well as marginal comments, metatext and flyleaves?

This section looks at how Latin and English are used in the manuscript, paying special attention to the passages that contain both languages. The aim is to find out what functions the two languages have, and whether one of them has uses which the other does not. The focus is mainly on what Schendl calls the *discourse functional-pragmatic* approach to code-switching, rather than the *grammatical-syntactic* approach (2002: 61), although I will comment on the syntax where relevant.

As is apparent from the previous sections, the manuscript is an anthology of texts in English and Latin, predominantly the latter. Only a handful of mixed language passages can be found in the manuscript. The best examples of code-switching and macaronic material come from the beginning of the manuscript, a short treatise on the different types of apothecaries' weights (scruple, drachm, pound etc.) used in the manuscript, in English, followed by a Latin recipe against jaundice. The text is a very common type which can be found in numerous manuscripts [emphasis mine].[7]

---

7   The electronic Voigts and Kurtz database recognises the incipit in seven other manuscripts: Wellcome Library, London Med. Soc. 131; Huntington, HM 19079; Bodleian, Ashmole 1389; Bodleian, Douce 304; Bodleian, Rawlinson D. 678; Glasgow University Library, Hunter 95 (T.4.12); BL, Add. 30338).
     eVK gives the following manuscripts for the latter incipit: Huntington, HM 19079; Bodleian, Ashmole 1389; Bodleian, Douce 304; BL, Add. 30338; Emmanuel College Cambridge 70; BL, Sloane 3171.

(5) þo wi3tes is strau(n)ge & harde to
     knowe y wole titil he(m) here /
     A povnde is þ(us) writen . lj .j.
     halfe a povnde þ(us) . lj.ss . Oþ(er) þ(us)
     lj.dj . A q(ua)rtro þ(us) q(ua)rt(er) .j. An
     vnce þus .ʒ .j. halfe an vnce
     þus   ʒ .ss or þus ʒ. dj /A drame þ(us)
     з j./ halfe a drame з.ss . or þ(us)
     з.dj ./ A scripule þ(us) Э . j. half a
     scripule þ(us) .Э ss . or þus Э dj ./
     A scripule weieþ a peny . & iij(e)
     sc(ri)pules ben a drame & viij drames
     a vnce & xvj vnces make(n)
     a povnde / and an handful is writen
     þ(us) m. & halfe an handful þ(us).
     m. ss. or þus .m. dj. & c(a)
     Optima medicina (pro) ict(er)icia .i.
     iaundise / R(ecipe) tarmarite .з.l.ss(...)(fol. 1r)

[The best medicine against ictericie, that is, jaundice. Take one and a half drachms
of turmeric(...)]

Voigts includes a slightly different version, from BL Sloane 3171 (not related to
the Sloane group), as an appendix. It is the only Middle English item in an
otherwise all-Latin codex. It begins "For to rede and undyrstonde þe wrytyng þt
comyþth [sic] hereaftyr and suche odyr wry3tynges as leches wryten in makyng of
here medycynes wheþer hyth be in englysse or in latyn(...)" and ends "(...)and þus
þey be wreten in latyn bokys" (1989b: 109).

The version in Trinity MS O.1.77 differs from the one quoted by Voigts in
keeping a low key about the language. Unlike Sloane 3171, it does not explicitly
call attention to the language with which the apothecaries' measurements are used.
This is despite the fact that it is found in a polyglot manuscript, in which language
use is more complex than in the monolingual Latin Sloane 3171. On the other hand,
this is in line with the multingualism of the manuscript, since this type of material
is essentially language-independent. Symbols, or sigils, used for measurements can
be read out aloud in English just as well as in Latin (see Voigts 1989b: 98).

The following passage, in the flyleaf following shortly after the previous
example, contains one of the few "intrasentential" (see Schendl 2002: 55)
switches in the manuscript [emphases mine].

(6)   *Ad rectificand(is) epar & ad illud*
      co(n)seruand(is) ab adustac(i)o(n)e & i(n)flacione
      R(ecipe) .li .j. de sug(er)loof .iiij.
      cocliaria plen(e) de saudres & iiij
      cocliare plen(e) de shawy(n)g of yue
      ry. & bete þe yu(er)y to smale poud(er)
      [2v]in a mort(er) & putte so(m)me of þe
      sug(er) w(ith)al. & aft(er) for ell(es) it wolle
      not be bete(n). & aft(er) þ(at) . put al i(n)
      a vessel & menge it toge(ede)r(is) &
      bete it to poud(er) til it be sotel.
      & take ha(lfe) di sponeful. or a sponeful
      at ones þ(er)of by day tyme
      or ny3t tyme as þe semeþ need(…). (flyleaves 2r-2v)

[For restoring the liver and for preserving it from burning and swelling. Take one pound of a loaf of sugar, four spoonfuls of sandalwood and four spoonfuls of shaving of ivory.(…)]

It is a recipe in which the language changes from Latin to Middle English in the middle of a sentence. The syntactic structure repeats the Latin phrase "cocliaria plene de" [spoonful of] twice, both times completing it with a Middle English phrase.[8] Syntactically the sentence is unified. The Latin verb "recipe" is represented with the common brevigraph, and the sentence continues a simple imperative, which is very typical for recipes, not the most syntactically complex of genres. The recipe continues in Middle English. The phrase "halfe a sponeful" occurs later in the same recipe, showing that the same information can also be communicated in Middle English. This type of usage is reminiscent of Voigts' category of "Mixed-language Texts Where the Alternation of Languages Appears to be Inadvertent" (1989b: 105) or Pahta's code-switched utterances in which the writer simply goes back and forth between English and Latin (2004: 94). The code-switching may be related to the specialist vocabulary, being either in English or in Latin (81), or simply to copying from a variety of exemplars.

---

8   I am grateful to Prof. Herbert Schendl for his feedback on the passage at the conference and pointing out to me the parallel syntactic structure of the phrases which contain the switch. He also suggested that the word 'saudre' might be considered as a switch into French. According to the MED, it has the following meanings (relevant here): "(a) Sandalwood, the wood of any of several trees of the species Santalum, esp. the white sandalwood (Santalum album) and the red sandalwood (Pterocarpus santalinus)(…) (b) powdered sandalwood(…)". The word is attested numerous times in recipes and medical texts in the 14th and 15th centuries, the earliest quotation dating from 1325. It seems to be well enough established to be treated as borrowing rather than a code-switch in the latter half of the 15th century.

The remainder of the introduction contains more recipes, a couple of which are in Middle English and the majority in Latin. All are scribbled together one after the other, without explicitly marked headings. The effect can perhaps best be described by the word macaronic. Intrasentential switches are often taken to imply good linguistic competence on the part of the text producer (see Schendl 2002: 56), and the effortless switching between the two languages in the introductory passage in the flyleaves suggests this. It is also noteworthy that many of the marginal comments are in Latin. For instance, the note on the position of Mars (see example two), containing the year 1459, occurs with the English astrological tract on the effects of the seven planets (see examples 10-12). By far the most common type of marginal comment are Latin recipes, also suggesting that whoever wrote them had a good command of the specialist vocabulary of medicine.

3.1.1. Text organising passages

(7)   Cui sit laus & gl(or)ia (per) to
        ti(us) mundi climata (et) (per)
        infinita seculo(rum) secula
        Amen/
        Explicit nobil(is) t(ra)ctat(us)
        mag(ist)ri Ioh(an)is de burgu(n)-
        dia co(n)t(ra) morbu(m) epidemi
        ale(m)(...)(fol. 72v)

[To whom be praise and glory through the regions of all the world and through the limitless ages of ages. Amen. Here ends the noble treatise of Master John of Burgundy against the epidemic sickness.]

Another instance in which Latin is used almost exclusively are the metatextual passages: incipits and explicits. These categories are similar to the examples given by Pahta (2004: 90-97). There are several reasons for the use of Latin in a context like this. They are traditional and formulaic, having been established over the course of several centuries, since Antiquity. Many of them also contain opening or closing prayers, which are likewise formulaic and related to the register of religion, another area in which Latin traditionally had a strong footing and well-established conventions (see 87-90). In terms of code-switching theory, the switches are thus multifunctional (see 77-78).

There is one instance of an incipit in English. Folio 27(v) contains an English passage which serves to mediate between two sections of the uroscopy treatise, which are both in English. It is underlined and rubricated like the equivalent Latin passages. The more technical part of the heading is in Latin, while the Middle

English one offers a freer description of the contents.

(8)   ¶Now folweþ þe sercles of
      .J(us). Circulus 1(us)   ¶þese vrynes.
      (fol. 27v)

The English version of the plague treatise by John of Burgundy contains a double transitional passage. The metatextual apparatus is in Latin, but the text itself begins "here begynneth(...)". It is a case of what is sometimes called flagged codeswitching (Voigts 1996: 818). This is the only instance in the manuscript in which the language of the treatise is introduced explicitly.

(9)   Iam i(n)cipit tractat(us)
      Ioh(an)is de burdega
      lia extract(us) i(n) lingua
      anglicana co(n)t(ra) morbu(m)
      [73r] pestilenciale(m) siue epide/
      HEre be ¶miale(m)//
      gynneth a noble
      tretys made of
      a good fisician John of bor
      deus. (fols. 72v-73r)

[Now begins the treatise of John of Burgundy excerpted in the English language against the pestilential or epidemic sickness.]

3.1.2. Endings for numerals and astrological words

Another instance in which the manuscript displays some free-ranging variation between Latin and Middle English are the inflections to numerals found in some of the texts. One of the instances can be seen in example eight above, which contains Latin "circulus" headings which are abbreviated with an "-us" brevigraph which resembles the numeral 9. It can be seen as formulaic text organising material connected to the metatextual elements in the manuscript, or otherwise, just as an example of conventionally inflecting ordinals. Numerals are an area of language use which are not necessarily language-specific (see e.g., Voigts 1989b: 95).

The superscript inflections indicating suffixes in some place seem to be in free variation in Trinity O.1.77 in folios 125(v) and 126(r), which are in the longer Middle English astrological treatise on the seven planets (see above). The text uses English inflection "in aquary" and the Latin "in aquario & capricorno" within only a couple of lines of each other.

(10)   dwellid i(n) eu(er)y sig
        ne xxx monethis.& whe(n)
        he regnyþ i(n) h(is) (pro)pir hous
        þ(at) is to sey **i(n) aquario & ca**
        p(ri)corno; þe(n) begy(n)ne grete
        [126r] harmes & myscheues w(ith)yn
        þe clymates of Þe erþe &
        þ(at) moste whe(n) he is **i(n) aq(ua)ry.** (fols. 125v-126r)

The same text contains numerals, which are abbreviated and have Latin inflections as superscript characters. For example, the following passage contains a numeral followed by the superscript "o" to mark the Latin inflection, as in Latin "secundo".

(11)   & xij houres & his course is **ij(o)**
        ȝere/.The children(n) of mars
        be of broune colo(ur) & þey be(n)
        gr(e)te debate(ur)s & (con)tagious
        peple (fol. 128v)

There are also opposite examples. In the following passage, the numeral 30 is abbreviated "xxx^{ti}," the superscript representing an English inflection.

(12)   science & craft(is) This pla
        nete goiþ h(is) course i(n) þe he
        ue(n) i(n) oon ȝere & he dwelliþ
        i(n) eu(er)y sygne xxx daies x.
        horis & **xxx(ti)** mynut(is). And a
        monge all þe planet(is) Þe
        so(n)ne disposiþ al man(er) best(is) (fol. 129r)

4. Conclusions

Reviewing the data examined in the previous sections, I will now attempt to answer the following questions:

How much can be assumed from manuscript features, related codices, and the use of Latin and Middle in the manuscript about the audience and the circumstances surrounding the production of Trinity College Cambridge MS O.1.77?
How can one relate this the socio-historical and linguistic context of the fifteenth century (based on other studies)?

First to briefly review the facts: the manuscript is written in a single hand by someone who appears to be a professional scribe. The manuscript has some decorated initials, normally the job of a specialist, and was charged separately. It shares a number of texts with one Sloane group core manuscript, 2320, and all of the sibling manuscripts. One of the sibling codices, Boston Countway MS 19, is of a slightly later date, 1468, and contains almost exactly the same texts copied in a single hand by a professional scribe known to have operated in the London area. Neither the scribe nor the commissioner, Sir John Paston, were medical practitioners.

Consequently, there is no reason to assume that the scribe or the commissioner and owners of Trinity MS O.1.77 have been professionally connected to medicine. The physical characteristics of O.1.77 along with what is known about the origin and provenance of Boston MS 19, and the fact that the same collection of texts can be found in all of the sibling manuscripts, would support a hypothesis that it was commissioned as a single item, a pocket-sized medical handbook, from a professional scribe, related to the professional book trade of 15th century, by an outside patron, who may or may not have had a professional connection to medicine, and it was used by someone who made notes on astronomical phenomena.

In contrast, the core manuscripts in the Sloane group contain several hands, usually linked to different languages (Voigts 1990: 30-31), and some may have originated as booklets (29), both of which would seem to speak of a longer and more complicated compilation process. Manuscript 2320 also shows signs of wear at the beginning of each gathering which may be signs of the manuscript having been used as an exemplar (29)

The audience for the vernacular treatises has received much attention. It is clear that medieval universities functioned in Latin, and education in them guaranteed full literacy in Latin (Pahta and Taavitsainen 2004: 15). It is also accepted that a driving force for translating material into the vernacular was making it accessible to a less Latinate audience (10-12). But what the exact nature of the readership below the university level was has caused a good deal of interest and speculation: how much literacy did the barber-surgeons, apothecaries, midwives, layman practitioners, empirics, wise women have and what kind of texts did they use (Pahta and Taavitsainen 2004: 16-17, Robbins 1970: 394)?

Trinity O.1.77 is predominantly a Latin manuscript, and whoever made the marginal comments in it had a good functional literacy in Latin, attested by marginal notes in Latin and the type of intrasentential code-switching between the two languages found in the flyleaves at the beginning of the manuscript. This, along with the known facts, agrees pretty well with the group Pahta and Taavitsainen consider to have the next highest level of literacy: learned aristocracy (2004: 17). Still, of course, the evidence is far from conclusive.

The manuscript comes from the latter half of the fifteenth century, a point at which vernacularisation "can be described as largely complete by 1475". Of the types described by Voigts (1989a), it falls under the majority, i.e. manuscripts which contain both Middle English and Latin. It is quite late in the period, and at that time, as the sizeable Trinity MS R 14.52 testifies, English could be used for even the most learned type of uses (Tavormina 2006: xii). The existence of manuscripts like Trinity O.1.77, on the other hand, speaks of the strength of the Latin tradition.

5. The digital edition

The digital edition which I am preparing will be designed in a way that it will function as reliable data for historical linguistics. This involves encoding sufficient amount of detail on linguistic variants without normalising, modernising, or emending the data, and keeping editorial interference transparent (see e.g., Kytö Grund and Walker 2007 or Lass 2004)

I am using TEI P5 –conformant XML tagging built on stand-off architecture. Features included in the base-level annotation are a graphemic transcription of the text (see e.g., Fenton and Duggan 2006), select manuscript features such as layout, and information about the manuscript and hand. Each word will also be tagged with a normalised form to facilitate linguistic research, and an ID which allows additional tagging by means of, for instance, POS tagging, semantic annotation or lemmatisation.

The development of the edition will take place in collaboration between the *Digital editions for corpus linguistics* (DECL) project, which aims to create a framework for producing online editions of historical manuscripts designed to meet the needs of corpus linguistics, using a more strictly defined subset of the TEI guidelines.[9]

My PhD project has both short- and long-term goals related to the study of multilingualism. Short-term aims include a more comprehensive and detailed look into the code-switching phenomena that have been described here. The XML tagging will enable corpus searches on features like marginal comments and metatextual passages (see 3.1. above). It will be easy to generate background information about the distribution across the various functions from the base-level tagging. The edition will make it possible to get information on features like spelling variation or syntactical complexity in English and Latin, in order to see whether the accepted general view that Latin was more regular is supported by quantitative data in the Latin and Middle English texts in this manuscript. In addition, the tagging will also make it possible to get quantitative information, for

---

9   The aims of the project are presented in more detail in Honkapohja, Kaislaniemi and Marttila (2009).

instance on which brevigraphs and contracted forms carry into the vernacular, and how frequently they are used.

Long-term goals, after finishing my PhD, include expanding the edition with other related multilingual medical and alchemical manuscripts in the Sloane group, which will increase the usefulness of the database, by allowing, for instance, comparative study of the same text in different manuscripts in the same group. One possibility would be to perform a LALME study on the English sections of all of the sibling group manuscripts, relating them to each other and dialectal locations, in order to see how this fits into the picture of a genesis in the London area. This could also be used as a starting point for a comparable study on Latin manuscripts in the group, in order to see how the variation in the two languages corresponds with one another. Another possibility is to make a computer-assisted stemmatological study to clarify the relations of the sibling group manuscripts to one another.

Other long-term goals are related to comparative studies between Middle English and Latin in scientific and medical writing over a longer period of time. One of the challenges will be finding data that is comparable. For classical Latin and Greek, there are plenty of resources, and corpora like MEMT and *A corpus of Middle English scientific prose* make a fairly good range of data for Middle English medical writing available. Data is currently very scarce on medieval scientific prose in Latin.[10]

References

Burnard, Lou – Katherine O'Brien O'Keeffe – John Unsworth (eds.)
  2006   *Electronic textual editing.* New York: MLA.
Dossena, Marina – Roger Lass (eds.)
  2004   *Methods and data in English historical dialectology.* Bern: Peter Lang.
Doyle, A. I.
  1956–1957   "The work of a late fifteenth-century English scribe, William Ebesham",
              Bulletin of the John Rylands Library Manchester 39: 298-325.
Fenton, Eileen Gifford – Hoyt N. Duggan
  2006   "Effective methods of producing machine-readable text from manuscript
              and print sources", in: Burnard, Lou – Katherine O'Brien O'Keeffe –
              John Unsworth (eds.), 241-253.

---

10 Some examples are to be found in the Corpus of Latin from Anglo-Saxon sources, which will be made available at the University of Helsinki (Olga Timofeeva; Matti Kilpiö). Syntactic comparisons will be facilitated by the Perseus Treebank. Philipp Roelli (University of Zürich) is also in the process of compiling a corpus of Medieval Latin scientific texts.

Getz, Faye
  1998   *Medicine in the Middle Ages.* New Jersey: Princeton University Press.
Griffiths, Jeremy – Pearsall Derek (eds.)
  1989   *Book production and publishing in Britain 1375-1475.* Cambridge: CUP.
Gray, Douglas – E. G. Stanley (eds.)
  1983.   *Middle English studies presented to Norman Davies.* Oxford: OUP.
  1989   *Book production and publishing in Britain 1375-1475.* Cambridge: CUP.
Harley, Martha Powell
  1982   "The Middle English contents of a fifteenth-century medical handbook",
           Medievalia 8: 171-188.
Harris, Kate
  1989   "Patrons, buyers and owners: the evidence for ownership, and the rôle of
           book owners in book production and the book trade", in: Griffiths,
           Jeremy – Derek Pearsall (eds.), 163-200.
Honkapohja, Alpo – Samuli Kaislaniemi – Ville Marttila
  2009   "Digital editions for corpus linguistics: Representing manuscript reality
           in electronic corpora", in: Jucker, Andreas H. – Daniel Schreier –
           Marianne Hundt (eds.), 451-475.
James, Montague Rhodes
  1902   *The western manuscripts in the library of Trinity College, Cambridge.
           A descriptive catalogue.* (Volume III. Containing an Account of the
           Manuscripts Standing in Class O). Cambridge: CUP.
Jucker, Andreas H. – Daniel Schreier – Marianne Hundt (eds.)
  2009   *Corpora: Pragmatic and discourse. Papers from the 29th Internationl
           conference on English language research on computerized corpora
           (ICAME 29). Ascona, Switzerland, 14-18 May 2008.* Amsterdam/New
           York: Rodopi.
Kytö, Merja – Peter Grund – Terry Walker
  2007   "Regional variation and the language of English witness depositions
           1560–1760: constructing a 'linguistic' edition in electronic form", in:
           Pahta, Päivi (et al.) (eds.).
Lass, Roger
  2004   "Ut custodiant litteras: Editions, corpora and witnesshood", in: Dossena,
           Marina – Roger Lass (eds.), 21-48.
Manzaloui, Mahmoud (ed.)
  1977   *Secretum secretorum. Nine English versions.* Vol. 1: Text. (Early English
           Text Society 276). Oxford: OUP.
McIntosh, Angus
  1983   "Present indicative plural forms in the Later Middle English of the North
           Midlands", in: Gray, Douglas – Eric Gerald Stanley (eds.), 235-244.
Minkova, Donka – Robert Stockwell (eds.)
  2002   *Studies in the history of the English language: A millennial perspective..*
           Berlin/New York: Mouton de Gruyter.

Minnis, Alistair J. (ed.)
  1989   *Latin and Vernacular. Studies in Late-Medieval texts and manuscripts.*
          Bury St. Edmunds: D. S. Brewer.
Mooney, Linne R.
  1995   *The index of Middle English prose. Handlist XI: Manuscripts in the
          library of Trinity College, Cambridge.* Cambridge: D. S. Brewer.
Pahta, Päivi
  2004   "Code-switching in medieval medical writing", in: Taavitsainen, Irma –
          Päivi Pahta (eds.), 73-99.
Pahta, Päivi – Irma Taavitsainen (eds.)
  2004   "Vernacularisation of scientific and medical writing in its sociohistorical
          context", in: Taavitsainen, Irma – Päivi Pahta (eds.), 1-18.
Pahta, Päivi – Irma Taavitsainen – Terttu Nevalainen – Jukka Tyrkkö (eds.)
  2007   *Towards multimedia in corpus studies.* [Studies in Variation Contacts and
          Change in English 2. Helsinki: Research Unit for Variation, Contacts and
          Change in English (VARIENG)]. Available at: http://www.helsinki.fi/
          varieng/journal/volumes/02/kyto_et_al.
Robbins, Rossell Hope
  1970   "Medical manuscripts in Middle English", *Speculum* 45.3: 393-415.
          Available at: http://www.jstor.org/stable/2853500
Schendl, Herbert
  2002   "Mixed-language texts as data and evidence in English historical
          linguistics", in: Minkova, Donka – Robert Stockwell (eds.), 51-78.
Taavitsainen, Irma
  2004a   "Transferring classical discourse conventions into the vernacular", in:
          Taavitsainen, Irma – Päivi Pahta (eds.), 37-72.
  2004b   "Scriptorial 'house-styles' and discourse communities", in: Taavitsainen,
          Irma – Päivi Pahta (eds.), 209-240.
Taavitsainen, Irma – Päivi Pahta (eds.)
  2004   *Medical and scientific writing in Late Medieval English.* Cambridge: CUP.
Tavormina, Teresa M. (ed.)
  2006   *Sex, aging, & death in a Medieval medical compendium. Trinity College
          Cambridge MS R.14.52, Its texts, language, and scribe.* Arizona:
          ACMRS.
Voigts, Linda Ehrsam
  1989a   "Scientific and medical books", in: Griffiths, Jeremy – Derek Pearsall
          (eds.), 345-402.
  1989b   "The character of the carecter: ambiguous sigils in scientific and medical
          texts", in: Minnis, Alistair J. (ed.), 91-109.
  1990   "The 'Sloane Group': Related scientific and medical manuscripts from
          the fifteenth century in the Sloane Collection", *The British Library
          Journal* 16: 26-57.
  1996   "What's the word? Bilingualism in Late-Medieval England", *Speculum.
          A Journal of Medieval Studies* October 1996: 813-826.

Waley Singer, Dorothea
    1919   "Survey of medical manuscripts in the British Isles dating from before the sixteenth century", *Proceedings of the Royal Society of Medicine* 12: 96-107.

CORPORA, ONLINE-RESOURCES & CATALOGUES

A corpus of Middle English scientific prose
    Compiled at the University of Malaga.
    <http://hunter.filosofia.uma.es/manuscripts>
eTK
    A digital resource based on Lynn Thorndike and Pearl Kibre, *A catalogue of incipits of Mediaeval scientific writings in Latin* (Cambridge, MA: Mediaeval Academy. 1963) and supplements. <http://cctr1.umkc.edu/cgi-bin/search>
eVK2
    An expanded and revised version of Linda Ehrsam Voigts and Patricia Deery Kurtz, *Scientific and medical writings in Old and Middle English: An electronic reference* CD (Ann Arbor: University of Michigan Press, 2000). < http://cctr1.umkc.edu/cgi-bin/search>
The Middle English dictionary
    <http://quod.lib.umich.edu/m/med/>
MEMT Middle English medical texts.
    2005   Taavitsainen, P. Pahta and M. Mäkinen (eds.) CD-ROM. Amsterdam: John Benjamins.
Perseus Treebank
    <http://nlp.perseus.tufts.edu/syntax/treebank/>
Text encoding initiative (TEI)
    <http:/www.tei-c.org>

On the pitfalls of interpretation: Latin abbreviations in MSS of the *Man of Law's tale*

Justyna Rogos, Adam Mickiewicz University, Poznań

ABSTRACT

Manuscript production in the medieval period was largely determined by the need for economy –
both in terms of time necessary for completing the copy and space on the vellum, covered in the
process. This requirement could be met by means of a complex, yet readily interpretable system of
abbreviations, originating in the Roman times and further developed in medieval Latin. (Petti
1977: 22) English scribes also frequently referred to that system, "adopting both [the] rules and the
signs which were readily transferable." (Petti 1977: 22) Importantly, with the degree of admissible
orthographic variability in Middle English a definitive and all-applicable interpretation of
particular abbreviation symbols is not feasible. Yet, editions of Middle English works fail to
"transcend what the manuscripts actually offer us" (Edwards 2000: 78) by silently expanding
abbreviations and assigning them specific alphabetical and (by implication) phonic values.
Electronic editions, on the other hand, offer the user an unprecedented possibility of juxtaposing
the actual manuscript with a transcription possibly inclusive in rendering the graphemic and
graphetic realities of that manuscript. This paper addresses the issue of treatment of Latin-based
abbreviations in preparing an electronic edition of the *Man of Law's tale* and presents the rationale
for the Man of Law's tale Project's decision to avoid interpreting abbreviation symbols in
transcriptions of Chaucer's manuscripts.

KEYWORDS: graphete; Latin abbreviations; Man of Law's tale; Middle English manuscripts;
transcription

1. Abbreviation as a graphetic element

Middle English manuscripts have been typically approached quite as if they were
linguistic informants in fieldwork linguistics, appreciated "more for what clues
they may furnish about the spoken language than for the sake of anything they tell
us about written language as such." (McIntosh et al. 1986: 5) This overreliance on
evidence which is secondary in nature masks an important property of the textual
tissue of a MS, namely the fact that its variable spelling(s), quite apart from
encoding some features of the spoken language, provide direct information about
the *written language* as a system *sui generis*. Importantly, re-directing the
analytical perspective towards an independent study of the orthographic layer of a
MS justifies the inclusion of distinctions which have been traditionally deemed
negligible as non-systemic within the phonic framework. The value of *graphetic*
analysis, which is concerned with variations in letter-forms and symbols used for
abbreviation, is manifested in at least two ways. Most importantly, it allows for
systematizing orthographic inventories of particular scribes in the form of

linguistic profiles, which could provide insights into the dialectal repository of the copyists and/ or their exemplars. This, in turn, might be an aid to ascertaining relations between witnesses of a polytextual work and reconstructing the process of its transmission. (Rogos 2009: 86)

This paper investigates one of the most conspicuous and, at the same time, most problematic graphetic elements of a Middle English MS – abbreviation symbols. Pointedly, this feature of MSS is not replayed in standard editions of Middle English works, which typically implement a wholesale 'graphemicisation' of both letter shapes and marks of abbreviation. This approach, as will be demonstrated further, is inherently flawed: first of all, it introduces a faulty parallelism between alphabetic and iconographic elements (i.e. between grapheme variants and abbreviations, respectively). Secondly, by silently expanding abbreviations, commonly practiced in conventional editions, the relation between form and function of individual abbreviation symbols is trivialised. As the following study will demonstrate, abbreviations are typologically and interpretatively complex entities, which deserve a separate consideration within the broader graphem(at)ic analysis.

2. Abbreviations in the *Man of Law's tale* MSS

As remarked by Petti (1977: 22), abbreviations fulfilled one of the main prerequisites of medieval MS production – economising on time and space available for writing. In order to meet this requirement, English scribes could resort to a complex system of abbreviations, developed in Latin scribal tradition, like, e.g., <p̄> (used for the sequences 'per', 'par', 'por'), <p̰> ('pro'), <⁹> ('us', 'os'), <9> ('cum', 'con', 'com') or <ẏ> ('is', 'es') (Martin 2007), which were readily understood and applied in pre-determined contexts. Characteristically, Middle English scribes were less than consistent in their use of Latin abbreviations and felt free to modify the form and/ or function of a given symbol. Roberts (2005: 10) attributes this discrepancy between Latin originals and their Middle English renditions to differences in the level of orthographic stability of the two languages: whilst the fairly stable orthography of Latin allowed a straightforward interpretation of abbreviations, the degree of admissible variability in Middle English spelling (coupled with the non-alphabetic character of abbreviation elements) makes the interpretation of such symbols to a certain degree speculative.

The following discussion capitalizes on transcription procedures implemented by the Man of Law's tale (MLT) Project team, transcribing the MSS of Chaucer's *Man of Law's tale* for the purposes of the envisaged electronic edition of all extant *Canterbury tales* MSS. The analysed sample comprises 17 MSS, representing all genetic families in Manly and Rickert's (1940) classification of the MSS in question.

Table 1. The corpus.

MS family	MSS
a	Fi, Ha1, Ma
b	He, Ne, Ld1, Se
c	Se
d	En2, Ry2, Lc, Ha2
independent	Hk, Ha5, Ph2, En3, Ps

Since the electronic format is inherently more inclusive and multidimensional than it is possible for conventional editions, transcriptions performed by the project team could also reach beyond the fairly uncontroversial level of graphemic analysis and incorporate some potentially (or actually) significant features of the graphetic level, like Latin-based abbreviations. As the goal of our transcriptions is maximal fidelity in rendering the MS reality, a set of conventions has been devised specifically for encoding such elements. Thus, e.g., superscript characters (*superscript letters* in Petti's (1977) terminology), which truncate the sequences of vowel + <r> are marked by means of <[sup]i[/sup]>, <[sup]u[/sup]>, <[sup]a[/sup]> and <[sup]e[/sup]>, respectively. Brevigraphs (*special signs* or *symbols*), in turn, are rendered by means of macro characters, formally reminiscent of their MS counterparts; hence, e.g., <p> for the sequences 'per', 'par', 'por'; <ꝑ> for 'pro', <ɣ> for 'is', 'es'; <ꝰ> for 'us', 'os'; <ꝯ> for 'cum', 'con', 'com' or <ꝛ> for the sequence 'er' or 're'. The following discussion focuses on the first four abbreviations as symbols utilised most frequently in the studied corpus.

2.1 p ('per', 'par', 'por')

This symbol represents the sequences 'per', 'par', or 'por'. (Martin 2007) In the MLT MSS it is never used in latter context, as demonstrated by juxtaposing the truncated forms with their unabbreviated counterparts, e.g.,

(1)   Empouꝛ <L 58, 150> vs. Emperouꝛ <L 856, 862> (MS He)
       Pfey <L 12> vs. Perfay <L 939> (MS Se)
       Pfay <L 12> vs. par fay <L 751> (MS Ps)

It is noteworthy, however, that abbreviation here is lexically, rather than morphologically triggered, i.e. it is not so much the availability of specific grapheme combinations ('per', 'par' or 'por') as the incidence of specific words that effect abbreviating. Thus, for instance, all MSS in the corpus abbreviate the word EMPERO(U)R, albeit not all of them do so indiscriminately. Pointedly, the only orthographic variant attested for the relevant grapheme sequence in the unabbreviated forms of this lexeme is 'per' (*Emperoū* (Ph2, He); *Emperoure* (Ld1); *Emperours* (Ne, Ps)). Therefore, arguably, there is little interpretative ambiguity as to the correct expansion of this particular symbol.

Similarly unambiguous are the abbreviated instances of the item PROSPERITE: whenever the truncated form alternates with full form or the latter is the only available form in the MS, the grapheme sequence constituting potential input for abbreviation reads 'per', rather than 'par' or 'por'. Likewise, for PERFECCIOUN, which appears as *p̸feccioū* (Se, Fi, En3, En2, Ha5, Hk), *p̸fectioū* (Ld1, Lc), *p̸feccoū* (Ph2, Ha1), p̸feccyon (Ps) or *p̸feccion* (Ry2), the only available spelling for the full form is 'per' (*perfeccion* (Ne); *perfecciouñ* (He)).

Yet another context for the application of <p̸> is exemplified by the lexeme DEPART-. Here, the only attested spelling for the otherwise abbreviated grapheme sequence is 'par'. Thus, in MSS En3, Ha5, Lc, Fi line 9 reads *departeth*, whereas MSS Ma, Ne, Ph2 and He in that same line have *departith*. Other unabbreviated forms of that lexeme appear as *departyng(e)* or *departing(e)* (En3, Lc, Ld1, Ma, Ne, Ps, Fi, He), *depart* (Ld1, He, Ph2), *departe* (Ps) or *departed* (Ne, Fi).

A different interpretation of the symbol <p̸>, however, seems to be available for the second most frequently 'p̸-truncated' lexeme, namely PARFAY. Abbreviated forms of this word are attested in four orthographic variants: *p̸fai* (Ld1, Ma), *p̸fay* (Ps, Ry2, Fi, Ha2, He, En3, En2, Ha1, Ha5), *p̸faye* (Se) and *p̸fey* (Ne, Se, Ha1, Ha5, Lc). Some MSS abbreviate all instances of this type (MSS Fi, He, Ha5) others do it occasionally (En3, Ha1, Lc, Ld1, Ma, Ne, Ps, Ry2, Se, Ha2), some (Ph2 and Hk) – never, even though <p̸> is applied to other lexemes in those MSS (e.g., p̸de in Ph2; p̸auenture in Hk). It is also worth pointing to the MS-dependent orthographic variability of the available full forms: *parfay* (En3, Ne, Ha2), *par fay* (Ps), *parfai* (Ld1), *par fai* (Ld1), *parfey* (Ma and Lc), *par fey* (Hk). In some contexts this variability reinforces the orthographic mismatch in pairs of abbreviated and unabbreviated witnesses of this type: p̸fay – *parfey* (Lc, Ma) or p̸fey – *parfay* (Ne) (however, MSS En3, Ps and Ha2 contrast the contracted and full forms as p̸fay – *parfay*, whilst MS Ld1 the two forms are paired as p̸fai and *par fai* respectively). This kind of variation notwithstanding, the grapheme sequence susceptible to truncation in those MSS is always 'par'. This interpretation, however, is not the only one available, as the examples of MSS Se and Ph2 demonstrate. In the former MS, the sole unabbreviated form is *perfay*. Ph2, in turn, never abbreviates this particular lexeme but encodes it in both available spellings: *perfay* and *parfay*.

The only case in which <p̸> could be expanded as 'por' is the lexeme TEMPORAL. The abbreviated form *tempall(y)* appears in 5 MSS in the corpus (Ne, Fi, En3, Ha1, Ha5), whereas in other MSS the full forms are always spelled with the 'por' sequence: hence, *temporał* (Hk, Ma, Ha2) and *temporal(le)* (Lc, Ps, Se; Ph2). Remarkably, though, the same token appears in MS He as *temperałły*.

2. 2 ₚ ('pro')

This symbol is seldom used in MLT MSS; in virtually all MSS in the corpus (except for Ph2, Ha2, and Ry2, where the relevant line is missing from the MS) it is applied for the nonce-occurring item PROPHETE in line 126. The sole unabbreviated instance is in MS En3, where the lexeme reads *prophete*. Moreover, MSS Hk, Lc, Ha1 and Ma abbreviate the token PROSPERITE as *ₚsperite(e)* (Hk and Ma) or *ₚspite* (Ha1, Lc) (compare with *prosperite* En3, Ld1, Ha2, He, Ph2; *prospite* Ha5, Ne, Se; *prospyte* in Fi and *prosperytee* in Ps). Yet another '*ₚ*-abbreviated' item is PROTECTIOU(N), attested as *ₚteccioune* (Hk), *ₚtectioū* (Lc) and *ₚteccyou* (Ma) respectively (compare with *proteccioū* in En3, En2, Ph2, Ha5; *proteccion* in He, Ne, Se; *protectoū* in Ha1; *protectioū* in Ld1 or *proteccyon* in Ps). As suggested by the orthographic shape of full forms attested both in MSS which abbreviate PROPHETE and/ or PROTECTIOUN and in full forms of the two lexemes, for both items in question the most likely interpretation of <ₚ> seems to be the alphabetical sequence 'pro'.

However, apparently this interpretation is not the only one available, as in MS Ps one can find the form *ₚpose*, which in all other MSS reads *purpos(e)* (except for Ha5, which has *pourpos*).Therefore, it could be argued that in that particular MS the *ₚ*-symbol encodes also the 'pur' rather than 'pro' graphemic sequence – an interpretation not available for the original Latin mark.

2. 3 ɣ ('is', 'es') and ⁹ ('us', 'os')

In the Latin system of abbreviations the two symbols abbreviated distinct sets of grapheme sequences: <ɣ> was used for the *-is*, *-es* sequences and <⁹> – for *-us*, *-os*. It is quite remarkable, however, that in the MLT MSS the latter symbol is at times applied in contexts available for <ɣ>. The two abbreviations have been attested in 9 analysed MSS, although in some of them these are nonce occurrences (such is the case with <⁹> in MSS Ha2 and Ry2, as well as with the symbol <ɣ> in Se).

As far as <ɣ> is concerned, scribes of MLT MSS seem to be motivated by lexical, rather than graphemic or morphological considerations in employing this symbol. Although MSS in question display quite considerable variability in abbreviating specific lexemes with the *-is* or *-os* sequence, there are a few items whose abbreviated forms recur in all or some analysed MS witnesses. Thus, e.g., *cristɣ* is attested in all relevant MSS; *tydingɣ/ tidingɣ* - in all MSS except Ld1; *kyngɣ/ kingɣ* - in all except Ph2; *marchauntɣ* (all MSS except Ne and Ry2) or *thyngɣ* (in MSS Fi and Ne). Crucially, this abbreviation symbol is not decodable into an unambiguous graphemic sequence, as both *-is* and *-es* appear in full forms of lexemes which in other MSS are abbreviated. Accordingly, e.g.,

(2)   <L 26> Yoũr <u>baggy</u> be not fylled witħ almes as (Fi)
       <L 26> Your <u>bagges</u> be nat , feld with ambes as (En3)
       <L 26> 3owῑ <u>bagges</u> betħ not fyllyd w[sup]t[/sup] Amys Ace (Ha1)

The same full form appears in MSS Ha1, Ha5, Hk, Lc, Ps, Se.
     On the other hand, MSS Ne, Ha2, He2 and Ph2 display the following full forms:

(3)   <L 26> Your <u>baggis</u> bitħ not fillid w[sup]t[/sup] ambes aas (Ne)
       <L 26> Your <u>baggis</u> beth not fulfillyd with ambes aas . (Ha2)

Similarly, for the item WORK, both the ending *-is/-ys* and *-es* have been attested whenever the full form appears:

(4)   <L 66> To ałł <u>werky</u> vertu ys her gyde (Fi)
       <L 66> To alle hir <u>werkys</u> vertu is his guyde (Ps)
       <L 66> To al her <u>workis</u> vertu is her guyde (He)
       <L 66> To ałł hir <u>werkis</u> , v²tu is hir guyde (En3); similarly, Ph2

(5)   <L 66> To al her <u>warkes</u> vartu ys her gyde (Ha1)
       <L 66> To alle hir <u>werkes</u> vertu is hir gyde (Ne)
       <L 66> To alle hire <u>werkes</u> vertu is here gide (En2)

Similar forms occur in MSS Ha5, Lc, Ld1, Ma, Ry2 and Se.
     <^{9}> is attested only in 4 MSS, with MS Ha2 displaying but one instantiation of this symbol (*Pyrr^9*). Interestingly, the other 3 MSS, Fi, Ry2 and Ha1, are highly idiosyncratic in their choice of lexemes for the ^{9}-abbreviation, never overlapping in this respect. For instance, where Fi has *pyto^9* <L 351 and 1016>, Ha1 has *pytus* and *pytuos* respectively (*pitous* in Ha2 and Ry2). Likewise, *þ^9* from MS Fi is rendered as *þus* or *thus* in other MSS. On the other hand, where Ha1 has *P²r^9* <L 190>, *Iuli^9* <L 302>, *Maurici^9* <L 625> and *olyfern^9* <L 842>, Fi has *pyrrys*, *Iulius*, *Mauricius* and *Olyfernῑ* respectively (*Iulious*, *Mauricyus* and *Olefernus* in Ha2 and Ry2). Moreover, not only is MS Fi quite exceptional in terms of the frequency of use of <^{9}> but it seems that this symbol has a wider frame of reference here, overlapping with the referent of <ɣ>.
     Thus, among the most frequent forms with <^{9}>, e.g., where Fi has *godd^9* <L 235, 425, 588, 774, 840> (in other MSS this lexeme alternates with *cristis*); Ne, Ps, Se, Ha2, He, Ph2 have *goddis*; Ha5, Hk, Lc, Ld1, Ma – *goddes*; whereas Ry2 has *godd^9* in <L 235 and 840> but *goddes* in <L 774> and Ha1 has three variant forms: *goddis*, *goddys*, *goddes*. Moreover, compare the forms for WOUND:

(6)   <L 5> That veray nede vnwrappeth thi <u>wound</u>[9] hydde (Fi)
       <L 5> That veray nede vnwrappith al þi <u>woundy</u> hid (Ph2)
       <L 5> Þat verry nede vnwrappith al þi <u>woundis</u> hid (Ne)
       <L 5> That v[2]ray nede vnwrappeth alle þi <u>woūdis</u> smerte . (Ha2)
       <L 5> Þat verray nede vnwrappith al þi <u>woundes</u> hid (Ld1)
       <L 5> That verray nede vnwrappeth al þi <u>wounde</u> hid (Lc)
       <L 5> That verray neede vnwrappeth , al thi <u>woūde</u> hed (En3)
       <L 5> Þat wery nede vn̄ wrappyd al þy <u>woundyd</u> (Ha1)

To give one more example, *schipp*[9] <L 73> in MS Fi is *schippes* (En2, Hk, Lc, Ld1, Ma, Ne, Ry2, Se), *shippez* (Ps), *shipes* (Ha5), but also *shippis* (En3, Ha2, He), *shepis* (Ha1) and *shippy* (Ph2).

3. Conclusion

This brief overview of the interpretative pitfalls awaiting transcribers of Middle English MSS has hopefully proven that orthographic analysis of scribal copies can only be comprehensive if it provides tools for the description of meaningful sub-graphemic phenomena. That these tools have been hitherto largely absent from similar analyses is manifest in the long-standing convention of subsuming all kinds of graphetic phenomena under the non-discriminatory label of graphemic variants, which would be quite unreflectively endowed with specific alphabetic (and – by implication – phonic) interpretation, without reference to actual MS evidence.

The analyzed MSS not only show a demonstrable lack of context-dependent consistency in the application of the discussed Latin abbreviations, but orthographic variability characterising the non-abbreviated counterparts of truncated word forms puts into question the soundness of re-encoding MS abbreviations as unambiguous graphemic strings, which is the usual practice of standard editions of Middle English MSS. As illustrated, both the distribution and the degree of admissible interpretative variability of abbreviation symbols in MLT MSS suggest that these characters should be treated as iconographic rather than merely orthographic elements, with a much wider scope of interpretation than has traditionally been granted.

References

Edwards, Anthony S. G. (ed.)
  2000   "Representing the Middle English manuscripts", in: Pearsall, Derek (ed.),
              65-79.
Manly, John M. – Edith Rickert (eds.)
  1940   *The text of the Canterbury tales: Studied on the basis of all known
              manuscripts. Vol. 2. Classification of the manuscripts.* Chicago:
              University of Chicago Press.
Martin, Charles Trice.
  2007   *The record interpreter: A collection of abbreviations, Latin words and
  [1892]   names used in English historical manuscripts and records.* Baltimore:
              Clearfield.
McIntosh, Angus – M. L. Samuels – Michael Benskin (eds.)
  1986   *A linguistic atlas of Late Mediaeval English. Vol. 1. General
              introduction, index of sources, dot maps.* Aberdeen: Aberdeen University
              Press.
Pearsall, Derek (ed.)
  2000   *New directions in later medieval manuscript studies. Essays from the
              1998 Harvard Conference.* Woodbridge: York Medieval Press.
Petti, Anthony G.
  1977   *English literary hands from Chaucer to Dryden.* Cambridge,
              Massachussetts: Harvard University Press.
Roberts, Jane
  2005   *Guide to scripts used in English writings up to 1500.* London: British
              Library.
Rogos, Justyna
  2009   "Transcribing and editing graphetic detail in the manuscripts of
              Chaucer's *Man of Law's Tale*", *Medieval English Mirror* 6: 79-86.

Patterns of loan-influence on the Medieval English plant names, with special reference to the influence of Greek

Hans Sauer, University of Munich (LMU) / Wyższa Szkoła Zarządzania Marketingowego, Katowice

ABSTRACT

Medieval English is here understood in the sense of Old English plus Middle English. About 2500 Medieval English plant names are attested, ca. 900 Old English ones and ca. 1800 Middle English ones – the discrepancy in the sum stems from the fact that many OE plant names died out, but ca. 200 survived into Middle English. For a number of reasons it is impossible, anyway, to give precise numbers: For example, it is not always clear whether a Latin or French word should be regarded as a loan-word into English or as a foreign word used in an English context. Some of the OE and ME plant names were common and frequently used, whereas others are attested rarely or just once (*hapax legomena*).

Many OE and ME plant names are native or formed with native elements, but many are also due to loan-influence. During the OE period, Latin was the main donor language; during the ME period, French was the main donor language. The influence of Celtic and Old Norse on plant names was very small, almost negligible.

Typologically, the following distinctions can be made: loan-words (which formed the majority); loan-formations (with subdivision into loan-translations, loan-renditions, and loan-creations); loan-meanings (very rare among the plant names); borrowed word-formation patterns (rare); borrowed morpho-semantic patterns (apparently also rare), and hybrid formations.

The present paper focuses on Greek influence on the OE plant names. Greek influence was usually indirectly via Latin, i.e. a number of OE plant names go back to Latin names and some of those Latin names in their turn go back to Greek (and some of the Greek names came from still other languages, but I do not go into this aspect here).

Roughly 92 OE plant-names ultimately go back to Greek; these are listed, described and discussed. There is a general list and there are also specific lists of loan-words, loan-formations (e.g., OE *hundes-heafod* after L *canis caput* after Greek *kynokephalos*), hybrid formations (e.g., *ciris-beam* 'cherry-tree') and words certainly or possibly changed due to popular etymology (folk etymology, e.g., *bisceopwyrt* from *hibiscum*). Most of the 92, namely ca. 69, are loan-words, whereas ca. 23 are (certain or possible) loan-formations. Among the latter, the loan-translations form the majority, followed by the loan-renditions; there is just one case of a (possible) loan-creation. A few of those loan-formations look as if they had been translated not from Latin but directly from Greek – this is striking because it is usually assumed that the learned Anglo-Saxons knew Latin but not Greek (apart from archbishop Theodore and Hadrian). Occasionally both a loan-word and a loan-formation based on it are attested (e.g., *cuneglæsse – hundestunge*). There is also a number of hybrid formations, i.e. compounds consisting of a loan-word plus a native word (e.g., *cipe-leac*). Most of these, however, have not been counted among the ca. 92 plant names going back to Greek (apart from those cases where the loan-word is attested only in a hybrid formation but not independently). Especially hybrid tree names are often pleonastic (e.g., *ceder-treow*), but the second, native element serves as a kind of explanation to the first, borrowed element.

Many of the plant-names ultimately derived from Greek still exist in Modern English. Relatively few of them, however, show an unbroken tradition from Old English to Modern English. The majority died out after the OE period, but was re-borrowed or reinforced from Latin or French during Middle English or (Early) Modern English.

KEYWORDS: Old English, Middle English, Latin, Greek, French, plant names, loan-words = borrowings, loan-formations, loan word-formation patterns, hybrid formations, re-borrowings, word-formation, popular etymology = folk etymology

1. Introduction: period, material and research

The term Medieval English is used in at least two different ways: Some authors apply it just to Middle English (ca.1100-ca.1500), with respect to the plant names for example Hunt 1989, whereas others apply it to the period comprising Old English (ca.450 - ca.1100) as well as Middle English, i.e. ca.450 - ca.1500 – I prefer the second usage because it implies a sort of continuity between the Old English and the Middle English periods.[1]

Old and Middle English plant names are attested in a variety of sources, Old English plant names for example in the Late Old English medico-botanical texts (especially the following four: *Herbarium pseudo-apuleii*, *Bald's leechbook*, *Lacnunga*, *Peri didaxeon*), but also in charters, in charms, in some of the poetry, and in glossaries (Latin – Old English), e.g., in the *Épinal-Erfurt glossary* (ca.700; the earliest English text of any length) or in Ælfric's *Glossary*;[2] there was even a specific plant name glossary, the *Durham plant name glossary*. In Middle English there are a number of trilingual plant name glossaries, e.g., the *Trilingual Harley glossary* (Latin – French – English),[3] and there are also general glossaries, dictionaries, poetry and prose where plant names have been preserved.

---

1   Although, of course, there were also dramatic changes due to the Norman Conquest, which affected the language, too. Another distinction would be between Early Middle Ages and Later Middle Ages. The term 'Dark Ages' is often used for the Early Medieval period, but nevertheless I find it a rather negative term. And Anglo-Saxon is, of course, another alternative for the period between ca.449 and 1066. – For a critical look at the present article and for helpful suggestions my thanks are due to Ulrike Krischke, Elisabeth Kubaschewski, Gaby Waxenberger, and Katharina Wolff and I am also grateful to M LC 1970.

2   The *Épinal-Erfurt glossary* is an example of an alphabetical glossary, whereas Ælfric's *Glossary* is an example of a class glossary, i.e. a glossary arranged according to semantic fields (which, of course, do not always agree with our modern ideas about the structure of semantic fields). See, e.g., Sauer 2009.

3   See Hunt 1989; on the *Trilingual Harley glossary* also Sauer 1996.

The most comprehensive modern collection and study of the Old English plant names is still Bierbaumer 1975-1979. This is now being expanded and turned into an electronic corpus by the 'Dictionary of Old English plant names project'.[4] The *ThOE* = *A thesaurus of Old English* by Roberts, Kay & Grundy 1995, lists Old English plant names in vol. I under section 2. Life and death, 02. creation, 02.07 a plant (pp. 96-114). A thorough study of the complex Old English plant names has just been completed by Ulrike Krischke.[5] The largest collection of Middle English plant names is Hunt 1989 (see also section 2.3 below). *The historical thesaurus of the Oxford English dictionary* (2009) has recently been published. It covers semantic fields across the entire history of the English language but I did not have the chance to use it for the present article as far as plant names are concerned.

2. Numbers, frequencies and problems

Almost 2500 Medieval English plant names are attested, ca.900 Old English plant names and ca.1800 Middle English plant names, i.e. there are roughly twice as much Middle English plant names than Old English ones. Many Old English plant names were no longer used after the Norman Conquest, but ca.200 Old English plant names lived on in Middle English, i.e. ca.1600 out of the 1800 were newly formed or newly borrowed in Middle English. About 400 plant names were borrowed from French during the Middle English period, but in documents from the period one cannot always be certain whether a French plant name should be regarded as a borrowing in Middle English or still as a French term; see (3) below.[6] More than 80 Old English plant names ultimately go back to Greek; these are listed and discussed in sections 6-7 below.

Some of the Old and Middle English plant names are attested frequently, others rarely or just once (*hapax legomena*).[7] Some of the *hapax legomena* occur only in glosses and glossaries, and some were perhaps simply created in order to render a Latin plant name, e.g., OE *candelwyrt* 'candlewort' for L *herba lucernaria* in the *Épinal-Erfurt glossary*. The *DOE* (Cameron et al. 2003): s.v. *candelwyrt* explains that it may have been used for making candles, but in view of its rarity and the context of its transmission this seems unlikely for Anglo-Saxon England; it was probably just coined to render *herba lucernaria*.

For a number of reasons it is impossible to give precise numbers; some of these reasons are:

---

4   See, e.g., Bierbaumer and Sauer et al. 2008; Sauer and Krischke 2009.
5   Krischke 2010; publication is in preparation.
6   This is the reason why Hunt 1989 does not distinguish between English and French plant names; see also Sauer 1996.
7   *Hapax legomena* are here not normally marked as such, however; for a list of *hapax legomena* among the Old English plant names see Krischke 2010: 357-360.

(1) Borders of the word-field: Plant names can be regarded as a word-field. As with many word-fields there is a core area and a marginal area, and it is difficult to draw the borderlines of the field. (a) Central are, of course, the names of plants (*fennel, lily, oak, rose* etc.). (b) The names of parts of plants (*blossom, leaf, root, stem* etc.) should probably also be included, as well as the names for natural products of plants (*apple, cherry, nut, pear* etc.). (c) Less central are, for example, names for a collectivity of plants and for places where plants normally grow (*garden, forest, meadow, wood* etc.). (d) Probably to be excluded are colour terms (*blue, green, red, yellow* etc.), although plants usually have one or more colours. (e) The *ThOE* in its section on plants also lists, for example, adjectives such as *lifleas* 'lifeless', *wilde* 'wild', and verbs such as *growan, (ge)weaxan* 'to grow', etc., but again it is doubtful whether such terms should be included.[8] In the present article, I shall concentrate on the names of plants and their fruits and largely exclude the other categories.

(2) Variants of the same name or different names: Sometimes it is unclear whether we have to do with variants of the same name (spelling variants, morphological variants etc.) or with different names. For example OE *crawan leac* and *crawe-leac* are morphologically different: *crawan leac* is a compound with the first element in the genitive, whereas *crawe-leac* is a compound with the first element in the nominative (the much more frequent case), but both have the same meaning 'crow garlic' and could therefore be regarded as variant forms (as for example Clark Hall does) – the question then still is which one should be regarded as the basic form (probably *crawe-leac*).

(3) Foreign word or loan-word? It is not always clear whether a Latin or French plant name should be regarded as a borrowing into English or as simply as a Latin or French term in an English context. A plant name can usually be regarded as a loan-word if it has been phonologically or morphologically adapted to English (Old English, Middle English), but the question is more difficult to answer if it retains its original form. Thus OE *celendre* 'coriander, coliander' can be regarded as a phonologically adapted Latin loan-word in Old English (showing i-mutation), but the status of the original form *coliandrum* in Old English is less clear. *Lactucam* 'lettuce' in the Latin accusative form is regarded as a Latin word used in an Old English text (the *Herbarium*) by some scholars, but as a loan-word by others. Similar problems arise in Middle English with French plant names. Interestingly Hunt 1989 does not distinguish between English plant names and French plant names found in English sources, but subsumes both of them under the term 'vernacular' plant names. In the trilingual plant name glossaries such as the

---

8   *Wilde* of course has to be included if it forms the first part of a complex plant name, such as
      wilde lactuce 'wild lettuce'.

Trilingual Harley glossary (13th century) often the sequence of the names helps. It is usually Latin – French – English, e.g., *viola – viole – appelleaf*. But sometimes just two names are given, e.g., *apium – ache*; *bethonica – beteine*; *ruta –rue* – in these cases it is difficult to decide whether the second word is to be regarded just as a French word or as a French word that has also been borrowed into English. The question is complicated by the fact that some French names were borrowed earlier and others later. *Saxifrage* and *tansy*, for example, were eventually borrowed, whereas *mort ortie* lit. 'dead nettle' and *ortie griesche* were never borrowed. In the *Trilingual Harley glossary* the plant name *herb Robert* probably has to be regarded as a loan-word, whereas *herb beneit* and *herb John* probably were French words, just as *escume de or*, *muge de bois*. In some glossaries (but not in the *Trilingual Harley glossary*) the languages are indicated by labels such as Anglice – Gallice.[9]

(4) Reborrowings: Fairly many Old English loan-words from Latin were reinforced or reborrowed mainly via French and in a more or less different form during the Middle English or Early Modern English period, e.g., L *fica* > OE *fic*; ME *figue* > ModE *fig*; for further examples see 7.1. below.

(5) Other problems which I just mention but cannot discuss in detail include: (a) The identification of the plants is sometimes very difficult; see especially Bierbaumer 1975-1979. Some of the plants are very similar and accordingly hard to distinguish, and the Middle Ages did not yet have our modern botanical knowledge, although their knowledge should not be underestimated either. (b) The question of identification is sometimes connected with the question of synonymy and polysemy. Sometimes the same Latin name is rendered by different English names, e.g., *althaea officinalis – marshmallow*, *wild mallow*, *hollyhock*; conversely, sometimes different Latin names are rendered by the same English name, e.g., *consolida maior*, *acantum*, *bruscus* – OE *banwyrt*, ME *bonewort*. (c) It is not always certain whether and how far all the plants mentioned in the Old and Middle English sources were actually known in Medieval England. Some, for example, were probably just known from the Bible and other classical texts, but some were probably introduced by the missionaries or known through trade. (d) Nothing seems to be known about possible dialectal variation among the Old and Middle English plant names.

3. Donor languages

During the Old English period, Latin was the main language from which plant names were borrowed; Latin loan-influence on Old English plant names (including loan-words as well as loan-formations) even seems to have been greater than on the general Old English vocabulary. During the Middle English period, French was the main donor language. Greek influence was practically

9   See also Sauer 1996: 138-139.

always indirectly via Latin or, to put it the other way round: some Latin plant names in their turn go back to Greek; these are listed and discussed in sections 6-7 below. The influence of Celtic, Old Norse and other languages on English plant names was very small.[10] Among the names for parts of plants, *root* is a loan-word from Old Norse. Of course some plant names have a difficult or disputed etymology, for example: ME *arsesmart* could go back to an unattested Old English compound or to a Middle Dutch word (the *MED*: s.v. *ars-smerte* does not mention any etymology). OE *curmealle* seems to be a native name, but apparently does not have a clear Germanic antecedent.

4. Typology of loan-influence

With regard to the patterns of loan-influence, the basic distinction is between native words and loan-words. Loan-formations, loan-meanings (semantic loans) and hybrid formations cut across this distinction, however; in other words, loan-words represent direct influence and loan-formations, loan-meanings and hybrid formations represent indirect influence. A distinction which does not primarily pertain to the question of loan-influence is between morphologically simple (simplex) words and morphologically complex words (compounds, prefix-formations and suffix-formations). Loan-words, however, are often morphologically simplex, whereas loan-formations are usually morphologically complex. I shall now briefly sketch the typology of loan-influence:

(1) Loan-words: Here, form and meaning are taken over, e.g., *fennel* (from L *foeniculum* etc., lit. 'little hay') or *rose* (from L *rosa*). Some borrowed plant-names were taken over more or less unchanged, with simply the Latin ending omitted, e.g., L *costus* > OE *cost*, L *cuminum* > OE *cymen* (but with i-mutation), L *hysopus* > OE *hysope* 'hyssop', L *nardus* > OE *nard*, L *storax* > OE *stor*, whereas others were affected by later sound-changes, e.g., L *fenuculus* etc. > OE *finul, finol* etc. > ModE *fennel*. Thus the form was often adapted to the English phonological, orthographical or morphological conventions. Sometimes there seems to have been suffix substitution, i.e. the addition of a native Old English suffix instead of a Latin suffix or inflectional ending, e.g., L *asphaltum* > OE *spaldur*, L *castanea* > OE *cistel-*, L *galla* > OE *galloc, galluc*, L *persicum* > OE *persoc*. Some loan-words show partial adaptation to native words or to adapted loan-words, e.g., OE *solsece* < L *solsequium* 'heliotrope', lit. 'sun-follower', where L *sol* 'sun' was retained, but OE *sece* from *secan* 'seek, search' was substituted for L *sequi(um)* 'follow(er)'. The first element of OE *feferfuge* 'feverfew' < L *febrifugia* lit. '[plant] that makes the fever flee' is the loan-word OE *fefer* 'fever' < L *febris*. Forms such as *feferfuge* and *solsece* should probably

---

10   See Krischke 2010: 158-159.

be regarded as loan-words with partial adaptation (substitution) rather than as hybrid loan-translations (on these see (6) below), but they show how difficult it can be to draw the borderline. Some loan-words were apparently not borrowed as independent words; they only occur as (usually first) elements of hybrid compounds; see 7.1. below.

(2) Loan-formations: These are imitations of a foreign, in Old English usually a Latin word with native material, i.e. the form is new, but the meaning is borrowed. They can be subdivided into loan-translations, loan-renditions, and loan-creations: (a) Loan-translations have the closest formal correspondence to their (Latin, French) model and are accordingly easiest to recognize,[11] e.g., L *herba lucernaria* > OE *candelwyrt* lit. 'candlewort'; *viscum quercinum* > OE *acmistel* lit. 'oak-mistle'; L *rosa canina* > ME *hundes-rose*. As the examples show, the change of word-order, the replacement of a Latin adjective by an Old English noun, or the use of a noun in the genitive in Old English still warrant the inclusion of a formation among the loan-translations. (b) Loan-renditions only show a partial formal correspondence, e.g., L *apiago, apiastrum* > OE *beowyrt* lit. 'beewort, beeplant'; here the first element *api-* corresponds to OE *beo* 'bee', but the Latin name is a suffix formation (*-ago* or *-astrum*), whereas the Old English rendering is a compound consisting of two nouns (with *wyrt* 'wort, plant' as second element). (c) Loan-creations show no formal correspondence to their Latin models. They are the rarest group and certainly most difficult to recognize. A possible example is OE *wedeberge* for L *helleborum*. *Wedeberge* literally means 'mad-berry' – the connection perhaps is that *helleborum* was thought to be useful in curing mental diseases. See further 7.2 below.

(3) Loan-meanings (semantic borrowings): Here we have native English words (sometimes going back to Germanic) which took over their meaning from a foreign (usually Latin) word. There are several examples from the religious vocabulary, e.g., OE *synn* > *sin* for the Latin-Christian concept of *peccatum*. However, there seem to be extremely few instances of loan-meanings among the plant names.[12]

(4) Borrowed word-formation patterns (loan word-formation patterns): These are rare, because loan-formations are usually formed according to native patterns of word-formation. Borrowed word-formation patterns of course entail, at least originally, loan-translations. (a) A possible instance of a borrowed word-formation pattern from Latin is provided by the bahuvrihi nouns L *trifolium* – OE *þrilefe* lit. 'threeleaf'; L *quinquefolium* – OE *fifleafe* lit. 'fiveleaf'; L *septifolium* –

---

11   On the criteria for loan-formations see 5.1 below.
12   Krischke 2010: 167-168 considers *wingeard* in the meaning 'vine' as a semantic loan.

OE *seofonleafe* lit. 'sevenleaf'. Bahuvrihi nouns imply a possessive relation, i.e. 'a plant having three/five/seven leaves',[13] but the semantic head (i.e. 'plant') is not expressed on the surface. Semantically bahuvrihi nouns can also be seen as metonymic (pars pro toto) formations: A part, i.e. the leaves, stands for the entire plant. Whereas bahuvrihi adjectives, e.g., *anmod* 'of one mind' or *earmheort* 'humble, merciful' (lit. 'having a poor heart') were frequent in Old English, bahuvrihi nouns were rare. This and the close morphological correspondence make it likely that the pattern 'numeral + noun = plant name' is a loan word-formation pattern. (b) In Middle English, the so-called inversion compounds, where the head precedes the modifier, is also a borrowed pattern that goes back to French and is first attested in French loan-words, e.g., *herb John, herb Robert*. (c) In Middle English, the pattern noun + preposition + noun also seems to be due to French influence, e.g., *feuille de vigne*; *hyssop of the wood*. (d) The pattern 'noun + deverbal noun in *–end*' (or: 'noun + present participle in *–ende* used as a noun') is a native pattern, but the only two Old English plant names formed according to this pattern are *hapax legomena* and loan-formations: *men-lufigende* 'men-lover' < *philanthropos*; *sun-folgend* 'sun-follower' < *solsequium*.[14]

(5) Borrowed morpho-semantic patterns: In Old English, there are ca. nine compounds with 'earth' as their first element: *eorþ-æppel, -berige, -crop, -gealle, -hnutu, -ifig, -mistel, -nafole, -rima*. Since at least four of these are loan-formations (loan-translations) based on Latin names containing *terra*, the entire pattern may originally be due to the imitation of Latin plant names with *terra* or *terrestris*: L *malus terrae* > OE *eorð-æppel*; L *fel terrae* > OE *eorð-gealle*; L *hedera terrestris* > OE *eorð-ifig*; L *umbilicus terrae* > OE *eorð-nafola*; see Krischke 2010: 202-205, and 7.2 below.

(6) Hybrid formations: Hybrid formations are English formations which usually consist of a loan-word and a native word, e.g., *porleac* 'leek' from L *porrum* plus OE *leac* 'leek', or *ficwyrt* 'figwort' from L *ficus* 'fig, fig-tree' and OE *wyrt* 'wort, plant'. Usually the Latin word was also borrowed independently, as in *ficwyrt*, but there are also cases where a (Latin) loan-word occurs only within a hybrid formation, e.g., *cisirbeam, cirisbeam* 'cherrytree': *cisir, ciris* comes from L *cerasum*, but is only attested in this OE compound. There were also hybrid loan-formations, e.g., L *mentha aquatica* > OE *brocminte* 'brookmint', or L *lactuca silvatica* > OE *wudulectric* lit. 'woodlettuce'. On the status of *feverfuge* and *solsece* see (1) above.

---

13   More precisely, the names refer to plants the leaves of which are divided into three or five or seven parts.

14   See Krischke 2010: 325, and 7.2 below.

(7) Chronology: I shall not deal with questions of chronology here.[15] Some Latin words were borrowed on the Continent, i.e. into Germanic or West-Germanic before ca.450 (e.g., L *cuminum* > OE *cymen*; L *pirus* > OE *pere*), others into Old English through Celtic transmission, i.e. between ca.450 and ca.600 (e.g., L *humilus* > OE *hymele*; L *solsequium* > OE *solsece*), others into Old English during Christianization, i.e. ca.600 – ca.700 (e.g., *lilie, rose*), others during the Benedictine Reform, i.e. ca.955 – ca.1066 (e.g., *cucumer, organe*).

5. Some questions about loan-influence and special cases

(1) Loan-formation or independent formation? One question about loan-formations is, of course, how it can be shown that we actually have to do with a loan-formation and not with an independent native formation which is similar to a Latin word just by accident. Possible criteria are: (a) the close morphological correspondence; (b) that translators were experimenting and came up with several English renderings for the same Latin name, which shows that they had no fixed English term; (c) that the plant was not known in England and that the translators and glossators nevertheless tried to coin an English equivalent for a Latin word they came across, or that the plant was not known before but was introduced, for example, by the missionaries – this is, of course, often difficult to prove. With religious concepts such as L *omnipotens* it is usually easier to assume that they were not known to the Germanic tribes or to the Anglo-Saxons and were introduced by the missionaries, and that *almighty* accordingly is a loan-translation based on *omnipotens*. In the area of plant names we often have to do with probability, not with proof.

(2) Direction of translation: Normally Latin names were translated into Old English (or Middle English), but in some cases an Old English word may have been translated into Latin. Possible examples are: OE *attorlaþe* lit. '[plant] which is hostile to poison' (i.e. plant used as an antidote to poison) > L *venenifuga*; OE *sinfulle* 'houseleek', lit. 'always full' > L *sempervivus*; OE *fenminte* > L *menta aquatica*.

(3) Loan-formation immediately from Greek? Greek names were usually borrowed or translated into Latin and from Latin borrowed or translated into (Old) English. For Old English plant names which were perhaps immediately translated from Greek, see 7.2 below.

(4) Obscuration and popular etymology (folk etymology): Occasionally complex words were shortened and changed so that they were no longer related to the

---

15   See, e.g., Krischke 2010: 155-163.

words of which they originally consisted. A well-known example is *lord* from OE *hlaf-w(e)ard*, lit. 'bread-guardian' (*hlaf* > *loaf*; *w(e)ard*: related to *ward, warden*). Popular etymology (folk etymology) is the opposite phenomenon; here words which are no longer transparent (native words and loan-words) are changed and remotivated so that they resemble existing words wholly or partly; the phonological similarity is, however, usually more important than semantic coherence or probability. Sometimes words seem to have been obscured first and then re-motivated by popular etymology (and then obscured again). OE *gundeswylige* 'devourer of pus' may have been obscured even in Old English, because later it was changed into OE *grundeswylige* lit. 'devourer of ground', but in ModE it was once more obscured into *groundsel*. *Wermod* (cf. G *Wermut*) seems to consist of *wer* 'man' and *mod* 'mind, spirit' (ModE *mood*), but 'man's mind' does not make much sense with respect to a plant name; perhaps it is a reformation by popular etymology of a form originally meaning 'bitter plant'. Later it was reformed by popular etymology again to ModE *wormwood*. Loanwords which were perhaps obscured in Middle English are, for example, *dandelion* < *dent de lion* < *dens leonis*, or *feltere* < *fel terrae*. For Latin loanwords of Greek origin which were reformed by popular etymology in Old English see 7.4 below.

6. Plant names of Greek origin attested in Old English and later

Roughly 92 Old English plant names are loan-words or loan-formations ultimately going back to Greek, although they were usually immediately borrowed from Latin, thus the sequence is Greek > Latin > Old English. Moreover there are several hybrid compounds with words ultimately borrowed from Greek (also via Latin). Some of the Greek names in their turn had been borrowed from other languages, but I shall not go into this question here. In the present section I give an inventory of the Old English plant names of ultimately Greek origin; in the following section 7 I attempt a classification according to the system outlined in section 4 above. Some of the Old English plant names of Greek origin live on in Modern English, and many were reinforced from French or Latin in Middle English or later; I have also noted this. I have tried to be comprehensive, but of course I can lay no claim to completeness. One problem is to distinguish loan-words into Old English from Latin (ultimately Greek) words in an Old English context (see 2.3 above and Feulner 2000: 459-477); another is that the Greek origin of some words is very uncertain.[16] I have tried to exclude words that belong to these categories. The Old English as well as the Latin and Greek forms often existed in several variant forms; I have not noted all of these, nor do I discuss all the phonological phenomena and

---

16   E.g., *arod, bulut, camedris, cameleon, cawlic, cymed, pentafilon, plume/plyme*; see Feulner 2000: 393-441.

problems. For the following survey I am indebted to the studies by Feulner 2000 and Krischke 2010, which are in a way complementary: Feulner deals mainly with loan-words, whereas Krischke deals mainly with complex plant names, including loan-formations and hybrid formations. I have tried to include both aspects, i.e. simplexes as well as complex plant names.

Plant names of Greek origin attested in Old English:

1. *agrimonia* 'agrimony' < L *argemonia, agrimonia* < Gk *argemone*. Reborrowed in ME from French and from Latin.
2. *alexandr(i)e* 'horse-parsley, alexanders' < L *alexandrinum* < Gk *alexandros*. Used as a plant-name in Latin (not yet in Greek). ModE *alexanders* was reborrowed in Middle Engish from French and Latin.
3. *alwe, alewe* etc. 'aloe' < L *aloe* < Gk *aloe*. In ME reinforced from French *aloes*.
4. *ambrosie* 'ambrosia' < L *ambrosia* < Gk *ambrosia*. Reborrowed in Early ModE.
5. *ameos, ami* 'bishop-weed' < L *ameos* < Gk *ami*.
6. *amigdal, magdala* 'almond' < L *amygdala* < Gk *amygdale*. OE hybrid compound: *magdala-treow* 'almond-tree' (with initial vowel omitted). ModE *almond* was borrowed in Middle English via French.
7. *aprotane, oportanie, prutene* 'southernwood' < L *abrotanum* < Gk *abrotonon*. OE *prutene* is a shortening of *aprotane* (with initial vowel omitted).
8. *armele* 'wild rue' < L *harmala* < Gk *harmala*.
9. *asaru* 'asarabacca, hazelwort' < L *asarum* < Gk *asaron*. See *hæselwyrt* below.
10. *balsam(um)* 'balsam, balm, balsam-tree' < L *balsamum* < Gk *balsamon*. *Balm* borrowed in ME via French; *balsam* reborrowed in Late ME from Latin.
11. *balsemite, balsminte, balsmeþe, baldsmiþe* etc. 'watermint' < L *balsemita* < Gk *balsamon*. *Balsmeþe* is perhaps a popular etymology with association to *smeþe* 'soft, soothing'.
12. *bisceopwyrt* 'hibiscus': probably by popular etymology with association to *bisceop* 'bishop' and *wyrt* 'wort, plant'; based on L *hibiscum* < Gk *hibiskos*. OE hybrid compounds: *bradbisceopwyrt, feldbisceopwyrt, superne bisceopwyrt*. *Hibiscus* borrowed in ModE from Latin.
13. *boxtreow* 'box-tree' (*box* is homonymous with *box* 'receptacle'): OE hybrid compound (pleonastic; second element explains that the first element refers to a tree); *box* < L *buxus* < Gk *pyxos*.
14. *bradeleac* lit. 'broad leek': possibly loan-translation < L *ampeloprasum* < Gk *ampeloprason*, lit. 'vine-leek', confused with 'broad leek'.

15. ***cannon*** 'reeds, cane' < L *canna* < Gk *kanna*. ModE *cane* was borrowed in ME via French.

16. ***cassia*** 'cassia, wild cinnamon (?)' < L *cassia* < Gk *kassia*. Reinforced from Latin in EarlyModE (16th century).

17. ***ceasteræsc, ceasterwyrt*** 'hellebore': hybrid compounds; first element probably by popular etymology (homonymy with *ceaster* 'castle, town') < L *cestros* < Gk *kestron* 'betony'.

18. ***ceder*** 'cedar' < L *cedrus* < Gk *kedros*; OE hybrid formations: *cederbeam*; *cedertreow* 'cedar tree' (pleonastic; second element explains that the first element refers to a tree). Reborrowed in ME via Old French.

19. ***cel(l)endre, coliandre, coriandre*** 'coriander' < L *coliandrum, coriandrum* < Gk *koriandron*. OE *celendre* shows i-mutation; both *celendre* and *coliandre* show dissimilation (which had already occurred in Latin). *Coriander* was borrowed in ME via French.

20. ***celeponie, celedonie, cylepenie*** 'celandine' < L *chelidonia* < Gk *chelidonion*. *Celandine* was borrowed in ME via F *celidoine*.

21. ***centaurie*** 'common centaury' < L *centauria* < Gk *kentaureion*. *Centaury* was reborrowed in ME from Latin.

22. ***cerfelle, cerfille, fille*** 'chervil' < L *cerefolium, chaerephyllum* < Gk *chairephyllon*; OE hybrid formations: *wuducerfille, wudufile* (the latter shortened from *wuducerfille*), *reade wudufille*. ModE *chervil* apparently developed from the OE form.

23. ***ciepe, cipe*** 'onion, shallot' < L *cepa* < Gk *kepe, kapia*; OE hybrid formation: *cipeleac* (pleonastic; the second element explains that the first is a kind of leek).

24. ***ciper-sealf*** 'henna-ointment': *ciper* < L *cypros* < Gk *kypros*. Hybrid compound.

25. ***ciris, cirse, ciser*** 'cherry' < L *cerasum* < Gk *kerasos*; OE *ciser* shows metathesis; OE hybrid formations: *cirisæppel, cirisbeam, ciserbeam, ciristreow*; *cherry* was reborrowed in ME from F *cerise*, which was taken as a plural, and the singular *cherry* was derived by backformation (cf. *pea*: see *pise* below).

26. ***cisten, cistel*** 'chestnut (tree)' < WGmc **kastinja* < L *castanea* < Gk *kastanea, kastáneion*; OE hybrid formations: *cistenbeam* and *cistelbeam* 'chestnut tree' (pleonastic; the second element explains that *cisten* is a tree), *stan-cysten*. *Cisten, cistel* is only attested as the first (or second) element of these compounds. The first element of ModE *chestnut* was reborrowed in ME from OldF *chastaine*.

27. ***cod-æppel***: *cod-* 'quince' < L *cydonium, cotonium* < Gk *kydonion*; *cod(d)-æppel* is an OE hybrid formation (hybrid loan-rendition); *cod-* is not attested independently. In *god-æppel* the first element has been changed by popular etymology from *cod-* to *god-* 'God'.

28. **corn-** < L *cornus* < Gk *kranos*; only in the OE hybrid compound *corntreow* 'cornel-tree'. Homonymous with *corn* 'corn, grain'. Reborrowed in Early ModE.

29. **cost** 'costmary' < L *costus, costum* < Gk *kostos*. OE hybrid group: *englisc cost*. ModE *costmary* is a Late ME compound of *cost* + *Mary*.

30. **cristalle** 'a plant' < L *crystallion* 'a plant' < Gk *krystallion* 'ice, crystal'.

31. **crocc, crog, croh** 'saffron' < L *crocus* < Gk *krokos*. *Crocus* was reborrowed in ModE from Latin. OE hybrid compound: *collon-croh* 'water-lily'.

32. **cunelle, cunille** 'wild thyme' < L *cunila* < Gk *konile*. OE hybrid compound: *wudu-cunille*.

33. **cuneglæsse** 'hound's-tongue' < L *cynoglossum* < Gk *cynoglossos*; for an OE loan-translation: see *hundestunge*.

34. **curmealle** 'centaury': *curmealle seo mare* lit. 'the bigger centaury': perhaps a loan-formation < L *centauria major*; *curmealle seo læsse* lit. 'the lesser centaury', cf. *lytle culmille*: perhaps a loan-formation < L *centauria minor*.

35. **cymen, cumin** 'cumin' < L *cuminum* < Gk *kyminon*. OE hybrid group: *superne cymen*. ModE *cumin, cummin* reborrowed in ME via French *cumin*.

36. **dracan-blod** 'dragon's blood tree' lit. 'dragon's blood': perhaps OE hybrid loan-translation < L **draconis sanguis* < Gk *haima drakontion*.

37. **dracentse** 'dragonwort' < L *dracontea* < Gk *drakontion*.

38. **ele** etc. '(olive) oil' < L *olium, oleum* < Gk *elaion, elaifon, elaina*. OE hybrid formations: *elebeam* and *eletreow* 'olive tree'. *Oil* and *olive* were borrowed in ME via French.

39. **elehtre** 'lupine' < L *electrum* < Gk *elektron*. As a plant-name in Old English.

40. **elene, eolone** 'elecampane' < L *inula* < Gk *helenion*. OE hybrid compound: *horselene* 'elecampane'.

41. **elleborum** 'hellebore' < L *elleborum* < Gk *helleboros*. Reborrowed in ME via French and in EarlyModE from Latin and Greek. See *wedeberge* below.

42. **eorþnafola** 'asparagus': loan-translation < L *umbilicus terrae* < Gk *ges omphalos* or *omphalokarpos*.

43. **fenogrecum** 'fenugreek' < L *foenum graecum* lit. 'Greek hay': this is a Latin formation, but obviously refers to a plant that came from Greece. *Fenugreek* was reborrowed in ME via French *fenugrec*.

44. **fifleafe** 'potentilla, cinquefoil': loan-translation < L *quinquefolium* < Gk *pentaphyllon*: See also *seofonleafe*, *twileafe*, and section 4.4 above, section 7.2 below.

45. **fille**: see *cerfille*.

46. **fingeræppla** 'fingershaped fruits, dates': perhaps a loan-rendition based on L *dactylus* < Gk *daktylos*.

47. ***foxes-glofa*** 'foxglove': perhaps a loan-rendition due to a misunderstanding of Gk *manikos* 'mad' or *manikon* 'a plant the juice of which maddens' as L *manicae* 'glove'. See also *glofwyrt*.

48. ***gingifer, gingiber*** 'ginger' < MedLat *gingiber, zingiberi* < Gk *zingiberis*. ME *gingivere* was reinforced from French.

49. ***glofwyrt*** 'lily of the valley' lit. 'glovewort': loan-rendition < L *manicon* < Gk *manikon* 'a plant the juice of which maddens', which was confused with L *manicae* 'glove'. See also *foxes-glofa*.

50. ***godæppel***: see *codæppel* above.

51. ***hæselwyrt*** 'asarabacca, hazelwort': Perhaps a folk-etymology based on L *asarum* < Gk *asaron*. See *asaru* above.

52. ***hafocwyrt*** 'a plant', lit. 'hawkswort': perhaps loan-rendition < L *hieracium* < Gk *hierakion*.

53. ***hræfnes-fot*** 'ravensfoot, cinquefoil': perhaps a loan-rendition of L *polypedium, polypodium* < Gk *polypodion* 'a kind of fern', lit. 'many-foot'.

54. ***hundesheafod*** 'snapdragon' lit. 'hound's head': loan-translation < L *canis caput* < Gk *kynokephalos*.

55. ***hundestunge*** 'dog's tongue' lit. 'hound's tongue': loan-translation < L *lingua canis* < Gk *kynoglosson, kynoglosse*.

56. ***leonfot*** 'lion's foot': hybrid loan-tranlation < L *pes leonis* < Gk *leontopodium*.

57. ***lufestice*** 'lovage' lit. 'love-stitch': popular etymology based on L *lubisticum* for *levisticum* < Gk *oxylapathum*. ModE *lovage* was borrowed in ME from French (there were several variant forms).

58. ***magdalatreow***: see *amygdale*.

59. ***menlufigende***: loan-translation, probably based on Gk *philanthropos* (there does not seem to be a L **amans hominum*).

60. ***minte*** 'mint' < WGmc **minta* < L *menta, mentha* < Gk *minthe*. Several OE hybrid compounds: *brocminte, feldminte, fenminte, horsminte, tunminte* etc.

61. ***murra, myrre*** 'myrrh' < L *myrrha* < Gk *myrre*. Reinforced in ME from French.

62. ***naeglaes***: mistake for *cuneglæsse*, see above.

63. ***nard*** 'spikenard' < L *nardus* < Gk *nardos* (in OE: the Latin ending was omitted). Reborrowed in ME from Latin.

64. ***oleastrum*** 'wild olive tree' < L *oleastrum*: a derivation from L *olea* < Gk *elaia* 'olive, olive tree'.

65. ***organe*** 'origanum, wild marjoram' < L *oreganum* < Gk *origanon*. The OE form lives on as dialectal *organ*; the ModE form *origanum* was reborrowed from Latin in EarlyModE.

66. ***peonie*** 'peony' < L *peonia* < Gk *paionia*. The ModE form was assimilated to the Latin form.

67. ***pepones*** 'water-melons' < L *pepon* < Gk *pepon*.

68. **pepor, pipor** 'pepper': borrowed into WGmc from L *piper* < Gk *peperi*. ModE *pepper* arose in ME from the OE form.

69. **persoc** 'peach' < L *(malum) persicum*, based on Gk *Persis*. OE *persoc* shows suffix substitution. OE hybrid formation: *persoc-treow*. ModE *peach* was borrowed in ME from F *peche*.

70. **petersilie** 'parsley' < Romance **petrosilium* < L *petroselinum* < Gk *petroselinon*. ModE *parsley* seems to be a blend of the OE form and Old French *peresil*. See also *stanmerce* below.

71. **pise** 'pea' < L *pisa, pisum* < Gk *pison*. OE hybrid compound: *musepise* lit. 'mouse-pea'. ModE *pea* is a backformation from *pease*, which was regarded as a plural form (cf. *cherry*: see *ciris* above).

72. **plume, plyme** 'plum, plum-tree' < L *prunus, prunum* < Gk *proumne, proumnon*. OE hybrid formations: *plumsla, plumtreow*.

73. **prutene**: see *aprotane*.

74. **pyretre** 'feverfew' < L *pyrethrum* < Gk *pyrethron*.

75. **rude, rute** 'rue' < L *ruta* < Gk *ryte*. ME *rute*. OE hybrid compounds and groups: *feldrude, wilde rude*. ModE *rue* was reborrowed in ME from French.

76. **scamonia** 'scammony' < L *scamonia* < Gk *skammonia, skammonion*. ModE *scammony* was reborrowed in ME from Latin and French.

77. **scearpe docce** lit. 'sharp dock, sharp sorrel': loan-formation < L *lapathum acutum* < Gk *oxylapathon*.

78. **senep, sinap** 'mustard' < L *sinapis* < Gk *sinapi*.

79. **seofonleafe** lit. 'sevenleaf': loan-translation < L *septifolium* < Gk *heptaphyllon*. See also *fifleafe* and *twileafe*.

80. **sicomorus, sycomer** 'sycamore, sycomore' < L *sycomorus* < Gk *sykomoros, sykomoron*. ModE *sycamore* was reborrowed from French in ME.

81. **sigelhweorfa** 'heliotrope': loan-translation < L *solsequium* < Gk *heliotropion*. See also *solsece* and *sunfolgend*.

82. **solsece** 'heliotrope' < L *solsequium* < Gk *heliotropion*. See also *sigelhweorfa* and *sunfolgend*.

83. **spaldur** 'a thorny plant, balsam' < L *asphaltum* < Gk *aspalthos*. Omission of initial vowel in OE, plus suffix substitution.

84. **stanmerce** 'parsley': loan-translation < L *petroselinum* < Gk *petroselinon*. See also *petersilie* above.

85. **stor** 'incense' < L *storax, styrax* < Gk *styrax*.

86. **sunfolgend** 'heliotrope': loan-translation < L *solsequium* < Gk *heliotropion*. See also *sigelhweorfa* and *solsece* above.

87. **terebintina, terebintion** 'terebinth' < L *terebinthus* < Gk *terebinthos*. ModE *terebinth* was reborrowed in ME from French.

88. *twileafa* lit. 'two-leaf': loan-rendition < Gk *diglosson* lit. 'two-tongued'. Perhaps translated directly from Greek, because there does not seem to be a corresponding Latin form.

89. *wedeberge* 'white hellebore': perhaps a loan-creation based on L *helleborum album* < Gk *helleboron*.

90. *wududocce* 'sorrel', lit. 'woodsorrel': probably a loan-translation < L *lapathum silvaticum*. *Lapathum* < Gk *lapathon*.

91. *wudufille*: see *cerfille*.

92. *ysope* 'hyssop, ysop'< L *hyssopus* < Gk *hyssopos*. Reinforced in ME from French (*ysope*), and later assimilated to the Latin form.

7. Categories of the Old English plant-names going back to Greek

Many of the categories mentioned in sections 4-5 above are attested among the Old English plant names ultimately going back to Greek. The loan-words form the largest group (ca.69), followed by the certain or possible loan-formations (ca.23). There are also many hybrid compounds, and a smaller number of loan-words changed by popular etymology (folk etymology; ca.6), as well as a few doublets consisting of loan-word plus loan-formation based on the Latin or Greek original (ca.5).

(1) Loan-words: Many of the ultimately Greek loan-words in Old English still exist in Modern English; some died out. *Cost-* (in ModE *costmary*), *minte* (ModE *mint*), *pepor* (ModE *pepper*), *pise* (ModE *pea*, plur. *peas*) and *plum* (ModE *plum*) apparently show continuity from Old English to Modern English. Many, however, have no unbroken tradition from Old English onwards, but were reborrowed in Middle English or even in Early Modern English (mainly in the 16th century) via French or Latin; these have been marked with RB (for Re-Borrowing). A few show suffix-substitution in Old English (*spaldur* < L *asphaltum*); a few show omission of the initial vowel (also *spaldur* < L *asphaltum*; furthermore *prutene* from *aprotane*; *magdala-* from *amigdal*); some were only borrowed as first elements of compound but not independently: *ceaster-(æsc)*, *ceaster-(wyrt)*, *cisir-(beam)*, *cisten-*, *cistel-(beam)* (RB: *chest-nut*), *corn-(treow)*. The list of loan-words is: *agrimonia* (RB: *agrimony*), *alexandrie* (RB: *alexanders*), *alwe* (RB: *aloe*), *ambrosie* (RB: *ambrosia*), *ameos*, *amigdal/magdala*, *aprotane/prutene*, *armele*, *asaru*, *balsam(um)* (RB: *balm, balsam*), *balsemite* etc., *bisceopwyrt* (RB: *hibiscus*), *box-treow*, *cannon*, *cassia* (RB: *cassia*), *ceder* (RB: *cedar*), *cellendre* etc. (RB: *coriander*), *celeþonie* etc. (RB: *celandine*), *centaurie* (RB: *centaury*), *cerfelle* etc. (RB: *chervil*), *ciris* (RB: *cherry*), *cisten-*, *cistel-(beam)* (RB: *chest-nut*), *corn-(treow)*, *cost-* (ModE *cost-mary*), *cristalle*, *crocc* (RB: *crocus*), *cunelle*, *cuneglæsse*, *cymen* (RB: *cumin*), *dracentse*, *ele* (RB: *oil*), *elehtre*, *elene*, *elleborum* (RB: *hellebore*), *fenogrecum* (RB: *fenugreek*), *gingifer* (RB: *ginger*), *lufestice* (RB: *lovage*), *murra* (RB: *myrrh*), *minte* (ModE *mint*), *nard* (RB: *nard*), *oleastrum*, *organe* (RB: *origanum*), *peonie* (RB: *peony*), *pepones*, *pepor* (ModE

pepper), *persoc, petersilie* (RB: *parsley*), *pise* (ModE *pea*, pl. *peas*), *plume, pyretre, rude* etc. (RB: *rue*), *scamonia* (RB: *scammony*), *senep, sicomorus* (RB: *sycamore*), *solsece, spaldur, stor, terebinthia* (RB: *terebinth*), *ysope* (RB *hyssop*).

(2) Loan-formations: The following 23 formations are probably or possibly loan-formations. Mostly the Latin form in its turn is a loan-formation based on a Greek word (compound). Normally the Old English forms imitate the Latin form, but in a few instances the translation may have been based directly on the Greek form: In the case of *haima drakontion* > *dracan-blod, philanthrophos* > *menlufigende*, and *diglosson* > *twileofa*, there does not seem to be a corresponding Latin form; in the case of *ampeloprasum* > *brade-leac, hieracium* > *hafoc-wyrt, petroselinum* > *stanmerce* the original meaning of the Latin form (itself borrowed from Greek) can only be understood with a knowledge of Greek. These formations are interesting because it is generally assumed that the learned Anglo-Saxons knew Latin but no Greek.[17] The pattern 'numeral + noun ('leaf')' = plant name (bahuvrihi compounds, i.e. 'plant having two etc. leaves'), *twi-leafa, fif-leafe, seofon-leafe* seems to have been borrowed from Latin as a word-formation pattern, see 4.4 above. The formations of the pattern 'noun in the genitive + noun' are all exocentric (i.e. the element 'plant' is not expressed on the surface) and include a reference to an animal: *dracan-blod, foxes-glofa, hræfnes-fot, hundes-heafod, hundes-tunge, leon-fot*, but only some of them are based on a Latin genitival group: *hundes-heafod* < *canis caput*; *hundes tunge* < *lingua canis; leon-fot* < *pes leonis*. As is to be expected, the loan-translations are the most frequent group (14 formations), followed by the loan-renditions (7 formations); but there is just one doubtful case of a possible loan-creation (*wedeberge*). For details, see Krischke 2010: 366-369.

(i)   *brade-leac* lit. 'broad leek' < L *ampeloprasum* < Gk *ampeloprason* lit. 'vineyard-leek'. Loan-rendition: *leac* translates *prasum*, but *brade* 'broad' does not translate *ampelo-* 'vineyard'.

(ii)   *curmealle*: (a) *seo mare curmealle* < L *centauria major*; (b) *curmealle seo læsse* < L *centauria minor*. These forms (loan-translations) seem to be based on Latin, but *centauria* originally is a Greek word (*kentaurion*).

(iii) *dracan-blod* lit. 'dragon's blood' < L **draconis sanguis* < Gk *haima drakontion*: hybrid loan-translation.

(iv)   *eorþ-nafola* lit. 'earth-navel' < L *umbilicus terrae* < Gk *omphalokarpos* lit. 'navel-fruit': loan-translation.

(v)   *fif-leafe* lit. 'fiveleaf' < L *quinquefolium* < Gk *pentaphyllon*: Loan-translation.

---

17   With the exception of Theodore of Tarsus and Hadrian; see, e.g., Krischke 2010: 102-103.

(vi)   *finger-æppla* lit. 'finger-apple' (for 'dates') < L *dactylus* < Gk *daktylos* 'finger'. Perhaps a loan-rendition: finger translates *dactylus*, but *æppla* was added.

(vii)   *foxes-glofa* lit. 'fox's glove': perhaps a misunderstanding of Gk *manikos* 'mad' or *manikon* 'plant the juice of which causes madness' as L *manicae* 'glove'. Perhaps a loan-rendition: *glofa* translates *manicae*, and *foxes* was added. See also *glof-wyrt*.

(viii)   *glof-wyrt* lit. 'glove-wort, glove-plant': Perhaps a loan-rendition based on a misunderstanding: Gk *manikos* 'mad' or *manikon* 'plant the juice of which causes madness' was understood as L *manicae* 'glove', and *wyrt* was added. See also *foxes-glofa*.

(ix)   *hafoc-wyrt* lit. 'hawk-wort' < L *hieracium* < Gk *hierakion* 'hawk-wort'. Perhaps a loan-rendition: Gk *hierax* is the 'hawk' or 'falcon', the suffix *-ion, -ium* was rendered by the word *wyrt*.

(x)   *hræfnes-fot* lit. 'raven's foot' < L *polypedium, polypodium* < Gk *polypodion* lit. 'many-foot'. Perhaps a loan-rendition: *fot* translates *pedium*, but *hræfn* ,raven' does not correspond to *poly-* ,much, many'.

(xi)   *hundes-heafod* lit. 'dog's head (hound's head)'< L *canis caput* < Gk *kynokephalos*. Loan-translation.

(xii)   *hundes-tunge* lit. 'dog's tongue (hound's tongue)' < L *lingua canis* < Gk *kynoglosson*. Loan-translation.

(xiii)   *leon-fot* lit. 'lion-foot' < L *pes leonis* < Gk *lentopodium*. Hybrid loan-translation.

(xiv)   *men-lufigende* < Gk *philanthropos* lit. 'lover, friend of men'. Loan-translation, probably based on the Greek word, because there does not seem to be a L *amans hominum*.

(xv)   *scearpe docce* lit. 'sharp dock, sorrel' < L *lapathum acutum* < Gk *oxylapathum* lit. 'sharp dock'. Loan-translation.

(xvi)   *sigel-hweorfa* lit. 'sun-turner' < L *solsequium* < Gk *heliotropion*. Loan-translation.

(xvii)   *seofon-leafe* lit. 'sevenleaf' < L *septifolium* < Gk *heptaphyllon*. Loan-translation.

(xviii) *stan-merce* lit. 'stone-smallage, stone-celery' < L *petroselinum* < Gk *petroselinon*. Loan-translation.

(xix)   *sunfolgend* lit. 'sun-follower' < L *solsequium* < Gk *heliotropion*. Loan-translation.

(xx)   *twi-leafa* lit. 'two-leaf' < L *diglosson* < Gk *diglosson* lit. 'two-tongue(d)'. Loan-rendition: *twi-* translates *di-*, but *leafa* is 'leaf' and does not translate *glosson* 'tongue'.

(xxi)   *wede-berge* lit. 'mad-berry' < L *elleborum (album)* < Gk *helleboros, helleboron* (from *helleros* 'bad'; second element apparently unclear). There is no formal correspondence. It has been suggested that this may be one of the rare cases of a loan-creation among the Old English plant-names, the connecting idea being that the plant was used to cure madness/mental disease, but Krischke 2010: 250-251 is not convinced of this.

(xxii) *wudu-docce* lit. 'wood-dock, wood-sorrel' < L *lapathum silvaticum; lapathum* < Gk *lapathon* 'dock, sorrel'. Loan-translation.

(3) Hybrid formations, i.e. formations consisting of a loan-word and a native word, are, e.g., (without claim to completeness):[18] (a) the first element is a loan-word: *box-treow, ceaster-æsc, ceaster-wyrt, ceder-beam, ceder-treow, cipe-leac, ciris-æppel, ciris-beam, ciris-treow, cisten-beam/cistel-beam, cod-æppel, corn-treow, ele-beam, ele-treow, magdala-treow* (see: *amigdal*), *persoc-treow, plum-sla, plum-treow*; (b) the second element is a loan-word: *brad-bisceopwyrt, feld-bisceopwyrt* etc., *wudu-cerfille, wudu-cunille, hors-elene, broc-minte, feld-minte* etc., *muse-pise, feld-rude*. Some loan-words were not taken over independently, but occur only as first element of hybrid compounds: *ceaster-* (homonymous with *ceaster* 'castle, town'), *cisten-/cistel-, cod-, corn-*. Especially with tree-names such as *ceder-beam, ceder-treow, persoc-treow* etc., the second element strictly speaking is often pleonastic, i.e. the first element refers to a specific tree (for example the *cedar* is a kind of tree) and the second element states again generally that it is a tree, but since the first element is a loan-word, the second element can be seen as an explanation of the first element. Moreover, in Latin and Greek the first element is sometimes ambiguous, because it can refer to the tree or its fruit, and sometimes it refers only to the fruit or product of the tree (*ciris-, cisten-, ele-*) and therefore a word for 'tree' as second element also serves to clarify the meaning.

(4) Popular etymology (folk etymology): Ca. seven borrowed names ultimately from Greek were probably changed due to the process of popular etymology, where a word which is not or no longer understood is reformed so that it resembles common words. Since there was no fixed spelling (no orthography) in Old English, it is, however, not always possible to say with certainty whether the folk etymology was really intended.[19]

(i)   *balsmeþe* and *balseminte* < *balsemite*: the second element in *balsmeþe* was apparently adapted to the adj. *smeþe* 'smooth, soft'; the second element of *balseminte* was apparently adapted to the noun (plant name) *minte*.

(ii)   *bisceop-wyrt* lit. 'bishop-wort' < *hibiscum*: *hibiscum* was probably changed to *bisceop* 'bishop' and *wyrt* 'wort, plant' was added for clarification.

---

18   See Krischke 2010: 361-364.
19   See Krischke 2010: 365.

(iii)   *ceaster-æsc, ceaster-wyrt*: the first element is from L *cestros* < Gk *kestron* 'betony'. It was changed to *ceaster* 'castle, town'; the second element was added for clarification.

(iv)   *god-æppel* was changed from *cod-æppel* to become 'God's apple'; *cod* was not borrowed independently into Old English and thus is a blocked (unique) morpheme.

(v)   *hæsel-wyrt*: the first element was perhaps changed from L *asarum* to become 'hazel', and the second element was added. See Krischke 2010: 216 f.

(vi)   *lufe-stice* lit. 'love-stitch' was probably changed from *lubisticum*. Similarly G *Liebstöckel* lit. something like 'love-plant'.

(vii)   *peter-silie* from *petroselinum*. Perhaps the first element was recognised as the name Peter.

(5) Doublets: Sometimes there were in Old English loan-words as well as the corresponding loan-formations (or folk-etymological re-formations) based on the Latin (or Greek) source of the loan-words (see the preceding sections):

(i)   *cuneglæsse – hundes-tunge* lit. 'dog's tongue'
(ii)   *elleborum – wede-berge* lit. 'madberry'
(iii)   *petersilie – stan-merce* lit. 'stone-smallage'
(iv)   *sol-sece, sigel-hweorfa*, and *sun-folgend* lit. 'sun-seeker, sun-turner, sun-follower'
(v)   *asaru – hæsel-wyrt* lit. 'hazelwort'

References

DICTIONARIES

Cameron, Angus – Antonette diPaolo Healey et al.
    2003   *Dictionary of Old English*. (Letters A-G). Toronto: Pontifical Institute of
    [1986]   Medieval Studies. Available at: http://www.doe.utoronto.ca/.
Hall, Clark J.R.
    1960   *A concise Anglo-Saxon dictionary*. (4th ed. with a supplement by H.D.
            Meritt). Cambridge: Cambridge University Press.
Kurath, Hans – Sherman Kuhn – Robert E. Lewis (eds.)
    1952-2001   *Middle English dictionary*. Available at: http://quod.lib.umich.edu/
            m/med/.

Onions, C.T. (ed.)
  1966   *The Oxford dictionary of English etymology.* Oxford: Oxford University
          Press.
Roberts, Jane – Christian Kay – Lynne Grundy
  2000   *A thesaurus of Old English.* 2 vols. Amsterdam – Atlanta, GA: Rodopi.
  [1995]

STUDIES

Bierbaumer, Peter
  1975-1979 *Der botanische Wortschatz des Altenglischen.* 3 vols. Bern and
             Frankfurt/Main: Lang.
Bierbaumer, Peter – H. W. Klug (eds.)
  2009   *Old names – new growth: Proceedings of the 2ⁿᵈ ASPNS conference.*
          Frankfurt am Main: Lang.
Bierbaumer, Peter – Hans Sauer et al.
  2008   "Old English plant names go cyber: The Graz-Munich dictionary
          project", in: Lendinara, Patrizia (ed.), II: 43-62.
Biggam, C.P. (ed.)
  2003   *From earth to art: The many aspects of the plant-world in Anglo-Saxon
          England.* Amsterdam: Rodopi.
Cowie, Anthony (ed.)
  2009   *The Oxford history of English lexicography.* 2 vols. Oxford: Clarendon.
Feulner, Helene
  2000   *Die griechischen Lehnwörter im Altenglischen.* (TUEPh 21). Munich: Lang.
Fisiak, Jacek (ed.)
  1996   *Middle English miscellany: From vocabulary to linguistic variation.*
          Poznan: Motivex.
Hunt, Tony
  1989   *Plant names of Medieval England.* Cambridge: Brewer.
Krischke, Ulrike
  2010   *The Old English complex plant names: A linguistic survey.* [Unpublished
          doctoral dissertation]. University of Munich (LMU).
Lendinara, Patrizia (ed.)
  2008   *... un tuo serto di fiori in man recando: Scritti in Onore di Maria Amalia
          D'Aronco.* 2 vols. Udine: Forum.
Sauer, Hans
  1996   "English plant names in the thirteenth century: The trilingual Harley
          vocabulary", in: Fisiak, Jacek (ed.), 135-155.
  2003   "The morphology of the Old English plant-names", in: Biggam, C.P.
          (ed.), 161-179.
  2009   "Glosses, glossaries, and dictionaries in the Medieval period", in: Cowie,
          Anthony (ed.), I: 17-40.

Sauer, Hans – Ulrike Krischke
    2004   "Die altenglischen Pflanzennamen aus linguistischer und lexiko-
                graphischer Sicht", *Sudhoffs Archiv* 88: 175-209.
    2009   "The dictionary of Old English plant names or The Graz-Munich
                dictionary project", in: Bierbaumer, Peter – H.W. Klug (eds.), 145-180.
Wollmann, Alfred
    1990   Untersuchungen zu den frühen lateinischen Lehnwörtern im
                Altenglischen: Phonologie und Datierung. (TUEPh 15). Munich: Fink.

'Tomarȝan hit is awane': Words derived from Old Norse in four Lambeth Homilies

Richard Dance, St Catharine's College, Cambridge

ABSTRACT

This paper investigates some issues connected with the medieval English lexical material that scholars have derived from the early Scandinavian languages, focusing on four texts copied c. 1200. The twelfth century is an important period in the history of the 'Norse-derived' element in the English vocabulary, when a number of important words are first securely attested. But the textual witnesses have been relatively underexplored from this point of view, especially when it comes to copies of works other than the major 'new' (East Midland) compositions. As recent work on the textual culture of the period has demonstrated, there is a wealth of other extant manuscripts containing English writings; and these manuscripts, often featuring what have previously been dismissed as 'late' or 'corrupt' copies of Old English material, stand to make a significant contribution to our conception of how the English language developed, including how Norse-derived vocabulary was adopted beyond the area of 'the Danelaw'. My main focus in this paper is upon four of the homilies in London, Lambeth Palace Library 487, specifically those pieces which contain reworked pre-Conquest textual material, and whose Norse-derived lexis has not been analysed in detail before. The identification of these lexical items poses numerous challenges; I present them in the light of an experimental typology for the labelling of words purportedly originating in or influenced by the Scandinavian languages, which aims to bring processes of etymological attribution to the surface. I also explore the textual circumstances of these words' attestation, contexts which in important respects act as precursors to the better-known literary-stylistic and lexical traditions of thirteenth-century South-West Midland works like *Ancrene Wisse*, but where individual word choices need to be understood against a complex background of scribal responses to inherited material.

KEYWORDS: Old English, Middle English, Old Norse, language contact, lexical borrowing, etymology, Lambeth Homilies.

1. Preliminaries

In this paper I shall investigate a small corner of the lexical material that scholars have derived from the early Scandinavian languages. Broadly-speaking, my focus will be upon the twelfth century, a potentially very important but often neglected period, and specifically upon a case-study of four short texts copied *c.* 1200 whose Norse-derived words have not been fully analysed before.[1] My main

---

1   Note that I use the inelegant but unambiguous term "Norse-derived word" to refer generally
     to lexis borrowed from or influenced by Old Norse in any of the ways that this is possible,
     i.e., encompassing what conventional taxonomy distinguishes as "loanwords proper" next to
     "loan shifts" (semantic loans and loan translations), and at whatever remove from the original

business is to provide an annotated list of these words, which includes two *hapax legomena* (the partial Norse origin of one of which is suggested here for the first time). In the accompanying discussion I shall also contemplate some of the principles and problems which attach to the study of a lexical corpus like this. I shall pay special attention to the methods used to identify Norse input into English vocabulary, and which underpin the establishment of any such corpus, since the attribution of Norse origin can be a very difficult matter whose pitfalls are too seldom advertised; the (experimental) typology I shall use to annotate my data responds to these problems. I shall also probe some aspects of the distribution of these words, the situations in which we meet them, and how these relate to the larger historiographical narratives scholars have constructed about English vocabulary and textual culture in this period, paying particular attention to a comparison with the lexis of the thirteenth-century South-West Midland traditions surveyed in Dance (2003). My interest will therefore be 'etymological' in a broad and applied sense.[2] The quotation in my title, from Lambeth Homily II, may (perhaps) be translated as 'tomorrow it is uncertain'. This phrase is offered both as an instantiation of and a motto for the intractability of some of the evidence for the adoption and early usage of words derived from Old Norse, and hence of the difficulties facing us as etymologists; for, while I shall suggest that *awane* may itself be one of those words, its identification and its translation are indeed matters of some doubt for us coming upon it several centuries later.

2. Contexts

2.1 Scandinavian influences and twelfth-century textual culture

The twelfth century is a site of considerable interest for students of Anglo-Scandinavian language contact. Perhaps the chief focus of this interest has been upon a small handful of epigraphic texts from the beginning of the century, which constitute the latest evidence for a form of Old Norse being spoken in parts of England. I shall not deal with this material further here save to note that, by c. 1100, such meagre evidence as we have for the use of Old Norse is confined to the extreme North-West of the country.[3] For the great majority of England, we normally assume that Anglo-Norse linguistic contact was by this time long in the

---

act of borrowing (in terms both of word-formation processes and diffusion from one English dialect to another).

2   For some recent discussion of the role of the etymologist see Durkin (2009: esp. 31–33).

3   See especially the incisive discussion in Parsons (2001), building on and responding to earlier work by Ekwall (1930) and Page ([1971] 1995), and the treatment of Old Norse language death in Townend (2002: esp. 201–210). On the Scandinavian runic inscriptions in England, see especially Holman (1996), Barnes (2004: 131–2), Barnes and Page (2006) and Townend (2002: 193–4).

past, and belonged mainly to the ninth and tenth centuries; and it is to this period that we usually trace the first adoption of the bulk of the Norse lexical material that was borrowed by English. Nonetheless, it is well known that the Old Norse loans visible in the mainstream of the Old English textual record are much fewer, and different in kind, from those attested once Middle English literary traditions get into full swing in the thirteenth and fourteenth centuries. A distillation of orthodox thinking on the subject is conveniently provided by Burnley (1992: 418–419):

> Perhaps the most striking feature of the lexical legacy of Scandinavian is the extent to which its emergence into written English is delayed. The major period of population mixing is over before the Middle English period begins, yet although the evidence of close contact is apparent quite early in Middle English from influence on word formation, function words and syntax, relatively few Scandinavian lexical loans (perhaps 150 ...) appear in Old English texts; indeed surprisingly few make their appearance until at least a century and a half after the Norman Conquest ... Scandinavian words filtered slowly into the written language only after the Conquest, when training in the West Saxon standard was terminated and scribes began once more to write on a broader range of topics in the forms of their own local dialects.[4]
>
> (Burnley 1992: 418-419)

Given this cleavage between "Old" and "Middle", the twelfth century – conventionally understood as the interface, the "transition" (or sometimes just the gap) between the two canonical periods of medieval English – ought to be crucial if we seek to understand the adoption of those Norse loans which are nowhere to be seen in texts produced before the Norman Conquest, but which are commonplace in the major written traditions of the thirteenth century. It is easy enough to draw up a list of common words such as that in Table 1 below, all of which are generally recognized as deriving from Old Norse and which are first attested in twelfth-century manuscripts; details of first record follow *MED*, including dating and title stencils.[5]

---

4   The most important discussions of Norse-derived words recorded during the Old English period are Hofmann (1955), Peters (1981a, 1981b), Kastovsky (1992: 320–336), Wollmann (1996) and Pons Sanz (2000, 2007a). On the Middle English (and medieval Scots) evidence see especially Björkman (1900–1902) and Rynell (1948), and further Hug (1987), Skaffari (2001), Dance (2003), Kries (2003). On differences between the Old and Middle English material see further Townend (2002: 201–210).

5   Throughout this paper I follow philological convention by citing Old Icelandic forms to represent suggested Norse etyma for early medieval borrowings into English, noticing the reflexes of other dialects or reconstructed earlier forms where the differences are significant.

Table 1. Some Norse-derived words first recorded in twelfth-century manuscripts

ME word (*MED* s.v.)	sense	etymology	first attestation(s)
bōnd (n.)	bond	cp. OIcel *band*	*a*1126 *Peterb.Chron.* (LdMisc 636)
bōn (n.2)	request, prayer	cp. OIcel *bón*	*c*1200 *Orm.*(Jun1)
flitten (v.)	move, go, flit	cp. OIcel *flytja*	*c*1200 *Orm.*(Jun1)
geinen (v.)	profit, be of use	cp. OIcel *gegna*	*c*1200 *Orm.*(Jun1)
loue (adj.)	low	cp. OIcel *lágr*	*c*1175 *Body & S.(1)* (Bod 343)[6]
lōn(e (n.1)	loan	cp. OIcel *lán*	*c*1175(?OE) *Bod.Hom.*(Bod 343)
nai (interj.)	no, nay	cp. OIcel *nei*	*c*1200 *Orm.*(Jun1)
rōte (n.4)	root	cp. OIcel *rót*	*a*1131 *Peterb.Chron.* (LdMisc 636)
sēmen (v.2)	seem, appear, befit	cp. OIcel *sœma*	*c*1200 *Orm.*(Jun1)
skil (n.)	reason, purpose, skill	cp. OIcel *skil*	a1150(c1125) *Vsp.D.Hom.Elucid.*(Vsp D.14)
wing(e (n.)	wing	cp. OIcel *vængr*	*c*1200 *Orm.*(Jun1)

Naturally, a bald list like this can tell us relatively little. There have been a small number of more detailed studies, dedicated to the Norse-derived lexis *in situ* in particular twelfth-century texts: notable is Brate's 1884 monograph on *The Orrmulum* (one of the pioneering studies of Norse-derived vocabulary),[7] as is recent work on the Peterborough continuations of the *Anglo-Saxon chronicle* (Kniezsa 1994). But, as has so often been true of literary-critical investigations of this period, scholarly energy has been directed to these major "new" compositions, usually celebrated as the first *bona fide* texts in Middle English, and therefore to the effects of contact in the East Midlands; and this may be regarded as symptomatic of a relative lack of interest in, and to an extent the intransigence of, most of the other material from this time. There is a remarkable wealth of originally Old English texts variously copied, recopied, altered and recontextualized, and which survive in more than fifty manuscripts produced between the Norman Conquest and the beginning of the thirteenth century (Treharne 2001: 403), a period sometimes designated "the long twelfth century". These texts have long been the "poor relation" in studies of early English literary culture and language history, partly at least because they fit so

---

6   MED also records an onomastic usage from "(1170) *EPNSoc.5* (North Riding Yks.)".
7   See also the important remarks in Townend (2002: 208–209).

awkwardly into the period typologies we habitually use: they can be and have been classed as either Old English and Middle English (or both, or neither). Nonetheless this is a considerable body of material, which has far-reaching implications for our understanding of the "interwoven continuity and transformation of English linguistic and cultural identity" (Swan 2006: 152) during this crucial period (for general discussion see especially Swan and Treharne 2000, Irvine 2000, Treharne 2001, 2006b, 2006c and 2009, Swan 2005 and 2006, Da Rold 2006). For the historian of early English vocabulary, these texts represent very substantial early evidence for the occurrence of Norse-derived words outside the area of the Danelaw, especially in the South-West Midlands and the South-East. It is therefore especially important that the texts and the manuscripts containing them are now being opened up to sustained and detailed scrutiny. To be celebrated for its focussed and thorough survey of the manuscripts is the "Production and Use of English Manuscripts 1060–1220" project,[8] which has been preceded and accompanied by a number of associated text-critical analyses (several of which are cited below). And of course access to many of these texts and their linguistic features has been exponentially improved courtesy of the first fifty-or-so years' coverage of the *Linguistic atlas of Early Middle English (LAEME)*.[9]

In this paper I shall dig into a small number of these "transitional" texts, in order to interrogate the evidence they provide for the influence of Old Norse on medieval English lexis and, as far as possible, to assess some of the difficulties we encounter when we try to use this evidence to construct narratives about English vocabulary in the twelfth century. Burnley's formulation as quoted above, about Norse-derived words appearing more abundantly in English texts "when training in the West Saxon standard was terminated and scribes began once more to write on a broader range of topics in the forms of their own local dialects", inevitably elides a great deal of complicated actual linguistic usage: the transition from writing in "West Saxon" to "their own dialects" encompasses quite a long period, and a series of complex appropriations of the Old English literate past virtually as multi-faceted as there were scribes involved. To some extent, studying their outputs just goes to reinforce the old truism that the history of a language is in real terms the history of language usage; but this has especially important consequences in a period for which so much of the surviving evidence is embedded in a relatively small number of challenging textual incarnations.

---

8   See the project website at <http://www.le.ac.uk/ee/em1060to1220>, last accessed April 2010.
9   See the website at <http://www.lel.ed.ac.uk/ihd/laeme1/laeme1.html>, last accessed April 2010.

2.2. The Lambeth Homilies and this study

My focus here is upon four of the so-called "Lambeth Homilies" (hereafter LH). The homilies, seventeen in total, are preserved (together with a copy of the *Poema Morale*) in London, Lambeth Palace Library 487 ff. 1r-59v (L).[10] These texts were copied by a single hand, usually now dated c.1200 (the very beginning of the thirteenth century or a little earlier). On linguistic grounds Sisam (1951) divided them into two principal groups (and further sub-groups), which she traced to different exemplars. *LAEME* also treats the homilies as constituting two slightly distinct scribal dialects (conflated as index nos. #2000, #2001), both localized for mapping purposes to the same grid reference (372 262 E) in North-west Worcestershire (though an origin anywhere in the borders of Herefordshire, Shropshire and Worcestershire would be plausible, and Worcester itself is a good candidate; see especially Laing 2008: 2-3, 125-30).[11] The last few years have seen a flowering of scholarly interest in the textual and literary contexts of the homilies, from a variety of angles: see especially the work of Swan (1997, 2000, 2006: 161-164, 2007a: 41-42, 2007b and forthcoming) and the important studies by Millett (2005 and 2007), Treharne (2006a), Wilcox (2000a) and Hanna (2009).[12] These cast significant new light on the intellectual background of the texts, as well as their production and use, which can be understood in several, interlocking milieux. Millett (2007) has cogently argued for a diocesan pastoral context, which would be in keeping with the mixture of "older" and "newer"

---

10   They are edited by Morris (1868), and in part (items I, V, VI, IX, X, XVI and XVII) by O'Brien (1985); Mary Swan is currently preparing a new edition. A microfiche facsimile is published in Wilcox (2000b). See further Hill (1972: 271–273) and Pickering and O'Mara (1999: 40–43). For recent accounts of the palaeography and codicology of the manuscript see notably Wilcox (2000b: introductory booklet 72–75), Hanna (2009), and also the remarks in Swan (2007b: 411–412).

11   Laing (2008: 2–3) remarks: "For the SW Midlands, surviving early Middle English texts in somewhat differing forms of language outnumber the most likely places of origin of written local dialect systems. The complex of texts that include those in London, Lambeth Palace Library 487, London, British Library, Cotton Nero A xiv, London, British Library, Cotton Caligula A ix, part I (Laȝamon A), and part II (*Owl and the Nightingale*) are all very similar to each other, and also to the language of the Worcester Tremulous Hand and other material with Worcester associations. It is possible that varying Worcester language is what this complex may represent." For other discussions of localization, and further references, see notably Hill (1977: 108–109), O'Brien (1985: 7–11), Laing (1993: 111), Dance (2003: 61), Laing and Lass (2003: 266), Laing (2004: 72–3). For a detailed survey of orthography/phonology and morphology, see O'Brien (1985: 12–113).

12   For a pioneering linguistic study drawing on *LAEME* data, which includes Lambeth 487, see Hotta (2009). Versions of homilies VII, XIII, XV, XVI and XVII are also found amongst the "Trinity Homilies" in Cambridge, Trinity College B.14.52, ed. Morris (1873), *LAEME* Index nos. #1200, #1300; see e.g. Laing and McIntosh (1995), Laing 2008: 31–34, Millett (2005 and 2007), Treharne (2006a).

elements in the collection; Swan underlines the plausibility of Millett's case, and also points towards the suitability of the manuscript's contents for private reading by female recluses (2005, 2006: 160–161, 163–164, 2007a: 42). It is unlikely that the seventeen homilies appeared as a single collection before the production of L, whose scribe is best understood as a *literatim* copyist uniting material from two exemplars (see above, and Hanna 2009 on the codicological evidence for the scribe's activities). But, though Sisam (1951) emphasized apparent differences in the date and outlook of these two earlier collections (believing X, and hence the LH "A" texts, to be older and more backward-looking than Y, and hence the LH "B" group),[13] recent studies have instead stressed their commonalities, including the extent to which they have been influenced by new "scholastic" preaching techniques deriving from the Continent; there are indeed grounds to believe that X and Y were themselves produced in the same place and with access to the same source materials (see especially Millett 2007: 62–63, and Laing 2008: 126).

To my knowledge, no thorough survey of the Norse-derived words in the full set of homilies has been undertaken. Rynell's study (1948: 211–216) is valuable, but records only those items which feature in the specific semantic fields it samples.[14] In my doctoral work on the major thirteenth-century South-West Midland traditions (published as Dance 2003), I included eight of the Lambeth Homilies (items I, III, IV, V, VIII, XII, XIII, XIV), on the grounds that they did not contain material demonstrably reworked from extant Old English sources and did not themselves survive in non-South-West Midland recensions (see Dance 2003: 61–63).[15] But this leaves plenty of ground still to cover, and it seemed to me worthwhile to turn in this paper to a particularly challenging sub-set of the remaining homilies, in order to consider their vocabulary in the light both of my earlier work and that of a more fully developed model of etymological analysis. The texts in question are the four pieces which most manifestly contain "updatings" of material originally composed in the Old English period, as detailed below;[16] I shall refer to them hereafter with the abbreviation LH(OE). Rubrics and lineation follow Morris (1868); Sisam's (1951) textual sub-groupings are in brackets.

13　And see also Hotta (2009: 84), who finds that the nominal morphology of the B group texts is (slightly) more "advanced" than that of the A group.

14　Of the items recorded in the catalogue in section 4 below, Rynell notices only *forlaʒe, laʒe, ulaʒeliche, þrel* and (uncertainly) *ongein*.

15　NB I was following Sisam's (1951) account of these texts' attestations, and hence missed (as she did) the fact that there is also a version of LH.XIII amongst the "Trinity Homilies"; see Millett (2007: 126).

16　Sisam (1951: 110 n. 4) also felt that items I and III "certainly go back to Old English", but offered no evidence; on I see also Swan (2007b: 407), but O'Brien (1985: 62–64). Treharne (2006a: 233–235) has recently suggested that a few lines from Ælfric's Catholic Homily II.7 (*Dominica .i. in quadragesima*; Godden 1979: 60–66) might lie (fairly indirectly) behind Lambeth item III.

II *Hic dicendum est de quadragesima* (A1)

Contains (13/15–15/5) a reworked version of almost all of the English text of
Wulfstan's Homily 19 (*Be Godcundre Warnunge*; Bethurum 1957: 251–254). For
a detailed consideration of Wulfstan's text and the reviser's use of it, see Wilcox
(2000a: 87–96). (*LAEME* index no. 191.)

IX *In die pentecosten* (A2)

A revised version of Ælfric's Catholic Homily I.22 (*In die sancto pentecosten*;
Clemoes 1997: 354–364).[17] On the revisions in L see especially Swan (2000: 71-
76), and the brief remarks in Sisam (1951: 112 n.1), O'Brien (1985: 299).
(*LAEME* index no. 198.)

X *De octo uiciis et de duodecim abusiuis huius seculi* (A2)

A revised version of the composite Ælfrician homily *De octo uitiis et de duodecim
abusiuis* (printed in Morris 1868: Appendix II; ultimately composed of material
from four different Ælfrician texts).[18] On the composite homily and its L revision
see especially Swan (forthcoming), and the brief remarks in Sisam (1951: 112
n.1), O'Brien (1985: 305–307) (plus the discussion of compilation history in
Kleist 2009). (*LAEME* index no. 199.)

XI *Dominica v. quadragesimæ* (A3)

Contains two brief excerpts (121/32–34, 123/3–17, 21–24) revised from Ælfric's
Catholic Homily I.14 (*Dominica palmarum*; Clemoes 1997: 290–298). For
discussion of this and other revisions of this Ælfrician text, see Swan (1997), and
also the remarks in Treharne (2006b: 344–345). (*LAEME* index no. 200.)

Though these four pieces are alike in their re-use of pre-Conquest homiletic
material,[19] the ways in which this happens are in important respects distinct. Item
IX is the most straightforward example of an "updated" copy of an Old English
text, with some very numerous and often very interesting changes to the Ælfrician
original, applied consistently throughout. It may be contrasted with Item II, which
appropriates almost all of a Wulfstan homily but embeds it in a much longer and
apparently later text; and Item XI, which is also mostly original apart from its
insertion of two excerpts derived from another Ælfric homily. Item X is a

---

17   See also the parallel text printed by O'Brien (1985: 159–96, discussed at 150–157).
18   See also the parallel text printed by O'Brien (1985: 203–250, discussed at 197–201).
19   Swan (2007b: 407) emphasizes the similar ways in which Items IX, X and XI modify their
      sources.

particularly complex creature, a revised version of what was already an Old English composite reworking of four original Ælfrician texts stitched together. In examining all these texts one may refer to the thorough recent attempts by Swan (1997, 2000, forthcoming) and Wilcox (2000a) to characterize the nature of the updatings and reworkings that they represent: they have been variously felt, for instance, to introduce a more "informal" style, with a penchant for the occasional extra intensifying phrase, but also for the addition of quotations in Latin that speaks to a confident and interventionist revisionism that Swan has suggested might be the result of memorial transmission. Collectively and individually, these homilies are therefore a valuable source of information for those trying to understand literary culture in the period which may be thought of both as separating and connecting the "classical" Old English textual tradition and nascent Middle English ones. Looking backwards from the twelfth century, we can compare the "updated" portions of these texts with earlier copies of the same pieces by Ælfric and Wulfstan; and, looking forwards in time, we can put them next to major thirteenth-century written traditions from precisely the same part of England, including the AB texts, Laʒamon's *Brut* and the output of the Tremulous Hand of Worcester. Amongst other things, it will therefore be interesting to compare the forms and usages of the Norse derivations in our Lambeth texts with their occurrences in this more famous corpus; I shall return to these matters in section 5 below.

3. Etymologies, methodologies and typologies

3.1 Identifying Norse-derived lexical material

Before we can embark upon an analysis, of course, we need first to describe the set of probable Norse-derived words in these texts – and how we go about this task is a matter of fundamental importance. There are several ways in which we might wish to approach and to classify this group of lexemes. A useful point of entry is Fischer's "typology of typologies" of lexical borrowings in English, a summation of the sorts of questions scholars have asked of loaned material more generally. Fischer (2001) divides the main approaches into three groups:

(1) the morpho-etymological
i.e., classifying borrowings by their morphological structure (loanwords proper next to the several varieties of what are usually called "loan-shifts", i.e., loan-translations, semantic loans, loan-blends, etc.)

(2) the lexico-semantic
i.e., classifying the eventual lexical and semantic consequences of borrowing for the vocabulary of the recipient language (especially how a loaned item competes with and/or comes to dominate existing native expressions for a given concept)

(3) the socio-historical (sociolinguistic)
i.e., classifying contact situations and their effects on the processes via which
loaned material was transferred between the two systems (e.g. the relative status
of the two languages, the "intensity" of contact, distinguishing recipient-language-
led "borrowing" from shift-based interference, etc.)

All these categories are of course relevant to the history of the Anglo-
Scandinavian contact and its consequences for the English lexicon, and (2) will be
one of my focuses in section 5 below.[20] But since Fischer's typologies are
designed to be generic, and to be applicable to lexical borrowing into English of
any origin, they do not expose the issue facing the student of Norse loans in
particular, which arises directly out of the very peculiar circumstances of Anglo-
Norse interaction: how do we identify Norse input into English lexical material in
the first place?

The extent of the uncertainty can be indicated by reference to the catalogue of
Norse-derived material offered in section 4 below. This is a breakdown of all the
suggestions for Norse influence on the lexis of LH(OE) which I have traced in
previous scholarship, including editions, dictionaries, and etymological and other
studies. As will be obvious from a glance at the catalogue, some entries are much
more secure than others, or at least some have been ascribed to Norse much more
consistently than have others: comparing etymological attributions, only about
seven or eight items would be confidently derived from Norse by all commentators,
but that number rises to at least thirty-one if one brings in all suggestions down to
the most speculative. The confident derivation of early English words from Old
Norse is so problematic, of course, for reasons that will be familiar. The most
important is perhaps the sheer similarity of Old English and Viking Age Norse in
terms of inherited phonology, morphosyntax and lexis.[21] However we envisage the
effects of this for communication between speakers (whether we have in mind some
sort of mutual intelligibility or not),[22] the similarities of the two language systems
have obvious consequences not only for the relatively effortless movement of words
and other linguistic material between them, but moreover for our ability to
recognize that this is what has happened in a particular case. This capacity is
degraded still further by the patchiness of the record of both languages in the
periods before and during which, and for the parts of England in which, contact
mainly took place. These factors conspire to make it difficult to demonstrate that a

---

20 For recent discussion of (1) with respect to Norse-derived material, see e.g. Dance (2003: 74,
    91–97, 100–103). On (3), see especially the important conclusions in Townend (2002: 201–
    207), and further Dance (2003: 99–103). For a helpful recent overview of the study of
    language contact phenomena by the English etymologist, see Durkin (2009: 132–78).

21 Townend (2002: 19–41) provides a detailed comparison of Old English and Viking Age
    Norse.

22 See the thorough review of the evidence by Townend (2002: 181–185 for conclusions).

word-form or usage first attested in the textual record in the period from later Old English onwards must derive from Norse, rather than its being a hitherto unrecorded native item, or a convergent development in the two languages – and in some dubious cases we are left in the dark about whether either language is really a plausible source.[23] These are well-known problems, but I labour them here because, in the face of them, the tools we do use to try to identify *bona fide* instances of Norse input take on a special importance.

Still the most significant discussion of the principles is Björkman's *Scandinavian loan-words in Middle English* (1900-1902), which is impressively clear-sighted and remains exceptionally valuable. As Björkman sets out the criteria, by far the best evidence is provided by phonological and/or morphological developments diagnostic of a Norse rather than an Old English descent from Proto-Germanic, i.e., features which, provided we are confident about the identification of a word's Germanic root, cannot have come about in the native language (see Björkman 1900-1902: 30-85). Any purported Norse loans for which no formal, comparative criteria are applicable are inevitably far less secure, and have tended to be classified not primarily according to any particular "test", but by the relative degrees of conviction scholars attach to their inclusion; hence Björkman's two further sections, where he deals with words he regards as of greater likelihood ("tolerably certain") to show Norse input (1900-1902: 199-225) and of lesser likelihood ("possibly borrowed") (1900-1902: 226–258). These assessments are made on the grounds of whatever further evidence is available, most often drawn from distribution, that is the dialectal range shown by the given word in English and/or the distribution of its cognates in Germanic (words found mainly in the North and East of England are held to be more likely to show Norse input, as are words only found in Norse and English, and not elsewhere in West Germanic). Criteria like these are helpful in principle, and can provide useful if limited corroboration; but they remain ultimately circumstantial, and Björkman's own cautious take on their value is often overlooked ("Such tests are, however, all more or less unreliable"; 1900-1902: 197).[24] Arguing for Norse derivation on the basis that a word is recorded mainly in the areas of heaviest Scandinavian settlement is, furthermore, of limited value when one is examining texts from quite different parts of the country. Since the publication of Dance (2003), I have (re-)examined the etymologies of a large number of purported Norse loans.[25] This has involved analysing not only most of the words treated by Björkman but also numerous suggestions made in assorted scholarly sources since, and contemplating the various grounds on which all these items have been derived from Norse has led me to experiment with levels of classification additional to

---

23 For a general account of the problems, see Björkman (1900-1902: 8–12).
24 For some further discussion of these issues, see Dance (forthcoming 1).
25 I am in the process of making a detailed study of the several hundred instances in *Sir Gawain and the Green Knight*; see Dance (forthcoming 2).

Björkman's. Specifically, I suggest one might insert a layer of formal description in between Björkman's superordinate level of categorization (does a "phonetic test" apply or not?) and his subordinate one (where he turns to circumstantial distributional tests), in an attempt to boil down what seem to me to be the underlying (and largely unspoken) principles of attribution. In what follows I shall describe this expanded system of classification. It should be stressed that it is still very much experimental; it seems to me to have certain advantages when setting out the evidence for putative Norse-derived lexis in a textual corpus of the sort under consideration here, but if it is to be applied more widely it must of course be refined by being tested on much larger sets of words. I should also like to emphasize that by proffering some new (or really just additional) ways of labelling this loaned material I do not intend to suggest that I have "solved" any of the problems inherent in their analysis – in many respects quite the reverse. It must be reiterated that the very nature of the evidence makes identifying possible cases of Norse input very difficult, and one of our main tasks is to make sure we recognize all the ways in which it *is* difficult. I do not, therefore, offer any new species of evidence, but instead I am intent upon approaching the data more explicitly from an etymological point of view, and presenting a corpus of words in such a way that the decisions made by etymologists are as visible as possible.[26]

Taking into account the information encountered by the etymologist in the first instance, words perhaps showing Norse input seem to me consistently to divide into four broad groups, here labelled A, B, C and D. The differences between them are, on the one hand, to do with the relationship between the attested Old English and Old Norse lexicons, and on the other our grasp of a word's identity and ulterior etymology. I shall describe each group in turn, taking examples from LH(OE) where possible; further discussion of these words will be found in the catalogue in section 4 below.

3.2 Towards a revised etymological typology

3.2.1 Type A: formal comparative evidence

There is a fundamental division between words of Type A and the other categories, corresponding to Björkman's first-order distinction between items whose Norse derivation is evidenced by "phonetic tests" (and other formal features), and those for which no such support is forthcoming. **Type A** words are therefore defined as offering formal comparative evidence for derivation from Old Norse, i.e., one or more distinctive Old Norse phonological and/or morphological developments not supposed to have occurred in Old English. This Type may be sub-divided as follows:

---

26   For some further discussion of these principles and preliminary accounts of the revised system presented below, see Dance (forthcoming 1 and 2).

A1 = phonological criteria, e.g. ME *greiðen* 'prepare' (cp. OIcel *greiða*, OE *gerād*);

A2 = morphological criteria, e.g. ME *wiʒt* 'valiant' (cp OIcel *vígt*, neut. of *vígr*);

A3 = phonological *and* morphological criteria, e.g. ME *haʒer* 'skilful' (cp. OIcel *hag-r*; an Old English cognate would have shown palatalization of *-g*).

The LH(OE) words placed unambiguously in this category are *gersum* (A1) and *þrel* (A1), and note also *gist* (see discussion under item 7 below). Note that some applicable criteria have sometimes been regarded as more compelling than others, i.e., a characteristically Old Norse outcome of a phoneme like PGmc /ai/ (as in ME *greiðen* cited above) is in theory more impressive than failure of palatalization of PGmc */g/ (as in e.g. *gersum*), which is more widespread in the Germanic languages and hence easier to imagine in some variety of Old English (see for instance Lass 2007: 20-21); but to the best of our knowledge all these features are genuinely indexical of Norse rather than English developments, and hence these words all form a distinct category from the point of view of etymological approach. Note further that formal "tests" are naturally only as reliable as our confidence in the orthographic representation of sounds in the texts under scrutiny; see the remarks under items 7 and 14 in the catalogue below.

3.2.2 Absence of formal comparative evidence: Types B, C and D

Where formal evidence of this calibre is wanting, the case for Norse derivation is never on so firm a footing. But, starting from the problems faced by the etymologist at first blush (rather than the various types of further evidence that we might look to in order to help us solve those problems), I suggest three further broad categories:

Type B contains lexemes whose Germanic root is not recorded in Old English in the period before contact with Norse begins to have an effect, but it is recorded in Old Norse; loan from Norse into English has therefore been proposed to account for this. The case is obviously strongest (and almost always accepted, in fact) for items whose Norse equivalent is frequently attested and lexicalizes a relatively common concept, meaning that the chances of this root having existed but gone unrecorded earlier in Old English are usually reckoned to be remote (though of course this is not impossible, especially given the gaps in our record). The best examples in the LH(OE) corpus are *grið* and *saht* (catalogue items 8 and 13); other very familiar words of this sort include ME *taken* 'take' (cp. OIcel *taka*), ME *ille* 'bad' (cp. OIcel *illr*). In some such cases, evidence from English dialect distribution is helpful corroboration of what we suspect: *ille* is a very good example, the majority of whose earlier Middle English attestations belong to the North and East (see *MED*: s.v. *il(le* (adj.), *OED*: s.v. *ill* (a. and n.)). But for the other words mentioned here this is not the case, including for *taken*, which is widespread from surprisingly early on in its recorded English history (see *MED*: s.v. *tāken* (v.), *OED*: s.v. *take* (v.), Peters 1981a: 98). Regardless of distribution, these words are all strong contenders for Norse derivation (they are here designated by a single **B**). There are, however, weaker cases to be made for a number of items of this broad Type. These are the words that tend to be argued about, because they stand for less commonly used concepts, and it is therefore less surprising to find them attested late and sparsely (e.g. ME *glam* 'din, merrymaking', cp. OIcel *glam(m)*; see *MED*: s.v. *glam* (n.), *OED*: s.v. *glam* (1)); or whose failure to appear earlier in writing is explicable on other grounds, e.g. ME *hore* 'prostitute, fornicator', LH(OE) *heore* (catalogue item 10), which it is not hard to imagine being deliberately avoided as uncouth or taboo. In such cases early distribution is sometimes invoked as helpful, though its value is limited in the case of rare (northern) words like *glam*, and/or it can complicate the picture (as with *hore*, which does have cognates across West Germanic, perhaps inclining us further to regarding it as an unattested native word). I have designated words of this more contentious type with a double **BB**.[27]

Type C words are different in a way which I take to be fundamental, given that the root of these words *is* attested earlier in Old English. So rather than using Scandinavian input to account for wholly new morphemic material, one is arguing here for loan or influence from Old Norse in order to explain a novelty in one or more of the following:

    C1 = derivational form;
    C2 = orthographic (phonological) form (where this does not constitute a decisive "test");
    C3 = sense;
    C4 = formation of compound or phrase;
    C5 = frequency.

A large number of the suggestions for Norse borrowing fall into this category, in fact, and some are much more contentious than others. The most secure words (here distinguished as **C**) are usually those showing a stem formative (theme) not otherwise found with the given root in Old English, or at least only to produce words in a very different sense area. It is still, of course, possible for these apparently new developments to be native formations not recorded earlier, but items in this category are generally (though not in all cases universally) accepted as showing Norse input. Good examples are ME *cost* (an *a*-stem presupposing PGmc **kust-a-z*, when the nearest Old English formation is an *i*-stem, *cyst* <

---

27 In some cases, especially ideophones, a native origin seems altogether more plausible than a loan, e.g. ME *wharren* 'whir' (cp. Dan *hvirre*; see MED: s.v. *wharren* v., OED: s.vv. *whar* v., *whirr*, *whir* v. (adv., int.)), and a third sub-category (**BBB**) might be useful in order to indicate their tenuous position; but I have found no such items in LH(OE).

PGmc **kust-i-z*) (catalogue item 2) and *laӡe* and its relatives, including the hapax *forlaӡe* (equivalent formations on the Germanic *lag-* root only mean 'sea' in earlier Old English) (catalogue items 4, 11, 16). *Laӡe* is moreover associated with Scandinavian legal practice in its earliest English occurrences, another very useful piece of corroboration. Other items of Type C are less compelling. In cases like *fere* and *genge* (catalogue items 3 and 5), derivations on the same stems *are* to be found (earlier) in Old English, but some aspect of their usage (including the sense) is noticeably different. Such words are generally, though by no means universally, ascribed an Old Norse origin; I have designated them **CC** to indicate the relatively less compelling nature of their claim. There is then a large group of further suggestions, more contentious still, whose form or sense or usage differs relatively little from those of their counterparts in (earlier) Old English, in ways that are just as (and perhaps more) readily explicable by endogenous changes in the native language (sub-type **CCC**). These developments have nonetheless, if sporadically, been accounted for in the scholarship by positing Norse influence – thus e.g. ME *borde* in the sense 'table', ME *uppon* as a compound preposition (catalogue items 18, 30).

Type D, finally, contains items whose etymology is in a variety of ways much harder to grasp, and which may perhaps best be classed as "obscure". In some cases the form and sense of the English word are easy to establish, but any really convincing etymology is difficult to arrive at. A famous case is ME *loupe* 'loop', which perhaps has some connection with ON *hlaup*, 'leap', but whose sense has more in common with Sc. Gael. *lūb*, 'a loop, bend' (or compare MDu *lūpen*, 'lie in wait'?); see *MED*: s.v. *loupe* n.1, *OED*: s.v. *loop* n.1. Such instances may be designated **D1** or **DD1**, depending on the plausibility with which Scandinavian origin can be invoked. Alternatively, a word may be elusive because it is hard to know how we should interpret it in context, and hence which is the most viable etymon of two or more possible roots whose origins may in themselves not be controversial. This is especially likely when we have a *hapax legomenon* like *awane* in LH.II (catalogue item 1), whose etymology depends on the relative plausibility of competing readings in context. In this part of the text, which is an addition to the Wulfstanian original, the homilist is enjoining a sinner to repent now while he can, rather than putting it off until another day, because "to dei he mei, tomarӡan hit him is awane" ('today he can, tomorrow it is uncertain (?wanting) for him'; 21/24–25). *OED* and *MED* both derive the element *-wane* from Old English *wana* 'lack, want', and thus translate *awane* as 'wanting, lacking'. But there are reasons to doubt this identification: there is no recorded Old English construction *a-wana*, and more to the point Old English short /ɑ/ before a nasal usually appears spelt <o> in Lambeth 487. A better analogue might be sought in Old English *ǽwēne* 'doubtful', which could be argued to give a better sense in context: the homilist is then not suggesting that the opportunity for repentence will definitely not be available tomorrow (which could hardly be predicted), but that one can never be sure, the future is always in doubt. If a connexion with Old English *wēne* is to be entertained, then the vocalism of *awane* can best be explained by influence from the early Middle English variant *wan*, *wone* 'expectation', which occurs several times in thirteenth-century South-West Midland texts, and derives from ON *ván* (in itself it is a Type A1); but it is very hard to say for sure. Such cases are labelled **D2** or **DD2**, again depending on the plausibility of claims for Norse input (see also *sterliche*, catalogue item 27).

3.2.3 Further remarks

These four Types therefore represent the broad categories used to classify the various possible Norse-derived words in our four Lambeth texts, which are detailed in the catalogue that follows. Each word is labelled to show the nature of the etymological evidence for its (putative) input from Old Norse, primarily according to the types and sub-types of A, B, C and D as described. Additional evidence that may be brought to bear in weighing the probability of Norse borrowing, and whose value has been referred to above, is appended to these labels where relevant:

(a)   the Old Norse word belongs to a different derivational class from the nearest Old English word in the equivalent semantic area (e.g. the Old Norse word is an *i*-stem, the only known Old English forms are *a*-stems);
(b)   cognates are known for the supposed Old Norse-derived element (in substantially the same stem-form and sense) in West Germanic;
(c)   the distribution of the supposed Old Norse-derived element is principally confined to the North and/or East Midlands in the onomastic record;
(d)   the distribution of the supposed Old Norse-derived element is (otherwise) principally confined to the North and/or East Midlands in the lexical record;
(e)   there is an association with a demonstrably (Viking-Age) Scandinavian "cultural artefact", including association with Scandinavian practices in the word's earliest English usage.

What I hope should be obvious from this attempt to systematize some of the principles behind the classification of even a very small corpus of words is just how much there is for etymologists to argue about when it comes to the evidence for Scandinavian input. Lexical and especially semantic systems being as complex as they are, no typology by etymology can be any more than a brusque simplification. Each of my rough groupings contains within it a wide range of more or less plausible contenders for Norse derivation, and in the end we must of course take each word's history individually, on its own merits; the application of a system, and my use of some labels, is intended as a way of charting this complex terrain, not a denial of its complexity. But my hope is that it is at least useful to recognize broadly similar groups of etymologies where arguments are of the same order, and moreover to advertize our problems as clearly as possible. In many instances, even the majority, a definitive conclusion is impossible: on the basis of this evidence alone, we cannot say for certain that a word's history really did or did not have Scandinavian input. In this respect, decisions about what to include in a list of "Norse loans" can depend less on the etymological evidence *per se* than on one's attitudes towards wider historical linguistic principles, particularly one's faith in the idea of language contact as an engine of change, and more narrowly on the idea of Old Norse influence on the medieval English lexicon;[28] where we draw the line might also have to do with the nature of the study, with whether we are interested in exploring the maximal possible extent of "Norse impact" or in tracing the specific biographies of the most secure examples.[29] But, whatever the case, it should be our ambition to go into any analysis with as clear-sighted a view as possible of the nature of the evidence for deriving words from Norse, and make absolutely clear how we have established our corpus. For the purposes of the present investigation, I have divided my material so as to separate off (what I regard as) the least secure suggestions (those labelled CCC and DD); the etymological evidence for these items is summarized (4.2 below), but their textual contexts and attestation history are not detailed, and they will not be pursued in my subsequent discussion of context and distribution (section 5).

4. Words derived from Old Norse in LH.II, IX, X, XI: Catalogue and notes

For all items treated in this section, a headnote lists: lexical item (given in a non-oblique form where this is attested or may uncontroversially be deduced); part of speech; sense; frequency in LH(OE) by text (followed by attested inflexional forms if different from that at the head of the entry); etymological category (refer to section 3.2 above).[30] An etymological description follows. For items in section 4.1 I have then supplied a digest of further information. "Context" describes the immediate textual environments for each attestation, together with information about the reading of the Old English source where relevant (in the case of LH.X,

---

28   For some further discussion of the implications, see Dance (forthcoming 2). For a notably sceptical take on invoking contact-based explanations in general, see Lass (1997: esp. 201-209), and cp. further Lass (2007: 18-21).

29   Studies interested in the etymologies of Middle English words primarily from other points of view, e.g. so as to trace phonological and morphological pathways of development from Proto-Germanic, can afford to set the bar very high, since they need not specify Old Norse input except in the most robust instances of formal divergence from expected native patterns. See the discussion of etymological labelling for the purposes of *LAEME* in Lass (2007: 18-21).

30   Here and throughout, all citations of LH readings are taken from Morris (1868) (referred to by page/line), checked against the electronic texts supplied by *LAEME* and against O'Brien (1985) where possible.

the Old English text is quoted at sufficient length for the effects of changes to the rhythm and alliteration of the Ælfrician original to be gauged). "Lexical field" provides a reference number for what seem to me the most appropriate categories in the *Historical thesaurus of the Oxford English dictionary* (*HTOED*), followed by a short description of the competition between the lexical item in question and its (near-)synonyms; these notes focus on the text(s) in which the Norse-derived item is attested, but also offer information for the other LH(OE) texts where helpful. The remaining elements of each entry refer to the attestation of the item elsewhere. Where relevant, its occurrences in Lambeth Homilies other than LH(OE) are noticed first, with frequencies and spelling variants.[31] A summary of the word's broader "Attestation history" follows, focusing on its earlier occurrences (if any). There is then ("EME SWM texts") a summary of its appearances and behaviour (including semantic and stylistic) in the other major thirteenth-century South-West Midland texts (excluding LH), as treated in Dance (2003) (where further details may be sought).[32]

4.1 Items accepted as (probably) Norse-derived

1. **awane**; adj.; ?'uncertain'; 1LH.II [D2]

Etymology: *OED* (s.v. *a-wane* advb. phr.) derives from OE *an, on* + *wana*, 'lack, want', *MED* (s.v. *awane* adj.) from '?OE *$\bar{a}$-wana, $\bar{æ}$-*'; both translate as 'wanting' or 'lacking' (*MED* 'Of an opportunity to do sth.: lacking'). But the recorded OE *ǣwēne* 'uncertain' (itself a *hapax*; see *DOE*: s.v.) is perhaps a better analogue. The LH form would in that case appear to show influence from SWM eME *wan, wone* 'expectation', from Old Norse (A1), cp. OIcel *ván* (see Björkman 1900–1902: 83–84). This would help to explain the <a> in LH *awane*, which would be an unusual outcome of OE short /a/ before a nasal in this dialect (contrast <wone> 'lack' < OE *wana*, LH.IX 91/23).

---

31   NB for these purposes I have surveyed all the homilies, not only those treated in Dance (2003).

32   These texts are as follows. *Ancrene Wisse* (AW): A = Cambridge, Corpus Christi College 402 (*LAEME* #272); C = London, British Library, Cotton Cleopatra C. vi (*LAEME* #273, 274, 1700); G = Cambridge, Gonville and Caius College 234/120 (*LAEME* #276); N = London, British Library, Cotton Nero A. xiv (*LAEME* #245). The "Katherine Group" (KG): B = Oxford, Bodleian Library Bodley 34 (*LAEME* #1000); R = London, British Library, Royal 17 A. xxvii (*LAEME* #260, 261, 262). The "Wooing Group" (WG): L (Lambeth 487 hand B, *LAEME* #189); N (Nero A. xiv, *LAEME* #1800); R (Royal 17 A. xxvii, *LAEME* #261). (AW, KG and WG are collectively described as the "AB group".) Laȝamon's *Brut* (LB): version in London, British Library, Cotton Caligula A. ix, Part I (*LAEME* #277, 278). Glosses of the "Tremulous Hand" (TH): various manuscripts, *s.* xiii^in, Worcester (see Dance 2003: 65–67). The "Worcester Fragments" (WF), in Worcester Cathedral, Chapter Library, F. 174, copied by the Tremulous Hand (*LAEME* #172).

Context:　　　In an original part of LH.II, in the (proverbial?) saying "to dei he mei. Tomarȝan hit him is awane" ('today he can, tomorrow it is uncertain (?wanting) for him'; 21/24–25).

Lexical field:　　*HTOED* 02.01.13.08.05 (adj.) (imperfectly known, uncertain).[33] No obvious synonyms in LH(OE).

Attestation history:　　*Hapax legomenon.*[34] (The fairly widespread ME *wan, wone,* 'expectation' (etc.) is first recorded in LB, and its variant *iwan, won* in *c*1200 *Wor.Serm.*in *EGSt.7* (Wor Q.29); see Dance 2003: 386, *MED*: s.vv. *wōn(e* n.3, *iwōn* n.).

2. **cost**; n.; 'manner, means'; 1LH.II (dat. **coste**) [C1a]

Etymology:　　Very likely from Old Norse, cp. OIcel *kostr*, 'choice, condition, means' (rather than from an unrecorded Old English *a*-stem formation on PGmc **kust-* as opposed to the attested *i*-stem OE *cyst* 'excellent thing', (rarely) 'choice' (*DOE*: s.v.)). See *OED*: s.v. *cost* n.1, Björkman (1900-1902: 247); *MED*: s.v. *cost* n.1 refers in its etymological note only to the late Old English instances of *cost*.

Context:　　In original part of LH.II, in the adverbial phrase "alre coste" ('in any manner, by any means', 21/9).

Lexical field:　　*HTOED* 01.05.05.20 (n.) (manner of action/operation). No obvious synonyms in LH.II (not quite a match for **forlaȝe**). LH.X has the near-synonym *wise* 'manner' 2x.

Elsewhere in the *Lambeth Homilies*:　　**cost** 1LH.III.

Attestation history:　　Several occurrences in later Old English texts (*DOE*: s.v. *cost* n.2, Peters 1981a: 89, Pons-Sanz 2007a: esp. 163-164, 208-209, 240), followed by a number in Middle English (*MED*: s.v. *cost* n.1).

EME SWM texts:　　LB (both in formulaic "cost nan oðer").

33　See also 02.01.10.03 (adj.) (equivocal, ambiguous), and 02.01.13.08.06 (adj.) (unreliable). If the sense is 'lacking' then see HTOED 01.05.07.04.04 (adj.) (absent) or 01.06.06.08|04 (adj.) (deficient, wanting).

34　OED records an instance of a modern word <awane> from 1876 under the same head (s.v. *a-wane* advb. phr.), but it seems unhelpful to treat this as the "same" lexeme, even if derivation of both from OE *wana* were granted.

3. **fere**; adj.; 'sound, healthy'; 1LH.II [CC3]

Etymology: Some input from Old Norse, cp. OIcel *færr* 'capable, fit (for use)', is often supposed, though note that there is an OE *-fēre* recorded in the sense 'accessible' (*DOE*: s.v. *gefēre* adj.), so any Old Norse influence does not necessarily extend further than the semantic. See *OED*: s.v. *fere* a., *MED*: s.v. *fēre* adj., Björkman (1900-1902: 237), Orel (2003: s.v. **fōriz*), Pons-Sanz (forthcoming 1).

Context: In original part of LH.II, in the enumerative phrase "hal. & fere. & strong. & stelewurðe" ('healthy and sound and strong and robust', 25/12).

Lexical field: *HTOED* 01.02.01|0.3.01 (adj.) (healthy). For LH.II synonyms (esp. *hal*) in collocation, see Context.[35]

Attestation history: Several occurrences in later Old English texts (*DOE*: s.v. *fēre* adj., Peters 1981a: 97), followed by a number in Middle English (*MED*: s.v. *fēre* adj.).

EME SWM texts: AW and LB. Subordinate in lexical fields next to *hal*, *sund*, *hail* (and NB collocation *hal and fere* in AW, viz. AW.A 4.402).

4. **forlaȝe**; n.; 'means, opportunity, wherewhithal'; 1LH.II [C1a/4]

Etymology: *MED*'s suggestion of derivation from Old Norse, cp. OIcel. *forlag* 'provision for living, means of subsistence', pl. *forlǫg* (*MED*: s.v. *forlaȝe* n.; Zoëga 1926: s.v.), seems the most reasonable available (Morris's translation 'liberty' (18/22) appears to be a gloss from context). Clearly native Old English formations on PGmc **lag-* belong to declensions with *i*-mutation (e.g. OE *ealdorlegu* 'course of one's life'), apart from *lagu* 'sea' (see e.g. Orel 2003: 231).

Context: In original part of LH.II ("forþon *crist* us haueð iȝefen muchele mare blisse & forlaȝe on þisse liue to biȝeten heouene riche"; 'because Christ has given us much greater happiness, and the means in this life to obtain the heavenly kingdom', 19/22).

Lexical field: Nearest *HTOED* field perhaps 01.05.05.14.01.01.04 (n.), particularly |04 ((a) means), |04.06 (available means/a resource).[36] No clear synonyms in LH(OE) (not quite a match for **cost**, etc.).

---

35   Note also the negative expressions of this field in LH(OE), viz. *untrummen* LH.IX 1x, *untrumnesse* LH.IX 1x, *unhalne* LH.X 4x, *seke* LH.X 1x.
36   See also 01.05.03.07|.04 (n.) (chance/opportunity) and 01.05.05.22 (n.) (ability/capacity /power).

Attestation history: A *hapax legomenon* (not in *OED*).

5. genge; n.; 'troop'; 1LH.IX [CC3]

Etymology: Derivation from Old Norse, cp. OIcel *gengi* 'help, company', is often suggested, and is plausible given that none of the recorded native formations on the *geng-* stem (e.g. OE *genge* 'privy' and *gegenga* 'companion') is very close in sense; but several authorities are equivocal. See *OED*: s.v. *ging* n., *MED*: s.v. *ging(e* n., Peters (1981a: 94), Dance (2003: 422–423).

Context: Replaces Ælfric *werod* in reference to Pharaoh's army (87/15; cp. Clemoes 1997: 354 line 13).

Lexical field: *HTOED* 03.03.12.01|02 (n.) (an army); cp. also the less specific 03.01.04.01.01 (n.) (a company/body of persons). Elsewhere in this (approximate) field, LH.IX has *ferde* 2x, *fereden* 1x, *ifereden* 1x, *iferende* 2x; see Table 5 and discussion below. LH.X has *here* 1x.

Attestation history: Several occurrences in later Old English (*DOE*: s.v. *genge* n.1, Peters 1981a: 94; cp. also Wulfstan *gegenge*, but see Pons-Sanz 2007a: 62); in fourteenth-century Middle English, particularly to be found in texts from the North/North-Midlands (*MED*: s.v. *ging(e* n.).

EME SWM texts: 15x in LB, 1x in KG (*Seinte Marherete*, both B and R); outnumbered by its (approximate) synonyms (*hird*, *floc*, *here*) in these texts.

6. gersum; n.; 'treasure, wealth'; 2LH.IX [A1]

Etymology: Derivation from Old Norse (cp. OIcel *gersemi*, *gørsemi*, OSw *gørsum*) is guaranteed by comparison with OE *gearw-*. See Björkman (1900–1902: 152), *OED*: s.v. *gersum* n., *MED*: s.v. *gersum(e* n., Dance (2003: 79).

Context: Both replace Ælfric *feo(h)* (91/35, 101/8; cp. Clemoes 1997: 357 line 92, 363 line 243).

Lexical field: *HTOED* 02.07.05.01 (n.) (wealth/riches), and the sub-sense 02.07.05.01|11.01 (n.) (treasure);[37] cp. also the less specific 02.07.03 (n.) (possessions/property). In this general field, LH.IX also has *feh* 1x, *e(a)hte* 6x; see Table 6 and discussion below. LH.II has **ehte* 1x (MS <ehee>), *wela* 1x and *istreon* 2x; LH.X has *welan* 3x, *ehte* 7x, *feh* 1x, *maðmas* 1x, *gold hord* 1x.

---

37   See also 02.01.15.07.08.11|05 (n.) (thing of worth).

Attestation history: Several occurrences in late Old English texts (*DOE*: s.v. *gærsum*, *gærsuma*, *gærsume*; Peters 1981a: 97) and elsewhere in Middle English; relatively infrequent after the thirteenth century, mainly in northern/eastern and/or alliterative texts (*MED*: s.v. *gersum(e* n.).

EME SWM texts: Frequent (AW, KG, LB and WF). Vying with plentiful competition in lexical field (inc. *weole*, *gold*, *tresor*). First syllable spelt variously including with <e> (the favoured AB and AW.C form), <a> (favoured by AW.N) and <æ> (the spelling of WF); LB shows all three, with a preference for <æ>; see further Dance (2003: 117–118).

7. **gist**; n.; 'visitor, stranger'; 1LH.X (pl. **gistas**) [C2]

Etymology: Derivation from Old Norse (cp. OIcel *gestr*) rather than from a form of OE *giest* is guaranteed by initial /g/, but I have resisted an A1* label in this instance owing to (very) occasional substitution of <g> for <ȝ> in the orthography of L (see e.g. <forliger> at LH.X 103/12, and cp. **ongein** (item 26 below)). Nonetheless <g> and <ȝ> are normally kept distinct in this manuscript, and I know of no spellings of ME *gest*, *gist* which certainly signify /j/ (see *OED*: s.v. *guest* n.), so it is overwhelmingly likely that /g/ is the sound intended. See Björkman (1900-1902: 152-153), *OED*: s.v. *guest* n., *MED*: s.v. *gest* n., Dance (2003: 79).

Context: Replaces "Ælfric" *cuman*: cp. "& þet mon gistas underuo. & to seke monan ga. oðer sarine frefrað" ('and by receiving strangers and visiting a sick person or comforting one in pain', LH.X 109/36–111/1) with "& on cumliðnysse. þæt man cuman underfo. & gif man seocne geneosað. oððe sarigne frefrað" ('and in hospitality by receiving strangers and if one visits a sick person or comforts one in pain', Morris 1868: 300, lines 16-17).

Lexical field: *HTOED* 03.01.04.06.03|12.03 (n.) (stranger/outsider), and cp. also 03.11.02.08.02 (n.) (guest). No competition from synonyms is evident in LH(OE).

Attestation history: See *MED* (s.v. *gest* n.) for (purported) occurrences earlier in Middle English, including the *Trinity Homilies* (though it is difficult to judge the evidence of some earlier twelfth-century and Old English spellings of the initial consonant, for reasons set out under Etymology above);[38] very widespread thereafter.

---

38   Here and in what follows I have classified the *Trinity Homilies* as a slightly earlier witness than LH, following the dating adopted by *LAEME* (C12b2 for Trinity, C13b1 for Lambeth); but in practical terms the two are very close.

EME SWM texts: Variously, inc AW and TH (and in the derivative *gistninge* in LB), where it is the only item in this lexical field. TH replaces the phrase *cumena huse* with *gistena huse* ('house of guests') in a gloss in Cambridge, Corpus Christi College 178. Derivatives on this stem are consistently spelt with an <e> in AW.A, C and G, but with <i> in AW.N, LB and TH (see Dance 2003: 423).

8. **grið**; n.; 'peace'; 1LH.II (dat. **griðe**) [B]

Etymology: Almost certainly derived from ON *grið* (ultimate etymology uncertain). See Björkman (1900-1902: 163), *OED*: s.v. *grith* n., *MED*: s.v. *grith* n., Pons-Sanz (2007a: 56-58).

Context: As in Wulfstan source (see Pons-Sanz 2007a: 200), in phrase "on griðe & on friðe" (LH.II 13/19, Bethurum 1957: 252-253, lines 50-51).

Lexical field: 03.01.07.06 (n.) (absence of dissension/peace).[39] The only direct synonym in LH.II is *frið* in the same phrase (see Context), and note also the verbal derivative *friðian* 1x (as in Wulfstan source). Elsewhere in this approximate field, LH.IX has the noun *sibsumnesse* 4x (3x in the sense 'unity', 1x more clearly 'peace'), beside the adjectives *isibsum* ('peaceful, peaceable') 1x and *isome* ('in concord, as one') 1x; LH.X has *isibsum* 2x.

Elsewhere in the *Lambeth Homilies*:   **grið** 4LH.IV, **griþ** 1LH.VIII.

Attestation history: Common in later Old English, especially in the works of Wulfstan (see *DOE*: s.v. *griþ* and various derivatives; Peters 1981a: 89; Pons-Sanz 2007a: 125-158), followed by a number of occurrences in Middle English (*MED*: s.v. *grith* n.)

EME SWM texts: Very frequent (plus numerous compounds and sub-derivations), esp in LB (140x in total), where it dominates synonyms (*frið*, *some*, *sahte*); there are also several occurrences across the AB group, which however tends to prefer other words (esp. *sahte*, *sahtnesse*). Collocation with *frið*, often as a rhyming pair, is very common in LB.

9. **heordom**; n.; 'fornication, prostitution'; 1LH.X [BBb]

Etymology: Perhaps to be associated with ON *hóra* (or specifically its derivative *hórdómr*) (see **heore** below).

---

39   And see also 01.05.05.15|02.03 (n.) (guaranteed security).

Context: Replaces "Ælfric" *forliger*: cp. "He scal biwerian widewan &
steopbern & stale aleggen & heordom for-beodan" ('he will protect widows and
orphans and stop stealing and forbid fornication/prostitution', LH.X 115/19–21)
with "He sceal beon bewergend wydewena & steopcilda. & stala alecgan. &
forliger gewitnian" ('he will be the defender of widows and orphans and stop
stealing and forbid fornication', Morris 1868: 302 lines 34-35).

Lexical field: *HTOED* 03.05.05.07.02.03|01 (n.) (fornication/adultery),[40] or
perhaps more specifically 03.05.05.07.02.04 (n.) (prostitution). LH.X otherwise
retains *forliger*, *forliʒere* 2x from its Ælfrician source (OE *forliger*); see Table 4
and discussion below. LH.II has *forleʒen* 1x.

Elsewhere in the *Lambeth Homilies*:   **hordom** 1LH.III, 1LH.VI, 1LH.VIII.

Attestation history: Found early in Middle English in Orrm and the *Trinity
Homilies*, and thereafter relatively widespread (see *MED*: s.v. *hōredōm* n.).

EME SWM texts: AW (C shares the LH.X spelling in <eo>). No evident
competition from synonyms.

10. **heore**; n.; 'prostitute, (female) fornicator'; 1LH.X (gen. pl. **heoranna**) [BBb]

Etymology: Perhaps derived from ON *hóra* as often assumed, but a case can
be made for native origin (based on recorded cognates elsewhere, viz. OFris *hōr*,
OS *hōr-hūs*, OHG *huor*, Go *hors*). See *OED*: s.v. *whore* n., Dance (2003: 426–7),
Orel (2003: s.v. **xōran*), Pons-Sanz (forthcoming 2).

Context: Replaces "Ælfric" *myltestrena*: cp. "He buleð [= befuleð?] þene
mon & maceð of cristes leoman heoranna leoman; & of godes husa gromena
wuniunge" ('It defiles (?) the man and makes prostitutes'/fornicators' limbs out of
Christ's limbs, and the dwelling of torments out of God's house', LH.X 103/12-
14) with "& he befylð þone mannan. & macað of cristes limum myltestrena lima.
& of godes temple. gramena wununge" ('and it defiles the man and makes
prostitutes'/fornicators' limbs out of Christ's limbs, and the dwelling of torments
out of God's temple', Morris 1868: 296 lines 21-22).

Lexical field: *HTOED* 03.05.05.07.02.03|02.04.02 (n.) (female fornicator),[41] or
more specifically 03.05.05.07.02.04|06 (n.) (a prostitute). Elsewhere in this
general field, LH.X retains *forliʒeres* 1x from its Ælfrician source (OE *forligeras*);
see Table 4 and discussion below.

---

40   Cp. also 03.05.05.07.02.03|02 (n.) (fornication).
41   Or see more generally 03.05.05.07.02.03|01.02 (n.) (fornicator/adulterer).

Attestation history: Occasionally in late Old English (and cp. *horcwene, horing*), see Pons-Sanz (forthcoming 2); widespread in Middle English (see *MED*: s.v. *hōr(e* n.2).

EME SWM texts: A few occurrences in AW and LB (LB 1x shares the <eo> spelling), where the word dominates over synonyms (chiefly *hearlot*).

11. **laȝe**; n.; 'law'; 19LH.II, 2LH.IX, 8LH.X (pl. **laȝe, laȝen**) [C1abe]

Etymology: Almost certainly to be associated with ON **lagu* (cp. OIcel *lǫg*). Clearly native Old English formations on PGmc **lag-* belong to declensions with *i*-mutation (e.g. OE *ealdorlegu* 'course of one's life'), apart from *lagu* 'sea' (see e.g. Orel 2003: 231); but cp. also OS *aldor-lagu*. See *OED*: s.v. *law* n.1, Björkman (1900-1902: 249), *MED*: s.v. *laue* n., Pons-Sanz (2007a: 61).

Context: LH.II: 11/17, 11/29, 13/1, 13/25, 15/8 (2x), 15/11, 15/15, 15/17 (2x), 15/22, 15/27, 17/1, 17/10, 17/24, 17/31, 19/13, 19/30, 25/4; 1x (13/25) as in Wulfstan source, others in original parts of text (note also that the instance of OE *lagu* at Bethurum (1957: 254 line 72) has been omitted by a rewritten passage in LH.II). LH.IX: 87/3, 87/19; both replace Ælfric *æ*. LH.X: 105/9, 109/3, 109/26, 117/36 (2x), 119/2, 119/6, 119/12; all replace "Ælfric" *æ*, bar 1x (105/9) more loosely for "Ælfric" *gesinscipe* 'marriage'.

Lexical field: *HTOED* especially 03.04.13 (n.) (law).[42] The nearest synonym in LH(OE) is *e* (< OE *æ*), which appears 7x in LH.IX; see Table 4 and discussion below.[43]

Elsewhere in the *Lambeth Homilies*:   **laȝe** 11LH.I, 2LH.IV, 1LH.V, 1LH.VI, 4LH.VIII, 1LH.XIII, 1LH.XIV (i.e., 21x in total).

Attestation history: Widespread in late Old English (Peters 1981a: 90; Fischer 1989; on its use by Wulfstan see Pons-Sanz 2007a: esp. 68-125) and thereafter in Middle English (see *MED*: s.v. *laue* n.).

EME SWM texts: The noun and its various derivatives are very frequent in all traditions, including 29x TH glosses, all bar one replacing OE *æ* (see Dance 2003:

---

42   Note also the more specific 03.04.02.01|15.04 (n.) (a regulation/rule), 03.04.13|11 (n.) (edict/decree/ordinance/institute), and 01.07.04.01.03|09 (n.) (God's law), 03.07.00.20 (n.) ([religious] law).

43   Closely related in sense are a number of words for 'decree, commandment', etc., viz. *bebode/bibode* (5x LH.II, 3x LH.IX, 4x LH.X, 2x LH.XI), *ibode* (1x LH.II), *heste* (8x LH.II, 2x LH.XI), *isetnesse* (2x LH.IX, 3x LH.X).

364). Very much the dominant option in its lexical field, except in KG where it competes with *lei*. Spellings follow the expected patterns for late OE [ɣ]: <lahe> is the preferred form in AB texts, <laȝe> in AW.C and LB (and LH; see above), whereas AW.N and TH consistently opt for <lawe> (a minority variant also in LB).

12. **loftsong**; n.; 'song of praise'; 1LH.IX (dat. **loftsonge**) [C1a]

Etymology: OE *lof-sang*, most likely showing the influence of ME *loft* 'sky' < ON *loft* (contrast OE *lyft*) (*MED*: s.v. *lōf-sōng* n.; though see Dance 2003: 432-433).

Context: Replaces Ælfric *lofsangum* (99/28, cp. Clemoes 1997: 363 line 228).

Lexical field: *HTOED* 03.07.03.04.01 (n.) (hymn). No direct synonyms; the nearest competition in LH.IX is provided by *herunge* 'thanksgiving, celebration' (1x).

Attestation history: *MED* (s.v. *lōf-sōng* n.) records a small number of further occurrences in <loft->, mostly in early Middle English; earliest otherwise is the *Trinity Homilies*.

EME SWM texts: A small number of occurrences in AW.A (1x only), KG and LB, which do not have direct competition from synonyms (but cp. *leof-song* 1x in LH.I; Dance 2003: 220n).

13. **saht**; adj.; 'reconciled, at peace'; 1LH.II (pl. **sahte**) [B]

Etymology: Probably from ON **sahtr* (cp. OIcel *sáttr*), though for a sceptical view see Pons-Sanz (2007a: 244 and forthcoming 1). Ultimate etymology disputed: perhaps < PGmc **sanxt-* as traditionally ascribed (e.g. Björkman 1900-1902: 100), or perhaps < **saxt-* (so *OED*: s.v. *saught* a., *saught* n., Orel 2003: 312, and cp. Go *unsahtaba* 'indisputably').

Context: In original part of LH.II (15/33).

Lexical field: *HTOED* 03.01.07.06 (adj.) (free from dissension/peaceful) and the more specific 03.01.07.06|02 (adj.) (not at variance). No direct synonyms in LH.II. Elsewhere in this approximate field, LH.IX has the adjectives *isibsum* ('peaceful, peaceable') 1x and *isome* ('in concord, as one') 1x, and the noun *sibsumnesse* 4x (3x in the sense 'unity', 1x more clearly 'peace'), with which cp. also **grið** above; LH.X has *isibsum* 2x.

Elsewhere in the *Lambeth Homilies*:   not found as a simplex adj., but cp. **unisahte** 1LH.III (and the verb *sahtnien* 1LH.III, *isehtnede* 1LH.VIII).[44]

Attestation history: Frequent in later Old English texts (see Peters 1981a: 91, Pons-Sanz 2007a: 244); for widespread Middle English occurrences see *MED*: s.v. *saughten, isaughten, isehten* but note Dance (2003: 373n).

EME SWM texts: The adjective is found only in LB, and dominates in its lexical field (but cp. the nouns *sahte* and *sahtnesse* and the verb *sahtni*, which are more widespread and in some texts have more lexical competition). Spellings of the stem in <a> are the norm in the AB tradition, AW.C and AW.G; AW.N and WF prefer <ei>; LB varies between <æ>, <e> and <a>, with a strong preference for the former; see Dance (2003: 121).

14. **tiðinge**; n.; 'tidings, news, happenings'; 1LH.IX [CC2]

Etymology: ON derivation ought to be guaranteed for forms of this word with medial /ð/ (cp. OE *tīd*), though the morphology of ON *tíðendi* has here been adapted on the model of OE *-ing(e)* words; see *OED*: s.v. *tiding*, Björkman (1900-1902: 166-167), Dance (2003: 80). But, though unambiguous instances of eME medial /ð/ are recorded (e.g. <tiþinge> 2x AW.N), the graphs <ð> and <d> are sometimes used interchangeably in the LH scribal dialects (cp. e.g. 99/3 <icunðliche>, 99/4 <icundeliche>), and so it is difficult to be certain that /ð/ is the sound intended.

Context: In the construction "alle þam þet þeos tiðinge iherdon" ('all those who heard these tidings', LH.IX 93/7–8), revising Ælfric's "eallum ðe þæt geaxodon" ('all who found out about that', Clemoes 1997: 358 line 101).

Lexical field: 03.08.05.09 (n.) (news/tidings). No direct synonyms in LH(OE).

Elsewhere in the *Lambeth Homilies*:   None in this form (but cp. **tidinge** 1LH.VII).

Attestation history: Forms with a medial fricative are first recorded in this period (*MED*'s other earliest form (s.v. *tīding(e* n.) is c1200 *Wor.Serm.in EGSt.7* (Wor Q.29), 114 *tiþinge*).

EME SWM texts: Several examples in <ð> or <þ> (majority in LB and AW.N), next to others in <d> (but the etymology of these variants, which go back

---

44   The form <setnesse> in LH.XIV also seems to be a spelling, probably erroneous, of the noun *sahtnesse*; Dance (2003: 138-139).

to later Old English, is a more difficult proposition; see *OED*: s.v. *tiding*, Björkman 1900-1902: 167). No clear synonyms in this precise sense.

15. **þrel**; n.; 'slave, thrall'; 1LH.XI (pl. **þrelan**) [A1]

Etymology: Derivation from Old Norse (cp. OIcel *þræll*) is convincingly demonstrated on phonological grounds by several Old and early Middle English spellings, whether the Old Norse word derives from PGmc **þranhil-* (traditionally ascribed; see e.g. Björkman 1900-1902: 19 and n. 2) or from **þrahil-/þragil-* (see now Orel 2003: 424, and cp. OHG *dregil*); see further *OED*: s.v. *thrall* n.1 (a.1), Pons-Sanz (2007a: 58-59).

Context: In original part of LH.XI. Occurs in doublet "of þeowan and of þrelan" ('of slaves and of thralls'; 123/30).

Lexical field: 03.04.09.03|06 (n.) (slave). The only synonym in LH.XI is *þeow* 1x, which occurs in collocation with *þrel* (see Context). Otherwise in LH(OE) we find *þeowa* (1x LH.X), next to forms of *þe(o)wdome* (3x LH.IX) and the verbs *þeowest* (1x LH.II) and *[þ]enien* (1x LH.X), plus forms of the compound *larðeu* (2x LH.IX, 3x LH.X).

Elsewhere in the *Lambeth Homilies*:   **þrel** 1LH.IV, and see further **þreldome** 1LH.XIV, **þrel-weorkes** 1LH.IV.

Attestation history: Widespread in later Old English, especially in the works of Wulfstan (see Peters 1981: 93, Pons-Sanz 2007a: esp. 181-189 and 2007b), and common thereafter (see *MED*: s.v. *thral* n.1).

EME SWM texts: Common, with multiple occurrences (and several derivatives) in AW, KG and LB, and used by TH to gloss OE *þeowas* in Oxford, Bodleian Library Junius 121. Largely dominant over forms of *þeow*, including elsewhere in LH, except in SM (where it is noticeably the subordinate choice), and in LB (where the two are roughly equal). Collocates with *þeow* and derivatives several times (see Dance 2003: 244, 256). Spellings vary: AW.A uniformly has <ea>, but there is variation between <ea> and <a> in B; AW.N has only <e> (as does the one TH gloss); AW.C and AW.G have both <e> and <a> spellings, as does LB (see Dance 2003: 121).

16. **ulaȝeliche**; adv.; 'unlawfully'; 1LH.X [C1abe]

Etymology: Formed on **laȝe** (and cp. OIcel. *úlǫglíga*). (NB LH <u-> seems almost certain to be an error for *un-*, rather than a direct borrowing of ON *ú-* as

negative prefix (otherwise exceptionally rare in English; see Townend 2002: 208).
O'Brien (1985: 241, her line 345) prints <u[n]laȝeliche>, and see also the
marginal annotation at Morris (1868: 115/31).)

Context:　　　Replaces "Ælfric" *uneawfæstlice*: cp. "wa þere þeode þer þe
king bið child. & þer þa aldormen etað on erne marȝen ulaȝeliche" ('woe to that
people where the king is a child and where the noblemen eat in the early morning
unlawfully', LH.X 115/30-31) with "wa þære leode þar se cining bið cild; & þar
þa ealdormenn etað on ærnemergen uneawfæstlice" ('woe to that people where
the king is a child and where the noblemen eat in the early morning unlawfully',
Morris 1868: 303 lines 8-10).

Lexical field:　　*HTOED* 03.04.13.09.01 (adv.) (illegally). No evident synonyms
in LH(OE).

Attestation history:　　Apart from the SWM texts (see below), *MED* (s.v.
unlaulĩche adv.) records this word only from Orrm and *a*1225(*c*1200) *Vices &
V.(1) (Stw 34)*).[45]

EME SWM texts:　　2x in KG (1x each in *Seinte Katerine* and *Hali Meiðhad*).
No direct synonyms.

4.2 Other suggestions

17. **and**; conj.; '(and yet) if'; 1LH.II [CCC3]
MED (s.v. *and*, sense 5 [a]) suggests a conditional sense for *and* at LH.II 23/20, a
usage which ODEE (s.v. *and*) notes may show "reinforcement" from the
conditional senses of ON *endi* or *en*(*n*). But usages of this sort are found
sporadically throughout Old English; and moreover the LH.II instance in question
can be read as a straightforward 'and' (see further *DOE*: s.v. *and, ond*, sense B.1.c).

18. **borde**; n.; 'table'; 1LH.X [CCC3]
OED (s.v. *board* n) suggests input from ON *borð* in order to account for the
development of the 'table' sense by OE *bord*. But *DOE* (s.v. *bord*) in fact records
several unambiguous instances of *bord* meaning 'table' from relatively early
contexts.

19. **crune**; n.; 'crown'; 1LH.XI [CCC2]

A Norse input (cp. OIcel *krún*) into the form of this word, otherwise derived from
OFr *coroune*, has been suggested. But this seems unnecessary: the Old Norse

---

45　O'Brien (1985: 135 [her line 129]) inserts a further instance of <unlaȝeliche> in order to
　　make good an apparent failure of sense, but her wording is speculation.

word is itself recorded fairly late, perhaps via MLG *krūne* (see de Vries 1962: s.v. *krún*), and compare further *AND*: s.v. *corone* (1) which records eleventh-century Anglo-French spellings <croune, crowne>.

20. **deruenesse**; n.; 'hardship, affliction'; 1LH.II [CCC1d]
There may perhaps be some input from Old Norse if this word is a derivation (partly) upon the Middle English adj. *derf* (with influence from ON *djarfr*, see Dance 2003: 348), as *MED* (s.v. *derfnes(se)*) suggests. But given the LH spelling in <-ue->, the main ingredient seems more likely to be the stem of the verb OE (Angl.) *derfan*.

21. **fikenung**; n.; 'deceit'; 1LH.X (dat. **fikenunge**) [CCC1]
Sometimes (see Dance 2003: 393 n.32) derived from ON *fíkja* 'move quickly', but OE *gefic* 'deceit' predates Norse influence (see *DOE*: s.v.), so only the fact of a verbal form (plus perhaps the *-n-* infix) stands in favour of ON input.

22. **fore**; n.; 'fear'; 1LH.IX [CCC2]
Perhaps to be equated with later ME *fore* with /ɔː/, itself perhaps from ON *fár* (though see Dance 2003: 405n). But this instance (LH.IX 97/33) is usually interpreted as a form of ME *fere* < the cognate OE *fǣr* 'calamity, danger', i.e., showing <o> for <e> (thus O'Brien 1985: glossary s.v.).

23. **godemon**; n.; 'good man (as term of address)'; 5LH.II (pl. **godemen**) [CCC4]
MED (s.v. *gōd man*, *gōd-man* phr. & n.) compares to OIcel *góðmenni*, but there is no compelling reason to see the Norse compound as other than an independent parallel (cp. also MDu. *goedman*; *OED*: s.v. *goodman*).

24. **herebureʒen**; vb.; 'to lodge'; 1LH.II (pres. 2 sg. **herebureʒest**) [CCC4]
Has sometimes been supposed to show Old Norse input (e.g. *OED*: s.v. *harbour* n1), but this is probably unnecessary (see Dance 2003: 449).

25. **icruned**; vb. (pp.); 'crowned'; 1LH.XI [CCC2]
Has been associated with Old Norse (cp. OIcel *krún*, or vb. *krýna*), but see **crune** above.

26. **ongein**; prep.; 'against, in exchange for'; 1LH.II [CCC2d]
The <g> in <ongein> at 17/22 could conceivably show Old Norse input (cp. OIcel. *í gegn*). But it is a unique variant, next to multiple others in this text and L at large with <ʒ> (e.g. 21/10 and 11), and otherwise unknown in the eME SWM tradition (and rare in the South and West until c.1400; see *MED*: s.v. *ayēn* adv., *LALME* dot map 220); an isolated confusion of <g> and <ʒ> is thus a more plausible explanation.[46]

---

46   Examination of the manuscript facsimile (Wilcox 2000b) at f. 5v line 19 confirms the reading

27. **sterliche**; adv.; 'strongly, harshly'; 1LH.X [DD2]
Perhaps this form represents a derivation on OE *stēor* (so O'Brien 1985: glossary s.v., also an option suggested by *MED*: s.v. *stērlī* adv.), though if so the spelling with <e> is unexpected; or perhaps it is an error for *sternliche* (another *MED* suggestion) or *stercliche*. Conceivably, it is in fact a mistake for *storliche*, a Norse-derived word (cp. OIcel *stórr*) found in the KG (1x *Seinte Katerine*; the simplex *stor* and adjectival derivative *storlic* are to be found alongside the adverb in the eME SWM corpus, see Dance 2003: 377). (Appears in an addition to the "Ælfric" text.)

28. **þarua**; n.; 'pauper'; 1LH.X [CCC2]
O'Brien (1985: 16) raises the possibility that the <a> in this form (rather than regular <ea> from OE *þearf*) "may be a re-formation of the OE word under the influence of the ON verb *þarf*, 'it is necessary'", but thinks it more probable that the influence is simply from a dialect of English in which OE /æɑ/ had monophthongized to /a/; and it is indeed very uneconomical to adduce Norse input here.

29. **umbe**; prep.; 'about, concerning'; 1LH.IX, 1LH.X [CCC2]
Later ME spellings in <u> implying a back vowel /u/ (in dialects which do not otherwise spell the reflexes of OE /y/ with a <u>) are sometimes said (e.g. Björkman 1900-1902: 224, *OED*: s.v. *umbe* prep. and adv.) to show influence from ON *umb* (later *um*). But the extent of Norse input is debatable even in such instances, and unnecessary in the case of SWM eME texts, where <umbe> would be the expected spelling of OE *ymbe*; see Dance (2003: 407).

30. **uppon**; prep.; 'upon, on, to'; 3LH.II, 1LH.IX; **uppen** 1LH.II [CCC4d]
OED (s.v. *upon* prep.) uniquely suggests influence from ON *upp á* in the cementing of the OE *upp(e) on* as a compound, but a wholly native development seems sufficiently to explain ModE *upon*.

31. **wei**; interj.; 'alas'; 1LH.II [CCC2]
This form has sometimes been compared to ON *vei*, but is sufficiently explained as an emphatic variant of OE *wā* (see Dance 2003: 441).

<on gein>, printed <ongein> by Morris (1868, 17/22) (followed by Rynell 1948: 211 [and n. 85]), against *LAEME* (Index no. #2000) <onʒein>.

5. Contexts and distribution

All the items in section 4 above have at least some claim on derivation from Norse, but the case for those in 4.2 seems to me too negligible to pursue further in a short paper. It is therefore only the sixteen words detailed in 4.1, which are themselves (it must be remembered) attributed Norse input on various etymological grounds and with different degrees of conviction, that I shall treat in this section. Drawing on some of the information about context and broader attestation history digested in 4.1, I shall here make a (necessarily brief) consideration of these items' occurrences in LH(OE), and compare these to the occurrences of the same and closely-related words elsewhere, paying particular attention to the thirteenth-century South-West Midland corpus surveyed in Dance (2003), including a number of other Lambeth Homilies.

As a way into exploring their wider connections, one very simple method of sorting and grouping the words in our corpus is by date of first attestation. Table 2 below attempts this by conventional period labels; for further details see the information in section 4.1.

Table 2. LH(OE) Norse-derived words (section 4.1 above): period of first attestation.

later OE texts	earlier "ME" texts	contemporary (c.1200)	*hapax legomena*
cost	gist	tiðinge	awane
fere	heordom		forlaȝe
genge	loftsong		
gersum	ulaȝeliche		
grið			
heore			
laȝe			
sahte			
þrel			

Presented in this way, our "transitional" Lambeth homilies might seem rather backward-looking in their lexical make-up: although they contain two *hapax legomena*, the great majority of their Norse borrowings have been in written circulation since the eleventh century or earlier ("Old English"), and of the remainder only *tiðinge* first appears otherwise in texts dated c.1200[47] (the same may be said of the stem of *awane*, if I am correct in identifying it as ME *wan, wone*). Two of the fourteen non-hapaxes represent derivations on bases also attested in LH(OE), i.e., the abstract noun *heore-dom* (cp. *heore*) and the negative adverb *u[n]-*

---

47   Though on the date of the *Trinity Homilies* (*gist, loftsong*) see note 38 above.

laʒe-liche; but these derivations are themselves not new.[48] Several of the items first attested in Old English texts, furthermore, are well-known cases which belong to conceptual areas usually (not to say stereotypically) associated with material loaned from Norse in this period, viz. law and arbitration (*grið*, *laʒe*, *sahte*), social roles and relationships (*gist*, *þrel*) and military activity (*genge*), rather than to others amongst the much wider range of concepts lexicalized by Scandinavian-derived words in Middle English (for a typical discussion, see Kastovsky 1992: 333-336).

But closer examination of these words' textual contexts begins to dispel at least some of this impression of conservatism. A number of these items are indeed first recorded in the Old English period, but most are not widespread or frequent in the pre-Conquest homiletic tradition; and their novelty in texts of this sort is evident from how often they owe their appearance in LH(OE) to a reworking of Old English source material, or to the composition of original passages. Only two occurrences (of two items) continue the wording of the Old English source (see the entries for *grið* and *laʒe* above, and notice that a further instance of OE *lagu* has in fact been lost in the process of rewriting in LH.II).[49] By contrast, there are 24 occurrences (of 7 different items) in original parts of LH.II and LH.XI, and 19 instances (9 different items) are replacements for different words or constructions in the four homilies' Old English sources. There is therefore a strong case that all 16 items represent the active usage of the revisers of the homilies, and it appears that many were consciously enlisted (by writers at least somewhere on the chain of transmission of these texts from the Old English originals to the present copy) to serve as "updatings" of Old English lexical material into a form more acceptable to contemporary readers. Five are found *per se* in other Lambeth Homilies, plus one derivative on a recurring base (*sahte* next to various other *saht-* words), and one close but etymologically distinct variant (*tiðinge* next to *tidinge*). Note also that *grið*, the only item to appear in LH(OE) solely in a phrase which continues its Old English source, appears less like an instance of constrained selection when put next to its five other appearances in LH at large.

That the temptation to read "retrospective" features in the *Lambeth Homilies* (whether reworked or apparently new compositions) ought not to be over-indulged at the expense of their other connections has been repeatedly stressed in recent scholarship exploring the role of these texts in contemporary literary culture (see especially Millett 2007, Swan 1997, 2000, 2007b, forthcoming). The homilies in Lambeth 487 have, in particular, been fruitfully read in terms of their continuity with the linguistic, textual and intellectual tradition behind the "AB

---

48 It is generally best to assume that these affixed forms were generated in English, once the Norse-derived base words had been naturalized, even though both have parallels in literary Old Icelandic; and see the discussion in Dance (2003: 94-97).

49 NB also the loss in revision of two forms of *tofesian*, sometimes argued to be a Norse loan, from the Wulfstan source (Bethurum 1957: 253, lines 55 and 63); but for counter-arguments see Pons-Sanz (2006).

group" (Millett (2007: 63) has recently referred to them as "successive products of the same diocesan *milieu*"). In this light, it is noteworthy that every one of the 14 non-hapaxes in our Norse-derived corpus recurs at least once in the AB group, Laʒamon's *Brut* and the output of the Tremulous Hand, several many times over. Five of these items (*fere*, *genge*, *gersum*, *gist*, *loftsong*) are found in LH(OE) but not in the LH texts surveyed in Dance (2003), and so supply new connections between the lexis of LH as a whole and the broader South-West Midland corpus. This strengthens still further one's impression of the essential similarity of the vocabulary in this group of texts, even if the Norse-derived words in LH remain markedly less numerous and diverse than in the other traditions (for a discussion see Dance 2003: 277-278).[50]

Various comparisons with the language of these thirteenth-century South-West Midland written traditions can be pursued. At the level of orthography, it is well understood that both scribal dialects identified in LH bear strong similarities to those of near-contemporaries usually localized in northern Herefordshire, southern Shropshire and northern Worcestershire, especially the spellings of the Caligula A. ix version of Laʒamon's *Brut*, the version of *Ancrene Wisse* and related AB group texts in Nero A. xiv, and the Tremulous Hand (see Laing 2008: 2-3, cited in note 11 above). The spellings of LH(OE) Norse-derived words only go to reinforce these similarities, especially noteworthy being their participation in lexically-specific patterns of variation. A good example is *gist*, whose LH.X spelling with <i> aligns with one of the two major orthographic variants found in the broader corpus (agreeing with consistent <i> spellings of *gist-* in AW.N, LB and TH, in contrast with the consistent <e> in AW.A, C and G). Notice further *þrel*, whose form in LH.XI is in agreement with the consistent preference for spellings in <e> across LH, and which is once again also the only spelling in AW.N as against variation between <a> and <ea> forms elsewhere in thirteenth-century South-West Midland texts. There is also perhaps *tiðinge*, if <ð> really does represent /ð/, since spellings implying a fricative pronunciation are attested more frequently in LB and N than elsewhere. But not quite everything points in the same direction: LH.IX *gersum* twice with <e> looks more like the AB spelling than the preferences of LB, N or TH; and the spelling of *saht-* words is variable, the LH.II form agreeing with AB, AW.C and G, and LH.III, but the LH.VIII alternative having more in common with AW.N and WF.

The connections of our LH(OE) Norse-derived words with these other South-West Midland traditions can also be pursued if we consider in more detail the contexts of their usage, and probe the factors that might have governed their

---

50   There are several plausibly Norse-derived items not found in LH(OE) but recorded elsewhere in LH, the most significant probably being *taken* 'take' (cp. OIcel *taka*; 1LH.III), *bone* 'prayer, request' (cp. OIcel *bón*; 3LH.III), *casten* 'throw' (cp. OIcel *kasta*; 2LH.V) and *baþe* 'both' (cp. OIcel *báðir*; 1LH.XIV); but these are relatively infrequent and outnumbered by available synonyms in LH at large (see further Dance 2003: esp. 277).

occurrence. When it comes to texts that represent revisions of older written material, such an investigation does not only involve us in mapping what Fischer calls "lexico-semantic" relationships: in addition, that is, to assessing these words' place in their lexical fields next to competing synonyms, and their stylistic context, we must also take into account the evidence for how redactors responded to the earlier, Old English text, what they kept and what they changed, as part of what may be a complex and multi-layered transmission to the present scribal copy. These things, taken together, constitute the multifarious factors bearing on what is sometimes called "reader-response" (for general discussion see Swan forthcoming), and are responsible for what Laing describes as "the variation that results from the intricacies of language use" – in terms of textual history, "diastratic" variation (2004: 49). In the light of these things, we must naturally be careful not to regard our texts simplistically as evidence of one individual's linguistic usage, at least not necessarily of his active usage. But, with these caveats, it is possible to suggest a number of ways in which our LH(OE) Norse-derived words slot into text-cultural and lexical frameworks in L comparable to those of the more famous thirteenth-century South-West Midland corpora. Our data in these four short texts is inevitably limited, but it hints at corresponding semantic and stylistic systems, and at participation in similar traditions of responsiveness to earlier patterns of word usage. Take for instance *gist*: its use in LH.X as a replacement for its composite Ælfrician source's *cuman* 'guests, strangers' mirrors the same substitution in a gloss by the Tremulous Hand in Cambridge, Corpus Christi College 178 (*gistene huse* for *cumena huse*); and it shows the same apparent dominance in its lexical field, there being no competing words for 'guest' in either LH(OE) or the wider thirteenth-century South-West Midland corpus. Similarly, the use of *fere* in the enumerative phrase "hal & fere & strong & stelewurðe" (LH.II) calls to mind this word's similar range of competing synonyms in the thirteenth-century South-West Midland material (its only appearance in AW comes in the phrase "hal & fere"). And the collocative company kept by *grið* in LH.II ("on griðe & on friðe", continuing its Wulfstanian source) is a very frequent feature of the word's appearance in LB. Similar things are true for *þrel*, whose LH.XI attestation in the collocation "of þeowan & of þrelan" mirrors the common pairing of *þrel-* and *þeow-* in thirteenth-century South-West Midland texts (KG and LB), and also perhaps reflects its use to gloss *þeow* by TH (once in Oxford, Bodleian Library Junius 121); but in the case of this word there is a markedly higher rate of competition from native synonyms in LH(OE) than was apparent in the LH texts surveyed in Dance 2003 (see note 54 below).

Unsurprisingly, however, connections are not always anything like as easy to make as this, and consistent mappings from one user to another, and one tradition to another, can be elusive. For texts with such a complex transmission, it can be extremely difficult to access the motivations for a given choice of a given word, when any usage can be contingent upon a range of variables which may have been clear to the redactor as he wrote but which quite naturally are now lost to us. Certainly, if we are expecting responses to the words in an Old English source to be uniform, for Word X always to be replaced with the same Word Y in even a single text copied c.1200, then we are in for a rude awakening, and in this regard getting to the bottom of a redactor's lexical repertoires and preferences is rather difficult. A startling example is provided by the occurrences of *laȝe* 'law' in LH(OE), even if we confine ourselves to a relatively simple lexical field analysis and consider the relationship of this word with only its most obvious native synonym, ME *e* (< OE *ǣ* 'law'). There are 29 occurrences of *laȝe* in LH(OE) (plus one of the derivative adverb *ulaȝeliche*), next to only 7 of *e* (plus one of the compound *eubruche* 'adulterer'), as detailed in Table 3 below.

Table 3. ME *laȝe* vs. *e* in LH(OE).

text	*laȝe*	*e*
LH.II	19	(1x *eubruche* 'adulterer')
	(1x as in Wulfstan source; 18x "original")	
LH.IX	2	7
	(both replacing Ælfric *æ*)[51]	(all retained from Ælfric)
LH.X	8	0
	(7x replacing "Ælfric" *æ*, 1x for *gesinscipe*)	
	and	
	1x *ulaȝeliche*	
	(replacing "Ælfric" *uneawfæstliche*)	

In terms of relative frequency this is the sort of distribution we might expect in texts copied c.1200, by which stage the native *e* had long since ceded dominance of this lexical field and, with the exception of the specific sense of 'marriage', had been overtaken by *laȝe* (see Fischer 1989, and further Pons-Sanz 2007: 68-124, 231-235). Moreover, this picture seems in keeping with the situation in the broader thirteenth-century South-West Midland corpus, where *laȝe* has become absolutely victorious; in historical terms, its use to replace OE *ǣ* very regularly in the glosses of the Tremulous Hand looks like a more consistent outcome of the tendency displayed probably only slightly earlier in LH.IX and X. But the "variability" in the pattern of replacement of *æ* in LH(OE) is, as will be observed, entirely due to LH.IX, which is the only text anywhere in Lambeth 487 to use *e* in the sense 'law'. And the effect on the chain of evidence of perhaps one individual redactor's responses becomes more marked still when we notice that these seven retentions of

---

51   And notice that LH.IX 89/29 *trowfeste* is a replacement for Ælfric's *eawfæste* in the sense 'faithful, pious'.

e appear in close succession on just one folio (f. 31) where, having changed the first two of Ælfric's uses of *ǣ* in the homily to *laʒe*, the text subsequently retains the Old English word.[52] Quite why some scribe (or, conceivably, someone glossing a manuscript of the Old English version of the text) decided to let the word that must have been acceptable to him in his "passive" repertoire stand here and nowhere else is of course difficult to answer. It may be (as Sisam thought; 1951: 112) because he had by now "got his eye in" to the text and, after having decided he knew what he needed to substitute for Old English *ǣ*, felt that he would be able to do this *ex tempore* as part of a future preaching performance without having manually to change each case of *ǣ* in a longish run of them.[53] However we choose to explain it, this instance of a lexically-specific "lapse" in updating complicates the apparent relationship between two synonyms, compelling us to assess in the light of a particular act of language usage relative frequencies that we would otherwise be minded to view merely as evidence of historical tendencies in an ongoing lexico-semantic competition.

There are other complex, apparently inconsistent relationships between the lexis of Old English source and updated Lambeth homily. Notice, for instance, the words used for 'prostitute, fornicator' and the related abstract 'prostitution, fornication' in LH.X, as set out in Table 4:

Table 4. Words for 'fornicator' and 'fornication' in LH.X and the corresponding words in the Old English source.

LH.X		"Ælfric"
103/12	forliger	forliger
103/13	heoranna	myltestrena
105/8	forliʒere	forliger
115/20	heordom	forliger
117/30	forliʒeres	forligeras

The reviser (or perhaps a succession of revisers) of LH.X replaces *myltestre* in his Ælfrician source once with a form of *heore*, and the abstract *forliger* once with *heoredom*, but seems otherwise to have been content to let formations on the *forliger* base stand. The replacements are very likely to have been motivated by the obsolescence of OE *myltestre* and *forliger*, both of which *MED* (s.v. *miltestre* n., *forliʒer* n.) records no later than *c.* 1225, mainly in copies of Old English material. I can find no occurrences of either word elsewhere in LH or in the other South-West

---

52 The occurrences are as follows: *laʒe*, 87/3 (f. 30v), 87/19 (f. 31r); *e*, 87/22 (f. 31r), 89/5, 89/8, 89/10, 89/11, 89/12, 89/13 (f. 31v).

53 The choice between *laʒe* and *e* in this period is potentially complex, and necessitates a wider-ranging survey of textual contexts, including of semantic and stylistic factors; see Dance (forthcoming 3) for discussion.

Midland texts treated in Dance (2003), which prefer *heore* and *heoredom* to express these concepts, and it looks very much as though these were the words in the LH.X reviser's active repertoire. But the superficial impression given by LH.X is of more competition in this field, and of a more old-fashioned lexical stock, owing to the fact that he was sometimes willing to be led by the wording of his source, which he accepted at least passively (as was the case with *e* in LH.IX).[54] This is in keeping with the general behaviour of the text, as discussed by Swan (forthcoming), who finds that the reviser is inconsistent in the degree to which he maintains features of his Old English source, including its rhythm and alliteration (see further O'Brien 1985: 305-306). The alliteration seems in fact to be retained in three of the five instances dealt with here (at 103/13, where the replacement happens not to disrupt it,[55] at 105/8[56] and at 117/30[57]), but in the remaining two cases it is disturbed, either by the introduction of the Norse-derived item (115/20)[58] or by other changes (103/12);[59] it is therefore difficult to argue that the retention of the Old English words, where this happens, is motivated by stylistic factors.

If we turn to the (loose) lexical field to which *genge* belongs, as illustrated in Table 5, other explanations suggest themselves for the complex relationships between LH text and Old English source.[60]

---

54   Similar things may be said of the lexical field to which *þrel* belongs. Taking LH(OE) as a whole, the one instance of *þrel* in LH.II looks like an unusual choice next to a number of native-derived synonyms, which is at odds with its dominant position in some other texts in the South-West Midland corpus, including the other LH surveyed in Dance (2003). But of the native synonyms in this broad field, only the verb *þeowest* (1x LH.II) and one instance of *þeowdome* (LH.IX) occur in sections of original composition; contrast *þeowa* (1x LH.X), *þeowdome* (2 further examples in LH.IX; 1x = Ælfric *þeowte*) and the verb *þenien* (1x LH.X), all of which continue the wording of their Old English sources.

55   See the LH.X and OE texts compared under 4.1 item 10 above; the alliteration seems to be on the *l* of *limum ... lima*.

56   Compare OE "þæt se læweda hine healde buton forligre on rihtum gesinscipe mid gesceadwisnysse" (Morris 1868: 297 lines 27-28) with LH.X "þet þe leawde mon hine halde butan forliȝere on rihte laȝe and mid isceadwisnesse" (105/8-9). The LH version arguably extends the alliteration onto *laȝe*, though of course it disrupts the original's pairing of *gesinscipe ... gesceadwisnysse*.

57   Compare OE "þurhwuniað on steore & gewitodlice beoð swylce forligeras gif ge libbað butan steore" (Morris 1868: 304 lines 7-8) with LH.X "Ðurh-wuniað on steore and ȝe beoð swilche forliȝeres. ȝif ȝe libbað butan steore" (117/29-30).

58   See the LH.X and OE texts compared under 4.1 item 9 above; the alliteration of the OE text seems to be on the *l* of *alecgan ... forliger*.

59   Compare OE "Se oðer leahter is forliger" (Morris 1868: 296 line 20) with LH.X "Þa oðer sunne forliger" (103/11-12).

60   There are yet other words in LH.IX referring to groups and assemblies, but these largely continue the Old English original, viz. *hired* 4x (all as Ælfric), *folkes gaderunge* 1x (as Ælfric), *(i)laðunge* 2x (both as Ælfric), *isomnunge* 1x (Ælfric *heap*).

Table 5. Words for 'troop, company' in LH.IX and the corresponding words in the Old English source.[61]

LH.IX		Ælfric
87/13	ferde	fyrde
87/15	genge	werod
89/1	ferde	leode
91/32	fereden	geferræden
93/33	ifereden	geferræden
101/3	iferende	werod
101/4	iferende	werod

LH.IX uses the (likely) Norse loan *genge* once to replace *werod*, but there is no automatic "equivalence" between the two: even though the revised text appears to dislike OE *werod* and always removes it,[62] it opts instead for *iferende* as a replacement twice later on, and elsewhere has other preferences. The explanation seems likely to be semantic. The first three instances in Table 5 refer to Pharaoh's army, and it therefore looks as though an LH.IX reviser has in these cases chosen words which could specifically denote a military force (see *MED*: s.v. *ferd(e* n.2 and *ging(e* n.); indeed at 89/1 he has signalled this meaning more explicitly than did Ælfric, who used the more generic *leod* 'people'. It is not obvious why he chooses *genge* at 87/15, unless in an attempt to mirror the lexical variety in his source (for "fyrde ...werod" read "ferde ...genge"), but it may be noted that *genge* is likewise only an occasional choice in this field in the wider South-West Midland corpus. By contrast, at 91/32 and 93/33 the homily refers not to an armed force but to the company of the apostles, and it is thus entirely in keeping with the sense for a reviser to continue the words he found in his source (*fereden, ifereden,* literally 'fellowship, a group of comrades'). He also prefers a relatively non-specific word for 'company' at 101/3-4 (*iferende*), which refers to a large group of converts, evidently deciding that an equivalent that continued the potential military connotations of Ælfric's *werod* would in this case have been inapposite.[63]

---

61 Note another instance of *werod* in the OE source, in a passage rewritten to provide more explanation in LH.IX (cp. OE "þæt modige werod" (Clemoes 1997: 358, line 112) with LH.IX "þe engles of eofone for heore modinesse" (93/17-18)).

62 It is not necessarily the case that he regarded *werod* as simply obsolescent; even though the word is not recorded by MED later than the early thirteenth century other than in set phrases/compounds with *engel* (see MED: s.v. *wēred* n.), it is attested several times in South-West Midland texts (LB, AW, SW), albeit nowhere else in LH.

63 NB that O'Brien (1985: 193, 194; her lines 317, 318) emends both instances of *iferende* to *ifereden*, evidently agreeing with Morris's suggestion (see his marginal note to 101/3) that *iferende*, which is found nowhere else as a noun in Middle English, is an error (and *LAEME* follows suit by tagging *iferende* as a descendant of OE *ferræden*). If such is the case, it is possible to argue that an LH.IX reviser intended to link the company of the apostles

For a still more complex set of relationships with the lexis of the source text, compare the occurrences of *gersum* and related words in the same homily (Table 6):

Table 6. Words for 'property, wealth, treasure' in LH.IX and the corresponding words in the Old English source.[64]

LH.IX		Ælfric
91/18	ehte	æht
91/18	feh	feoh
91/22	ehte	æht
91/24	wurð	wurð
91/33	ehte	landes wurþes
91/35	gersum	feoh
93/1	þinge	þing
101/8	gersum	feoh
101/10	eahte	gestreonum
101/11	ehte	goldhord
101/12	eahte	gold

The Old English version of the homily uses a number of words for material possessions and wealth, which at first sight seem practically synonymous: only one (*gestreon*) is usually translated 'treasure', but it varies with more specific words for actual embodiments of wealth (*gold, goldhord*), more general denotations of the monetary value of that wealth (*feoh, wurð, landes wurðes*) and hypernyms for material possessions (*æht, þing*). One would be forgiven on the basis of a bare list for assuming that all these words essentially refer to the same thing, especially when one glances at the pattern of LH.IX reactions to these Old English items. Sometimes, especially earlier in the text, the revised text retains Ælfric's choices, but at other times it replaces them: *gersum* is used as an equivalent for *feoh* twice, but elsewhere the preference seems to be to substitute *gold* and various 'treasure' words with the generic *e(a)hte*. But closer attention to the contents of the homily and its arguments uncovers a more subtle set of relationships, and a more precisely controlled series of lexical choices. The section of the text from 91/15-93/8 focusses on the crowds of converts at and

---

described at 91/32 and 93/33 with the crowd of converts at 101/3-4 by selecting (forms of) the same word for both. But for an alternative view see *MED*: s.v. *iferen* (v.), which designates the two LH instances of *iferende* under (c): "*ppl. iferende*, as noun: a group of people having a common faith, a fellowship", and hence differentiates them from its entry s.v. *ferrēde(n* n. I have been unable to find LH *iferende* in *OED*.

64   NB a further instance of OE *æht* at Clemoes (1997: 358 line 108), which has been lost in LH.IX owing to a reviser's shortening of the original's description of monastic life (93/12-14).

shortly after Pentecost receiving baptism and following the apostles (ultimately from Acts 2, 4 and 5; Godden 2000: 177-179). To demonstrate their commitment, they sell their material possessions and give the proceeds to the apostles. At this point in the narrative, the Old English text consistently refers to the possessions that have been sold with the word *æht*, and uses a word denoting monetary value (*feoh* or *wurð*) to describe what is given to the apostles.[65] LH.IX follows this pattern closely, choosing the same words as Ælfric at 91/18 (*ehte, feh*), 91/22 (*ehte*), 91/24 (*wurð*) and 93/1 (*þinge*), but at 91/35 instead replacing OE *feoh* with *gersum*, a substitution repeated at 101/8 in the same context. It is clear therefore that *gersum* is not intended here as a generic word for 'treasure',[66] but has the same force as OE *feoh* and *wurð*, i.e., indicating the value in monetary terms of what has been sold. For this specific denotation, it seems therefore that the LH.IX redactor (if one reviser is indeed responsible for all these alterations) has begun by repeating the words in his Old English source, but by 91/35 has decided that he in fact prefers his own word *gersum* – perhaps an effect comparable to the observable phenomenon of scribes "reading their way in" to the orthography of an exemplar, and at a certain stage more confidently asserting their own identity (see the types of scribal behaviour discussed notably in Benskin and Laing 1981, Laing 2004).

This neat pattern, contrasting words for possessions and their material value, seems to break down elsewhere in the LH version of the text. In the other instances in Table 6, that is, the LH revision seems excessively fond of *e(a)hte* 'possessions', using this item to replace Old English words for monetary value (*landes wurþes*) and for 'treasure' and gold (*gestreonum, goldhord, gold*). But these instances of substitution seem to me to say less about competition in specific lexical fields than they do about the interpretation of the narrative, and about a reviser's willingness to recast its emphasis. The 91/33 use of *ehte* relates to the couple Ananias and Sapphira, who decide not to give up quite everything they own. Ælfric describes what they want to keep as *landes wurþes*, i.e., the monetary value of their land; but by preferring plain *ehte* LH.IX makes a different and perhaps more self-consistent sense, since it is precisely their *ehte*, their possessions, that the other converts give away, and this duplicitous pair's attempt to hang onto some of their material goods makes a more explicit contrast with the underweight resultant *gersum* (OE *feoh*) which Ananias brings before an unfooled St Peter at 91/35. It is perhaps clearer still what the reviser is about at the end of the homily, which returns to the topic of material wealth in its conclusion. Compare the Old English and Lambeth versions of the following passage:

---

65   The distinction is not consistently made in Ælfric's Vulgate source, but compare Acts 4.34 (*possessores agrorum aut domorum ... vendentes adferebant pretia*); Godden 2000: 178.

66   And hence that MED's assignment of one of these LH.X instances to its sense 1(b) "*coll.* treasure, valuables, movable possessions" is potentially misleading.

Ða geleaffullan brohton heora **feoh**. 7 ledon hit æt þæra apostola foton; Mid þam is geswutelod þæt cristene menn ne sceolon heora hiht besettan on woroldlicum **gestreonum**; ac on gode anum; Se gitsere þe besett his hiht on his **goldhorde** he bið swa swa se apostol cwæð. þam gelic ðe deofolgild begæð; Hi heoldon þæt **gold** unwurðlice for þan ðe seo gitsung næfde nænne stede on heora heortan;

(Clemoes 1997: 363, lines 243-249)[67]

Ða ileaffullen brohton heore **gersum** & leiden heo et þere apos*t*lan fotan. Mid þan is itacned þe*t* cristene men ne sculen heore bileafe bisettan on þere weordliche **eahte**; ac on heore gode ane. þe ȝitsere þe biset his iþonc on his **ehte**; he bið þes deofles bern buten he hit iswike; forðon heo þe*t* þa ȝitsunge heolde*n* heore **eahte** unwur[ð]liche nefde nenne stude; on heore heortan. [*sic*, for "heo heolde*n* heore eahte unwurðliche forðon þe*t* þa ȝitsunge nefde nenne stude on heore heortan"]

(LH.IX 101/7–13)[68]

Here, the Lambeth text's consistent replacement of treasure/gold words by *e(a)hte* has the effect of making Ælfric's references to wealth read more uniformly, rendering more explicit the identical significance of the various types of riches to which the Old English version elegantly but more dilutely points. Moreover, by deliberately recasting these as references to *e(a)hte* 'possessions, what one owns', the reviser expressly recalls the terms of the pentecostal narrative on which this concluding section is an exegesis: *gersum* was placed at the apostles' feet, as is reiterated at 101/7; but the means by which this was obtained, the thing that was given up in order to procure it, was the people's *e(a)hte* – and as the reviser insists, it is that which is to be eschewed in search of salvation.[69]

In summation, patterns of lexical substitution can rarely be interpreted straightforwardly in "lexico-semantic" terms, or as giving us unmediated access to some writer's unconstrained choices. Unpredictable, "differential" mappings from source to revision signify the extent to which writers like the redactor(s) responsible for LH.IX were embedded in reading and reperforming earlier English material, and tell us something about the range of their options to do so passively or more actively at the level of the individual word. Sometimes they retain the

---

67 'The faithful brought their money, and laid it at the apostles' feet. By that is symbolized that Christian people ought not to put their hope in worldly treasures, but in God alone. The miser who puts his hope in his gold-hoard is, as the apostle said, like one who practices devil-worship. They [i.e., the faithful] regarded that gold as valueless because avarice had no place in their heart.'

68 'The faithful brought their money, and laid it at the apostles' feet. By that is symbolized that Christian people ought not to put their faith in worldly possessions, but in their God alone. The miser who sets his thoughts on his possessions is the devil's child unless he desists. They [i.e., the faithful] regarded their possessions as valueless because avarice had no place in their hearts.'

69 For further discussion of the stylistic and exegetical strategies of the LH.IX reviser(s), see Swan (2000: 71-76).

reading of their exemplar, sometimes they replace individual items of vocabulary (for which they may have several alternatives according to precise sense), sometimes they rework the emphasis of the text altogether, and we should not expect always to be able to tell what they intended in any given instance.

6. Concluding remarks

I have argued in this paper that the textual culture of the "long" twelfth century, including the four homilies mainly at issue, is a significant body of evidence for understanding the history of Old Norse-derived lexical material in English, but that its study poses a number of problems. On the one hand there is the complex and frustrating (and ubiquitous) series of issues that confront us when we try to decide which words we really should derive from Old Norse in the first place. The difficulties of this identification process cannot and should not be underestimated; but, experimentally at least, I have suggested some approaches to labelling the data so as to help render the nature of the task as transparent as possible. On the other hand there are the further historiographical aspects of such a study, attempting to chart the adoption and spread of "Norse borrowings" by a survey of their distribution in the medieval English textual record. Large-scale historical-lexicographical work perhaps inescapably gives the impression that time and space are the key variables in understanding this distribution, and these things are of course extremely important if we hope to isolate the major trends, to paint the big picture. But when we approach our words via their occurrences in a small number of actual texts, we find of course that their "biographies" are in detailed terms inseparable from their contexts of usage, and in tracing the reasons for that usage we are drawn into trying to account for all the interacting contingencies that bear on it, which in the context of English text production in the twelfth century can be exceptionally complicated. Current research is, rightly, encouraging us to see the textual culture of this time as more and other than a period in which "debased", "late" Old English hesitantly gave way to an embryonic Middle English, and we need to be able to view the evidence for lexical developments in the same light: as the output of a living community of readers/writers/speakers with complex relationships of their own, to each other as well as to the past traditions to which they responded. Projects like "The Production and Use of English Manuscripts 1060-1220" and *LAEME* are equipping us with the tools with which to undertake increasingly sophisticated accounts of the lexical circumstances of this crucial period, enabling investigations that go far beyond the small etymologically-delimited sub-set to which I have confined myself in this paper, and this is a very exciting prospect. Realistically, our understanding of this material is in many details still *awane*, but by this I mean to imply that it is productively and challengingly 'uncertain', and certainly not just obscurely 'lacking'.[70]

---

70   I am very grateful to colleagues whose advice and assistance have improved this paper,

References

Adams, Jonathan – Katherine Holman (eds)
 2004   *Scandinavia and Europe 800–1350: Contact, Conflict, and Coexistence.*
          (Medieval Texts and Cultures of Northern Europe 4.) Turnhout:
          Brepols.
Barnes, Michael P.
 2004   "The Scandinavian languages in the British Isles: The runic evidence",
          in: Adams, Jonathan – Katherine Holman (eds.), 121-136.
Barnes, Michael P. – R. I. Page
 2006   *The Scandinavian runic inscriptions of Britain.* (Runrön 19.) Uppsala:
          Institutionen för nordiska språk, Uppsala universitet.
Beadle, Richard – A.J. Piper (eds.)
 1995   *New science out of old books: Studies in manuscripts and early printed
          books in honour of A. I. Doyle.* Aldershot: Scolar Press.
Benskin, Michael – Margaret Laing
 1981   "Translations and *Mischsprachen* in Middle English manuscripts", in:
          Benskin, Michael – M.L. Samuels (eds.), 55-106.
Benskin, Michael – M.L. Samuels (eds.)
 1981   *So meny people, longages and tonges: Philological essays in Scots and
          Mediaeval English presented to Angus McIntosh.* Edinburgh: M. Benskin
          and M. L. Samuels.
Bergs, Alex – Laurel Brinton (eds.)
 forthcoming *The historical linguistics of English: An international handbook.* Vol. 1.
          (Handbooks of Linguistics and Communication Science). Berlin and New
          York: de Gruyter.
Bethurum, Dorothy (ed.)
 1957   *The homilies of Wulfstan.* Oxford: Clarendon Press.
Björkman, Erik
 1900-1902 *Scandinavian loan-words in Middle English.* 2 vols. (Studien zur
          englischen Philologie 7, 11.) Halle: Max Niemeyer.
Blake, Norman (ed.)
 1992   *The Cambridge history of the English language.* Vol. 2: *1066–1476.*
          Cambridge: Cambridge University Press.
Bøgholm, Niels – Aage Brusendorff – C. A. Bodelsen (eds.)
 1930   *A grammatical miscellany offered to Otto Jespersen on his seventieth
          birthday.* Copenhagen: Levin and Munksgaard; London: George Allen
          and Unwin.
Brate, Erik
 1884   *Nordische Lehnwörter im Orrmulum.* (Sonderabdruck aus den Beiträgen
          zur Geschichte der deutschen Sprache und Literatur 10.) Uppsala: Halle.
Burnley, David
 1992   Lexis and semantics, in: Blake, Norman (ed.), 409-499.

---

notably Christine Franzen, Bella Millett, Sara Pons-Sanz, Mary Swan and Elaine Treharne.

Clemoes, Peter (ed.)
  1997   *Ælfric's Catholic homilies, The first series: Text.* (EETS s.s. 17). Oxford: Oxford University Press.
Clemoes, Peter – Kathleen Hughes (eds.)
  1971   *England before the Conquest: Studies in primary sources presented to Dorothy Whitelock.* Cambridge: Cambridge University Press.
Dance, Richard
  2003   *Words derived from Old Norse in Early Middle English: Studies in the vocabulary of the South-West Midland texts.* (Medieval and Renaissance Texts and Studies 246). Tempe, Arizona: Arizona Center for Medieval and Renaissance Studies.
  forthcoming 1   "English in contact: Norse", in: Bergs, Alex – Laurel Brinton (eds.).
  forthcoming 2   *"Tor for to telle*: Words derived from Old Norse in *Sir Gawain and the Green Knight*", in: Putter, Ad – Judith Jefferson (eds.)
  forthcoming 3   "*Laȝe* and *e* in the twelfth century", *New Medieval Literatures* 13.
Da Rold, Orietta
  2006   "English manuscripts 1060 to 1220 and the making of a re-source", *Literature Compass* 3/4: 750-766.
Diaz Vera, Javier E. (ed.)
  2001   *A changing world of words: Studies in English historical lexicography, lexicology and semantics.* Amsterdam and New York: Rodopi.
Doane, A.N. – Kirsten Wolf (eds.)
  2006   *Beatus Vir: Studies in Early English and Norse manuscripts in memory of Phillip Pulsiano.* (Medieval and Renaissance Texts and Studies 319). Tempe, AZ: Arizona Center for Medieval and Renaissance Studies.
Dossena, Marina – Roger Lass (eds.)
  2004   *Methods and data in English historical dialectology.* (Linguistic Insights 16). Bern: Peter Lang.
Durkin, Philip
  2009   *The Oxford guide to etymology.* Oxford/New York: Oxford University Press.
Ekwall, Eilert
  1930   "How long did the Scandinavian language survive in England?", in: Bøgholm, Niels – Aage Brusendorff – C.A. Bodelsen (eds.), 17-30.
Fischer, Andreas
  1989   "Lexical change in late Old English: From *æ* to *lagu*", in: Fischer, Andreas (ed.), 103-114.
  2001   "Lexical borrowing and the history of English: A typology of typologies", in: Kastovsky, Dieter – Arthur Mettinger (eds.), 97-115.
Fischer, Andreas (ed.)
  1989   *The history and the dialects of English, Festschrift for Eduard Kolb.* (Anglistische Forschungen 203). Heidelberg: Carl Winter Universitätsverlag.

Fuster, Francisco Fernández Miguel – Juan José (eds.)
  1994   *English historical linguistics 1992: Papers from the seventh International conference on English historical linguistics, Valencia, 22–26 September 1992*. Amsterdam/Philadelphia: Benjamins.
Godden, Malcolm (ed.)
  1979   *Ælfric's Catholic homilies, The second series: Text*. (EETS s.s. 5). London: Oxford University Press.
  2000   *Ælfric's Catholic homilies: Introduction, commentary and glossary*. (EETS s.s. 18). Oxford: Oxford University Press.
Graham-Campbell, James – Richard Hall – Judith Jesch – David N. Parsons (eds.)
  2001   *Vikings and the Danelaw: Select papers from the proceedings of the thirteenth Viking congress, Nottingham and York, 21–30 August 1997*. Oxford: Oxbow.
Gunn, Cate – Catherine Innes-Parker (eds.)
  2009   *Texts and traditions of Medieval Pastoral Care, Essays in honour of Bella Millett*. Woodbridge: York Medieval Press.
Hanna, Ralph
  2009   "Lambeth Palace Library, MS 487: Some problems of early thirteenth-century textual transmission", in: Gunn, Cate – Catherine Innes-Parker (eds.), 78-88.
Hill, Betty
  1972   "Early English fragments and manuscripts: Lambeth Palace 487, Bodleian Library Digby 4", *Proceedings of the Leeds Philosophical and Literary Society, Literary and Historical Section* 14: 269-280.
  1977   "The twelfth-century *Conduct of life*, formerly the *Poema morale* or *A moral ode*", *Leeds Studies in English* 9: 97-144.
Hofmann, Dietrich
  1955   *Nordisch-Englische Lehnbeziehungen der Wikingerzeit*. (Bibliotheca Arnamagnæana 14.) Copenhagen: Einar Munksgaard.
Hogg, Richard M. (ed.)
  1992   *The Cambridge history of the English language*. Vol. 1: *The Beginnings to 1066*. Cambridge: Cambridge University Press.
Holman, Katherine
  1996   *Scandinavian runic inscriptions in the British Isles: Their historical context*. (Senter for middelalderstudier, Skrifter 4). Trondheim: Tapir.
Hotta, Ryuichi
  2009   *The development of the nominal plural forms in Early Middle English*. (Hituzi Linguistics in English 10). Tokyo: Hituzi Syobo.
Hug, Sibylle
  1987   *Scandinavian loanwords and their equivalents in Middle English*. (European University Studies 21.62). Bern/Frankfurt am Main/New York/Paris: Peter Lang.
Irvine, Susan
  2000   "The compilation and use of manuscripts containing Old English in the twelfth century", in: Swan, Mary – Elaine M. Treharne (eds.), 41-61.

Jorgensen, Alice (ed.)
forthcoming   *Reading the Anglo-Saxon chronicle: Language, literature, history.*
               (Studies in the Early Middle Ages). Turnhout: Brepols.
Kastovsky, Dieter
1992   "Semantics and vocabulary", in: Hogg, Richard M. (ed.), 290-408.
Kastovsky, Dieter – Arthur Mettinger (eds.)
2001   *Language contact in the history of English.* (Studies in English Medieval
               Language and Literature 1). Frankfurt am Main: Peter Lang.
Kennedy, Ruth – Simon Meecham-Jones (eds.)
2006   *Writers of the reign of Henry II: Twelve essays.* (The New Middle Ages).
               New York and Basingstoke: Palgrave Macmillan.
Kleist, Aaron J
2009   "Assembling Ælfric: Reconstructing the rationale behind eleventh- and
               twelfth-century compilations", in: Magennis, Hugh – Mary Swan (eds.),
               369-398.
Kleist, Aaron J (ed.)
2007   *The Old English homily: Precedent, practice, and appropriation.*
               Turnhout: Brepols.
Kniezsa, Veronika
1994   "The Scandinavian elements in the vocabulary of the Peterborough
               Chronicle", in: Fuster, Francisco Fernández Miguel – Juan José (eds.),
               235-245.
Kries, Susanne
2003   *Skandinavisch-schottische Sprachbeziehungen im Mittelalter: der
               altnordische Lehneinfluss.* (NOWELE supplement 20). Odense:
               University Press of Southern Denmark.
Laing, Margaret
1993   *Catalogue of sources for a linguistic atlas of Early Medieval English.*
               Cambridge: D. S. Brewer.
2004   "Multidimensionality: time, space and stratigraphy in historical
               dialectology", in: Dossena, Marina – Roger Lass (eds.), 49-96.
2008   "Index of sources", in: LAEME (date of access: April 2010).
Laing, Margaret – Angus McIntosh
1995   "Cambridge, Trinity College, MS. 335: Its texts and their transmission",
               in: Beadle, Richard – A.J. Piper (eds.), 14-52.
Laing, Margaret – Roger Lass
2003   "Tales of the 1001 nists: The phonological implications of literal
               substitution sets in some thirteenth-century South-West Midland texts",
               English Language and Linguistics 7: 257-278.
Lass, Roger
1997   *Historical linguistics and language change.* (Cambridge Studies in
               Linguistics 81). Cambridge: Cambridge University Press.
2007   "The corpora of etymologies and changes", in: LAEME (date of access:
               June 2009).

Magennis, Hugh – Mary Swan (eds.)
    2009   *A companion to Ælfric.* (Brill's Companions to the Christian Tradition 18). Leiden/Boston: Brill.

Magennis, Hugh – Jonathan Wilcox (eds.)
    2006   *The power of words: Anglo-Saxon studies presented to Donald G. Scragg on his seventieth birthday.* Morgantown WV: West Virginia University Press.

Millett, Bella
    2005   "The discontinuity of English prose: structural innovation in the Lambeth and Trinity homilies", in: Oizumi, Akio – Jacek Fisiak – John Scahill (eds.), 129-150.
    2007   "The pastoral context of the Trinity and Lambeth Homilies", in: Scase, Wendy (ed.), 43-64.

Morris, Richard (ed.)
    1868   *Old English homilies and homiletic treatises (Sawles Warde, and Þe Wohunge of Ure Lauerd: Ureisuns of Ure Louerd and of Ure Lefdi, &c.) of the twelfth and thirteenth centuries, edited from MSS. in the British Museum, Lambeth, and Bodleian Libraries; with introduction, translation, and notes.* (EETS o.s. 29 and 34). London: N. Trübner and Co.
    1873   *Old English homilies of the twelfth century, second series, from the unique MS. B. 14. 52 in the library of Trinity College, Cambridge.* (EETS o.s. 53). London: Trübner and Co.

Nielsen, Hans F. – Lene Schøsler (eds.)
    1996   *The origins and development of emigrant languages. Proceedings from the second Rasmus Rask Colloquium, Odense University, November 1994.* Odense: Odense University Press.

O'Brien, Sarah M.
    1985   "An edition of seven homilies from Lambeth Palace Library MS 487". [D.Phil. diss.]. University of Oxford.

Oizumi, Akio – Jacek Fisiak – John Scahill (eds.)
    2005   *Text and language in Medieval English prose: A festschrift for Tadao Kubouchi.* Frankfurt: Peter Lang.

Orel, Vladimir
    2003   *A handbook of Germanic etymology.* Leiden and Boston: Brill.

Page, R. I.
    [1971]   "How long did the Scandinavian language survive in England? The epigraphical evidence", in: Clemoes, Peter – Kathleen Hughes (eds.), 165-181.
    1995   Reprinted with a Postscript in: Parsons, David (ed.), 181-196.

Parsons, David N.
    1995   *Runes and runic inscriptions: Collected essays on Anglo-Saxon and Viking runes.* Woodbridge: The Boydell Press.
    2001   "How long did the Scandinavian language survive in England? Again", in: Graham-Campbell, James – Richard Hall – Judith Jesch – David N. Parsons (eds.), 299-312.

Peters, Hans
1981a   "Zum skandinavischen Lehngut im Altenglischen", *Sprachwissenschaft* 6: 85-124.
1981b   "Onomasiologische Untersuchungen zum skandinavischen Lehngut im Altenglischen", *Sprachwissenschaft* 6: 169-185.
Pickering, O. S. – V. M. O'Mara
1999   *The index of Middle English prose, Handlist XIII: Manuscripts in Lambeth Palace Library, including those formerly in Sion College Library.* Cambridge: D. S. Brewer.
Pons-Sanz, Sara M.
2000   *Analysis of the Scandinavian loanwords in the Aldredian glosses to the Lindisfarne gospels.* (Studies in English Language and Linguistics, Monographs 9). Valencia: Lengua Inglesa, Universitat de València.
2006   "OE *fēs(i)an* / ME *fēsen* revisited", *Neophilologus* 90: 119-134.
2007a   *Norse-derived vocabulary in Late Old English texts: Wulfstan's works, a case study.* (NOWELE supplement 22). Odense: University Press of Southern Denmark.
2007b   "A reconsideration of Wulfstan's use of Norse-Derived terms: The case of *prǽl*", *English Studies* 88: 1-21.
forthcoming 1   "Norse-derived vocabulary in the Anglo-Saxon chronicle". In: Jorgensen, Alice (ed.).
forthcoming 2   "A brief etymological note on OE *hore* and its word-field", *Anglo-Saxon.*
Pulsiano, Phillip – Elaine M. Treharne (eds.)
1998   *Anglo-Saxon manuscripts and their heritage.* Aldershot: Ashgate.
2001   *A Companion to Anglo-Saxon literature.* Oxford: Blackwell
Putter, Ad – Judith Jefferson (eds.)
forthcoming   *Multilingualism in Medieval Britain, 1100-1400: Sources and analysis.*
Rynell, Alarik
1948   *The rivalry of Scandinavian and native synonyms in Middle English, especially 'taken' and 'nimen' (with an excursus on 'nema' and 'taka' in Old Scandinavian).* (Lund Studies in English 13). Lund: Håkon Ohlssons Boktryckeri.
Scase, Wendy (ed.)
2007   *Essays in manuscript geography: Vernacular manuscripts of the English West Midlands from the Conquest to the sixteenth century.* Turnhout: Brepols.
Sisam, Celia
1951   "The scribal tradition of the *Lambeth homilies*", *Review of English Studies* n.s. 2: 105-13.
Skaffari, Janne
2001   "Touched by an alien tongue: Studying lexical borrowings in the earliest Middle English", in: Diaz Vera, Javier E. (ed.), 500-521.
Swan, Mary
1997   "Old English made new: One catholic homily and its reuses", *Leeds Studies in English* n. s. 28: 1-18.

1998	"Memorialised readings: Manuscript evidence for Old English homily composition", in: Pulsiano, Phillip – Elaine M. Treharne (eds.), 205-217.
2000	"Ælfric's *Catholic homilies* in the twelfth century", in: Swan, Mary – Elaine M. Treharne (eds.), 62-82.
2005	"Imagining a readership for post-Conquest Old English manuscripts", in: Thompson, John – Stephen Kelly (eds.), 145-157.
2006	"Old English textual activity in the reign of Henry II", in: Kennedy, Ruth – Simon Meecham-Jones (eds.), 151-168.
2007a	"Mobile libraries: Old English manuscript production in Worcester and the West Midlands, 1090–1215", in: Scase, Wendy (ed.), 29-42.
2007b	"Preaching past the Conquest: Lambeth Palace 487 and Cotton Vespasian A. XXII", in: Kleist, Aaron J (ed.), 403-423.
forthcoming	"Lambeth Palace 487 item 10 and reading for the ear".

Swan, Mary – Elaine M. Treharne (eds.)

| 2000 | *Rewriting Old English in the twelfth century*. (Cambridge Studies in Anglo-Saxon England 30). Cambridge: Cambridge University Press. |

Thompson, John – Stephen Kelly (eds.)

| 2005 | *Imagining the book*. Turnhout: Brepols. |

Townend, Matthew

| 2002 | *Language and history in Viking Age England: Linguistic relations between speakers of Old Norse and Old English*. (Studies in the Early Middle Ages 6). Turnhout: Brepols. |

Treharne, Elaine

2001	"English in the post-Conquest period", in: Pulsiano, Phillip – Elaine Treharne (eds.), 403-414.
2006a	"The life and times of Old English homilies for the first Sunday in Lent", in: Magennis, Hugh – Jonathan Wilcox (eds.), 205-240.
2006b	"Reading from the margins: The uses of Old English homiletic manuscripts in the post-Conquest period", in: Doane, A.N. – Kirsten Wolf (eds.), 329-358.
2006c	"Categorization, periodization: The silence of (the) English in the twelfth century", *New Medieval Literatures* 8: 247-273.
2009	"Making their presence felt: Readers of Ælfric, *c.* 1050–1350", in: Magennis, Hugh – Mary Swan (eds.), 399-422.

Wilcox, Jonathan

| 2000a | "Wulfstan and the twelfth century", in: Swan, Mary – Elaine M. Treharne (eds.), 83-97. |
| 2000b | *Wulfstan texts and other homiletic materials*. (Anglo-Saxon Manuscripts in Microfiche Facsimile 8). Tempe, AZ: Arizona Center for Medieval and Renaissance Studies. |

Wollmann, Alfred

| 1996 | "Scandinavian loanwords in Old English", in: Nielsen, Hans F. – Lene Schøsler (eds.), 215-242. |

DICTIONARIES AND ELECTRONIC RESOURCES

AND = *Anglo-Norman dictionary*, William Rothwell and Louise W. Stone, T. B. W. Reid (eds.). London: Modern Humanities Research Assocation, 1992. 2nd ed., Stewart Gregory, William Rothwell and David Trotter (eds.). London: Maney, 2005–. <http://www.anglo-norman.net/>, accessed December 2009–April 2010.

DOE = *Dictionary of Old English: A–G* on CD-ROM, Angus Cameron, Ashley Crandell Amos and Antonette diPaolo Healey (eds.). Toronto: Pontifical Institute of Mediaeval Studies for the Dictionary of Old English Project, 2008.

HTOED = *The historical thesaurus of the Oxford English dictionary*, Christian Kay, Jane Roberts, Michael Samuels and Irené Wotherspoon (eds.). 2 vols. Oxford: Oxford University Press, 2009.

LAEME = *A linguistic atlas of Early Middle English, 1150–1325*, Margaret Laing and Roger Lass (eds.), version 2.1. Edinburgh: The University of Edinburgh, 2008. <http://www.lel.ed.ac.uk/ihd/laeme1/laeme1.html>, accessed June 2009–April 2010.

LALME = *A linguistic atlas of Late Mediaeval English*, Angus McIntosh, Michael Benskin and M. L. Samuels (eds.), with the assistance of Margaret Laing and Keith Williamson. 4 vols. Aberdeen: Aberdeen University Press, 1986.

MED = *Middle English dictionary*, Hans Kurath, Sherman M. Kuhn and Robert E. Lewis (eds.). Ann Arbor: University of Michigan Press; London and Oxford: Oxford University Press, 1956–2001. <http://quod.lib.umich.edu/m/med/>, accessed December 2009–April 2010.

ODEE = *The Oxford dictionary of English etymology*, C. T. Onions (ed.), with the assistance of G. W. S. Friedrichsen and R. W. Burchfield. Oxford: Clarendon Press, 1966.

OED = *The Oxford English dictionary* (first published as *A New English Dictionary on Historical Principles*), James A. H. Murray, Henry Bradley, W. A. Craigie and C. T. Onions (eds.). Oxford: Clarendon Press, 1928. 2nd ed., J. A. Simpson and E. S. C. Weiner (eds.), Oxford: Oxford University Press, 1989. 3rd ed. in progress. <http://dictionary.oed.com/entrance.dtl>, accessed December 2009–April 2010.

The production and use of English manuscripts 1060 to 1220. <http://www.le.ac.uk/ee/em1060to1220>, accessed December 2009–April 2010.

de Vries, Jan
    1961   *Altnordisches etymologisches Wörterbuch*. Leiden: E. J. Brill.
Zoëga, Geir T.
    1926   *A concise dictionary of Old Icelandic*. Oxford: Clarendon Press.

On the Scandinavian origin of the Old English preposition *til* 'till'

Marcin Krygier, Adam Mickiewicz University, Poznań

ABSTRACT

The paper revisits the origin of the English preposition 'till', commonly claimed to have resulted from a merger of Old English *til* and Old Norse *til*. An analysis of the data from the DOE corpus shows that the role of the Old English preposition in the process is rather unlikely, and *till* should be viewed as a direct borrowing from Old Norse.

KEYWORDS: loanword, grammatical borrowing, preposition, Old English, Old Norse

1. Introduction

The process of borrowing of grammatical words is generally viewed both as exceptional and as indicative of intimate language contact. The history of the English language provides exactly the right context, namely the long-lasting contact between the speakers of Old English and Old Norse, which is said to have exerted profound influence on the structural make-up of English. It is therefore the more surprising that, with the exception of personal pronouns, these structural borrowings have not been subjected to more than a perfunctory scrutiny, especially as they might have wider theoretical implications.

The aim of this paper is to review the accepted etymology of one of these non-lexical borrowings, the preposition *till*. This particular word is said to have had a mixed history, descending from homophonous Old English and Old Norse prepositions – the explanation which has remained unchallenged since the publication of the *Oxford English Dictionary*; therefore, data from the *DOE* corpus (Cameron et al. (ed.) 1981) will be used to test its validity. Regardless of the status of PDE *till* as a borrowing, a native word or a mixture of the two, the analysis should contribute to a better understanding of the process of structural borrowing in general.

2. Preposition borrowing and the typology of borrowability

The issue of what constitutes suitable material for borrowing is not a new one. Hock's statement that "anything can be borrowed: lexical items, morphemes, morphological rules, phonemes, phonological rules, collocations and idioms, and morphosyntactic processes" (Hock 1991: 384) encapsulates the general belief into the ability of languages to exchange material of any type, depending on contact conditions. Hock himself goes on to place a number of restrictions on this statement, pointing out that basic vocabulary tends to resist borrowing better than specialised forms of discourse, even though he himself uses the case of Scandinavian borrowings in English as a counterexample. More recent work seems to suggest that the borrowing of closed set items may be more common in the languages of the world than has been previously suspected; Thomason and Everett's (2001) work on Pirahã, for example, contains a claim that in this particular language the entire pronominal system has been borrowed from the neighbouring Tupi language. Although doubts continue to linger about the viability of Everett's analyses in general (Everett 2005, 2009; Nevins – Pesetsky – Rodrigues 2009), it is just one out of many examples which support Lass's borrowability hierarchy: Noun > Adjective > Verb > Adverb > Preposition (Lass 1997: 190).

Obviously, this hierarchy is only one of many, and it is really questionable whether a universal ranking of borrowable forms can ever be set up, bearing in mind the extent of variation present in languages of the world. Nevertheless, the location of prepositions as a category to the far right of the alignment suggests that preposition borrowing will be a relatively infrequent phenomenon; Hornero Corisco (1997) goes even as far as to claim that "as function words, prepositions are crosslinguistically hardly ever borrowed, the process taking place here is one of calquing; these formations do not introduce foreign elements into the language, but they do introduce new forms." (Hornero Corisco 1997: 35) This statement is probably too general; a counterexample that has come to light recently is the borrowing of English prepositions into Acadian French (King 2008). Nevertheless, universally the process seems to be quite rare.

If this indeed is the case, the borrowing of Old Norse prepositions into Old and Middle English should be treated as exceptional on the one hand, but also as an opportunity to learn more about the nature of the process. It is agreed upon that in this particular case both intra- and extralinguistic conditions were especially favourable – the two languages were closely related, most likely to the point of mutual intelligibility, after the initial upheaval of Viking conquest and settlement the two populations quickly established a peaceful *modus vivendi*, and the social status of the speakers of the two languages was similar enough not to force issues of social and linguistic prestige into the picture (Townend 2002).

The overall result of the contact between Old Norse and Old English speakers constitutes a textbook example of adstratal contact situation. As Baugh and Cable stated,

> If further evidence were needed of the intimate relation that existed between the two languages, it would be found in the fact that the Scandinavian words that made their way into English were not confined to nouns and adjectives and verbs, but extended to pronouns, prepositions, adverbs, and even a part of the verb *to be*. Such parts of speech are not often transferred from one language to another
>
> (Baugh – Cable 2002: 102)

This passage, while in general true, has been however taken to be so obvious ever since that with the notable exception of personal pronouns grammatical borrowings from Old Norse have been perceived as not requiring a more detailed analysis. Prepositions of Scandinavian origin – not semantic calques in the Hornero Corisco (1997) sense, but a wholesale transfer of form and function in one package – have been prime victims of this neglect.

3. Views on the etymology of *til*

It will be best to start the discussion of the generally accepted etymology of *till* with the entry in the *Oxford English dictionary*, as its contents seem to have constituted the primary source for all the subsequent accounts.

Unfortunately, the *OED* does not provide much information on the provenance of the preposition, and the etymology section of the relevant entry basically sees it as a mixture of two words, Old Norse *til* and Old Northumbrian *til*: "ONorthumb. *til*, a. ON. *til* (...) Characteristically northern in reference to place or purpose (though in ME. occasionally midl. or south.); in reference to time, general Eng. from c1300, though now often superseded by the compound UNTIL" (*OED*: sv. *till*).

In the local function the presence of *til* in English is traced back by the editors of the *OED* to the *Ruthwell Cross* inscription, after which a gap of 400 years ensues, closed only by attestations in the *Ormulum*:

(1)   Hweþræ þer fusæ fearran kwomu æþþilæ til anum (*Ruthwell Cross*, a800)
(2)   He (...) stah þa siþþenn upp till heffne (*Orrmulum*, c1200)

Later, related senses 'conformably to, in accordance with' and 'to or for the purpose of, in order to be; to become' developed, both since becoming obsolete:

(3)   Ilk man (...) God made til his awen lyknesse (*The Prick of Conscience*, 1340)
(4)   þat he may at his ending haue heuin till his mede (*Minot, Poems*, a1352)

Another early sense of *til*, attested already in Old English, was to express the object of a verb of giving, telling and the like; the earliest instance of this function comes from the 10th century, and later attestations appear from the 13th century onwards:

(5)   þa cueþ til him þe hælend (*Lindisfarne Gospels*, c950)
(6)   He se33de þuss till himm (*Orrmulum*, c1200)

Finally in the 14th century *til* develops temporal senses as well:

(7)   Fro Eneas till Brutus tyme (*Robert Mannyng of Brunne, Chronicle*, c1330)
(8)   Sa þai sal tille domes day (*Cursor Mundi (F)*, c1375)

Outside of the *OED* it is surprisingly hard to find any reference to *til* beyond the mere mention of the fact that it is partially of Scandinavian provenance. Mitchell in his *Old English syntax* mentions *til* in the heading of the section devoted to *tō* together with its unstressed form *te* (Mitchell 1985: 498). Visser (1963-1973) does not discuss prepositions in a systematic fashion at all. Mustanoja's *A Middle English syntax*, the other major book devoted to the history of English syntax, offers the most generous extensive treatment of *til*, saying that

> *Till* (ON and Northumbrian *til*) is a typically northern preposition in all its functions
> down to c1300, since which time it has occurred in all dialectal areas in the temporal
> sense 'until'. In local and final use, although occasionally found in the Midlands and the
> South, it remains predominantly northern even in later times and can be said to serve as
> a northern equivalent of *to*.
>
> (Mustanoja 1960: 409)

The dependence of this passage on the *OED* entry is fairly clear.

General histories of English as well as specialised volumes devoted to Old and Middle English period do not fare much better. Baugh and Cable (2002) summarise the dominant approach in their discussion of Old Norse prepositions under the heading of 'Form words': "The preposition *till* was at one time widely used in the sense of *to*, besides having its present meaning, and *fro*, likewise in common use formerly as the equivalent of *from*, survives in the phrase *to and fro*. Both words are from the Scandinavian" (Baugh – Cable 2002: 102). Fisiak (1996) is silent on this issue, as are Mossé (1952), Campbell (1959), and Wełna (1996); it seems that for historical linguists prepositions as a category are not particularly fascinating.

Likewise, more recent discussions of the Middle English lexicon are not really different in this respect. Burnley's (1992) treatment of function words in the "Lexis and semantics" chapter of *The Cambridge history of the English language* (Blake (ed.) 1992) is limited to the following statement: "Some of this 'grammatical' borrowing has also survived into modern English: *til* (as a conjunction) (...)" (Burnley 1992: 421).

What is worrying here is the apparent regurgitation of the same set of facts, each cycle removing some details and offering its own generalisations; where the *OED* and Mustanoja (the first cycle) provide an analysis of temporal, dialectal, and functional properties of the preposition, Baugh and Cable (the second cycle) are content with a general statement, whereas Burnley's account (the third cycle) is extremely simple. The purpose and audience of the respective authors could have played some part in the selection of data for publication, yet they alone cannot explain this strange simplificatory tendency.

4. *Til* in Old English

It is clear from the discussion in section 3 above that the origin of *til* is seen as uncontroversial and the preposition is widely believed to be a combination of Northumbrian Old English *til* and its Old Norse equivalent. Such a picture is presented in those sources which at least passingly discuss the etymology of this word at all. However, it is equally clear that the consensus stems largely from the fact that all accounts ultimately derive from the *OED* entry for the preposition. Therefore, it seems worthwhile to return to the primary data and analyse the use of OE *til* as attested in the *DOE* corpus (Cameron et al. (ed.) 1981).

The DOE corpus contains 14 instances of the word, regardless of its function, listed chronologically as (9)-(22) below:

(9)   He aerist scop aelda barnum heben til hrofe, haleg scepen; tha middungeard moncynnæs uard, eci dryctin, æfter tiadæ firum foldu, frea allmectig (*Cædmon's Hymn*, Northumbrian, c750).

(10)   Krist wæs on rodi Hweþræ þer fusæ fearran kwomu æþþilæ til anum (*Ruthwell Cross* c750)

(10a) Crist wæs on rode Hwæðere þær fuse feorran cwoman to þam æðelinge (*Dream of the Rood*, 10th c., West-Saxon)

The first two instances, (9) and (10) are found in oldest surviving Old English texts, a Northumbrian version of Cædmon's *Hymn* and the *Ruthwell Cross* inscription; it is worth noticing that the Vercelli Book version of the relevant section of the *Dream of the Rood*, (10a), employs the standard OE *tō* rather than *til*.

(11)   Þat wil i be him þat me scop, Bot til an Ercebiscop (*King Æthelstan to St. John's, Beverley*, 925 (for 927 x 939), Sawyer 451)

(12)   And til þe seuen minstre Prestes þat serues God þar saint John restes þat give i God and saint John Her befor you euerilkan All my hest corn iueldeel, To uphald his ministre weel, þa four Threue be heuen kinge, Of ilk a plowgh of Estriding (*King Æthelstan to St. John's, Beverley*, 925 (for 927 x 939), Sawyer 451)

(13)   If it swa betid or swa gaas, þat ani man her again taas, Be he baron, be he erle, Clark, Prest Person or Cherel, Na be he na þat ilk Gome, I will forsoþe þat he come, þat wit ye weel or and or, Til saint John mynstre dor (*King Æthelstan to St. John's, Beverley*, 925 (for 927 x 939), Sawyer 451)

(14)   Swilk þan be sain John laghes, þat þe Chapitel of Beuerlik Til þe Schirref of Euerwik, Send þair writ son on an, þat þis mansedman betan (*King Æthelstan to St. John's, Beverley*, 925 (for 927 x 939), Sawyer 451)

(15)   And hald him þat is mi wilt Til he bet his misgilt (*King Æthelstan to St. John's, Beverley*, 925 (for 927 x 939), Sawyer 451)

The next five instances all come from a grant of privileges allegedly issued by King Athelstan to the monks at St. John's, Beverley, in the first half of the 10th century. However, even a cursory look at the relevant excerpts from that grant clearly shows the language to be much more modern in all regards than would be expected of a 10th century text. It is therefore unlikely to be authentic, and Witty (1921) sees it as an early 14th century forgery (Kelly (ed.) 1999). Consequently, these instances cannot be admitted as evidence for OE *til*.

(16)   Þanne, on achylle on til luches lege (*Queen Eadwig to the minster at Shaftesbury*, 956, Sawyer 630)

The next instance, (16) is taken from a Latin grant to the minster at Shaftesbury, issued by queen Eadwig in 956 and provided with a description of the bounds in English (Kelly (ed.) 1999). There are doubts as to the authenticity of these bounds, which are usually interpreted as added to an original Latin grant at a later date (Barker 1967, Kelly (ed.) 1996); forms such as *achylle* definitely point towards a date later that the middle of the 10th century.

(17)   ða forma uutedlice doege ðara ðorofra mæta geneolecdon vel eodon ða ðegnas to ðæm hælende cuoeðende huer wiltu þæt we gearuiga ðe til eottanne eastro (*Lindisfarne Gospels (Mt)*, late 10th c., (North) Northumbrian)
(18)   ða cueð til him ðe hælend alle ge ondspyrnise ge ðrowiges on mec in vel on ðasser næht awriten is forðon ic slæ hiorde & tostengcid vel tostrogden biað scip edes (*Lindisfarne Gospels (Mt)*, late 10th c., (North) Northumbrian)

The next two instances come from the *Gospel of Matthew* translated by Aldred in the second half of the 10th century and constituting part of the North Northumbrian *Lindisfarne Gospels*. (17) presents *til* as an infinitival marker, whereas in (18) it is a regular preposition in a local sense of 'to'.

(19)   So aftir strem til it shutt eft into Hensislade (*King Æthelred to St Frideswide's Abbey*, 1004, Sawyer 909)

(19) is an example of *til* as a conjunction, taken from the English descriptions of bounds in a Latin grant to the nuns of St Frideswide's Abbey, issued by king Æthelred in 1004. As with the Shaftesbury bounds, the bounds in this grant could have been added later (Whitelock (ed.) 1979); at any rate, their authenticity is not universally accepted (Kelly (ed.) 1999).

(20)   Forþon his mildheortnyss is mycel ofer us torhtlice getrymed, til mancynne, and soðfæstnys swylce dryhtnes wunað ece awa to feore (*P116, The Paris Psalter*, 11th c., West-Saxon)

(20) comes from the verse part of the *Paris Psalter*, BN 8824, dated to the 11th century and written in a predominantly West Saxon dialect of Old English.

(21)   & þar he nam þe biscop Roger of Sereberi & Alexander biscop of Lincol & te Canceler Roger hise neues. & dide ælle in prisun. til hi iafen up here castles (ASC E, 1137)

(22)   & hi of Normandi wenden alle fra þe king. to þe eorl of Ang[ae]u. sume here þankes & sume here unþankes. for he besæt heom til hi aiauen up here castles. & hi nan helpe ne hæfden of þe kinge (ASC E, 1140).

Finally, instances (21) and (22) are taken from the *Final Continuation* of the *Peterborough Chronicle*, i.e., MS. Laud of the *Anglo-Saxon Chronicle*, usually called the MS. E.

There is little doubt that charters and grants evidence has to be rejected, as most of them, (11)-(16), can be reasonably shown to be Middle English forgeries, and the remaining one, (19), can be dated towards the end of the Old English period at best. This leaves seven genuine examples – two very early ones from Northumbria, two late 10th century ones, also from Northumbria, one from the 11th and two from the 12th century. The latter three may be easily explained as Scandinavian borrowings due to the time of their attestation, and there is no need to postulate a native English form to explain their presence in the data. Consequently, the two instances of *til* from the *Lindisfarne Gospels* are crucial for the native interpretation of the preposition, as they constitute the only possible evidence of the survival of native *til* in the north of England.

However, that (17) and (18) are native forms does not seem likely. First of all, in the *Gospel of Matthew* Aldred uses 258 instances of *tō* as opposed to only 2 instances of *til*, both in contexts in which *tō* is favoured otherwise. Therefore, *til* cannot be realistically viewed as a variant with a specialised meaning. It is also hardly possible that it is just a mere variant of *tō* – in that case one would expect it to appear more often in the text. Finally, the early instances of *til* from the 8th century are used as an expression of purpose in (9) and in a local sense in (10); on the other hand in (17) *til* introduces an inflected infinitive, and in (18) it follows a verb of speaking in a quasi-phrasal construction. Thus, it is not possible to show any functional continuity between the early and the late Northumbrian examples of *til*.

The Scandinavian presence in Northumbria, on the other hand, foreshadowed by the Lindisfarne raid of 793, culminated in an utter disaster for the Anglo-Saxons at York in 867, after which defeat the kingdom passed into the Danish hands (Jones 1984: 218-229). At the time of writing the interlinear gloss to the *Gospel of Matthew* the Danes had been living in Northumbria for approximately a century and the presence of an occasional Old Norse form should not be surprising in the language of a monk from Chester-le-Street.

5. Conclusions

The early history of *til* serves as a perfect illustration of the need to constantly re-examine and review the surviving data. Otherwise excessive reliance on earlier studies could lead to repeating their findings together with their shortcomings.

A detailed analysis of the Old English data has shown that much of what is thought to be known about the fate of *til* is, to put it mildly, at odds with facts. Subsequent generations of scholars have placed too much reliance on their predecessors, producing increasingly generalised descriptions, as can be shown by juxtaposing three statements representing different stages of this process, from a relatively detailed account in the *OED* and Mustanoja (1960), through the "bare bones" approach of Baugh and Cable (2002), to a simplified statement by Burnley (1992).

The data, however, indicate that the situation was not only different but also more complex than it is customarily believed. The assumption that *til* was available to speakers of the northern dialects of Old English and that the contact with Scandinavians led to a mere expansion of a native pattern cannot be successfully defended.

The two earliest attestations of *til* should probably be seen as genuinely English. Although trade contacts between Scandinavia and England before the arrival of the Vikings have been amply attested (Jones 1984: 157-168), a Scandinavian borrowing in a highly formulaic, poetic language of early Old English verse does not seem very likely. Therefore, *til* in *Cædmon's Hymn* and the *Ruthwell Cross* inscription should be interpreted as survivals of an otherwise unattested poetic Old English *til*. There is, however, no argument for postulating the presence of the native word in later Old English, as the existing attestations are either spurious or late; moreover, the functional mismatch between early and late Old Northumbrian instances of *til* strongly suggests lack of continuity between the two sets of attestations.

References

Barker, E. E.
    1967   "The Anglo-Saxon Chronicle used by Æthelweard", *B.I.H.R.* 40: 74-91.
Baugh, Albert C. – Thomas Cable
    2002   *A history of the English language.* (5th ed.). London: Routledge.

Blake, Norman (ed.)
  1992   *The Cambridge history of the English language. Volume II: 1066-1476.*
          Cambridge: Cambridge University Press.
Burnley, David
  1992   "Lexis and semantics", in: Blake (ed.), 409-499.
Cameron, Angus – Ashley Crandell Amos – Sharon Butler – Antonette diPaolo Healey
          (eds.)
  1981   *The dictionary of Old English corpus in electronic form.* Toronto: DOE
          Project.
Campbell, Alistair
  1959   *Old English grammar.* Oxford: Clarendon Press.
Everett, Daniel L.
  2005   "Cultural constraints on grammar and cognition in Pirahã", *Current
          Anthropology* 46: 621-646.
  2009   "Pirahã culture and grammar: A response to some criticisms", *Language*
          85.2: 405-442.
Fisiak, Jacek
  1996   *A short grammar of Middle English. Part I: Graphemics, phonemics and
          morphemics.* (7th ed.). Warszawa: PWN.
Hock, Hans H.
  1991   *Principles of historical linguistics* (2nd ed.). Berlin: Mouton de Gruyter.
Hornero Corisco, Ana Mª
  1997   "French influence on English prepositions: A study of *Ancrene Wisse*",
          Studia Anglica Posnaniensia 32: 33-46.
Jones, Gwyn
  1984   *A history of the Vikings* (2nd ed.). Oxford: Oxford University Press.
Kelly, S.E. (ed.)
  1996   *The charters of Shaftesbury Abbey.* Oxford: Oxford University Press.
  1999   *The electronic Sawyer, an online version of the revised edition of
          Sawyer's* Anglo-Saxon Charters section one [S 1-1602]. Available at:
          http://www.trin.cam.ac.uk/chartwww/esawyer.99/esawyer2.html. (date of
          access 05/05/2010).
King, Ruth
  2008   "*Chiac* in context: Overview and evaluation of Acadie's *Joual*", in:
          Meyerhoff, Miriam – Naomi Nagy (eds.), 137-178.
Lass, Roger
  1997   *Historical linguistics and language change.* Cambridge: Cambridge
          University Press.
Meyerhoff, Miriam – Naomi Nagy (eds.)
  2008   *Social lives in language: Sociolinguistics and multilingual speech
          communities. Celebrating the work of Gillian Sankoff.* Amsterdam:
          Benjamins.
Mitchell, Bruce
  1985   *Old English syntax.* Oxford: Oxford University Press.

Mossé, Fernand
   1952   *A manual of Middle English*. Baltimore: Johns Hopkins Press.
Mustanoja, Tauno F.
   1960   *A Middle English syntax. Part 1: Parts of speech.* Helsinki: Société
             Néophilologique.
Nevins, Andrew – David Pesetsky – Cilene Rodrigues
   2009   "Pirahã exceptionality: A reassessment", *Language* 85.2: 355-404.
OED, the
   1997   *Oxford English dictionary (Second Edition) on CD-ROM*. Oxford:
             Oxford University Press.
Thomason, Sarah G. – Daniel L. Everett
   2001   "Pronoun borrowing", *Proceedings of the Berkeley Linguistic Society* 27:
             301-315.
Townend, Matthew
   2002   *Language and history in Viking Age England: Linguistic relations
             between speakers of Old Norse and Old English*. Turnhout: Brepols.
Visser, Frederikus Th.
   1963-1973 *A historical syntax of the English language*. Leiden: Brill.
Wełna, Jerzy
   1996   *English historical morphology*. Warszawa: Wydawnictwa Uniwersytetu
             Warszawskiego.
Whitelock, Dorothy (ed.)
   1979   *English historical documents c. 500-1042*. London: Routledge.
Witty, J. R.
   1921   "The rhyming charter of Beverley", *Transactions of the Yorkshire Dialect
             Society* 22: 36-44.

Anglo-Scandinavian language contacts and word order shift in early English

Izabela Czerniak, University of Eastern Finland, Joensuu

ABSTRACT

The current paper sheds light on one of the most significant changes in the English language occurring at the early stages of its development. An attempt will be made to trace the emergence of rigid SVO order in Early English, happening as a consequence of overt morphological simplification, which in turn was instigated by medieval Anglo-Scandinavian language contacts. The results of my searches through the prose parsed corpora of Old (YCOE[1]) and Middle (PPCME2) suggest a receding pattern for the SOV and an increasingly prevailing tendency towards SVO word order in the areas most open to language contact. However, some additional statistical calculations are necessary to fully account for the nature of the change.

KEYWORDS: coefficient of variation (CV), language contact, Scandinavian(s), influence, word order

1. Introduction

The word order change from a predominantly (S)OV to a predominantly SVO system which took place in Middle English has been widely recognised and the motivation behind the change hotly debated on for many years now. From a purely syntactic standpoint, there are as many as five different options which could be used to explain the change in question (not excluding the possibility of them overlapping one another). Firstly, the rise and stabilisation of VO has been attributed to the existence of 'afterthought-like elements', which appear postverbally, as proposed by Stockwell (1977). The second proposal involves the idea that the postverbal position was generalised from heavy to lighter objects (cf. Lightfoot 1979). Thirdly, the change from OV to VO might have been due to "processing problems" caused by the "consistent use of OV order for internally complex objects" (see Colman 1988). The fourth scenario promoting the emergence of VO could have been connected with the infrequence of OV in the main clauses which are the "prime environment guiding language learners." (Lightfoot 1991) Finally, (S)VO[2] order is claimed to have been reinforced by the

---

1   YCOE – *The York-Toronto parsed corpus of Old English prose* (available through Oxford text archive (http://www.ota.ahds.ac.uk/), and PPCME2 – *The Penn-parsed Helsinki corpus of Middle English*, second edition (obtained from http://www.ling.upenn.edu/hist-corpora/). They are parsed 'offsprings' of *the Helsinki corpus of English texts* (http://www.helsinki.fi/varieng/CoRD/corpora/HelsinkiCorpus/) with considerable additions (and deletions) to the content, making altogether almost 3 million word database to explore.

2   The placement of the subject in the sequence, although not directly involved in some of the

loss of overt case marking on noun phrases (NPs) (cf. Weerman 1989: 157-78; Kiparsky 1997 both quoted in Fischer et al. 2000: 173). Surprisingly, the last-mentioned reason seems to be the only one clearly aiming at connecting this sudden[3] syntactic change with a potential externally motivated factor, represented by language contact.

The present study is a part of a doctoral research investigating the changes in syntax as triggered and promoted by Anglo-Scandinavian language contacts and interpreted in the light of some models of linguistic change. The study focuses on subject and object inflections. One of the main aims is to investigate whether the inflectional erosion in Early English, which began in the northern part of the Isle (Milroy 1992a: 181-2 and Fischer 1992: 208, also Fisiak 2005: 60f; Thomason and Kaufman 1988: 126) further reinforced the stabilisation of the SVO order. More specifically, the research aims at finding out how far the pushing of the sentence elements towards a more analytical layout is a result of the necessity to differentiate the 'caseless' noun phrases. Furthermore, the study examines to what extent word order change in English could be seen as a follow-up to the process instigated by the Anglo-Scandinavian language contacts at that time. The loss of case inflections at the early stages of development of English has often been attributed to this particular contact situation (cf. Iglesias-Rabade 2003: 86). All in all, when dealing with contact-induced change, the outcome may both simplify as well as complicate the grammar of a language (cf. Thomason and Kaufman 1988: 28).

2. Method and points discussed

The present paper presents the results of the searches on the parsed prose corpora of Old (YCOE) and Middle (PPCME2) English for the rate of (S)OV and (S)VO as the sequences of (originally) inflected elements. It is a longitudinal comparative study of the word order shift and stabilisation based on these two databases. The output of the searches was filtered through the statistical measure of the coefficient of variation (CV), which enabled a proper translation of the numerical data into particular linguistic phenomena. The aim of the corpus investigation was to test whether the patterns of word order change coincided with the process of inflectional erosion. As will be seen, the corpus analysis helped to confirm that the attrition of grammatical markers, including those on NPs, and the rise of the new (S)VO word order converged in the same dialect sets which correspond to the areas of Scandinavian influence at these early periods. The impact regions

---

processes just outlined, will be stressed due to the choice of the current research hypotheses.

3   There are varying opinions about whether to treat this particular instance of word order shift as a rapid change or the process happening more gradually (cf. Fischer et al. 2000: 139). The view presented in this paper is leaning towards the idea that any linguistic change motivated by linguistic contact is taking a language cycle out of its *natural* tempo of development, thus accelerating the adoption of the new feature (cf. Trudgill 1983 in McMahon 1994: 266).

overlapped with Old English Northumbrian and (parts of) Mercian dialects, collectively referred to as Anglian. Later on, during the Middle English period, when the linguistic outcomes of the Scandinavian impact were especially visible, the influenced regions covered the North and (parts of) the East Midlands.

Before a detailed discussion of the results, I will outline some essentials of the corpus queries. Next, an explanation of how output has been managed will be provided, followed by the introduction and the application of the statistical tool. Before the results proper are presented, a brief description of the dialect samples will be given. Finally, I will present some preliminary conclusions arising from the data. Though not conclusive at this point of my research, they constitute a firm basis for further study on the topic.

3. Queries and the output management

The parsed nature of both corpora allows for searching of complex element strings, including word order patterns. In the current study, three element sequence queries of SOV[4] and SVO[5] were chosen to tackle the research hypothesis in general: two predominant word orders in the Old English period, the former giving way to the latter throughout the (first part of) the Middle English period, as the progressing inflectional erosion impaired[6] the possibility of 'free' ordering of sentential components. In addition, elements pairs were searched[7] for

---

4   Where subjects would be represented by 'NP-NOM' label (with some restrictions) in YCOE and 'NP-SBJ' in PPCME2; verbs, due to the fact that the surface order was still relatively 'free' in Early English, would need a separate verb phrase (VP) construction to account for a particular verb type; and finally, objects could be obtained by a definition file in YCOE (which included all NP possibilities assigned to objective case) and a label of 'NP-OB' in PPCME2. In addition, the negative particle was included in the forming of various VP types. (For more information on labels and definition files see: http://www.ling.upenn.edu/hist-corpora/annotation/index.html.)

5   Other word order combinations were also investigated, largely to examine whether the output conformed to what had already been established on the topic. These, however, will not be handled in the present paper.

6   Although the degree of inflectional erosion *per se* does not constitute a point in dispute in the current study, it is worth emphasising that regardless of the question which of the two factors (internal or external) specifically tipped the scale in favour of subsequent changes in syntax, the magnitude of morphological attrition, even if not leading to 'rampant ambiguity' (Fischer and van der Wurff 2006: 187-188), must have, at least, created syntactic uneasiness around the subject and object status of NPs. Once the case signalling procedure had been disturbed some other means of representation of case relations had to be considered (cf. Saitz 1955 in Bean 1983:115). Out of an array of, at times, complex syntactic rearrangements to rectify for lost items, the system eventually opted for the extension of a 'familiar' (cf. Fischer et al. 2000: 104) option – a (fixed) verb element intervention between subjects and objects.

7   Searches were carried out by means of the CS search programme distributed along with the two databases. The queries run on MS-DOS. (For more information see: http://corpussearch.

as well, including OV/VO – to specifically explore the shift of the object from the preverbal to postverbal position.

Both the searches and the output were generated in a manner to specifically fulfil the conditions of one of the research hypotheses where a connection between the case erosion and the growing prevalence of SVO order was checked. In this respect, only originally inflected sentence elements were included in the query lines (i.e. element strings would not contain, for instance, *that*-clauses which can perfectly function as objects). In addition, when measuring the rate of the particular word order sequence, the closest proximity of elements was emphasised. For this reason, the search function *iPrecedes*[8] was employed. It does not allow for any interruptions in the element string and the output produced comprises of only the items specified in the query line. This rather straightforward manner of extracting data was chosen in order to approach the scenario of possible   disruption   (SOV)   and   restoration   or   optimisation   (SVO)   of communicative capability on account of morphological simplification *only* (cf. Hock and Joseph 1996: 211; Danchev 1991: 108).

As the present study deals with word order patterns where particular sentence elements form longer strings, the search results needed to be confronted not with the overall number of words but with that of clauses per given text. The output is available, therefore, at three levels: the sentence level comprised of the total of all the matrix[9] and subordinate clauses found in a particular text and at matrix and subordinate levels separately. The comparison of scores between the sentence and matrix/subordinate levels helped to identify which of the latter two specifically contributed to the height of the final values. Further, the output was generated separately for sequences with and without empty categories (which include empty subjects and various kinds of traces).[10] As traces phonologically constitute a 'null' category, the twofold perspective was created in order to test whether there would be any differences in the output when sequences did or did not include covert items. Lastly, the tokens, i.e. the raw frequencies of occurrence of a particular feature, were normalised to adjust counts from texts of different lengths. In this respect, they could be compared properly (cf. Biber et al. 1998: 263). The lowest common base adopted for this purpose was 25 clauses (IPs). It allowed for an examination of the largest sample of texts combined from the two databases, with text specimens available in all dialects at the two distinct periods. Among subsequent data

---

sourceforge.net/index.html.)

8   'Immediately precedes' – one of the search functions in the CS query language.

9   In order to obtain an accurate number of clauses, a separate query was generated to account for every instance of a *complete* clause both at the matrix and subordinate levels.

10   Traces – essential theoretical devices in some approaches to syntax, along with other empty elements, are labelled in both corpora and unless the search specifies whether traces should not count in the total, the CS will include them by default. In order to count out the empty categories from the total a ' \ **' label needs to be added to the ignore list in the query lines.

management and interpretation procedures, though not yet tackled in the present paper, there will be additional normalisation of frequencies for other, larger common bases. Having to deal with high text length inconsistency within the two corpora, it is necessary to examine, in due course, whether and how frequency differences between particular dialect sets fluctuate for a given common base. By adopting a particular base for output management, the size of dialect samples will change, undoubtedly influencing the results for the distribution of a particular feature. What is more, the multiple common base approach will allow to observe whether the overall pattern of changes discussed remains stable throughout.

4. Coefficient of variation

In order to accurately observe the language change in the making, as laid out by frequency values in the overlapping dialect areas between the two periods, the output had to, additionally, be filtered through the statistical measure which would help to elicit the relevant facts from the results charts – the coefficient of variation (CV). The measure is defined as the ratio of the standard deviation to the mean. It is a useful statistic for comparing of the degree of variation from one data series to another. More specifically, the coefficient measures how much output values deviate from the estimated average of the feature found in a particular series. In the present study, CV shows how much frequencies calculated for individual texts differ from the average frequency estimated for the whole dialect set. The higher the value of CV, the bigger variation (or irregularity) is noted. Conversely, the lower the value of the coefficient, the more uniform display of the feature is found in particular dialect sectors. The ratio is multiplied by 100 and the deviation is expressed as a percentage of the mean (Frank and Althoen 1994: 58-9). When the measures are changed to per cents of their averages, direct comparisons of the representativeness of particular two averages can be made. By contrast, an attempt to compare the averages in respect to their validity by means of direct measures of dispersion would *not* provide any precision in interpretation of the data. (Balsley 1964: 91-92).

In order to illustrate how the tool works, Figure 1 and 2 below present the layout of normalised frequencies[11] for SVO sequence in the northern and southern Middle English dialects respectively at the sentence level (for element strings including traces). The bold vertical line stands for the average frequency in a particular dialect set. The length of columns on the right and on the left off the vertical line show higher or lower frequency values found in individual texts. The North (Figure 1) scores 6% for CV, showing a regular distribution of the investigated feature – the columns barely deviate from the vertical line (i.e. average), as opposed to the bars of the graph for the South (Figure 2), where the sways are bigger, hence the higher CV of 16%.

---

11 The graphs have been drawn on real output.

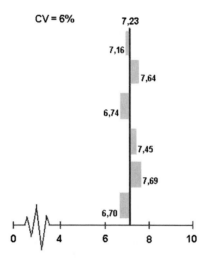

Figure 1. Coefficient of variation for the North - SVO at the sentence level with individual frequencies specified

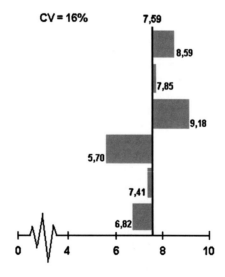

Figure 2. Coefficient of variation for the South - SVO at the sentence level with individual frequencies specified

The significance of reading of CV against frequencies will be exhaustively explained in the following paragraph, however, it is valuable to notice, already at this point, that just by solely relying on the (average) frequencies researchers are bound to inadequately (i.e. inaccurately) interpret results – the South, as indicated by average frequency values, scores higher for SVO than the North (exactly the opposite to what CV points to).

As regards the motivation for adopting of an additional measurement filter, the coefficient was employed in order to provide some more input as far as the character of variation was concerned. The tool proved especially useful when average frequencies in sets did not differ significantly from each other, which occurred frequently for normalised frequencies calculated on the currently adopted common base (25 IP). In this respect, CV helped to differentiate seemingly identical outputs. What is more, the coefficient properly translated the figures into facts. As the two databases present uneven distribution of texts per dialect, per time and per genre, any modification[12] to the length of particular samples changed the intensity of frequencies. Their values seemed too unstable to be solely used for the interpretation of linguistic phenomena. Further, apart from shedding light on the nature of the true variation, the coefficient was able to test the reliability of the output. It showed whether the high condensation of the feature per set was obtained from regularly (i.e. premeditatedly) distributed feature within texts, pointing to the reliability of results, as opposed to cases where values of frequencies for particular features within different dialect sectors fluctuated greatly, increasing, in this respect, the unreliability of the final output. The height of CV exceeding 60% equals with treading on the borderline between 'certain' and 'uncertain' (cf. Yamane 1973: 79). In this respect, any section which scored higher than the above threshold value should not be used to confidently predict changes.

5. Dialect sets, sample size and the genre problem

As dialect information is of crucial importance, the texts were, for the most part, divided by the linguistic region in both corpora, as indicated by the database

---

12   Changes to the size of particular samples, which determine the interpretation of results outlined in the current paper, involved only the clipping of the material to account for precise dialect information (see Section 5). Other sample normalisations will need to, subsequently, be considered as well, for instance section cuts to create equal time spans per set. (A number of texts of the OE corpus were composed at very early dates. However, they are not available in all of the dialects. The texts will have to be removed and the output obtained from these compared). Further, sample cuts will also entail exclusion of translated texts to estimate how much the layout of the feature could be influenced by the presence of foreign patterns, as introduced by translators.

compilers.[13] In this respect, the Anglian Northumbrian dialect developed into ME North (N[14]), Anglian Mercian evolved into East (EM) and West Midlands (WM). The Kentish (K) preserved its older name. Finally, OE West Saxon (WS) developed into ME South (S) (cf. Milroy 1992b: 172). Due to the fact that Anglian Northumbrian is not represented in YCOE, some modification in dialect samples was made to compensate for the absence and to make the comparison of data from the two corpora possible. Consequently, the Anglian dialect either branched into an overt Mercian (AM) set or into other, non-specified Anglian (NM) which contained texts from file clippings[15] (mostly comprised of smaller parts of charters and wills) and texts of mixed dialects one of which is West Saxon and the other, Anglian.[16] On the whole, the YCOE dialect sets differed greatly in size. The verified West Saxon set contained almost ¾ of all texts available in the database (41 instances). The non-specified Anglian comprised of only 9 texts, Anglian Mercian included 5 and Kentish as few as 4 texts. Fortunately, the PPCME2 material has a more uniform time frame and every dialect set was arranged to contain 6 texts of considerable size, except Kent where only 3 texts were available in the entire database. Lastly, since the distribution of texts per genre in the two databases is also quite uneven, it would be difficult, therefore, to objectively measure how much exactly the genre type will influence the preference for a particular word order sequence. It is possible, however, to roughly tell whether the variation in the distribution of a given word order within dialect sets is substantial enough to overcome the "genre bias". Some texts in the corpora are doublets available in different dialects. *The Mirror of St Edmund* (PPCME2) – a religious treatise written in the Northern and West Midland dialects, makes a good example. The frequency values at specific clause levels for these two versions differed enough to detect a particular dialectal "complexion". In this respect, if there were differences noted for the same text assigned to distinct dialects, the genre influence, although undoubtedly considerable in cases of word order distribution, could be set aside in the present study.

---

13   The information on dialects for YCOE comes from the Helsinki Corpus and is only given for the text which were included in that database. In PPCME2, most of the texts received the dialect tag from LALME (McIntosh et al. 1986). In the present study, only the specimens which could *clearly* be identified by a particular linguistic region were used for the analysis.

14   The letter code was employed for the sake of clarity in the output charts and graphs.

15   The nature of parsing allows for dissection of the original file as long as the parsing principle is respected and the relevant portion is picked out along with opening and closing codes.

16   Texts of mixed dialect always spoke in favour of the one other than the West Saxon. Most of the texts of OE corpus have a notable underlying West Saxon tint, therefore any other dialect marking is significant for the study.

6. Results

6.1. Normalised frequency values

When comparing the output of YCOE and PPCME2, the biggest growth in frequency values for SVO is, at all times, noted in the dialect sections corresponding to the areas of Scandinavian settlement whether sequences involve or exclude traces (Figure 3 and 4 below).

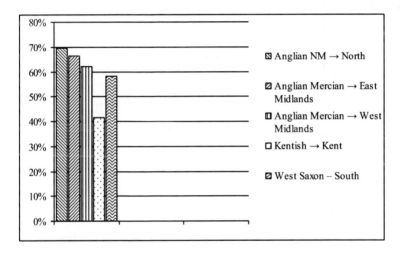

Figure 3. SVO frequency growth rate for the common base of 25 clauses (sentence level, with traces)

The gap between the Scandinavian impact areas and the rest of the dialect sections is wider for sequences excluding traces (Figure 4) – no other set experiences growth in SVO above 65%. Still, a slightly more diverse layout of values for SVO string with traces (Figure 3) does not, by any means, impair the leadership of the sets corresponding to regions of the Anglo-Scandinavian contact. Further, there is one more dialect set which exhibits a considerable increase in the preference for SVO – the West Midland section which used to be a part of the Anglian Mercian set.

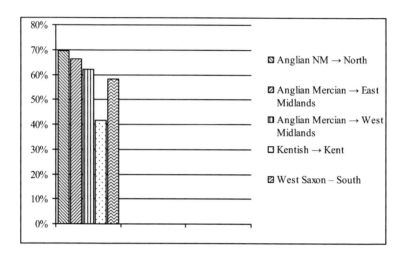

Figure 4: SVO frequency growth rate for the common base of 25 clauses (sentence level, no traces)

The remaining two, Kent and South, appear to be left behind. However, of these only the former could be regarded as conservative. Kent shows an adequate preference both for SVO as well as for SOV and this preference does not either fade or considerably strengthens with time. By contrast, with a steadily growing, and already quite significant preference for SVO, the West Saxon dialect never scores high enough for SOV and subsequently (represented as the Middle English South) is the first one to disfavour it, as can be seen from the detailed frequency charts below.[17]

F/25 IP	SOV	SOV mat	SOV sub	SVO	SVO mat	SVO sub
ANM	1.71	1.21	2.53	2.16	2.81	1.75
AM	3.98	3.71	4.34	2.39	3.36	1.43
K	3.56	2.55	4.29	3.41	3.77	3.11
WS	3.00	1.90	3.93	3.32	4.03	2.67

Figure 5. Frequency charts for SOV/SVO in YCOE (sentence,[18] matrix, subordinate clause levels specified)

---

17   The frequency charts present the sequencing option which includes traces. The non-traced perspective will only be mentioned in cases where the differences between the two layouts are significant.

18   The sentence level is always placed ahead of the matrix and subordinate levels in the charts.

The YCOE frequency table (Figure 5), on the whole, does not reveal significantly different values both for SOV and SVO. As expected, during the Old English period, SOV and SVO (along with other word order possibilities) are present in the syntactic scheme (cf. Fischer et al. 2000: 104) – the former prominent at the subordinate and the latter at the matrix level.

By contrast, for the Middle English database, the frequencies of SOV and SVO differ greatly from each other. The former substantially loses its strength to give way to the latter, which scores frequency values, at least, twice as high as those found in the samples of the Old English corpus.

F/25 IP	SOV	SOV mat	SOV sub	SVO	SVO mat	SVO sub
N	0.40	0.36	0.41	7.23	8.58	6.53
EM	1.02	0.96	1.00	7.03	7.85	6.32
WM	0.58	0.45	0.73	6.46	8.22	5.41
K	2.14	1.67	2.47	6.22	7.42	5.38
S	0.12	0.02	0.19	7.59	9.07	6.18

Figure 6. Frequency charts for SOV/SVO in PPCME2 (sentence, matrix, subordinate clause levels specified)

The highest average frequency for SVO is usually found first in the South and then immediately noted in the North and East Midlands at any but the subordinate level where the situation is reversed. The significance of the fact that SVO is particularly favoured in subordinate clauses in the dialects corresponding to the areas of Scandinavian influence should be strengthened with the remark that it is the East Midland set which, on the whole, scores the highest frequencies possible for individual texts in the entire corpus, not the North. Indeed, the two dialects form a truly 'Scandinavian contingent' in the output tables, as they tend to pair with the average values within different configurations. Finally, the diminishing preference for SOV comes as no surprise during the Middle English period. Majority of dialects score very low for that particular option.

6.2. Scale of variation in the two corpora – CV values as confronted with obtained frequencies

With the highest frequencies found in the South and with small differences in average values between particular dialect sets, it would be quite difficult to elicit significant facts supporting current hypotheses. In this respect, to fully grasp the nature of the changes in question, the normalised frequencies had to be contrasted with the values of the coefficient of variation. For YCOE (Figure 7), the level of fluctuation of values, is, on the whole, quite high (both for SOV and SVO). The high CV appears throughout the chart, especially for SVO within the Anglian sectors. Admittedly, an unusually high coefficient for the non-specified Anglian set (NM) could be the result of a 'tainted' sample (see Section 5). However, the second Anglian dialect, the Mercian set, is neatly represented and the fact that the dialect still shows substantial variation might be indicative of the subsequent changes in these areas. Lastly, when looking at CV at particular clause levels, out of the three, the matrix one reveals the most irregular output, both for SOV and SVO sequences.

CV (%)	SOV	SOV mat	SOV sub	SVO	SVO mat	SVO sub
ANM	42	59	33	74	119	40
AM	62	79	48	48	48	98
K	70	122	74	47	45	63
WS	35	86	33	34	41	39

Figure 7. Coefficient values for SOV/SVO in YCOE (sentence, matrix, subordinate clause levels specified)

Entering the Middle English period (Figure 8), there is an overall increase in the regularity for SVO[19] noted throughout. Each dialect set exhibits a more uniform distribution of individual frequencies. The CV values do not exceed 40% (West Midlands, sentence level) and can go as low as 6 % (North, sentence level), which equals with substantial stability. The Scandinavian North shows the most regularly distributed output, both at the sentence and subordinate levels, when compared with other sets. In fact, this dialect reveals, very consistently, a fairly stabilised output for SVO within all configurations (for sequences with and without traces). It is vital to account for the importance of this finding especially when CV values are confronted with the normalised frequencies. The latter would show higher average values first for the South, (not for the North), but, at the same time, they would be calculated out of an uneven collection of individual frequencies.

CV (%)	SVO	SVO mat	SVO sub
N	6	21	16
EM	26	25	29
WM	30	8	39
K	14	11	18
S	16	14	20

Figure 8. Coefficient values for SVO in PPCME2 (sentence, matrix, subordinate clause levels specified)

---

19 The coefficient values were not used to interpret results for SOV in the Middle English database. The average frequencies for that configuration of elements in PPCME2 are quite low (i.e. approaching zero). At this point, CV is (too) sensitive to small differences between sets and the obtained values do not properly indicate the degree of fluctuation.

As far as the results for OV/VO are concerned, the output for the pairs largely conforms to the one generated for sequences including subjects. The only significant and notably expected difference is that frequencies for pairs are higher than those for three element strings. When it comes to estimating of the level of variation, the coefficient shows a slightly stronger regularity for VO, especially in the dialect sets corresponding to the regions of Scandinavian influence.

7. Conclusions

The studies of morpho-syntactic changes in English have so far pointed to many internal factors behind the development of the language from the synthetic to the analytic type and to the establishment of the SVO order. Still, not many scholars dealing with the topic have made an effort to explain what specifically triggered the shift (cf. Fischer et al. 2000: 151). The results presented in the current paper suggest an external factor, the Anglo-Scandinavian language contacts, as a potential instigator of the change in question. Undoubtedly, some credit ought to be given to this particular instance of linguistic cross-encounters for intensifying the process of inflectional erosion in its early stages. Morphological simplification, especially the attrition of cases, could further lead to syntactic rearrangement, as a language tends to compensate for the loss of its vital components.

As previous studies have already shown that inflections began to erode first in the North, the current analysis of the parsed prose corpora of Old and Middle English has managed to reveal that the growing prevalence of the SVO word order from Old English onwards was similarly conditioned by geographical factors and that the two changes not only had a common starting point but that the latter developed faster in the dialects of the areas affected by the contact. The analysis focused on the processes of the attrition of case inflections and word order shifts in the same syntactic environment, namely, involving sequences of elements which were (originally) inflected. The use of the statistical measure of the coefficient of variation (CV) not only helped to properly interpret the output data but also added some more insight into the nature of these ongoing changes.

The results showed that the biggest growth in frequency values for (S)VO was found in the dialect sets corresponding to the regions once occupied by the early Scandinavians – the North and East Midlands. In addition, the two dialects exhibited a clearly visible preference for (S)VO at the subordinate clause level, especially the East Midland dialect. Furthermore, although the highest average frequencies for the feature were noted in the South, the 'Scandinavian contingent' always followed suit and eventually the highest frequencies for individual texts were found in the dialect set affected by the contact, viz. – the East Midlands. What is more, the coefficient of variation allowed to filter the input provided by the normalised frequencies and showed the most regular output, again, in the dialect section where the Scandinavian presence was felt most, the very same set which first started to shed inflections, i.e. – the North.

References

Anderson, John M. – Norman MacLeod (eds.)
  1988   *Edinburgh studies in the English language.* Vol. I. Edinburgh: John
          Donald.
Balsley, Howard L.
  1964   *Introduction to statistical method.* Totowa, N.J.: Littlefield, Adams & Co.
Bean, Marian C.
  1983   *The development of word order patterns in Old English.* Totowa,
          NewJersey: Barnes & Noble Books.
Biber, Douglas – Susan Conrad – Randi Reppen
  1998   *Corpus linguistics: Investigating language structure and use.* (Cambridge
          Approaches To Linguistics). Cambridge: Cambridge University Press.
Blake, Norman (ed.)
  1992   *The Cambridge history of the English language: Volume II 1066-1476.*
          Cambridge: Cambridge University Press.
Colman, Fran
  1988   "Heavy arguments in Old English", in: Anderson, John M. and Norman
          MacLeod (eds.), 33-89.
Danchev, Andrei
  1991   "Language change typology and some aspects of the SVO development
          in English", in: Kastovsky, Dieter (ed.), 103-124.
Fischer, Olga
  1992   "Syntax", in: Blake, Norman (ed.), 207-398.
Fischer, Olga – Ans van Kemenade – Willem Koopman – Wim van der Wurff
  2000   *The syntax of Early English.* Cambridge University Press.
Fischer, Olga – Wim van der Wurff
  2006   "Syntax", in: Hogg, Richard and David Denison (eds.), 109-198.
Fisiak, Jacek
  2005   *An outline history of English: Volume one – External history.* Poznań:
          Wydawnictwo Poznańskie.
Frank, Harry – Steven C. Althoen
  1994   *Statistics: concepts and applications.* Cambridge: Cambridge University
          Press.
Hock, Hans Henrich – Brian D. Joseph
  1996   *Language history, language change and language relationship. An
          introduction to historical and comparative linguistics.* (Trends in
          Linguistics. Studies and Monographs 93). Berlin and New York: Mouton
          de Gruyter.
Hogg, Richard – David Denison (eds.)
  2006   *A history of the English language.* Cambridge: Cambridge University
          Press.
Kamenade van, Ans – Nigel Vincent (eds.)
  1997   *Parameters of morphosyntactic change.* Cambridge: Cambridge
          University Press.

Kastovsky, Dieter (ed.)
    1991   *Historical English syntax.* Berlin: Mouton de Gruyter.
Kiparsky, Paul
    1997   "The Rise of Positional Licensing", in: van Kamenade, Ans and Nigel Vincent (eds.), 460-494.
Li, Ch. N. (ed.)
    1977   *Mechanisms of syntactic change.* Austin: University of Texas Press
Lightfoot, David
    1979   *Principles of diachronic syntax.* Cambridge: Cambridge University Press.
    1991   *How to set parameters: Arguments from language change.* Cambridge, Mass.: MIT Press.
Luis Iglesias-Rábade
    2003   *Handbook of Middle English: grammar and texts.* (LINCOM Studies in English Linguistics 05). Muenchen: LINCOM GmbH.
McIntosh, Angus – M.L. Samuels – Michael Benskin (eds.)
    1986   *A linguistic atlas of Medieval English.* New York: Aberdeen University Press.
McMahon, April. M.S.
    1994   *Understanding language change.* Cambridge: Cambridge University Press.
Milroy, James
    1992a   "Middle English dialectology", in: Blake, Norman (ed.), 156-204.
    1992b   *Linguistic variation and change: on the historical sociolinguistics of English.* Oxford: Blackwell.
Matti Rissanen – Merja Kytö – Leena Kahlas-Tarkka – Matti Kilpiö – Saara Nevanlinna – Irma Taavitsainen – Terttu Nevalainen – Helena Raumolin-Brunberg (eds.).
    1991   *The Helsinki corpus of English texts: Diachronic and dialectal.* Helsinki: The University of Helsinki
Saitz, Robert L.
    1955   *Functional word-order in Old English subject-object patterns.* [Unpublished dissertation]. University of Wisconsin.
Stockwell, Robert P.
    1977   "Motivations for Exbraciation in Old English", in: Li, Ch. N. (ed.), 291-314.
Thomason, Sarah – Terrence Kaufman
    1988   *Language contact, creolization, and genetic linguistics.* Berkeley, Calif.: University of California Press.
Trudgill, Peter
    1983   *On dialect.* Blackwell: Oxford.
Weerman, Fred
    1989   *The verb-second conspiracy: A synchronic and a diachronic analysis.* Dordrecht: Foris.
Yamane, Taro
    1973   *Statistics: An introductory analysis.* New York: Harper & Row.

CORPORA

Kroch, Anthony – Ann Taylor
    2000   *Penn-Helsinki parsed corpus of Middle English*. Philadelphia: Depart-
           ment of Linguistics, University of Pennsylvania.
Taylor, Ann – Anthony Warner – Susan Pinzuk – Frank Beths
    2003   *York-Toronto-Helsinki parsed corpus of Old English prose*. Department
           of Language and Linguistic Science, University of York.

In the realm of fantasy: *wyrm/worm* vs. *draca* and *dragon* in Medieval English

Justyna Karczmarczyk, University of Warsaw

ABSTRACT

In Medieval English words typically used to denote a dragon were *wyrm/worm*, *draca* and *dragon*. The present paper investigates these lexemes in order to establish the prototypical word for 'dragon' in Old English and Middle English. It also attempts to determine the temporal and, when Middle English is discussed, regional distribution of *wyrm/wurm*, *draca* and *dragon*, with due attention paid to orthographic variants. When accounting for the semantic and lexical changes, reference is made to Geeraerts's (1997) theory of meaning change.

KEYWORDS: dragon; loanword; meaning change; Middle English; Old English; prototype; rivalry; worm

1. Preliminary remarks

In the Middle Ages a large number of fantastic creatures were believed to inhabit unknown realms. Medieval art and literature teems with fabulous beasts of all kinds. One of the best known fantastic creatures is the dragon, a legendary monster which probably evolved from a snake in people's imagination (Shuker 1995: 11). It is normally "conceived as a huge, bat-winged, fire-breathing, scaly lizard or snake with a barbed tail." (*Britannica.com*) In Europe and the Near East the dragon, in general, evokes negative connotations: it is traditionally associated with danger, destruction and moral evil. (Simpson 2001: 17)

In Medieval English words typically used to denote a dragon were *wyrm/worm*, *draca* and *dragon*. The present paper investigates these lexemes with reference to prototypicality effects and also in order to determine their temporal and, when Middle English is discussed, regional distribution, with due attention paid to differences in spelling.

The linguistic material for the analysis comes from various electronic corpora. For Old English, the *Dictionary of Old English corpus* has been used. The Middle English data come almost exclusively from the *Innsbruck corpus of Middle English prose*. In addition, two poetic texts from the *Middle English compendium* have been examined. Texts with an unspecified dialect were not taken into consideration.

2. Native *wyrm/worm* for 'dragon'

According to the *Oxford English dictionary* (*OED*), the first occurrences of *wyrm* date back to the year 1000 approximately, which does not mean that the word was not used before that date, but simply no earlier manuscript containing this word has been preserved until modern times. The original meaning, according to the *OED*, was 'serpent, snake, dragon'. *An Anglo-Saxon dictionary*, on the other hand, does not mention the sense 'dragon' at all, assigning only the meaning 'reptile, serpent' to the noun. Genetically, *wyrm* derives from Gmc **wurmiz*, which is in turn related to Lat. vermis 'worm' (*The Oxford dictionary of English etymology*). Thus, the meaning 'dragon' of OE *wyrm* derives from the sense 'worm'. It was first applied to a real animal before denoting the mythical creature. Hughes (2000) does not mention the word *wyrm* or any other term for 'dragon'. As regards spelling, *An Anglo-Saxon dictionary* adduces three spelling variants of this lexeme, i.e. *wyrm*, *wurm* and *weorm*. No instances of *weorm* meaning 'dragon' have been found.

On examining *Beowulf*, the epic poem depicting the most famous dragon in Anglo-Saxon literature, one might draw a conclusion that OE *wyrm* was the prototypical word denoting the mythical creature and that the sense 'dragon' was in the core of the semasiological structure of *wyrm*. Reference is here made to the prototype theory of language change. (Geeraerts 1997)

Frequency counts reveal that in *Beowulf draca* 'dragon' appears 14 times, whereas native *wyrm* is used as many as 22 times with the same sense. The high frequency of occurrence of the lexeme is assumed to indicate its strong systemic position in the language. The higher the number of instances, the more prototypical a word is. *Beowulf*, however, seems to be an exception with regard to the frequency of occurrence of the native term. When other Anglo-Saxon texts are examined, it becomes clear that the frequency rate of this word is extremely low. It can be easily found that most occurrences come from *Beowulf*. Only 4 out of 26 instances have not been found in this epic poem. Cf. the list under (1), where the number of occurrences in particular texts appears in brackets:

(1)   The occurences of *wyrm* in Old English:
        Ælfric *Homily* 13 (1), Ælfric *Homily* 22 (1 and 1 *wurm*), *Beowulf* (22), *Psalms* (1).

Moreover, a closer look at the usage of both terms in Anglo-Saxon texts reveals that the native term was not used as freely as the Latin loanword. When the dragon in *Beowulf* is mentioned for the first time, *wyrm* appears before *draca*, but the Latin term is used in the second next sentence. The native term is also accompanied by the Latin loanword in Ælfric's homily *De falsis diis*. Cf.:

(2)   Đa wæs on þære byrig gewunod an *draca*, and þa babiloniscan bæron him
        mete, and hine for god wurðodan, þeah þe he *wyrm* wære.
                                          [Ælfric *Homily* 22, Pope 1967-1968, 676-712]

The native noun *wyrm* was probably considered an ambiguous term for 'dragon' already in Old English. Consequently, the Latin term often accompanied *wyrm* to avoid the reader's confusion and ensure that they would be properly frightened at the mention of a dragon and not, e.g., a worm.

The high frequency of occurrence of the native lexeme in *Beowulf* might stem from the fact that this is one of the oldest texts in Anglo-Saxon literature. It is possible that at a certain stage native *wyrm* had been the prototypical word denoting a dragon. As this epic poem is very old and might have been created even in the 8th century, certain archaic usages may have been preserved in its language, although the extant manuscript probably dates back to the early 11th century.

Moreover, different parts of the dragon's body are mentioned in the poem, except its legs. (Simpson 2001: 33) It is thus possible that OE *wyrm* usually denoted only a special kind of dragon, the serpent dragon. According to Shuker (1995: 11), from this specific type evolved all others. Still, it is not clear whether the *Beowulf* dragon might be classified as representing this particular type. Shuker describes serpent dragons as "Usually associated with rivers, lakes or the open seas, (...) huge, limbless and wingless entities, readily recognized by their dragonesque heads, which often sport horns, and their long crocodilian jaws." (Shuker 1995: 11) Not all of these characteristics may be applied to the *Beowulf* dragon, e.g., it does not live in water and certainly has got wings.

Wyrm denoting a dragon also appears in the compound *fahwyrm*, or *fagwyrm*, meaning 'basilisk', and literally 'serpent variegated in colour'. It is the equivalent of Lat. *basiliscus* (*DOE*). Shuker includes basilisks into the category of dragons, although, as he observes, such magical creatures "may not be true dragons in the strictest zoo-mythological sense." Still, he claims that they may be regarded as representing a type of dragon, as they "are as dramatically dragonesque in behaviour and appearance as any of their *bona fide* brethren" (Shuker 1995: 95); cf. (3), where *fagwyrm* appears in one sentence with *draca*, the name for a proper dragon.

(3)   Ofer nedran & *fagwyrm* gonges & trides leon & *dracan*.
         [*Psalms*, Bodleian Library, MS Junius 27, psalm 91, verse 13]

In Middle English, *worm*, although spelt differently than in Old English, could still denote a dragon. According to the *Middle English dictionary* (*MED*) 'dragon or dragonlike creature' was one of its main meanings, alongside e.g., 'serpent' and 'snake'. At that time, however, the number of possible meanings increased, which resulted in an even greater potential confusion. According to the *MED*, the lexeme had a large number of orthographic variants, but almost all of them are never found to carry the sense 'dragon'. In fact, *worm* carrying this sense appeared only once in Middle English prose, as *wurm* in *Seinte Marherete*. The manuscript, dating from 1225 approximately, represents the West Midland dialect. Only one occurrence in prose does not mean that the word was not used in this sense at all. The examples from the *Middle English compendium* under (4) show that it still occurred, although mostly in Middle English poetry. Of course, the data from this corpus are not complete and serve here to provide only two examples; cf.:

(4a)   He hade weryede the *worme* by wyghtnesse of strenghte,
        Ne ware it fore the wylde fyre þat he hym wyth defendez.
                              [*The Alliterative Morte Arthure*, Lincoln, Cathedral
                                                    Library, 91, p.62, lines 796-797]

(4b)   Sumwhyle wyth *wormez* he werrez, and with wolues als,
        Sumwhyle wyth wodwos, þat woned in þe knarrez, (…)
                                        [*Sir Gawain and the Green Knight*, B. L., Cotton
                                                          Nero A x, p.20, lines 719-720]

The data clearly demonstrate that ME *worm* was becoming an even more peripheral word for 'dragon' than in Old English. At the same time, the sense 'dragon' was gradually pushed further to the periphery of the semasiological structure of *worm*. This lexeme has survived until the present day, although its central meaning is different. Today it can denote a dragon only in archaic usage (*OED*). The usual meaning is 'small creeping animal' (*An etymological dictionary of the English language*), so the referent of *worm* seems to have first increased in size and then shrunk again to the size of a 'small creeping animal'.

3. Lat. *draca*

Another Old English lexeme denoting a dragon, *draca* is a borrowing from Lat. *dracō*, ultimately deriving from Gk *drakōn*. (Serjeantson 1935: 277) The Greek word probably means 'the sharp-sighted one' (*A comprehensive etymological dictionary of the English language*), so the dragon was traditionally associated with wisdom. The Latin loanword comes from the first, Continental, period of borrowing, which lasted until about 400 (1935: 271). In fact, the largest number of loanwords in Old English come from Latin (Kastovsky 1992: 300). Besides the sense 'dragon', *draca* could denote a battle standard with the image of this fantastic creature and it could also refer to Satan (*DOE*). The devil was metaphorically compared to the dragon, probably because both were imagined as the worst of all serpents and also because of the biblical tradition, especially present in the Book of Revelation. In certain cases *draca* could refer to Satan in the form of a dragon. While according to *An Anglo-Saxon dictionary*, *draca* could mean a 'serpent' as well, the *DOE* does not provide this last meaning at all. Still, this lexeme must have been considered less ambiguous than *wyrm* as, first and foremost, it referred to a dragon.

The Latin loanword and the native term are often used interchangeably. In *Beowulf* they even co-occur in four sentences. In one example, *wyrm* and *draca* can be found in an appositional structure:

(5)   *Dracan* ec scufun,
        wyrm ofer weallclif, leton weg niman,
        flod fæðmian frætwa hyrde.
                                [*Beowulf*, B. L., Cotton Vitellius A xv, lines 3031-3033]

Nevertheless, compounds are formed almost exclusively with *draca*, not *wyrm*. The examples in (6) denote 'foe-dragon', or 'hostile dragon', and 'dragon of the earth':

(6a)   Hordwynne fond
        eald uhtsceaða opene standan,
        se ðe byrnende biorgas seceð,
        nacod *niðdraca*, nihtes fleogeð
        fyre befangen (…)
                                [*Beowulf*, B. L., Cotton Vitellius A xv, lines 2270-2274]

(6b)   Bona swylce læg,
        egeslic *eorðdraca* ealdre bereafod,
        bealwe gebæded.
                                [*Beowulf*, B. L., Cotton Vitellius A xv, lines 2824-2826]

Compounding might be considered an indication that *draca* was used more freely than the native term and that, consequently, this lexeme should be regarded as a more basic and prototypical term for 'dragon'. Compounds with *wyrm* are, on the other hand, formed when the word means a 'snake' or a 'worm'. Cf. the examples under (7), where the meanings of the compounds are 'intestinal worm' and 'ringworm'.

(7a)   Wið þæt ymb þæne nafolan syn *rengwyrmas* genim þas ylcan wyrte
        hinnulan, cnuca on wine, lege to þam innoðe.
                                [*Herbarium*, B. L., Harley 6258 B]

(7b)   Wið *deawwyrme* sume nimað wearm cwead monnes þynne, bindað
        neahterne on, sume swines lungenne wearme.
                                [Bald *Leechbook*, B. L., Royal 12, D xvii]

The only exception when a compound with *wyrm* denotes neither a snake nor a worm is *fahwyrm*, i.e. 'basilisk'. This has already been discussed above.

The frequency of occurrence is, of course, another indication that the Latin loanword was the central term for 'dragon'. The frequency counts reveal that, including *draco(n)*, the most popular untypical spelling variant, *draca* occurred as many as 116 times in Old English literature. The distribution of this lexeme in particular texts is shown under (8):

(8) The occurrences of *draca* in Old English: *Anglo-Saxon chronicle D* (1); *Anglo-Saxon laws* (1); *Beowulf* (14); Byrhtferth *Manual* (1); *Canticles of the psalter* (1 *draco*); *Catholic homilies* (22); *Christ and Satan* (2); *Elene* (1); *Gospel of Nicodemus* (1); *Grammar* and *Latin-Old English glossaries* (5); Gregory the Great *Dialogues* (11); *Herbarium* (3); *Historia* ecclesiastica (...) (1); *Homilies of Ælfric* (...) (4); *Homilies* Willard (6); Homily *Easter Day* (1); Homily *Second Sunday in Lent* (1); *Ipswich stone* (1); *Marvels of the East* (1); *Maxims II* (1); *Old English Martyrology* (1); *Prognostics* (3); *Psalms* (3 and 3 *draco*); *St Machutus* (2 and 1 *dracon*); *St Margaret* (9); *St Michael* (2); *Solomon and Saturn* (1); *The Battle of Finnsburh* (1); *The Forty Soldiers* (1); *The Paris Psalter* (5); *The Vercelli Homilies* (5).

However, a large number of texts where this lexeme occurs have been translated from Latin. This fact obviously must have resulted in *draca* being chosen more frequently than its native equivalent.

Despite the high number of occurrences, it was not this lexeme which finally replaced the native term as *draca* did not survive beyond Old English. *Drake*, probably its descendant, not discussed in this paper, was employed in Middle English with the sense 'dragon', yet it failed to become the prototypical term probably due to pragmatic reasons. The conflict with *drake* 'male duck', a word of obscure origin, may have seriously contributed to its decreasing popularity. (Burnley 1992: 495)

4. Fr. *dragon*

In Middle English a new lexeme was introduced to refer to the mythical creature: the French loanword *dragon*. It was itself borrowed into French from Lat. *dracōnem*, the accusative of *dracō* (*A comprehensive etymological dictionary of the English language*). Serjeantson (1935: 5) observes that "it happens frequently (...) that a word is borrowed more than once from the same source (or from developments of this source)." She remarks that "English has a particularly large number of these 'repeated' loans (...)". The first recorded occurrence of this lexeme with the meaning 'dragon' dates back to 1225 approximately (*OED*). According to the *MED*, the basic orthographic form was *dragoun*. However, *dragon* is the form with the largest number of occurrences in the *Innsbruck corpus* and thus it is treated here as the most basic form. Under (9) are presented orthographic variants:

(9a)   Alas, douȝtur, swete derlyng, (...) nowe þou gost for to be deuowrid with a *dragon.*

[*Speculum Sacerdotale, Saint George*, B. L., MS Add. 36791, p. 131, lines 31-33]

(9b)   And it is seid in manye contreis that in the yle of Longo is y it the dough tyr of Ypocras in the liknesse of an orrible *dragoun*, and she is callid lady of that contre with the folk that wonede in that yle.

[Mandeville *Travels*, Bodleian MS E Musæo, 116 p. 17, lines 13-16]

(9c)   (...) my Lord Harry of Stafforth rod in a gown of cloth of tuyssew, tukkyd, furryd with sabulles, (...) and full of stons, (...), rydyng apon a sorellyd courser bardyd with a bayrd of goldsmythes wark, with rosys and *draguns* red.

[*The Paston Letters*, vol.6, Gairdner [1986], p. 173]

The orthographic variants under (9) are the first three provided by the *MED*. The variant under (9c) is, however, so marginal that in the *Innsbruck corpus* it occurs only in this example.

Like *draca* in Old English, *dragon* was more readily associated with the mythical creature than the increasingly ambiguous native term. As a consequence, it was used extensively. The occurrences of this lexeme in Middle English prose are listed in the Appendix. *Dragon* appears 80 times throughout the period, while its orthographic variant, *dragoun*, only 9 times, 8 times in the 14th and early 15th century. After this period only 1 occurrence of *dragoun* can be found. *Dragun* appears only once, in the 15th century, in *The Paston letters*, which represent the East Midland dialect. As regards dialectal distribution, it can be observed that in London and in the North, the *-oun* spelling variant does not occur, while in the East Midland both *-on* and *-oun* variants are used. As for other dialects, the data seem to be too scarce to draw any general conclusions.

Finally, in the course of Middle English, the French loanword replaced the native term, pushing the sense 'dragon' to the fringes of the semasiological structure of *worm*. A similar replacement did not take place when *draca* competed with the native term probably because "Medieval Latin as a dead language could not exert an influence comparable to that of Scandinavian or French." (Fisiak 2000: 81)

5. Concluding remarks

On the basis of the material examined, the following statements can be formulated:

1. The prototypical Old English word for 'dragon' was Lat. *draca*, not native *wyrm*. The evidence here comes from frequency counts, compounding and the fact that *wyrm* was often accompanied by the Latin loanword. *Draca* did not survive beyond Old English.

2. In Middle English the French loanword gradually pushed the meaning 'dragon' from the peripheries to the fringes of the semasiological structure of *worm*. As a consequence, today this word can be applied to the mythical creature only in an archaic context. It was the French and not the Latin loanword which eventually replaced the native term probably because at that time French had a greater impact on English.

3. *Dragoun*, unlike the basic orthographic variant, did not appear in all dialects. No occurrences in London and in the North were attested. This spelling ceased to be used towards the end of Middle English. *Dragun* appeared only once, in the East Midland dialect. The basic orthographic variant is the form still used today.

4. The distribution of *dragon* and *worm* in Middle English poetry and drama still needs to be investigated. The rivalry between ME *dragon* and *drake* should also be thoroughly examined.

References

SOURCES

Bosworth, Joseph – T. Northcote Toller
    1898   *An Anglo-Saxon dictionary*. Oxford: Oxford University Press.
Gairdner, James (ed.)
    1904   *The Paston letters*. Vol. 6. London: Chatto and Windus.
    [1986]   [Reprinted Gloucester: Alan Sutton Publishing]
Klein, Ernest
    1966-1967 *A comprehensive etymological dictionary of the English language*. Vol.
              1: A-K. Amsterdam: Elsevier Publishing Company.
Onions, Charles T. (ed.)
    1966   *The Oxford dictionary of English etymology*. Oxford: Oxford University
              Press.

Pope, John C. (ed.)
 1967-1968 *Homilies of Ælfric: a supplementary collection.* Vol. 2. London: Oxford
     University Press.
Skeat, Walter W.
 1879-1882 *An etymological dictionary of the English language.* Oxford: Clarendon
     Press.

ELECTRONIC SOURCES

Cameron, Angus (et al.)
 2003 *Dictionary of Old English on CD-ROM.* A-F. Toronto.
Healey, Antoinette diPaolo (ed.)
 1998 *Dictionary of Old English corpus.* University of Toronto.
Hoiberg, Dale (ed.)
     Britannica. Available at: http://www.britannica.com.
Markus, Manfred (ed.)
 2009 *Innsbruck corpus of Middle English prose.* (CD-ROM version 2.3).
     University of Innsbruck.
McSparran, Frances (ed.)
 1999 *Middle English compendium.* Available at: http://quod.lib.umich.
     edu/m/mec.
Simpson, John et al.
     The Oxford English dictionary online. Available at: http://dictionary.
     oed.com.

SPECIAL STUDIES

Blake, Norman (ed.)
 1992 *The Cambridge history of the English language.* Vol. 2: 1066-1476.
     Cambridge: Cambridge University Press.
Burnley, David
 1992 "Lexis and semantics", in: Blake, Norman (ed.), 409-499.
Fisiak, Jacek
 2000 *An outline history of English.* Vol. 1: External history. Poznań:
     Wydawnictwo Poznańskie.
Geeraerts, Dirk
 1997 *Diachronic prototype semantics. A contribution to historical lexicology.*
     Oxford: Clarendon Press.
Hogg, Richard (ed.)
 1992 *The Cambridge history of the English language.* Vol. 1: The beginnings
     to 1066. Cambridge: Cambridge University Press.
Hughes, Geoffrey
 2000 *A history of English words.* Oxford: Blackwell Publishers.

Kastovsky, Dieter
    1992   "Semantics and vocabulary", in: Hogg, Richard (ed.), 290-408.
Serjeantson, Mary Sydney
    1935   *A history of foreign words in English.* London: Routledge & Kegan Paul.
Shuker, Karl
    1995   *Dragons: A natural history.* London: Aurum Press.
Simpson, Jacqueline
    2001   *British dragons.* Ware: Wordsworth Editions and the Folklore Society.

Appendix

The occurrences of *dragon* in Middle English prose.

Date of MS	Text and dialect	*-on*	*-oun*	*-un*
1340	*Ayenbite of Inwyt* (K)	–	1	–
1350+	Mandeville's *Travels* (EM)	5	5	–
1400+	*An Alphabet of tales*, II (N)	5	–	–
a1400	*Lollard sermons* (M)	–	1	–
1400+	*Speculum Sacerdotale* (Lond.)	31	–	–
c1405	*The Parson's tale* (Lond.)	2	–	–
a1415	*The Lanterne of Liȝt* (EM)	–	1	–
1420-1500	*The Paston Letters* (EM)	–	–	1
c1422-c1454	*Liber de Diversis Medicinis* (N: Yorkshire)	1	–	–
1435	Richard Rolle *The fire of love* (EM)	1	–	–
1450+	*An alphabet of tales*, I (N)	5	–	–
a1450	*Richard Rolle of Hampole and his followers* vol. II (N)	1	–	–
c1450	*Speculum Christiani* (EM)	1	–	–
a1450	*Yorkshire Writers. Richard Rolle of Hampole* vol. I (N)	1	–	–
c1453-1454	Pecock *The donet* (EM)	1	–	–
c1460	*Saint George*, in *Three lives from the gilte legende* (WM)	12	–	–
c1462-1463	John Capgrave *Abbreuiacion of Chronicles* (EM)	4	1	–
c1483	*Quattuor Sermones* (Lond.)	1	–	–
1485	*Le morte d'Arthur* (Lond.)	6	–	–
1489	Caxton *Doctrinal of Sapience* (Lond.)	2	–	–
1490	Caxton *Eneydos* (Lond.)	1	–	–
Total		80	9	1

The Celtic hypothesis revisited: Relative clauses

Artur Bartnik, John Paul II Catholic University of Lublin

ABSTRACT

This paper deals with apparent Celtic influences in the history of early English relative clauses. It is argued that even though the two languages had close parallels in the relevant structures, this fact does not warrant a contact-based explanation, at least in Old and Early Middle English. Apparent similarities include the use of resumption and the spread of preposition stranding (cf. Filppula et al. 2008; Roma 2007). It will be shown that the former serves different purposes and the latter does not exhibit Celtic influence in English.

KEYWORDS: relative clause; Celtic languages; stranding, resumption

1. Introduction

This paper deals with relative clauses like those shown in (1)-(3):

(1)   The person he is in love <u>with</u>.
(2)   The person <u>with whom</u> he is in love.
(3)   That's the chap that <u>his</u> uncle was drowned

(Parry 1979: 146; Fippula 2008: 84)

Example (1) illustrates preposition stranding as the preposition *with* is stranded to the end of the clause. When the preposition, as in (2), is moved along with the wh-element, the structure is called pied-piping. In example (3), the indeclinable relative particle that is accompanied by a pronoun that indicates the genitival relation. Such "additional elements" that indicate case in relative structures are called resumptive pronouns.

Some scholars have attributed the spread of stranding in the history of English to Celtic influence since this option became more common in the course of history in both languages (cf. Filppula et al. 2008; Roma 2007 and references cited therein). Resumption, present in the histories of both languages, also might be the effect of Celtic influence (cf. Filppula et al. 2008).

In this paper I will argue that the hypothesis concerning the possible influence of Celtic on English in preposition stranding is not tenable. I will show that although both Early English and Early Celtic had resumptive pronouns and generalized preposition stranding, this change could not be due to Celtic influence.

In section 2 I will briefly sketch the relativization system in Old English. Section 3 examines relative constructions in Old and Middle Irish. In section 4 I will trace the basic changes that took place in both languages. Section 5 concludes.

2. Old English

In this section I will present the basic facts concerning stranding and resumption in relative clauses in Old English. In Old English the relativization system was fairly clear: preposition stranding, illustrated in (4), was obligatory with indeclinable *þe*-relatives:

(4)   *Seo gesihð <u>ðe</u> we god <u>myd</u> geseon scylon is angyt*
     the   sight   that we god with   see   shall   is under-
                                      standing
     'the sight that we shall see God with ___ is undestanding'
                                        (Sol. P.67.6; Allen 1980: 267)

In this example, the preposition *myd* 'with' had to be stranded because its object was relativized in the *þe*-relative clause. By contrast, in *se*-relatives (and also in the third major type, *se þe* relatives), that is relatives introduced by a declinable demonstrative pronoun, only pied-piping was available, as in (5):

(5)   *ðat he us ðingige wið ðone Heofonlican Cyning,*
     that he us intercede with the   Heavenly   King
     <u>for ðæs</u> naman he ðrowode
     for whose name   he suffered
     'that he intercede for us with the Heavenly King, for whose name he suffered'
                           (Alc.Th. Vol.1 p.434.35; Allen 1980: 271)

As for resumption in Old English, it was an available option, as shown in (6) and (7):[1]

---

[1]   Filppula et al. (2008: 85) actually gives example (i) below as an instance of "a repetitious pronominal reflex of the antecedent in the subordinate relative clause". This does not seem to be the case, though, as the dative of the underlined elements is purely coincidental and results from the syntax of the two predicates.
     swa bið eac <u>þam treowum</u> þe <u>him</u> gecynde biþ up heah to standanne
     so is   also to-those trees   that to-them natural is up high to stand
     'so it is also with trees to which it is natural to stand up straight'
                               (Bo 25.57.20, Traugott 1992: 229)

(6) | *Forðon ðe* | *hi* | *habbað* | *manega* | | *saula* | *on* | *heora* |
|---|---|---|---|---|---|---|---|
| Because that | they | have | many | | souls | in | their |
| *gewaldum* | *ðe* | *him* | *wile* | *git* | *God* | *miltsian* | |
| power | that | them | will | yet | God | have-mercy-on | |

'because they have many souls in their power that God will yet have mercy on'

(Blickling, p.47; Allen 1977: 93)

(7)	*ðæs*	*ædelan weres,*	*þone*		*Datianus*	*se casere*
the	holy man-GEN	whom-ACC		Datianus	the caesar
seofan	*gear*	*mid*	*unasæcgendlice*	*witum*	*hine*
seven	years	with	unspeakable	tortures	him-ACC
ðræde	*ðæt*	*he Criste widsoce*			
impelled	that	he Christ repudiate			

'of the holy man, whom Datianus the caesar impelled for seven years with unspeakable tortures to repudiate Christ'

(S.OET Mart. P. 178.40; Allen 1977: 93)

In example (6), the indeclinable particle *þe* relativizes the accusative *manega saula* 'many souls' and the case is repeated in the subordinate clause in the dative *him* 'them'. Example (7) exhibits the declinable demonstrative pronoun *þone*. Despite that, the additional accusative pronoun *hine* appears. Such examples show that resumptive pronouns are not exact copies of their antecedents: in (6), the cases expressed by the antecedent and the pronoun are different. In (7), the relativizer is a demonstrative pronoun, whereas *hine* is a personal pronoun (cf. also Allen 1977: 145-146).

Another important point is that resumption was not obligatory in Old English. Mitchell (1985: §2198-2199) notes that it was fairly rare, since it was found in less than five per cent of *þe* clauses in the prose. He adds that the use of an indeclinable particle followed by a pronoun showing the case relation might be dictated by stylistic, rhythmic or metrical considerations. Visser (1894: §604) agrees that it was not the main function of resumptive pronouns to signal the case of relativized items in *þe* relatives for two reasons. First, the indeclinable *þe* could relativize genitive, dative and accusative objects without resumptive pronouns as well. In fact, that was very common. In (8) below, the accusative object is relativized:

(8) | *Gemyne* | *he* | *þæs* | *yfeles* | *þe* | *he* | *worhte.* |
|---|---|---|---|---|---|---|
| remember | he | the-GEN | evil-GEN | that | he | wrought |

'Let him remember the evil that he wrought.'

(CP Sweet p.25.3; Allen 1980: 266)

Second, as shown in (7), even declinable relative pronouns could be used with resumptives. Such arguments confirm an optional status of this construction in Old English.

3. Old/Middle Irish

As distinct from Filppula et al., I use Old and Middle Irish for comparison, as these periods span more or less the same time as Old English. Filppula et al., who mainly discusses Welsh, is not very specific as far as chronology is concerned, though he stresses the possibility of earlier contacts between the languages.[2]

At the very beginning, it has to be pointed out that Celtic languages differ from Germanic languages in that they exemplify VSO order. Next, they employ very different means of expressing relativization from Germanic languages. For example, Old Irish used mutations[3] (that is, morphophonological means) to mark relative clauses. Specifically, as Thurneysen (1980: §494) describes, lenition was obligatory when the subject was relativized but optional in object relative clauses.[4] Nasalization, on the other hand, was optional with objects and obligatory with the antecedents designating more remote positions in the Relative Accessibility Hierarchy (cf. Keenan and Comrie 1977). Schematically, it can be presented as follows:

(9)   leniting relative clause   nasalizing relative clause
        Subject - DirObj-   IndirObj - Prepositional Obj -
                                       - Possessive NP - Object of Comparison

Apart from mutations, Old Irish used a wide range of other relative markers that accompanied mutations. For example, simple verbs usually required empty preverbs *no*, *ro* (verbal prefixes) or used special relative forms. I will not discuss these intricate means of expressing relativization since some of them were lost in the course of time (for example, object infixes) and had no counterpart in OE relatives (for a more detailed discussion of these relative strategies, see Thurneysen 1980).

In example (10) below, the subject is relativized. Hence lenition is obligatory. In (11), apart from the lented verb, the relativizing preverb occurs.

---

2   Old Welsh, the counterpart of Old English, has too few documents to draw conclusive evidence about relatives.
3   Celtic relative clauses use two types of mutations: lenition (marked by [L]), which involves "fricativisation of both voiced and unvoiced stops and /m/ and deletion of /f/, [and] nasalization (marked by [N]), [which] involves sonorisation of unvoiced and voiced stops and /f/." (Roma 2007: 249)
4   Strictly speaking, I mean direct objects here. The dative was almost never found except after a preposition in Old Irish (see below).

(10) *innaní*   *imm-e-*   *churetar*
      those-GEN   Rel part^L put
      'of those who are putting'

(Wb 5a5)

(11) *ind*   *huli*   *doíni*   *ro-*   *chreitset*
      the   all   men   Prev-RPart^L believe
      'all the men, who believed'

(Ml 60b16)

With all these differences, there was one relative construction that resembled OE relativization. Specifically, Old Irish had the indeclinable relative particle *-a* or *sa* (with nasalization of the following element) in pied-piping constructions, as in (12):

(12) *tre-*   *sa-*   *mbí*   *bethu*   *suthin*
      through-that^N be   life   eternal
      'through which life is eternal'

(Wb 23b5)

Preposition stranding was almost non-existent in Old Irish. On very rare occasions, it was found in structures with resumptive pronouns. Consider (13), where the pronoun is merged with the conjugated preposition:

(13) *nech*   *suidigther*   *loc*   *daingen*   *dó*
      Everyone   establish-Rel   place   strong   to-him
      'Anyone that a strong place is assigned to (him)'

(Ml 87d15)

Interestingly, such examples were not found in the oldest Old Irish text, the *Würzburg* glosses on the epistles of St. Paul, but in a later text, the glosses of *Milano*. This fact suggests a gradual development of preposition stranding, which gained ground in Middle Irish (that is still the Old English period).

Resumption was also manifested in genitival structures, but under some grammatical restrictions. As Thurneysen (1980: §507) remarks, "if the substantive to be defined is the subject of the clause and the predicate is an adjective, the copula has the relative form but the genitival relation remains unexpressed." This is exemplified in (14). By contrast, "if the substantive is a predicative nominative, the possessive pronoun is always inserted between the relative form of the copula and the substantive itself." (Thurneysen 1980: §507) Example (15) illustrates this point.

(14)   *don*   *bráthir*   *as*   *énirt*   *menme*
       To   the-brother   is-Rel   infirm   mind
       'to the brother whose mind is weak'
                                           (Wb. 10c1; Thurneysen 1980: §507)

(15)   *fir*   *as*   *a*   *c(h)athach*
       of the man   is   Rel-his   trespass
       'of the man whose trespass it is'
                       (Laws v.500, 13 (H.2.15); Thurneysen 1980: §507)

In sum, Old/Middle Irish and Old English seem to be very different in terms of relativization strategies, as Table 1 illustrates:

Table 1. Stranding and resumption in Old English and Early Celtic languages.

	Old English	Old/Middle Irish
Stranding	Þe relatives	Rare, possible only with resumptive pronouns (uninflected -a/-sa used in pied-piping structures)
Resumption	Possible in all cases (optional)	Rare with Preposition stranding Possible in some genitival relations (obligatory)

4. Changes

In this section I will sketch the most important changes that took place in Middle English and its parallel Celtic period.

As is well known, in Early Middle English there was a rapid growth of *þe*, also in relatives, later on replaced by the indeclinable *þat*, along with the rapid decline of inflections. Apart from the contexts defined in section 2, preposition stranding started to be used in inflected structures, with the introduction of *wh*-elements in Middle English relative clauses. In other words, it became more common.

Resumption strategies continued to be used in Middle English. Fischer (1992: 309) reports that they were used mainly with *þe* and, later, *þat* relatives to indicate case (mainly the genitive), as shown in example (16) (cf. also Mustanoja 1960). When *wh*-pronouns indicating case were introduced, Fischer further argues, resumption was no longer needed and disappeared. This cannot be the whole story, though. *Wh*-elements were introduced in the thirteen century and became common in the fourteen century (cf. Allen 1977), while resumption persisted until the eighteen century. One example of resumption with a *wh*-pronoun from the sixteen century is given in (17):

(16) *Ther-ynn wonyþ a   wyʒt,   þat   wrong   is   his   name,...*
      there-in lives   a   creature that   wrong   is   his   name
      'There lives a creature whose name is wrong'
      (Ppl. C (Hnt 143) i, 59; Fischer 1992: 309; Filppula et al. 2008: 87)

(17) *The erle of Angwyche ... <u>whom</u> the kynge had kept <u>him</u> with his brother and*
      dyvers other here in Ynglond
      (1556 Chron. Grey Friars (Camden) 46; Visser 1894: §607)

Examples such as (17) show that, just like in Old English, resumption was not used solely to indicate case with indeclinable relativizers because inflected *wh*-elements could be accompanied by resumptive pronouns.

The (Early) Modern Irish period, starting in the thirteen century, was parallel to the Middle English period. At that time there was also a rapid increase in the use of preposition stranding constructions, which were in the minority in the previous periods. Pied-piping became rare as it was only used in translated texts (cf. Roma 2007). Gradually, the relativization system took on the contemporary form both in Welsh and Irish. Specifically, in Modern Irish the indeclinable leniting particle *a* is used in direct relatives (when the direct object or subject are relativized), while in indirect relatives (when the genitive or dative are relativized) the indeclinable nasalizing particle *a* is necessary. Crucially, obligatory resumption in the form of either an additional possessive pronoun or an inflected preposition with an agreeing pronoun occurs in these constructions. Similarly, in Modern Welsh the leniting particle *a* is used in direct clauses, while in indirect clauses the non-nasalizing and non-leniting particle *y* is present. As in Irish, resumption is obligatory. Schematically, these changes are presented in Table 2.

Table 2. Relativization strategies in Modern Irish and Middle/Modern Welsh

	Direct relatives (accusative+nominative)	Indirect relatives (dative+genitive)
(Early) Modern Irish	a + lenition	a + nasalization + resumption
Middle and Modern Welsh	a + lenition	y (and its allomorphs) + resumption

Examples of these new strategies are shown below:

(18) *an fear a^L bhuail tú*
      'the man that struck you'

                              (McCloskey 1990: 18) [ModI]

(19)   *Sin   é   an fear   ar   thug   mé   céad   punt   dó*
        That is the man   Rel   give   I   hundred pound   to-him
        'That is the man I gave one hundred pounds to'
                                            (Roma 2007: 254) [ModI]

Interestingly, in some contexts, direct relatives can be ambiguous: example (20)
can mean either *The man who saw Seán* or *The man whom Seán saw*. In such
cases resumption and indirect relative markers are used to disambiguate the
context. Therefore example (21) can mean only the latter:

(20)   *An fear   a   chonaic Seán*
        the man   who(m)   saw   Seán
        'The man who/whom saw Seán'

(21)   *An fear   ar   chonaic Seán   é*
        The man   who   saw   Seán   him
        'The man whom Seán saw'

Again, it seems that resumption is obligatory and plays an important role in the
grammar of Celtic languages. In Welsh the situation is slightly different because
the resumptive strategy is not allowed in direct relatives (cf. Suñer 1998). The
reason for that might be that Welsh has a different indirect relative marker, *y*, and
it does not need an additional disambiguation marker.

5. Conclusion

To sum up, we find apparent similarities between Early Celtic languages and
Early English in two respects. First, resumption was used in relatives in both
languages. Second, preposition stranding became more common in the course of
time. However, these two superficial similarities could not be responsible for any
linguistic influence between these languages at that time because resumption,
though present in both languages, served different purposes. In Celtic it was
obligatory and used mainly for disambiguation: in Old Irish it played an important
grammatical role in some genitival constructions; in Modern Irish it is used in
stranding structures for oblique cases along with lenition/nasalization markers
(other relative markers were lost in the course of history). In Old and Middle
English, by contrast, the resumptive strategy did not serve to disambiguate the
contexts, as it could be used both with indeclinable and declinable relativizers.
Moreover, as reported by Visser (1894), it lost its significance and disappeared
circa the eighteen century from Standard English while in Irish it gained ground.
    The spread of indeclinable particles in English and, linked with that, the
spread of preposition stranding could not be influenced by Celtic languages for

two reasons. First, Filppula et al. himself admits that there might be a timing problem. (Filppula et al. 2008: 93) Specifically, preposition stranding seems to have been well established in Old English while its Early Celtic counterpart only started to develop at that time. Second, this spread started in the northern part of the country (cf. Allen 1977: 203), while Celtic influence was the strongest in the South West of England (also in Wales and Corwall). Thus a geographical factor also makes it unlikely that the changes were inspired by Celtic languages.

These considerations, however, do not preclude linguistic contacts in later periods. For, in example (3) taken from Welsh English, we clearly see a Celtic structure. Conversely, there are structures in colloquial Welsh (spoken mainly by teenagers) influenced by Modern English. This is illustrated in (22):

(22) *Cymraeg yw 'r iaith   rŏn   i 'n siarad   mewn*
      Welsh   is   the language was-Rel I-ing speak   in (no
                                                       agreeing pronoun)
      'Welsh is the language I was talking in'

                                                       (Willis 2000: 557) [ModW]

In (22) the preposition is uninflected and we have no resumptive pronoun. This suggests the influence of English.

What I suggest in this paper is that Celtic influence could not be responsible for the spread of preposition stranding in Old and Early Middle English, even though both languages used resumptive structures. However, I do not exclude contacts in later periods. This leaves room for further research.

References

Allen, Cynthia
      1977   *Topics in diachronic English syntax.* [Ph.D. diss.], Amherst: University
                 of Massachusetts.
      1980   "Movement and deletion in Old English", *Linguistic Inquiry* 11: 261-323.
Blake, Norman (ed.)
      1992   *The Cambridge history of the English language.* Vol. 2. Cambridge:
                 Cambridge University Press.
Filppula, Markku – Juhani Klemola – Heli Paulasto
      2008   *English and Celtic in contact.* London: Routledge.
Fischer, Olga
      1992   "Syntax", in Blake, Norman (ed.), 207-408.

Hendrick, Randall (ed.)
  1990   *Syntax and semantics. The syntax of the Modern Celtic languages.* New York: Academic Press.
Hogg, Richard (ed.)
  1992   *The Cambridge history of the English language.* Vol. 1. Cambridge: Cambridge University Press.
Keenan, Edward – Bernard Comrie
  1977   "Noun phrase accessibility and universal grammar", *Linguistic Inquiry* 8: 63-99.
McCloskey, James
  1990   "Resumptive pronouns, A'-binding, and levels of representation in Irish", in Hendrick, Randall (ed.), 199-248.
Mitchell, Bruce
  1985   *Old English syntax.* 2 vols. Oxford: Clarendon Press.
Mustanoja, Tauno
  1960   *A Middle English syntax.* Helsinki: Societe Neophilologique.
Parry, David
  1979   *The survey of Anglo-Welsh dialects. Vol. 2.* The South-West. Swansea: University Collage.
Ramat, Paolo – and Elisa Roma (eds.)
  2007   *Europe and the Mediterranean as linguistic areas: Convergences from a historical and typological perspective.* Amsterdam: John Benjamins.
Roma, Elisa
  2007   "Relativization strategies in insular Celtic languages: History and contacts with English", in: Ramat, Paolo and Elisa Roma (eds.), 245-288.
Suňer, Margarita
  1998   "Resumptive restrictive relatives: a crosslinguistic perspective", *Language* 74: 335-364.
Thurneysen, Rudolf
  1980   *A grammar of Old Irish.* Dublin: Institute for Advanced Studies.
Traugott, Elizabeth
  1992   "Syntax", in: Hogg, Richard (ed.), 168-289.
Visser, Fredericus Theodorus
  1894   *An historical syntax of the English language.* 4 vols. Leiden: EJ Brill.
Willis, David
  2000   "On the distribution of resumptive pronouns and wh-trace in Welsh", *Journal of Linguistics* 36: 531-573.

Indirect borrowing processes from Latin into Old English: The evidence of derived and compound nouns from the first book of Bede's *Ecclesiastical history of the English people* and its interpretation in the light of Naturalness Theory[1]

Anya Kursova, University of Pisa

ABSTRACT

Old English shows remarkable flexibility, resourcefulness and capacity for derivation and compounding. During the Old English period the language seems to rely on native material and prefer indirect borrowings (semantic loans and loan-formations) to direct borrowings. The phenomena of indirect borrowing are precious and interesting, because, as time passed, many of them disappeared being replaced by new waves of direct borrowings. An interesting question is: what is more natural for a language – to borrow a foreign word or to create a new term using the native material? In the present paper we are going to stop our attention on the derived and compound nouns of the first book of Bede's *Ecclesiastical history of the English people*, looking for their possible relationships to Latin models.

KEYWORDS: indirect borrowings; loan-formations (LFs); loan-translation (LTs); loan-renditions (LRs); loan-creations (LCs); semantic loans (SLs); word-formation; word-formedness; parallel developments; chains of indirect borrowings; redundant formations; Naturalness Theory; system-dependent naturalness; system-independent naturalness; transparency; biuniqueness; iconicity; indexicality; system-congruity; class-stability; naturalness conflicts; scales of naturalness for borrowings

1. Introduction

English has always been known as an insatiable borrower of vocabulary, and Latin as the most long-lasting donor of words to the English language. The interaction of the two languages though has not always been homogeneous.

The Old English period presents an interesting stage in the development of the language from the point of view of borrowing. Old English relies more extensively on native material expressing thus its preference for indirect borrowing processes (so-called semantic loans and loan-formations) as opposed to numerous direct borrowings and assimilation of foreign words observed during the Middle English period. Indirect borrowing processes may seem less evident and less significant when we speak about the contact of languages and its results, but in fact these phenomena stimulate creativity of a language and have more profound effects on its morphology.

---

1   I would like to thank Professor Antonio Bertacca for methodological and bibliographic suggestions and for continuous support and encouragement.

Dieter Kastovsky (1992: 309) mentions that we lack a full-scale investigation of loan-formations for the Old English period (the studies carried out so far are based on limited data). He also underlines that these all-pervasive processes by far outweigh the direct loans from Latin and it is necessary to study Old English word-formation and its relationship to Latin models systematically. So, there is still much to do in the field of analysis of loan-formations.

The main aim of the present paper is to enrich the analysis of loan-formations in Old English by application of Naturalness Theory and by analysing the data extracted from an electronic corpus of Old English.

2. Criteria of description and classification

Indirect borrowing processes are very complex and often present problems of delimitation, definition and classification. Thus, it is not easy to distinguish semantic loans from parallel independent developments of meanings of corresponding words in Latin and Old English or from mere translation of a foreign word by a semantically "nearest" native equivalent. It is difficult as well to decide whether a loan-formation is genuine or it is a mere parallel morphological development. The question that interests us in the present research is also whether the semantic loans and loan-formations that we find in Old English are isolated usages adopted by a single translator or the usages that pervade the entire vocabulary of the Old English texts that are available to us in the form of electronic corpora of Old English.

The most comprehensive study of indirect borrowings from Latin into Old English (based on Vespasian psalter) was undertaken by Helmut Gneuss. The results of his research are reflected in his work *Lehnbildungen und Lehnbedeutungen im Altenglischen* (1955). In Kastovsky (1992) we find a good description of indirect borrowing processes with reference to Gneuss (1955).

There exist some cases of doubt in definition and delimitation of indirect borrowing processes. Let us introduce immediately a basic terminology: leaving apart all the units larger then a morphological word/lexeme, one may subdivide all indirect borrowings into semantic loans (SLs) and loan-formations (LFs). Semantic loans in their turn are subdivided into analogical and substitutive, while loan-formations are represented by loan-translations (LTs), loan-renditions (LRs) and loan-creations (LCs).

We speak about a semantic loan in the case when an existing native lexeme adopts a meaning or a part of meaning of a foreign lexeme. If it shares some meanings with the model, and, on the basis of these common meanings, adopts another additional meaning from the model, then we have an analogical semantic loan. If, on the other hand, the native lexeme adopts additional meaning from the model without having any other meanings shared with the model, we speak about a substitutive semantic loan.

Loan-formations are in principle complex (derived or compound) formations newly created in the borrowing language on the model of lexical units of the donor language. All loan-formations can be accompanied by a semantic loan. This is the case when a complex word is not fully motivated, i.e. its meaning is not fully transparent and deducible from the sum of meanings of its component parts.

Some problems arise as to definition of different types of loan-formations. If in Kastovsky (1992: 315) we find that a loan-rendition may be a rendition of a simple word of a donor language by a complex (compound or derived) word in the borrowing language, in Gneuss (1955: 33) a loan-rendition by definition presupposes only derived and complex words as models (not simple ones though). Furthermore, in Gneuss (1955: 31) we find that only words/lexemes (compound or derived) may be the basis for a loan-translation, while Kastovsky (1992: 313) says that also syntactic groups (i.e. syntagmas) can be the bases for loan-translations. Gneuss (1955: 109) classifies such cases as loan-creations, while the cases when an Old English nominal syntagma translates a Latin compound he calls loan-renditions (Gneuss 1955: 114). However, among the compounds formed on the basis of Latin nominal syntagmas there may be cases of loan-translations (exact copies of the elements of a Latin syntagma) and cases of loan-renditions (quasi-exact copies of the elements of a Latin syntagma). It is possible that prior to becoming complex (compound) words, these indirect borrowings might have been nominal syntagmas also in Old English, and then they underwent the process of univerbation, turning into compounds. We will try to combine the classification of Gneuss (1955) with a more recent one of Kastovsky (1992). The classification that we obtain is as follows:

- LT: model – derived or compound word, or syntagma; replica – derived or compound word (all morphological constituents are semantically equivalent to those of the model);
- LR: model – simple, derived or compound word, or syntagma; replica – derived or compound word (al least one morphological constituent semantically corresponds to the model) ;
- LC: model – simple, derived or compound word, or syntagma; replica – derived or compound word (no morphological constituent of the replica semantically corresponds to the model, but the newly created word bears a new meaning borrowed from the donor language).

It is evident that in the above mentioned definitions we centre our attention on morphological structure of the words and on correspondence of morphological elements of a model and a replica. But what about semantics? Sometimes we come across situations when morphological constituents formally coincide, but the meanings of the constituent parts do not correspond perfectly to the meanings of the model constituents (i.e. we do not have a perfect equivalent of a part of the word, but a synonym). Let us take an example from Gneuss (1955: 31):

(1) OE *mildheortnes* 'mercy' – Lat. *misericordia* 'mercy'

Gneuss (1955: 31) describes it as a loan-translation. *Mildheort* 'gentle, mercyful' (*mild* 'gentle, mild, kind' + *heort* 'heart', already this word is a loan-translation) + *nes/nysse/nis* (a nominal suffix) is built on the Latin model: *misericors* 'merciful, pitiful' (*miser* 'poor, unhappy; suffering, mad of love' + *cor* 'heort') + *ia* (a suffix forming abstract deadjectival nouns). OE *mild* 'gentle, mild, kind' and Lat. *miser* 'poor, unhappy; suffering' can hardly be seen as having the same meaning/semantics. Nevertheless, Gneuss calls this case a loan-translation. A better equivalent seems to be the OE *earmheartnis/armhertnisse* (*earm/arm* 'poor, miserable, wretched') mentioned by Gneuss as really rare. Should we deduce from this example that a deviation in meaning does not really influence the classification, that the constituent parts must be at least synonymous in their lexical meaning and only morphological structure of the items really matters?

The problems do not finish here. Even if we centre our attention only on morphological structure of a word, we see that it is not always possible to state without a doubt the exact structure of a word. As mentioned in Kastovsky (1992: 313), some lexical items (e.g., Lat. *instruere, decipere, continere*, etc.) can be seen as complex (if we single out the prefixes) or as simple (if the prefixes are considered to be non-existent due to the fact that they lost their meaning). Since Latin prefixal verbs are often translated by Old English verbs with prefixes (sometimes redundant or without a specific meaning), we are going to stick to the point that such items are complex.

As far as suffixation goes, for uniformity reasons we shall regard *-nes, -dom, -had* and *-scipe* as suffixes, even if some of these suffixes were initially lexical items with full lexical meaning.

Another issue is the distinction between word-formedness and word-formation. Word-formedness represents the static approach and has to do with morphological structure of a word and its analisability, whereas word-formation is seen as a dynamic process and has to do with derivational patterns. Gneuss (1955: 34) in his analysis of indirect borrowings stresses the importance of paying attention to the correspondence between morphological structures of a model and a replica, not of word-formation patterns. So, he adopts the static approach. But Gneuss himself sometimes does not follow his principle of constructional equivalence (Gneuss 1955: 84):

(2) OE *gehalgung* 'consecration' – Lat. *sanctification* 'consecration'

He calls this case a loan-translation, but it is a loan-translation only dynamically (derivational patterns of both words are verb + suffix). Statically these words are not completely equal: OE *(ge)halg* + *ung* (prefix [optional] + root + suffix), Lat. *sanctus* + *fico* + *tio* (root + suffix [derived from verb *facio(facere)* 'to do'] +

suffix). So, statically we are dealing with a loan-rendition rather than a loan-translation. Probably, Gneuss in his analysis prefers to omit the prefix and single out another suffix in *(ge)halgung* (suffix *-ig* in *-halg-*), and then his static loan-translation is justified.

This discrepancy between derivational and structural approaches in classification is also underlined by Kastovsky (1992: 315). In Section 3 we are going to take into consideration both approaches, and, if there is a difference in these two approaches as to the classification, the labels will be given with reference to each of them. A more detailed discussion of this issue is offered in Section 4.2.

One more thing that has to be specified is the situation with conversion and back-formation. In literature conversion is frequently called "zero derivation", i.e. it is equal to suffixation and the suffix is zero in this case. Back-formation may also be seen as a case of negative suffixation, where a suffix is not added, but deleted. Since we should determine whether a word is a precise copy (loan-translation) or a quasi-precise copy (loan-rendition) of a model, we have to establish (for the dynamic approach) whether conversion and back-formation are instances of suffixation or they are separate derivational patterns. If they are instances of suffixation, than dynamically suffixation in the model and conversion in the replica is seen as a loan-translation. If they are not, in the same situation we have a loan-rendition. We will stick to the latter point of view, since we are operating in the framework Naturalness Theory, and in this theory conversion is not seen as a zero-derivation, but as a morphological metaphor (Dressler 2005: 269). The more detailed discussion of why conversion is not equal to suffixation is offered in Sections 4.5.

Of course, looking for indirect borrowings in a text one may be prone to mistake a simple translation by an Old English equivalent or a parallel development for an indirect borrowing. So, there should be certain criteria that permit us to discard the words that are unlikely to be indirect borrowings. Gneuss (1955: 38-40) suggests such criteria. They can be summarised as follows:

–   New notion. An indirect borrowing often represents a new notion, something unknown previously or something that belongs to a foreign culture. For instance, we can hardly sustain that OE *ondlifen* 'food, sustenance' is created to render the Lat. *victus* 'food, sustenance'. The Anglo-Saxons surely had had a word to express this meaning prior to the Roman influence. It is a very common notion since it has to do with eating and drinking which are necessary for life of any human being. We should take into consideration the culture and history of the nation that borrows words and of the nation that lends the model, because this information helps us to understand what was known and what was unknown to the borrowing nation.

- Perfect copy. An indirect borrowing is more sure so, if it presents a perfect copy of the model both structurally and semantically (though there is always a danger to mistake an independent parallel development of meaning or structure for an indirect borrowing (see Section 4.1.).
- Length and complexity. The longer and the more complex the word is, the more probably it is an indirect borrowing (a loan-formation).
- Other attempts at translation. If there are any other attempts at translation of a word, other variants that resemble the structure of the model, it is likely that the word is an indirect borrowing (variants of translations are more easily found in glosses and texts with several versions of translation).
- Group support. If there exist variants which resemble the structure of the Latin model in other related languages (languages of the same group, in our case, the Germanic languages), this may act as another proof of the fact that the model was really borrowed.
- "Monosemy". An indirect borrowing is more sure so, if it is "monosemic", i.e. if it has just one meaning.
- Rarity. For semantic loans and loan-formations accompanied by a SL, the rarity of occurrence of the new meaning in the texts may testify in favour of an indirect borrowing. Rarity of occurrence of a loan-formation may also testify to the fact that the word was indirectly borrowed, but here we have a problem: if the word is used once or just several times, it may not have been really accepted in a borrowing language and thus was not really a part of its vocabulary, but just an occasionalism, a word belonging to an author's idiolect.
- Productivity of pattern. If we presume that a word is an indirect borrowing, usually it is supposed to be built with the help of productive derivational patterns/derivational morphemes of the borrowing language.

Of course, it is difficult to find an indirect borrowing that would fit all these criteria perfectly, but it should fit at least some of them.

3. Analysis of some indirect borrowings found in the first book of the *Ecclesiastical history of the English people.*[2]

This section provides the following list of indirect borrowings found in the *Ecclesiastical history of the English people*:

---

2   The texts used for analysis are: *Venerabilis Baedae opera historica* by Plummer, C. and *The Old Enlgish version of "Bede's ecclesiastical history of the English people"* by Miller, T. The dictionaries used are: *Il vocabolario della lingua latina* by Castiglioni, L. and S. Mariotti, for Latin, *The students's dictionary of Anglo-Saxon* by Sweet, H. and *A concise Anglo-Saxon dictionary* by Hall, J. R. C. for Old English (for details see references). The corpus used for research of token frequency is the York-Toronto-Helsinki parsed corpus of Old English prose kindly provided by Oxford Text Archive.

(a) OE *mereswyn* 'porpoise, dolphin' – Lat. *delphin* 'dolphin' (from Gk.). LC. Corpus token frequency: 2. *Mere* 'sea, ocean' + *swyn/swin* 'wild boar, pig'. There existed in Old English also a direct borrowing from Lat. *delphinus* – OE *delfin* 'delphin' (Serjeantson 1935: 285).

(b) OE *meregrot* 'pearl' – Lat. *margarita* 'pearl' (from Gk.). LC (a case of folk-etymology). Corpus token frequency: 10. This word represents a borderline case between direct and indirect borrowing. *Mere* 'sea, ocean' + *grot/greot* 'particle; sand'. There existed in Old English also a direct borrowing from Lat. *perla* – OE *pærl* 'pearl' (Serjeantson 1935: 278). It is evident that the Old English equivalent resembles phonetically the Latin model. Thus, initially there might have been an attempt at direct borrowing and Old English acquired a loan-word from Latin. But then the word mutated and became clearly analysable (compound): *mere* 'sea' + *grot* 'pebble'. So, folk etymology may be seen as a case of loan-creation triggered by phonetic resemblance of parts of the model and some words of the borrowing language that become parts of the replica. But is it direct or indirect borrowing? Was it really a borrowing done by people who did not know much of Latin and who tried to give foreign words a motivation, being guided by its phonetic form and associations it produced? Or was it a conscious attempt of a bilingual translator to create a native word, a loan creation that happily resembled the original not only semantically but also phonetically? Anyway, it seems to be a very good compromise between direct borrowing and loan creation.

(c) OE *halwendnes* 'salubrity, healthyness' – Lat. *salubritas* 'sanity, salubrity, health'. LT (dynamic), LR (static). Corpus token frequency: 3. *Halwende* 'healing, salutary, wholesome, beneficial' (*hal* 'entire, whole; healthy, well, sound' + *wendan* 'to turn, go, return, change') + *nes/nysse/nis* (a nominal suffix) is built on the model of Lat. *saluber* 'healthy, wholesome, robust, saltary' (from *salvus* 'safe, healthy, whole, entire') + *tas* (a suffix used to form abstract nouns from adjectives).

(d) OE *hidercyme* 'arrival; advent (of Christ)' – Lat. *incarnatio* 'incarnation'. LR and SL (analogical) in its Christian meaning. Corpus token frequency: 7 (out of these, only one case may be considered a loan-rendition, other instances are semantic loans). This word is also found with the Latin equivalent *adventus* 'arrival' (in the syntagma *Ongolcynnes hidercymes* meaning 'the arrival of Angles'), so in this case *hidercyme* is a loan-rendition: OE *hidercyme* 'advent, arrival' – Lat. *adventus* 'arrival'. *Hider* 'hither, here' + *cyme* (a deverbal noun, from *cuman/cyman* 'to come') is built on the model of Lat. *advenio* (*advenire*) 'to arrive, come, reach' (from *ad* [a prefix used to form deverbal derivatives with the meaning of direction, approaching, bringing near] + *veneo* [*venire*] 'to come, arrive') + *tus* (a suffix of deverbal nouns denoting action or a suffix of abstract or collective nouns). *Hidercuman/hidercyman did not exist as a verb in Old English, so we cannot derive *hidercyme* from this verb, thus, it must be a loan-rendition. See also *menniscnys* ((f) in the present list).

(e) OE *eorðweall* 'earth-wall, mound' – Lat. *vallum* 'mound, bastion'. Hybrid LR. Corpus token frequency: 3. *Eorð* 'earth, soil, ground' + *weall* 'wall, dyke, earthwork, rampant, dam' (Hall 1916: 344); 'wall, rampant' (Sweet 1940: 201) (a direct borrowing from Lat. *vallum*) The first element of the compound may serve additional specification. In this case the compound results to be a redundant formation (precision type) and one must assume that OE *weall* meant any type of wall (if we fallow Sweet's dictionary) while Lat. *vallum* presupposed 'mound, earth construction' (for 'wall' there was Lat. *murus* 'wall of the city, house' and it was borrowed directly in Old English as *mur* 'wall').

(f) OE *menniscnys* 'human nature, humaneness, humanity; incarnation' – Lat. *incarnatio* 'incarnation'. SL (substitutive). Corpus token frequency: 215 (out of these 153 are semantic loans).

(g) OE *wæcce* 'keeping awake, vigil; religious vigil' (from *wacian* 'to be awake, keep watch') – Lat. *vigilia* 'insomnia, vigil; religious vigil'. SL (analogical) in its religious meaning. Corpus token frequency: 59 (out of these 50 are semantic loans).

(h) OE *underðeod(ed)* 'subject' (a noun) – Lat. *subiectum* 'subject'. LT . Corpus token frequency: 39. *Underðeod* (a noun derived from the past participle of *underÞeodan/underÞiedan/underÞydan* 'to subjoin, add, subjugate, subject, subdue', already this verb being a loan-translation from Lat. *subiogo [subiugare]* 'to subdue, subjugate': *under* 'under' + *Þeodan* 'to join, attach, engage' is built on the model of Lat. *sub* 'under' + *iugo [iugare]* 'to unite, connect, link') corresponds to the Lat. model *subjectum* (a noun derived from perfect participle of *subjugo*). See also *underÞeodnys* ((j) in the present list). There must be a chain of indirect borrowings in this case.

(i) OE *toslitnys* 'laceration, dissention' – Lat. *discerptio* 'laceration'. LT. Corpus token frequency: 1. *Toslitan* 'to tear to pieces, break, lacerate; sever, separate, destroy' (*to* [a preposition of motion, time, may be later – a prefix] + *slitan* 'to tear, rend, destroy, slander) + *nes/nysse/nis* (a nominal suffix) is built on the model of Lat. *discerpo(discerpere)* 'to tear into pieces, reduce to fine particles' (*dis* [a prefix meaning separation, division, negation, also with intensifying meaning] + *carpo [carpere]* 'to divide, tear to pieces, break') + *tio* (a suffix of deverbal nouns denoting action).

(j) OE *underÞeodnys* 'subjection, submission' – Lat. *subiectio* 'subjection'. LT. Corpus token frequency: 11. *UnderÞeodan* 'to subjoin, add, subjugate, subject, subdue' (*under* 'under' + *Þeodan* 'to join, attach, engage', already this verb being a loan-translation) + *nes/nysse/nis* (a nominal suffix) is built on the model of Lat. *subicio* (*subicere*) 'to submit, subject' (Lat. *sub* 'under' + *iugo* [*iugare*] 'to unite, connect, link') + *tio* (a suffix of deverbal nouns denoting action). See also *underðeod* ((h) in the present list).

(k) OE *forðgeong* 'progress, advance, success' – Lat. *processus* 'progress, success'. LR. Corpus token frequency: 10. *ForÞ* 'forwards, onwards, continually' + *gang/geong* 'going, progression' (from *gan* 'to go') is built on the model of Lat. *procedo* (*procedere*) 'to rise, pass, reach' (*pro* [a prefix meaning 'in front of, forwards' as well as temporal priority] + *cedo* [*cedere*] 'to arrive, pass, cease') + *tus* (a suffix of deverbal nouns denoting action or suffix of abstract or collective nouns). Hall (1916: 116) also gives the verb *forðgan* (*gan*) 'to procede, to go forth, advance' absent in Sweet (1940): *forÞ* 'forwards, onwards, continually' + *gan* (*gan*) 'to go, proceed', which may be a loan-translation on the model of Lat. *procedo* (*procedere*). So, the noun may be derived by means of subtraction from the verb, and we may have a chain of indirect borrowings in this case.

(l) OE *æfteryldo* 'old age, past time' – Lat. *retro aetas* 'past time'. LT. Corpus token frequency: 1. *Æfter* 'behind; after' + *yldo/ield(o)* 'period, age, time, old age' is built on the model of Lat. *retro* 'behind; after' *aetas* 'age, years, time, period, epoch'.

(m) OE *wællhreownys* 'ferocity, cruelty' – Lat. *crudelitas* 'cruelty, inhumanity'. LT (dynamic), LR (static). Corpus token frequency: 26. *Wællhreow* 'fierce, cruel' (*wæll* 'slaughter, carnage; bodies of those who have fallen in battle' + *hreow/hreaw* 'raw, not cooked', already this word may be a loan-rendition [see *crudelis* below]) + *nes/nysse/nis* (a nominal suffix) is built on the model of Lat. *crudelis* 'cruel, inhuman' (*crudus* 'raw, not cooked' [from *cruor* 'sangue'] + *elis* [a suffix used to derive adjectives from adjectives]) + *tas* (a suffix used to form abstract nouns from adjectives). There seems to be a chain of indirect borrowings in this case.

(n) OE *wiÞcoren* 'rejected, outcast' – Lat. *improbus* 'bad, evil, dishonest'. LT (static), LR (dynamic, if the pattern is not mistaken). Corpus token frequency: 2. *WiÞcoren* is the past participle of *wiÞceosan* 'to reject' (*wiÞ* 'against, opposite' [with negative meaning] + *ceosan* 'to choose, decide; accept' may already be a loan-translation). The Latin derivational pattern is *im* (=*in*, a prefix with negative/privative meaning) + *probus* 'good, honest'. Probably the translator considered this adjective as derived from the Latin verb *improbo* (*improbare*) 'to disapprove, reject, reprove' (which was in its turn analysed as derived from *probo* [*probare*] 'to prove, judge, evaluate, accept') with the help of the negative prefix *in*. But the reality is quite opposite: the Latin verb *improbo* is derived from the Latin adjective *improbus* + *o* (a suffix of the verbs of the 1st conjugation). There may be a chain of indirect borrowings in this case.

(o) OE *mæssesong* 'mass' – Lat. *missa* 'mass'. Hybrid LR. Corpus token frequency: 21. *Mæsse* 'mass' (a direct borrowing from Lat. *missa*) + *sang/song* 'song, singing'. Here we observe a hybrid loan-rendition and a redundant formation (precision type): *song* seems to be added for precision, better explanation of the concept, for the purpose of making the word more transparent, more understandable.

(p) OE *ordfruma* 'origin, originator, creator, chief' – Lat. *auctor* 'the one who makes grow; creator, founder; witness, source; master, model'. LC. Corpus token frequency: 34. *Ord* 'point, spear; source, beginning; chief, prince' + *fruma* 'beginning, origin; originator, creator, inventor, doer, maker'. The Latin model is as follows: *augeo* (*augere*) 'to grow, amplify, strengthen' + *tor* (a suffix used to form deverbal agent nouns). It seems to be a redundant formation (superfluous type), i.e. the parts are superfluous and repeat one another: *fruma* already means 'beginning, origin' but it is completed by *ord* which means 'origin, source' and makes the meaning more precise or intensifies it.

(q) OE *mæssepreost* 'mass priest, high priest' – Lat. *presbyter* 'priest' (from Gk.). Hybrid LR (double). Corpus token frequency: 427. *Mæsse* 'mass' (a direct borrowing from Lat. *missa*) + *preost* 'priest' (a direct borrowing from Lat. *presbyter*). It is a redundant formation (precision type): *mæsse* seems to be added for precision, better explanation of the concept, for the purpose of making the word more transparent.

(r) OE *cneoris* 'generation, family, race, tribe' – Lat. *generatio* 'generation, reproduction'. LR. Corpus token frequency: 53. *Cneo(w)* 'knee' + *ris(se)* (probably a noun derived from the verb *risan/arisan* 'to rise, stand up, get up; originate') may be built on the model of Lat. *genero* (*generare*) 'to generate, produce, derive, descend, create' (from *genus* 'knee' + *o* [a suffix of the verbs of the 1st conjugation]) + *tio* (a suffix of deverbal nouns denoting action).

(s) OE *monþwærnes* 'gentleness, good nature' (Sweet 1940: 114); 'courtesy' (Hall 1916: 198) – Lat. *mansuetudo* 'gentleness, goodness, meekness'. LT. Corpus token frequency: 19. *Monþwære/man(n)þwære* 'gentle, kind' (*mon/mann* 'man' + *þwære* 'united, harmonious, peaceful, pleasing, gentle, obedient') + *nes/nysse/nis* (a nominal suffix) may be built on the model of Lat. *mansues* 'obedient, meek, domesticated' (*manus* 'hand' + *suesco* 'get accustomed, be used to') + *tudo* (a suffix of abstract deadjectival nouns). There may be a chain of indirect borrowings in this case. The adjective may also be seen as a case of folk-etymology (compare *mannþwære* and *mansues*).

(t) OE *undeaðlicnes* 'immortality' – Lat. *immortalitas* 'immortality, eternity'. LT. Corpus token frequency: 20. *Undeaðlic/undeadlic* 'immortal' (*un* [a negative prefix] + *deaðlic/deadlic* 'mortal, subject to death, deadly' [*deað* 'death' + *(ge)lic* 'similar, equal'] may already be a loan-translation) + *nes/nysse/nis* (a nominal suffix) is built on the model of Lat. *immortalitas* 'immortality, eternity': *in* (a negative/privative prefix) + *mortalis* 'mortal' (*mors* 'death' + *alis* [a suffix of denominal adjectives]) + *tas* (a suffix used to form abstract nouns from adjectives). There may be a chain of indirect borrowings in this case.

(u) OE *oferflownis* 'superfluity, abundance, overflow' – Lat. *superfluitas* 'abundance, redundancy, overflow'. LR (dynamic, if we don not mistake the derivational patter), LT (static). Corpus token frequency: 21. *Oferflowian* 'to overflow' (*ofer* 'over, above, across' + *flowan* 'to flow, be abundant' may already be a loan-translation) + *nes/nysse/nis* (a nominal suffix) may be built on the model of Lat. *superfluus* 'excessive, redundant, superfluous' + *tas* (a suffix used to form abstract nouns from adjectives). However, it is possible that the translator mistook the derivational pattern and considered *superfluitas* as derived from *superfluo/superfluere* 'to overflow, be redundant' (*super* [a prefix meaning 'over, above'] + *fluo/fluere* 'to flow, run; be abundant') + *tas* (a suffix used to form abstract nouns from adjectives). In this case we have a perfect dynamic loan-translation. There may be a chain of indirect borrowings in this case.

4. Some conclusions and suggestions

On the basis of the data of Section 3 and other cases analysed some conclusions and suggestions can be made.

4.1 Parallel developments and mere translations

There is a number of cases where one can hardly exclude an independent parallel development:

(3) OE *wunenes* 'dwelling' – Lat. *mansio* 'stay; habitation, shelter, dwelling'

The structures of both words perfectly coincide: *wunian* 'to dwell, remain, continue, inhabit' + *nes/nysse/nis* (a nominal suffix) may be built on the model of Lat. *maneo* (*manere*) 'to remain, dwell, inhabit' + *tio* (a suffix of deverbal nouns denoting action). But the notion in question is so common and does not present any novelty in meaning, so it is very probably a parallel development. However, the token frequency of this word in the corpus is really low (only 10 matches), and this may speak in favour of indirect borrowing.

This is not the case with *wisdom*:

(4) OE *wisdom* 'knowledge, learning, experience' – Lat. *scientia* 'science, knowledge, cognition'

It may seem to be built on the Lat. model: *wis* 'learned, experienced, the one who knows' (from *witan* 'to know, understand, be aware of' [Hall 1916: 356]) + *dom* (a nominal suffix) corresponds to Lat. *sciens* 'learned, expert, informed, the one who knows' (from *scio* [*scire*] 'to know, understand') + *ia* (a suffix used to form deadjectival nouns and nouns derived from participles), but it is again a very common notion. Moreover, the word's token frequency in the corpus is really high (513 matches), which testifies to the fact that it was a pre-existing Old English word. Thus, here we have a sure case of parallel development.

Latin and OE seem to be typologically close, especially as far as derivation is concerned: compounding, common in Old English, is extremely rare in Latin, but in derivation both languages extensively use suffixation and prefixation. So, frequent correspondence between Latin agent suffix *-tor* and OE agent suffix *-end* seems quite normal, and the words with such a suffix in Old English may well be parallel developments.

There is also a number of cases where several Latin words that differ in structure but are synonymous in meaning correspond to one Old English word. In this case it is likely a pre-existing word used to translate the Latin words and not an indirect borrowing. For instance:

(5) *bebod* 'command, order, decree' – Lat. *mandatum* 'command, order'

Deverbal *bebod* (from past participle of *biddan* 'to ask, order, command, require' or *bebeodan* 'to command, ask, announce') translates the Latin deverbial *mandatum* (from perfect participle of *mando* [*mandare*] 'to send, order'). There are some other Latin correspondences to OE *bebod*: Lat. *iussum* 'order, command, law', Lat. *praeceptum* 'command, rule, teaching', Lat. *imperium* 'order, command'. Moreover, it is a common notion that does not present any novelty, so it seems rather a mere Old English equivalent used to translate the Latin words than an indirect borrowing.

4.2 Static and dynamic approaches

In Section 2 it was mentioned that there is a necessity to distinguish between the static and the dynamic approaches in the classification of the loan-formations. This distinction results really important. In some cases, the static and dynamic points of view do not contradict each other as to the classification:

(6) *hidercyme* 'arrival' – Lat. *adventus* 'arrival'

This case is a loan-rendition both from the static and the dynamic point of view. Statically, *hidercyme* is a loan-rendition, because its morphological structure is prefix + root: *hider* 'hither, here' (may be seen as a prefix) + *cyme* (a deverbal noun derived from *cuman/cyman* 'to come' with the help of back-formation). The morphological structure of the Latin model is prefix + root + suffix: *advenio* (*advenire*) 'arrive, come, reach' (from *ad* [a prefix used with deverbal derivatives with the meaning of 'direction to, approaching, bringing near'] + *veneo* [*venire*] 'to come, arrive') + *tus* (a suffix of deverbal nouns denoting action or suffix of abstract or collective nouns). So, the morphological constructions of the model and the replica do not coincide, and thus *hidercyme* is a loan-rendition from the static point of view. Dynamically, given that **hidercuman/hidercyman* does not exist as a verb (it was not found either in the dictionaries or in the corpus), we cannot derive *hidercyme* from the verb directly, thus, *hidercyme* must be derived from *hider* 'hither, here' (seen as a prefix) + *cyme* (a deverbal noun, from *cuman/cyman* 'to come' with the help of back-formation). That means that the derivational pattern of the replica is prefix + noun, while the Latin model has the derivational pattern verb + suffix: *advenio* (*advenire*) 'arrive, come, reac' + *tus* (a suffix of deverbal nouns denoting action or suffix of abstract or collective nouns). The two patterns do not coincide, so *hidercyme* is a loan-rendition also from the dynamic point of view.

However, there are other cases where the static and dynamic points of view do contradict each other as to the classification:

(7) *halwendnes* 'salubrity, healthyness' – Lat. *salubritas* 'sanity, salubrity, health'

Statically it is a loan-rendition, because the morphological structure of the replica is root + root + suffix (*halwende* 'healing, salutary, wholesome, beneficial' [*hal* 'entire, whole; healthy, well, sound' + *wendan* 'to turn, go, return, change'] + *nes/nysse/nis* [a noun suffix]) whereas that of the Latin model is root + suffix (*saluber* 'healthy, wholesome, robust, saltary' [from *salvus* 'safe, healthy, whole, entire'] + *tas* [a suffix used to form abstract nouns from adjectives]). The problem here is that both nouns are derived from an adjective with the help of a suffix, so why cannot it be a loan-translation if the derivation patterns coincide perfectly? From the dynamic point of view we may call this case a loan-translation, while from the static point of view (following Gneuss) the construction is considered a loan-rendition.

Thus, we see that if we take into consideration only the static approach, we miss out on derivation. Even if Old English translators created some words mechanically by simple joining of constituent parts corresponding to the parts of Latin models, we cannot claim that all indirect borrowings were coined in this way. Creation of a new word seems to be rather a dynamic process governed by certain derivational patterns and rules. The existence of chains of indirect borrowings proves this point. The words of a chain and their derivational patterns are related to each other, they could not have been coined separately by mechanical joining of constituent parts. In this case they could have resulted different in structure or pattern, but they do not.

4.3 Chains of indirect borrowings

In the descriptions of indirect borrowings in Section 3 the notion of chains of indirect borrowings was introduced. A chain of indirect borrowings is a set of several conjugate words that are borrowed indirectly and their word-formation patterns seem to be related to each other as well as to the model. Let us have a look at an example:

(8)   *wællhreownys* 'ferocity, cruelty' – Lat. *crudelitas* 'cruelty, inhumanity'

In this case we have a dynamic loan-translation and a static loan-rendition. The adjective *wællhreow* 'fierce, cruel (*wæll* 'slaughter, carnage; bodies of those who have fallen in battle' + *hreow/hreaw* 'raw, not cooked') is a loan-rendition on the model of Lat. *crudelis* (*crudus* 'raw, not cooked' [from *cruor* 'sangue'] + *elis* [a suffix used to derive adjectives from adjectives]) based on the correspondence of OE *hreow/hreaw* and Lat. *crudus*. The noun *wællhreownes* in its turn is derived from the adjective *wællhreow* + *nes/nysse/nis* (a nominal suffix) on the model of Lat. *crudelis* 'cruel, inhuman' + *tas* (a suffix used to form abstract nouns from adjectives) and dynamically is a loan-translation. The adjective and the noun, thus, present a chain of two indirect borrowings: first the adjective was borrowed indirectly from Latin, and then the noun was derived from the adjective, but also this one followed the Latin model.

Such chains prove that not always the process of indirect borrowing was a mechanic conjunction of constituent parts, but in many cases it was a deliberate process governed by certain derivational patterns. So, the dynamic aspect of indirect borrowing is also very important in the description of the phenomenon.

4.4 Mistaking of derivational patterns

A mechanical structural copying of a model (part by part) may seem to have had place in some cases, but even in such cases we may suspect that a translator followed a derivational pattern (even if it was mistaken). Let us have a look at the cases where static loan-translation is accompanied by dynamic loan-rendition, i.e. the cases when the constituent parts coincide perfectly, but the derivational pattern is different:

(9) *oferflownis* 'superfluity, abundance, overflow' – Lat. *superfluitas* 'abundance, redundancy, overflow'

This case combines static loan-translationa and dynamic loan-rendition. *Oferflowian* 'to overflow' + *nes/nysse/nis* (a nominal suffix) may be built on the Lat. model *superfluus* 'excessive, redundant, superfluous' + *tas* (a suffix used to form abstract nouns from adjectives). The word may seem mechanically created, but we may also suppose that the translator mistook the derivational pattern deriving Lat. *superfluitas* from the verb *superfluo* (*superfluere*) 'to overflow, be redundant' + *tas* (a suffix used to form abstract nouns) rather than from the adjective mentioned above, and then we have a perfect dynamic loan-translation instead of a loan-rendition.

The same is valid for *wiþcoren*:

(10) *wiþcoren* 'rejected, outcast' – Lat. *improbus* 'bad, evil, dishonest'

Wiþcoren is derived by conversion from the past participle of *wiþceosan* 'to reject' (*wiþ* 'against, opposite' [used as a prefix with negative meaning] + *ceosan* 'to choose, decide; accept' may already be a loan-translation). The Latin derivational pattern is *im* (=*in*, a prefix with negative/privative meaning) + *probus* 'good, honest'. The translator may have considered this adjective as derived from the Latin verb *improbo* (*improbare*) 'to disapprove, reject, reprove' which was in its turn analysed as derived from *probo* (*probare*) 'to prove, judge, evaluate, accept' with the help of the negative prefix *in*, and then we have again a perfect dynamic loan-translation in this case. But the reality is quite different: the Latin verb *improbo* is derived from the Latin adjective *improbus* + *o* (a suffix of the verbs of the 1st conjugation).

4.5 Conversion and suffixation

We should say that conversion is present in both Latin and Old English, but not always Latin conversion is rendered by conversion in Old English and Latin suffixation by suffixation in Old English. There are also cases when Latin conversion is rendered by Old English suffixation and Latin suffixation – by Old English conversion. The term "zero-suffix", as compared to materialised suffix, seems inappropriate in the framework of Natural Linguistics. Actually, we cannot consider conversion as zero-suffixation since suffixation is highly iconic, while conversion is non-iconic. Moreover, suffixation is also highly indexical, while conversion is much less indexical. We may conclude that conversion is a derivational mechanism absolutely different from affixation in the degree of naturalness. So, conversion and suffixation cannot be seen as equal derivational patterns, and only if Latin conversion is rendered by conversion in Old English (or Latin suffixation – by suffixation in Old English) we will speak of a dynamic loan-translation:

(11) *underðeod(ed)* 'subject' (a noun) – Lat. *subiectum* 'subject'

This case is a loan-translation. *Underðeod* is a noun derived from past participle of *underþeodan/underþiedan/underþydan* 'to subjoin, add, subjugate, subject, subdue' (already this verb being a loan-translation from Lat. *subiugo [subiugare]* 'to subdue, subjugate') by conversion. The Latin model *subjectum* is also a noun derived from perfect participle of the verb *subjugo* by conversion. Thus, we have an Old English past participle and a Latin perfect participle that, both by conversion, become nouns.

But if Latin suffixation is rendered by Old English conversion (or subtraction), or Latin conversion – by Old English suffixation, we have a dynamic loan-rendition:

(12) *forðgeong* 'progress, advance, success' – Lat. *processus* 'progress, success'

This case is a loan-rendition. Hall (1916: 116) and Bosworth and Toller (1898: 322) give the verb *forðgan (gan)* 'to procede, to forth, advance' absent in Sweet (1940): *forþ* 'forwards, onwards, continually' + *gan (gan)* 'to go, procede' must be already a loan-translation on the model of Lat. *procedo (procedere)*. If it really exists, then *forðgeong* is a noun formed from *forðgan (gan)* by means of subtraction. The Latin model, on the other hand, involves suffixation (see (k) in the list of Section 3). Thus we have a Latin suffixation rendered by Old English subtraction (and not by Old English suffixation, e.g., possible but non-existent loan-translation **forðgannes*), and consequently the word is a loan-rendition from he dynamic point of view.

4.6 Redundant formations

In some cases we note that Old English indirect borrowings are a little bit redundant, i.e. it seems that in search of transparency Old English translators in some cases went too far. Let us take some examples:

(13) *ordfruma* 'origin, originator, creator, chief' – Lat. *auctor* 'the one who makes grow; creator, founder; witness, source; master, model'

This case is a loan-creation. *Fruma* already means 'beginning, origin' but it is completed by *ord* which means 'origin, source' as though to make the meaning more precise or to intensify. We call such cases redundant formations (superfluous type): the constituent parts of such indirect borrowings are superfluous and seem to repeat one another (actually, they mean the same thing).

There are similar cases that are labelled as redundant formations (precision type). Their parts do not mean the same thing as in redundant formations of superfluous type but one part is added seemingly without necessity. Such addition is not provoked by the form of the Latin equivalent, but probably by its meaning and seems to have the purpose of better explanation and specification/sharpening of the meaning:

(14) *mæssesong* 'mass' – Lat. *missa* 'mass'

In this hybrid loan-rendition *song* seems to be added for precision, better explanation of the concept, for the purpose of making the word more transparent, more understandable.

4.7 Borrowed productivity

In our data from the first book of the *Ecclesiastical history of the English people* we find a great number of examples where Old English suffix *-nysse/nes/nis* corresponds to the Latin suffixes *-tio* and *-tas* in the formation of abstract nouns. Probably we may attribute the productivity of the Old English suffix *-nysse/nes /nis* to the influence of the productivity of the two Latin suffixes. There was another suffix in Old English with seemingly the same meaning *-þo/ðo*: e.g., *heihþo* 'height', *læþþo* 'hatred' (Kastovsky 1992: 338), but it was hardly as productive as *-nysse/nes/nis*. These are only suppositions for the moment, as well as the cases regarding frequent correspondence of Old English prefix *forð-* (and also *for-* [probably a reduced form of *forð* that appeared due to the assimilation]) and Latin prefix *pro-*.

5. Borrowing processes in the light of Natural Linguistics: looking for explanation

5.1 Introduction to Naturalness Theory

The questions that interest us in the present research are the following:

– What is more natural for a language – to borrow a foreign word or to create a new word for a new notion using the native material?

–   How can we explain the preference of indirect borrowing processes in Old
    English vs. the preference of direct borrowings in Middle English? What
    could have caused this change in preference?
–   Which mechanisms of indirect borrowing are more natural and which are less
    natural?

Fischer (2003: 102) notes that semantic typology, as well as morphological
typology of borrowings is purely descriptive. There are attempts to describe the
reasons for borrowing (cf. Weinreich 1964: 56-62), but "surprisingly little effort
has been devoted to the question of why certain types of borrowing seem to be
more frequent than others." (Fischer 2003: 100) The present research is an attempt
to bridge this gap.

We are going to compare the Old English and Middle English/New English
situations in the framework of Natural Linguistics. The choice of this framework
is justified by the openness of Naturalness Theory to other scientific disciplines
and theories and by its explanatory character. Natural Linguistics uses all types of
evidence and relies on results in many fields of research in order to explain how
different linguistic phenomena work and, what is more important, why they work
this way. Thus, Natural Linguistics integrates semiotics, markedness theory
(linguistic universals), typological theory (language types), theory of system
congruity (language specific competence), sociolinguistic and psycholinguistic
theories in search for explanations of linguistic phenomena. As well expressed by
Oswald Panagl, "a cumulative causality more genuinely accounts for the
phenomenon of linguistic change" (1987: 144).

Natural Linguistics uses two types of evidence that are equally important in
search for an explanation of morphological principles and preferences:

–   internal evidence: evidence within the linguistic system and within all
    components of the language (phonology, syntax, lexicon, morphology);
–   external evidence: psychological, neurological, cognitive, semiotic and
    sociolinguistic motivation of linguistic phenomena.
    The main concept of Natural Linguistics is naturalness. Natural means:
–   cognitively simple;
–   easily accessible (especially to children);
–   universally preferred (derivable from the human nature);
–   unmarked, or rather less marked.

Natural is not seen as a binary predicate (natural vs. unnatural), but as a gradient
one (more natural vs. less natural). Moreover, naturalness is a terminologically
flexible notion: when it is applied to Universal Grammar, we speak about system-
independent naturalness, but when it is applied to language-specific grammar, we
deal with system-dependent naturalness. The main purpose on Natural Linguistics

is to decide what is more or less natural with respect to Universal Grammar and/or language-specific grammar.

In the view of the fact that Natural Linguistics operates within a semiotic framework, we are to mention some important facts regarding language. There is a semiotic hierarchy of verbal signs:

- words are primary signs;
- morphemes and morphological rules are secondary signs;
- phonemes and phonological rules are tertiary signs.

This priority of words probably can explain why in the case of OE *mildheortnes* – Lat. *misericordia, mildheortnes* was preferred to more constructionally and semantically transparent *earmheortnes*. In the latter, all parts/morphemes of the model are faithfully copied and are transparent, but the meaning of the whole word in this case is not really deducible from the sum of the meanings of its parts. In the former, on the other hand, the meaning of the whole word is morphosemantically more transparent, even if the first morpheme does not precisely coincide in its semantics with the first morpheme of the Latin model. Thus, we see that the semantic transparency of the entire word is more important than the faithful rendering and semantics of the morphemes that constitute the word.

If we consider all borrowings as signs, we should also try to identify them with particular types of signs. Loan-translations, loan-renditions and loan-creations resemble icons, more precisely diagrams, which represent the relation of the parts of one thing (in our case, the model) by analogous relation in its own parts (in our case, the replica). This analogy can vary in the degree of precision that is the highest in the case of loan-translations and the lowest in the case of loan-creations. Icons are the most natural signs, so they should be preferred over other signs.

Semantic loans can be identified with indexes which stand for the object they refer to. Indexes are less natural than icons. Actually, all indirect borrowings are indexes as far as they refer to a model, but in semantic loans (especially, analogical semantic loans) this indexicality is very important. Analogical semantic loans presuppose the addition of a new meaning on the basis of the common meanings shared by the model and the replica. In this case, the new meaning is an index of the common shared meanings of the model and the replica. Substitutive semantic loans lack such indexicality and thus they are less natural than analogical semantic loans.

Direct borrowings, in their turn, can be identified with symbols – the least natural signs of all. They have only a conventional connection between the signatum and the signans since they usually lack morphotactic or morpho-semanatic transparency or motivation. In addition, non-nativised direct borro-wings, which retain phonetic and/or morphological characteristics of the source language, are less natural than nativised ones, which have been adapted to the native phonology and morphology. Nativised direct borrowings acquire certain characteristics (morphemes) that help to identify them with a certain class of native words.

Indirect borrowing processes usually presuppose a model (a word of a foreign language) and a replica (a corresponding word/meaning created in the borrowing language on the model of a word of a foreign language). So, these processes of copying of a model can be seen as legisigns. Legisigns are laws that are signs. They are conventional rules that connect signatum and signans. In our case, the signatum is the input of a respective rule and the signans is the output (actualisation in performance of a legisign).

Our task with respect to the borrowing processes, as mentioned above, is to decide what is more natural for a language – to borrow a foreign word or to create a new one using the native material. If we put the question this way (we are speaking in general, not considering any particular borrowing language that borrows words from a particular donor language), we should first rely on universal/system-independent naturalness.

5.2 System-independent naturalness

If we appeal to semiotics, in accordance with what we have said in Section 5.1., we are to presuppose the following scale of naturalness for borrowings (based on the notion of sign):

    Score 1: LTs
    Score 2: LRs
    Score 3: LCs
    Score 4: Analogical SLs
    Score 5: Substitutive SLs
    Score 6: Nativised direct borrowings
    Score 7: Non-nativised direct borrowings.

If, on the other hand, we appeal to system-independent naturalness theory, we should take into consideration certain principles of this theory, elaborated by Mayerthaler (1987: 48-50) (all principles are based on human perception):

(a) Principle of uniformity/biuniqueness. This principle presupposes the formula "one meaning – one form" and is based on biologically given preferences of the human brain for the uniform encoding which facilitates constant perception of objects.

(b) Principle of transparency states that a form is transparent if it obeys the principle of compositionality. Here we are to distinguish between:

- morphotactic transpatency which means the coincidence of the syllable boundaries with the morpheme boundaries;
- morphosemantic transparency which presupposes that the meaning of a complex word can be deduced from the meanings of its constituent parts.

(c) Principle of constructional iconicity: if (and only if) a semantically more marked category is encoded as more featured than a less marked category, the encoding is said to be iconic. Otherwise it is non-/countericonic. Human brain prefers iconic images.

The form is maximally unmarked if it fulfils all the above mentioned principles simultaneously. Otherwise, it is more or less marked. The principles mentioned above are given in the hierarchical order of priority.

Let us apply these principles to indirect borrowings:

Biuniqueness. Loan-formations (loan-translations, loan-renditions and loan-creations) are usually biunique. But the same can be said about direct borrowings which usually remain monosemic. Semantic loans, in their turn, are unique, and thus more ambiguous, and consequently less natural than the borrowings mentioned above.

Transparency. Morphotactically, loan-formations are usually quite transparent. We can speak about morphotactic transparency of semantic loans only in the case when they are complex words, but not when they are represented by simple words. As far as direct borrowings go, they usually lack morphotactic transparency and are seen as simple words. Morphosemantically, loan-formations usually have a high degree of transparency, while semantic loans may be less transparent (especially substitutive ones). Direct borrowings lack morphosemantic transparency at all.

Iconicity. We are to speak mainly of constructional iconicity which presupposes that addition in meaning should be paralleled by addition in form. From this point, loan-formations and direct borrowings are more iconic than semantic loans, in which addition in meaning is not paralleled by addition in form (no new words are created, but the existing words acquire new meanings). We may say that loan-renditions are less iconic than loan-translations, and loan-creations are the least iconic of the three. Semantic loans are rather non-iconic.

We may also add the principle of indexicality. This principles tells us that there should be direct reference of the signans (output) to the signatum (input). Optimally direct and close connection between signans and signatum is characteristic of a good index. As already mentioned above, all indirect and direct borrowings are indexes since they refer to their models in the source language. Loan-formations are good indexes as far as they show the above mentioned direct connection between signans and signatum. Loan-translations are the best indexes, loan-renditions are less indexical and loan-creations only indirectly refer to the model, and thus are bad indexes. Also direct borrowings show quite a good connection of the replica with the model. In semantic loans, as mentioned above, the new meaning acts as an index of the common, shared meanings in the model and the replica.

We may conclude, that the scale given above is valid also with respect to the principles of system-independent naturalness, though we may observe some changes in the bottom part of the scale:

Score 1: LTs are the most natural borrowings as far as they show high degree of iconicity, morphotactic and morphosemantic transparency and biuniqueness.

Score 2: LRs are less natural than LTs because they are less iconic than LTs, even though they may be equally transparent and biunique.

Score 3: LCs are even less natural than LTs and LRs since they are less iconic and have worse indexicality than that of LTs and LRs, even though they may be equally biunique and transparent.

Score 4 and 5: Direct borrowings (nativised and non-nativised) are less natural than LFs since they are morphotactically and morphosemantically opaque, even though they may be equally biunique and iconic.

Score 6 and 7: SLs (analogical and substitutive) are less natural than LFs and direct borrowings because, in the case of simple words, they totally lack morphosemantic and morphotactic transparency. But even if they are morphotactically and morphosemantically transparent (in the case of complex words), they are non-iconic and lack biuniqueness.

To resolve the problem of non-coincidence in the bottom parts of the naturalness scale based on the notion of sign and the naturalness scale based on the principles of system-independent naturalness, and arrive at a unified scale of naturalness, let us resort to the extralinguistic evidence. According to the Naturalness Theory, the things that are easier to handle for the human brain are more natural. Here we are to distinguish between the genotypical brain (the brain seen as an aspect of the human genotype [Universal Grammar]) and the phenotypical brain (the brain shaped in the course of acculturation in a given social and linguistic context [language-specific grammar]). What is more natural/easy for the human brain in general and what is more natural/easy for the brain of a speaker of a particular language and a member of a particular speech community – are two different things. In this section we are to speak about the genotypical brain.

All markedness relations are based on properties of the prototypical speaker which are biologically given and more or less culturally bound. If we speak about system-independent naturalness, we should consider first of all the biological core (human sensorium) and possibly exclude sociolinguistic factors. The more accessible any given entity is to the human sensorium, the less marked (more natural) it will be.

So, our prototypical speaker in this case will be a person who has a certain linguistic competence in his/her native language, but is hardly bilingual and even less so multilingual (as long as we are not talking about any particular donor language and borrowings may arrive from practically any language of the world).

Now we are to contemplate what is more natural for the kind of speaker we have described above – to borrow a foreign word or to create a new one in his/her own language to render describe a new notion.

We have mentioned that our speaker is hardly bilingual/multilingual, so every word of a foreign language, introduced in the borrowing language, let us say, by a translator, is a simple word for our prototypical speaker (he/she does not know any words, or morphemes, or morphological rules of the donor language, so he/she cannot analyse complex words and thus perceives them as simple).

Simple words are the hard core of storage. This means that they are not morphosemantically or morphotactically transparent, and they lack motivation. So they are more difficult to handle, especially if there is a large amount of them, because our memory has certain limits.

As we have mentioned, words have epistemological priority over morphemes, so we can hardly speak about borrowing of morphemes. Roberto Gusmani (1986: 137-165) insists that foreign morphemes penetrate into the borrowing language rather by induction than by simple borrowing. This means that when foreign words with one and the same morpheme (very likely a productive morpheme in the donor language) enter the borrowing language, these words may become analysable on the basis of this common morpheme. Thus, we cannot say that the morpheme was borrowed. It was rather induced in the recepient language from the borrowed words that with time became analysable.

If, on the other hand, rather than introducing a direct borrowing, a translator introduces an indirect one into the recepient language (a loan-translation, a loan-rendition or a loan-creation), the prototypical speaker is expected to have less difficulties in handling this item, as far as:

– it is formed with the help of the morphemes and according to the word-formation rules familiar to the prototypical speaker, so such a word is usually more transparent morphosemantically and morphotactically (it is motivated);
– it is biunique (at least at the moment when it is introduced);
– and it is very probably iconic.

As underlined by Kornexl (2003: 202), indirect borrowings possess a considerable amount of explanatory capacity, which is quite impossible in the case of direct borrowing.

As for semantic loans, they are easier to handle for the prototypical speaker than direct borrowings, since they are actually the words of his/her native language that he/she already knows (has in the storage). The speaker is only to add a new meaning and store it among the other meanings of a given word, whereas, in the case of direct borrowings, the speaker is not only to store a new meaning (or a shade of meaning), but he/she is also to store a new form (a foreign word), which is morphosemantically and morphotactically opaque.

So, speaking generally, probably indirect borrowings are less marked and more natural than direct one, since they seem to be more iconic and transparent. Another proof of this fact comes from the cases of popular etymology when speakers of a language, in search for transparency and iconicity, try to reinterpret a foreign word giving it motivation. This change is very natural, because it leads from what is more marked to what is less marked.

We must conclude, then, that in the light of system-independent naturalness (taking into account the notion of sign, system-independent principles of naturalness and external evidence), the scale of naturalness for borrowings is as follows:

Score 1: LTs
Score 2: LRs
Score 3: LCs
Score 4: Analogical SLs
Score 5: Substitutive SLs
Score 6: Nativised direct borrowings
Score 7: Non-nativised direct borrowings.

But if indirect borrowings are more natural, why do direct ones exist at all? The answer to this question lies in the following facts:

–   There exist naturalness conflicts, since within complex systems it is usually impossible to optimise several parameters simultaneously. For instance, semantic loans are indirect borrowings. They should be considered more natural than direct borrowings with regard to the parameter of linguistic economy, but on the parameter of biuniqueness a semantic loan, being a generator of polysemy, loses against a direct borrowing that is definitely more biunique. Or, in the case of *mildheortnes*, the indirect borrowing is morphotactically transparent, but morphosemantic transparency of the whole compound requires the sacrifice on the level of semantics of the constituent morphemes (the correspondence of the constituent parts of the model and the replica is not perfect).
–   There are also certain sociolinguistic and language-specific factors that influence the choice of one or another linguistic technique.

These factors are discussed below.

5.3 System-dependent naturalness

A concept of morphological naturalness based exclusively on system-independent factors is too narrow and often leads to incorrect predictions. Sometimes we come across certain morphological phenomena that do not differ in system-independent naturalness, but, nevertheless, speakers favour one of these phenomena. Here, system-dependent naturalness comes in play. Sometimes it may contradict universal morphological preferences.

In this section we are going to speak about the phenotypical brain (the brain shaped in the course of acculturation in a given social and linguistic context) and about what was more or less natural for the speaker of Old English and the speaker of Middle English, and not just for the speaker of any language.

In the Naturalness Theory, "unmarked" often means "frequent" and "marked" means "infrequent". Thus: more natural = less marked = more frequent (and viceversa, less natural = more marked = less frequent).

Let us first see the frequency of different types of indirect borrowings in Old English in Gneuss (1955) and in our data from the first book of the *Ecclesiastical history of the English people*:

In Gneuss (1955), out of 275 indirect borrowings:

- □ 103 are LTs;
- □ 82 are SLs;
- □ 79 are LRs;
- □ 11 are LCs.

In our data from the first book of the *Ecclesiastical history of the English people*, out of 153 supposed indirect borrowings:

- □ LTs are 65 (static) (77 dynamic);
- □ LRs are 46 (static) (34 dynamic);
- □ SLs are 23;
- □ LCs are 19.

Analysing this type frequency data we may say that the results obtained from Gneuss's data and from our data practically coincide. From the static as well as from the dynamic points of view, loan-translations are the most frequent type of indirect borrowings. Semantic loans must take the second place. Even if in our data they take the third place, this can be explained by the fact that our data is really limited for now and in our research we are more interested in loan-formations than in semantic loan. The third place is taken by loan-renditions, and loan-creations conclude the rating list. Thus, we have the following scale of naturalness for indirect borrowings in Old English based on type frequency:

        Score 1: LTs
        Score 2: SLs
        Score 3: LRs
        Score 4: LCs

With respect to the system-independent naturalness scale semantic loans have changed their place and have gone up the scale. Why so? Here, again, we are to find the answer in the conflict of naturalness parameters. We mentioned in Section 5.2. that semantic loans (analogical and substitutive) are less natural than loan-formations because they totally lack morphosemantic and morphotactic transparency, they are non-iconic and lack biuniqueness. But, on the other hand, we have to consider the principle of linguistic economy, and on this parameter semantic loans are much more natural than loan-formations because they do not create new words that have to be memorised/stored, but they use existing words, already stored in the memory of the speaker. Thus, the speaker has to memorise only a new meaning of an already existing word, and not a new word with a new meaning. So, we can see that in Old English the naturalness on the parameters of transparency, iconicity and biuniqueness is often sacrificed for the greater naturalness on the parameter of linguistic economy. This may also be connected with the fact that Old English is an inflecting/fusional language, and, according to Dressler, this language type is characterised by less iconicity, transparency and biuniqueness, i.e. these parameters are not valued very highly (1985: 342, 1987: 120, 2005: 278).

        Anyway, frequency considerations are not enough to state the degree of naturalness of a phenomenon. We are also to take into consideration different naturalness parameters that we have discussed in Section 5.2. and the principles of system-dependent naturalness.

        Wurzel (1987: 59-96) introduces two more principles for system-dependent naturalness in addition to those of system-independent naturalness discussed above:

–   system-congruity;
–   class-stability.

This principles have priority over system-independent principles, i.e. they rank higher.

5.3.1 System-congruity

When we speak about system-congruity, we must mention that any language has specific structural properties that determine its structural typology and distinguish it from other languages. These properties are called system-defining structural properties. When system-defining structural properties have been established, they form a classificatory matrix and it will be easy to determine to what extant individual morphological phenomena of the system correspond to them, that is to determine their system-congruity.

System-defining structural properties have a system-stabilising effect: languages always show the trend towards uniformity and decomposition of non-system-congruous phenomena.

Speakers of a language always favour those morphological phenomena which are intuitively more normal for them than others. Normalcy for a speaker depends on his/her linguistic experience, i.e. on the language-specific structural properties. So, normal also means the one that dominates in a given language and determines the structural typology of the language at a certain stage of its development. Properties that are most dominant are also most adequate/congruous for the system. Naturally, normalcy varies greatly from language to language, and also in diachrony, since a language may change its typology in time. We are to admit that what was normal for an Old English speaker, may not seem so normal to a Middle English speaker.

As mentioned above, indirect borrowings seem to be more natural than direct ones (from the point of view of system-independent naturalness). This reflects perfectly the situation in Old English, which abounds in indirect borrowings, and they are much more numerous than direct ones. But what is wrong with Middle English? Why does the language change the strategy and starts to prefer direct borrowings to indirect ones in the Middle English period? Why would a language change its strategy towards a less natural choice? This is the question that is to be answered with the help of Wurzel's system-dependent naturalness theory and typology.

In order to explain the difference regarding borrowing processes in Old and Middle English, we are to take into consideration:

- linguistic factors (typological differences between Old English and Middle English);
- extralinguistic factors (historical, sociolinguistic considerations).

Typological considerations are very important. We must mention that indirect borrowings (mainly, loan-translations, loan-renditions and loan-creations) have much to do with word-formation, since they are all complex words (derived or compound), created in Old English in order to render Latin models. So, we have to say something about naturalness in word-formation.

In Naturalness Theory word-formation is described in terms of word-formation rules which are represented by affixation or other operations such as conversion. The approach to word-formation is operational/procedural and functional. It stresses two main functions of the language:

- communicative function;
- cognitive function.

Word-formation serves both main functions.
Moreover, there are two specific main functions of word-formation:

- lexical enrichment: the formation of new words has to do with the cognitive function of language and is served best by labelling the concepts needed as precisely as possible;
- morphotactic (structural) and semantic motivation of existing words: it facilitates the communicative function as well as storage in memory and is performed best by very detailed description.

We may see that the consequences of the two functions (labelling and detailed description) come into conflict with one another, as far as the techniques very apt for labelling (the best being the coinage of simple names) are not very adequate descriptively, and good descriptive techniques are rather bad ways of labelling. Thus, there may be two situations:

- There are languages in which optimal labelling techniques are highly valued. This languages are usually of isolating type and have little word-formation. They use unmotivated terms, either inherited or loaned, and repetitive or abbreviatory devices.
- There are languages with high motivation. They are usually of polysynthetic/incorporating or introflecting type and tend to have rich word-formation.

Now let us use this information with regards to borrowing processes:

- in this respect, Old English (fusional/inflecting language) seems a language with high motivation and preference for descriptive techniques, and thus shows preference for indirect borrowings;
- whereas Middle English (already losing part of its fusional character and changing towards the isolating type) is a language with optimal labelling techniques and it prefers direct borrowings.

We may conclude that preference for descriptive techniques in word-formation is a system-defining structural property of Old English, while preference for labelling techniques is a system-defining structural property of Middle English. And in accordance with these system-defining structural properties, Old English and Middle English favour indirect and direct borrowings respectively.

New words are created in the language to satisfy the function of lexical enrichment. These words must be precise and reliable signs (biuniqueness is favoured) (Dressler 2005: 329-330). Indirect borrowings as well as direct borrowings tend to be biunique, so they are very reliable signs.

If we compare Modern English and Modern German (both are Germanic languages), we can see that German uses much more often the technique of indirect borrowing as compared to English (e.g., Engl. *television* vs. Germ. *Fernsehen*). Moreover, unlike in English, a great number of Old High German indirect borrowings "have apparently made their way into the common language and survived into Modern German." (Kornexl 2003: 209) This can hardly be explained with the help of extralinguistic factors. In this respect, a modern German speaker hardly differs much from an English speaker. The only extralinguistic factor that could have had some influence here is the want for purism in the language. Probably, the explanation lies in the fact, that German is a fusional/inflecting language that still prefers descriptive techniques, while Modern English is a language approaching the isolating type and thus it favours labelling techniques. The importance of taking into consideration the structure of the recipient language is also underlined by Diller who notes about the English verbs that "owing to morphological changes, especially the loss of the infinitive endings, the [English] language had become more hospitable to verbs of foreign origin." (2003: 59)

We can also observe the decomposition of non-system-congruous phenomena in Old English as well as in Middle English:

–   In Old English, direct borrowings that resulted to be non-system-congruous, sometimes were substituted by loan-creations or underwent the process of folk-etymology which gave motivation to unmotivated borrowed words and practically turned direct borrowings into indirect ones (see the case of *meregrot* and *mereswyn*, (a) and (b) in the list of Section 3).
–   Already in Middle English, many Old English motivated indirect borrowing were lost and substituted by direct borrowings (OE *mildheortnes* – ME *mercy*, OE *undeaðlicnes* – ME *immortality*).

Extralinguistic factors are also extremely important when we speak about the preference for certain borrowing processes. As Dressler notes, social factors are constitutive for language, and "they [extralinguistic factors] limit the choice of operations open to languages and favour/disfavour alternative operations" (1985: 288).

Let us compare the speaker of Old English and the speaker of Middle English, taking into consideration that we are interested in borrowing processes from Latin:

–   Old English speakers were the Anglo-Saxons who conquered the British Isles and were not really acquainted with Latin, since the Germanic tribes had never been conquered by the Roman Empire. Nevertheless, they had had some kind of contact with the speakers of Latin, because there were many Germans acting as mercenaries in the Roman Army and, of course, the Germans had some commercial contact with the Romans. But this influence can hardly be considered important and all-pervasive from the linguistic point of view. The British Romanised Celts were much more likely bilingual because their territory was conquered by the Romans and was made a part of the Roman Empire for a certain period. Latin was the language of the government and of the higher stratum of society, and everybody who wanted to improve his/her life had to learn Latin. When the Anglo-Saxons arrived in the British Isles in the 5th century they drove the Romanised Celts to the remote areas of the islands, so we cannot say that there was a close contact situation between the two tribal units which could have resulted in extensive lexical borrowing processes from the Celtic dialects or from Latin via the Romanised Celts into the Anglo-Saxon dialects. Thus, we can conclude that the Anglo-Saxons who lived in the British Isles were the speakers of Old English with a very limited (if any) knowledge of Latin, this knowledge mainly originating from the fact that Latin was the language of the church after Christianity was introduced into Anglo-Saxon society. As Otto Jespersen remarks: "People did not know so much Latin as they learned later, so these learned words, if introduced, would not have been understood." (1952: 44) And in addition he cites the words of Alfred the Great: "there were very few on this side of the Humber who could understand their [Latin] rituals." (Jespersen 1952: 44) Then he concludes: "it is rather the natural thing for a language to utilise its own resources before drawing on other languages." (Jespersen 1952: 44) But the thing is not as easy as it sounds. Here the term "natural" is definitely used in the sense of intuitively plausible and has nothing to do with the value it has today in Natural Linguistics. Furthermore, the capacity of the language to rely on its own resources prior to borrowing foreign words depends greatly on the particular extralinguistic situation and on the characteristics of the speakers of a given language.

–   As for the Middle English speakers, they witnessed the Norman Invasion and the introduction of French as the language of administration, court and army. Thus, French was much more institutionalised in the English society of that time, than Latin in Old English. Everybody who wanted to achieve something in life had to learn French. However, we cannot really speak about bilingualism here. Fischer remarks that "the native speakers of French never amounted to more than ten per cent of the population and bilingualism was not widespread." (2003: 109) Even less can be said about Latin, because in this case "we have an exceptional contact situation, the donor being a 'dead', though highly prestigious language, universally used in the church and functioning as the main idiom of learning in Anglo-Saxon England."

(Kornexl 2003: 196) The prestige of Latin was indisputable. Later, during the period of the Renaissance, "some, indeed, felt that English was in any case not an appropriate vehicle for the expression of the new learning." (Crystal 2005: 60) Crystal also discusses the 16th c. controversy over the use of foreign words in English and lists the supporters of foreign terms (e.g., Thomas Elyot, George Pettie) as well as the opponents (e.g., Thomas Wilson, John Cheke). Whatever the reasons are, "most of the native coinages invented by contemporary writers as alternatives to Latin loans have failed to survive." (Crystal 2005: 61) Moreover, from the 12th c. on we observe the growth of literacy in England. Schools were established in may towns and cities. Some were grammar schools independent of the Church, while others were attached to a cathedral. All of these schools taught Latin, because most books were written in this language. Latin was important, because it was the educated language of almost all Europe, and was therefore useful in the spread of ideas and learning. As already mentioned above, Latin was seen as a richer language than English or any other European language. So, probably the growth of literacy increased also the knowledge of Latin among the population of the country. And this growth continued in the following centuries, especially after the introduction of printing by William Caxton.

The above mentioned facts enable us to propose some conclusions:

–   For the Old English speakers, who were predominantly monolingual and little (if at all) acquainted with Latin, it must have been easier to deal with indirect borrowings rather than with direct ones. Probably, the presence of so many indirect borrowings in Old English is also justified by the fact that the main purpose of the translators at that time was to explain the things that otherwise remained unapprehended, whereas in the later periods "the main factor responsible for borrowing was not the need of the recipient language for new terms and concepts, but the desire to adorn the language" (Diller 2003:64). And this desire was satisfied by borrowing words directly from the highly admired Latin language;

–   For the Middle English speakers, who probably possessed greater literacy and were more acquainted with Latin, the situation changed. Latin, being a dead language, was mostly written and read. So, Latin words were mostly imported by educated people and for educated people. Latin words, morphemes and word-formation rules probably did not seem to an educated Middle English speaker so strange and foreign as they might have seemed to an Old English speaker. Even if they did, he/she had to cope with the situation. Thus, not all of the Latin words were seen as simple, non-transparent and unmotivated. This resulted in the fact that, through the knowledge of Latin, Latin words acquired transparency and motivation for educated Middle English speakers, and consequently there was less necessity to create new words in the native language to translate the new notions introduced by Latin terms. These terms were borrowed directly and did not present so much difficulty in handling them as it seemed to be the case in Old English.

We may say, that the Middle English preference for direct borrowings is rather unnatural from the point of view of system-independent naturalness, but it might be quite natural from the point of view of system-dependent naturalness.

If we take a look at the situation in sciences nowadays, we shall see that there are a lot of terms borrowed from foreign languages directly. Why so? Again, these terms may be absolutely opaque or even unknown to a layman, but quite transparent for a specialist in a certain field. Due to globalization, scientists and students of different scientific disciplines are nowadays quite bilingual, so it is not a problem for them to deal with foreign terms. Students of languages and computer programmers quite often use the techniques of code switching and code mixing properly due to their advanced bilingualism/multilingualism. Thus, bilingualism is a very strong extralinguistic factor that promotes the usage of the technique of direct borrowing. Unfortunately, we cannot rely on this factor while speaking about the history of English, since the situation of the past is not really clear and we have to rely only on written records which were preserved.

Prestige is another important extralinguistic factor that plays an important role in the preference for direct borrowings. When, having at our disposal a native equivalent term, we prefer to use a foreign one, we want to underline our acquaintance with a foreign language and its terminology (foreign terms often sound to us "more scientific" than native ones). Thus, to some extent, using foreign terms we are "boasting" of our competence in a foreign language.

5.3.2 Class stability

If we turn our attention to class stability, we should say that Wurzel's class stability has to do with inflectional morphology. All words according to their inflectional-morphological properties can be grouped into inflectional classes. Depending on what type of paradigm structure conditions hold for the respective inflectional classes, Wurzel (1987: 80) singles out:

- stable inflectional classes: classes whose paradigms follow the implicative pattern of a paradigm structure condition which exclusively applies or dominates the words with respective extramorphological properties;
- unstable inflectional classes: classes whose paradigms follow an implicative pattern which does not agree with the paradigm structure condition which dominates words having the respective extramorphological properties;

- stability-indifferent inflectional classes: classes of words with extra-morphological properties which lack a dominant paradigm structure condition.

The dominant paradigm structure conditions determine the direction of class changes in the inflectional system. There is a strong trend towards decomposing unstable and stability-indifferent inflectional classes. The transition from unstable to stable complementary classes normally happens by word-by-word transferral.

With respect to borrowings, we may suggest that there are two classes of borrowings:

- direct borrowings (subclasses: loam-translations, loan-renditions, loan-creations, analogical and substitutive semantic loans);
- indirect borrowings (subclasses: nativised and non-nativised direct borrowings).

In Old English, the most stable subclass is that of loan-translations. The other subclasses are unstable. In Middle English, the most stable class is that of nativised direct borrowings, other subclasses being unstable.

Also here we may observe the tendency towards decomposition of unstable classes. The analysis of Gneuss's data reveals that very often in Old English there were several attempts at indirect borrowing of certain words from Latin: certain semantic loans were accompanied by the attempts at loan-translation or loan-rendition (see Gneuss [1955], numbers 24, 25, 26, 36, 41, 85); loan-renditions accompanied by attempts at loan-tranaslation (Gneuss [1955], numbers 26, 97, 121, 133); loan-creations accompanied by attempts at loan-translartion (Gneuss [1955], number 145). From our data we may add that direct borrowings were often substituted by loan-creations (see (a) and (b) in the list of Section 3). So, there is an evident tendency towards decomposition of unstable classes of loan-renditions, semantic loans and loan-creations in favour of the stable class of loan-translations, and of direct borrowings in favour of loan-creations.

In Middle English, we witness the decomposition of the unstable class of non-nativised borrowings in favour of the stable class of nativised borrowings (e.g., *antennae > antennas*).

It is evident that stable classes act as attractors for the members of unstable classes.

5.3.3 Naturalness in word-formation

If we return to the question of naturalness in word-formation, we may add that determinative compounds, possessing great diagrammatic iconicity, are very frequent among loan-formations in Old English (e.g., *wingeard*, *sæwiht*, *mereswyn*, *meregreot*, *sealtseap*, etc.). As far as derivation goes, the majority of loan-formations are created by means of affixation, the most iconic derivational technique. The usage of non-iconic conversion in loan-formations in Old English is rather rare (e.g., *unterðeod*) as compared to affixation. Anti-iconic subtraction is encountered rarely in loan-formations (e.g., *forðgeong* from *forðgangan*).

We may conclude that, with regard to the parameter of iconicity, Old English favours more natural word-formation rules in the process of indirect borrowing.

As far as morphosemantic and morphotactic transparency goes, Old English compound loan-formations always aim at maximal transparency (both members of a compound must be transparent: e.g., *wingeard*, *sæwiht*, *mereswyn*, *sealtseaþ*, etc.). Again, let us turn our attention to the case of *mildheortnes* (see example (1)), where *mildheort* is morphosemantically more transparent/motivated than the alternative *earmheort*. The meaning of *mildheort* seems better predictable than that of *earmheort*; that is why it wins out over *earmheort*.

This tendency towards transparency and iconicity results in some cases in what is called above redundant formations, as well as in popular etymology. See again the case of *meregrot* ((b) in the list of Section 3): *mere* 'sea, ocean' + *grot/greot* 'particle, sand' is morphotactically transparent. Morphosemantically, it is probably not so transparent (it seems rather metaphoric), but still it is better than a completely opaque direct borrowing.

Old English derivational loan-formations also strive for maximal transparency. And of course the semantic transparency of the head is more important here than that of the non-head: in loan-formations affixes sometimes seem to be used randomly and are often ambiguous.

References

Bosworth, Joseph – T. Northcote Toller
    1898   *An Anglo-Saxon dictionary*. Oxford: Clarendon Press. Available at:
        http://www.beowulf.engl.uky.edu/~kiernan/BT/bosworth.htm (date of
        access: 28 January 2010).
Castiglioni, Luigi – Scevola Mariotti
    2007   *Il vocabolario della lingua Latina*. (4th edition). Milano: Loescher.
    [1966]
Crystal, David
    2005   *The Cambridge encyclopedia of the English language*. (2nd edition).
    [1995]   Cambridge: Cambridge University Press.
Diller, Hans-Jürgen
    2003   "Verbs of verbal communication in the English Renaissance: a lexical
    [2001]   field under language contact", in: Kastovsky, Dieter – Arthur Mettinger
        (eds.), 57-68.

Dressler, Wolfgang U.
    1985   *Morphonology: The dynamics of derivation.* Ann Arbor: Karoma
                Publishers.
    1987   "Word-formation as part of natural morphology", in: Dressler, W. (ed.),
                99-126.
    2005   "Word-formation in natural morphology", in: Pavol, S. & R. Lieber
                (eds.), 267-284.
Dressler, Wolfgang U. (ed.)
    1987   *Leitmotifs in natural morphology.* Amsterdam, Philadelphia: John
                Benjamins.
Fischer, Andreas
    2003   "Lexical borrowing in the history of English: a typology of typologies",
    [2001]   in: Kastovsky, Dieter – Arthur Mettinger (eds.), 97-115.
Gneuss, Helmut
    1955   *Lehnbildungen und Lehnbedeutungen in Altenglischen.* Berlin: Erich
                Schmidt.
Gusmani, Roberto
    1986   *Saggi sull'interferenza linguistica.* (2nd edition). Firenze: Le Lettere.
    [1981]
Hall, John R. Clark
    1916   *A concise Anglo-Saxon dictionary.* (2nd edition). New York: Macmillan
    [1894]   Company.
Hogg, Richard M. (ed.)
    1992   *Cambridge history of the English language.* Vol. 1. Cambridge: Cam-
                bridge University Press.
Jespersen, Otto
    1952   *Growth and structure of the English language.* Oxford: Basil Blackwell.
Kastovsky, Dieter
    1992   "Semantics and vocabulary", in: Hogg, Richard M. (ed.), 290-408.
Kastovsky, Dieter – Arthur Mettinger (eds.)
    2003   *Language contact in the history of English.* (2nd edition). Frankfurt am
                Main: Peter Lang.
Kornexl, Lucia
    2003   "*Unnatural words*? Loan-formations in Old English glosses", in:
    [2001]   Kastovsky Dieter – Arthur Mettinger (eds.), 195-216.
Mayerthaler, Willi
    1987   "Systen-independent morphological naturalness", in: Dressler, Wolfgang U.
                (ed.), 15-58.
Miller, Thomas
    1959-1963   *The Old English version of "Bede's ecclesiastical history of the English
                people".* London: Oxford University Press.
Panagl, Oswald
    1987   "Productivity and diachronic change in morphology", in: Dressler,
                Woldgang U. (ed.), 127-151.

Plummer, Charles
    1961   *Venerabilis Baedae opera historica*. Oxford: Oxford University Press.
    [1896]
Serjeantson, Mary
    1935   *History of foreign words in English*. London: Routledge and Kegal Paul.
Štekauer, Pavol – Rochelle Lieber (eds.)
    2005   *Handbook of word-formation*. Dordrecht: Springer.
Sweet, Henry
    1940   *The student's dictionary of Anglo-Saxon*. Oxford: Clarendon Press.
Taylor, Ann – Anthony Warner – Susan Pintzuk – Frank Beths (eds.)
                The York-Toronto-Helsinki Parsed Corpus of Old English prose.
                Available at: http://ota.oucs.ox.ac.uk/headers/2462.xml.
Weinreich, Uriel
    1964   *Languages in contact: findings and problems*. London, the Hague, Paris:
    [1953]   Mouton & Co.
Wurzel, Wolfgang U.
    1987   "System-dependent morphological naturalness in inflection", in: Dressler,
                Wolfgang U. (ed.), 59-96.

Why *ANGER* and *JOY*? Were *TĒNE* and *BLISS* not good enough?

Hans-Jürgen Diller, Ruhr-Universität Bochum

ABSTRACT

Joy (from Old French) and *anger* (from Old Norse) are clearly cases of "Foreign influence on Medieval English". But equally clearly the concepts which they represent were already represented in the Old English lexicon, as *blisse* (joy) and *tēona* or *wræþþu* (anger, wrath).

It seems reasonable to ask why the native words were replaced by foreign ones. To answer this question evidence has been collected from the quotations in *MED* online <http://quod. lib.umich.edu/m/med/>, probably the most comprehensive and balanced representation of Middle English. The tokens found are analysed according to word formation patterns and syntactic contexts. The sense development of *ANGER* and its family from 'sadness' to 'anger, irritation' is traced and explained in terms of the socio-psychological concepts of 'goal frustration' and 'status violation'. The establishment of both *ANGER* and *JOY* in the English emotion vocabulary testifies to a growing importance of the contrast between the human subject as experiencer and the conditions of the subject's experience.

KEYWORDS: *anger, tēne, joy, blisse/bless*, context, emotions, loanwords, *Middle English Dictionary* online, parts of speech, semipelagianism, word formation

We regard our emotions as perhaps the most fundamental part of our psychological makeup – certainly much more fundamental than concepts. And anger and joy are clearly among the most fundamental. Darwin ([1872] 1998) has taught us to recognize emotions in our animal cousins, but the idea that animals might form concepts still seems strange to most of us. A change in emotion labels suggests a very thoroughgoing re-interpretation which cries out for an explanation. But before we can even begin to identify the causes of such changes, we must try to find out how they took place. With the technical means available today, the best way to do this is a quotation search of the electronic *MED* ("*MED* online", "*eMED*") <http://quod.lib.umich.edu/m/med/>. *MED* online is no doubt the most searchable, the most comprehensive and probably the most balanced representation of ME that we have. To harvest it is fairly easy. You just key in your search strings in the appropriate boxes. You must spend some thought, though, on the selection of the search strings – ME spelling variants being what they are. Still, the much more laborious and error-prone part of the operation consists in separating the wheat from the chaff. When we have eliminated all our spurious matches and multiple matches we may be left with anything between 70 and 7 % of the original intake. Unfortunately, the wealth of data which the *eMED* can provide is not without negative consequences. It requires a very detailed analysis of a very small selection of lexemes.

The structure of the paper is practically pre-ordained by the title. It will be divided into two main sections:

(1) *TĒNE* and *ANGER*
(2) *BLISS* and *JOY.*

Within each of these sections I will analyse parts of speech and word formation as well as syntactic contexts. The order of these sub-sections will vary according to the special characteristics of each word family.

1. *TĒNE* and *ANGER*

Table 1 shows the highly uneven distribution of *TĒNE* and *ANGER* in prose and verse, a point to which we will return in passing (for a fuller treatment cf. Diller forthcoming b).[1]

Table 1. *ANGER* and *TĒNE* in MED quotations

	verse	prose	total	ratio
TĒNE	525	88	613	6 : 1
1150-1299	23	40	63	0.6 : 1
1300-1600	502	48	550	10.5 : 1
ANGER	320	235	555	1.4 : 1
1150-1299	0	5	5	0 : 5
1300-1600	320	230	550	1.4 : 1

1.1. Parts of speech and word formation

Table 2 and Figure 1 show the various Parts of Speech and Word-Formation patterns that are generated by *TĒNE* and *ANGER*. Table 2 shows that both bases are used in broadly the same structures, whereas Figure 1 makes it very clear that there are certain quantitative differences, which will turn out to be highly significant.

---

1   A similar discrepancy between ME prose and verse can be observed for *mōd*. For its demise in ME prose cf. Diller (2006: 61; 2007a: 18–20; 2008a: 51); for its continuing use in ME poetry cf. Diller (2007b: 130).

Table 2. *TĒNE* and *ANGER*: POS, Word Formation

	pattern[2]	TĒNE		ANGER	
1.	n	tene	421	anger	281
2.	(n)n	tenereden	1	angernesse	1
3.	(n)aj	teneful	29	angerful	8
4.	(n)av		0	angerly	11
5.	((n)aj)av	tenefully	8	angerfully	1
6.	aj	tene	14	angry/i	132
7.	(aj)n		0	angriness	5
8.	(aj)av	tenely	2	angre/ily	14
9.	av	tene	1		0
10.	v	tenen	131	angren	100
11.	(v)av		0	angurdly	2
12.	(V)ing	tening	4		0
13.	?		3		1
14.	**Total**		**614**		**556**
15.	**aj+av**		**54**		**146**

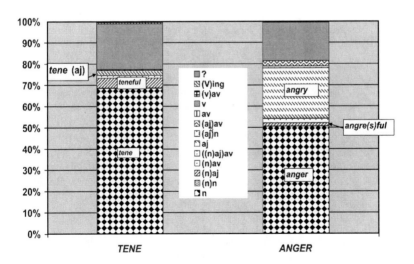

Figure 1. *TĒNE* and *ANGER* in *MED* quotations: percentages of POS and word formation patterns

---

2 Pattern notation: Expression within parentheses: POS of simple lexeme; expression after closing parenthesis: POS generated by suffix.

For both bases the simple noun is by far the most common structure, but the adjectives are more interesting. This is chiefly due to the importance of *angry*, but *tēneful* and *angerful* also deserve a comment. *Angerful*, in spite of its rarity, has considerable diagnostic value for the semantic difference between *anger* and *tēne*. *Angerful* always means 'full of sorrow or anxiety', never 'full of anger' in the modern sense. It thus testifies to the precedence of the 'passive' sense of *anger*, which tallies with the evidence of ON (cf. Zoëga [1910] 2004; Diller forthcoming a). It describes a passive emotion rather than an active one, and it describes the state of the Experiencer of that emotion.

For *angry* the *MED* lemma does give a second sense which is glossed, *int. al.*, as 'noisome, vexing', in which it colligates with the Causer rather than the Experiencer, but my survey of *MED* quotations yielded only five attributive adjectives that could be glossed as 'anger-causing' – exactly one-ninth of all occurrences. With *tēneful*, on the other hand, the causative sense is the usual one. This will become even clearer when we consider the syntactic contexts, to which we will turn in sub-section 1.2.

1.2. Syntactic contexts

1.2.1. Contexts of the adjectives

Since I have already dealt with the adjectives at some length, I will continue with them. For reasons of time and space I will confine myself to attributive adjectives. I have tried to categorize the nouns taking those attributes. The result can be seen in Table 3.

The broad categories of Table 3 are of course open to debate. But one thing should emerge very clearly: the nouns taking *angry* as an attribute, the 'carriers' of anger so to speak, form a highly unified group. Almost half of them (12+3+7=22) designate human beings, another 18 (7+11) are closely related to human beings. The group of "others" amounts to only one-ninth of the total 45. Like *angerful*, *angry* describes the state of mind of people or, even more commonly, their mental disposition. The noun phrases represented by Table 3 are clear evidence of what at the end of Section 1.1 we could only suspect: the typical 'carrier' of anger is the human person – in marked contrast to *tēne*, where the "others" make up almost one-half (10 out of 19).

Tēne is typically not what a person experiences, but what is done, or rather may be done, to a person. Whether the 'thing-done-to' is actually experienced is another matter and not really part of the meaning of the phrase. One example must suffice to illustrate this point: There is a *tenefull toure* in the alliterative *Wars of Alexander*, whose inmates have their hands and feet cut off – surely enough to inspire *tēne*, in this case dread or fear.

Table 3. (Designates of) nouns taking *angry* or *tene(ful)* as an attribute

Categories	exemplars			
	angry		*tene(ful)*	
1. human beings	*man, men*	12		0
	folk	3		0
	cook, daughter, niggard, sire, waster, wife, wight	7	warrior (*wye*)[3]	1
2. (products of) human activities	bite, chiding, dream, fight (*stour*), language, trick (*jape*), word	7	*labour* (2), *travail, tale* (2), text (*tixte*), touch	7
3. parts or aspects of the human person	face (*cheere* 3, *visage* 1) heart (3, + 1 *corage*), mood (2), snout (1)	11	*tach* [=nature, disposition], disease	2
4. others	beast, fates (*Parcas*), manner (*wise*), thing, wound	5	event (*þynges* [=pagan statues crumbling]), place (**tene**), thicket (**tene greue**), time, tool, tooth (a bear's), tower (2), way	9
Sum		**45**		**19**

Þare was a tenefull toure & tulkis in-closid:
Sum ware þe handis of-hewen [=had their hands cut off], & sum [þe] hoȝes [=heels] [wantid];
Sum þe eȝen, sum þe eres & egirly cries
On Alexsandire eftir help, & he þam all liuers [delivers, frees].
He wepis on þam for wa, said, 'wa is me, my childire!'
And of his talentis he takis ten thousand [ilkane].
(Duggan and Turville-Petre (eds.), ll. 3276–3281 [= Skeat (ed.), ll. 3149–3154])

1.2.2. Contexts of the nouns

The noun contexts are shown in Table 4. Their number is far too large to be exhausted in this paper. I begin with a general observation, which formally is in stark contrast to what we have seen in Table 3, though semantically it points in the same direction: while the adjective *angry* has a strong preference for a small group of well-defined contexts, the noun *anger*, by contrast, occurs far less often than *tēne*, but in more than twice as many contexts.

---

3   Italics: original ME words, roman: ModE equivalents.

Table 4. Contexts of the nouns *ANGER* and *TĒNE* in *MED* quotations

	Slot/construction	ANGER			Total Slot/constr.	TĒNE		
1.	**Pat**			2	**2**			
2.	**Pred**			5	**5**			
3.	**PrepPhr**	1.	after	1				
4.		2.	by	3				
5.		3.	for	58		1.	for	47
6.		4.	from	5		2.	from	10
7.		5.	in	57		3.	in	40
8.		6.	in(to)			4.	in(to)	5
9.		7.	into			5.	into	2
10.		8.	of	45		6.	of	39
11.		9.	(full of	1)[4]		7.	(full of	3)
12.		10.	out of	3		8.		
13.		11.	through	1				
14.		12.	to	4			*to*	*39*
15.		13.	(until	1)				
16.		14.	upon	1				
17.		15.	with	23		9.	with	46
18.	**Total PrepPhr**	16.	without	1	**202**			**228**
19.	**oj**	17.	avenge	2		10.	*avenge*	*10*
20.						11.	avoid	3
21.		18.	cause	1				
22.		19.	*cease*	*1*				
23.		20.	charge	1				
24.		21.	*destroy*	*1*				
25.		22.	*do*	*1*		12.	*do*	*30*
26.		23.	*endure*	*1*				
27.		24.	*expel*	*2*				
28.		25.	*feel*	*1*				
29.		26.	forget	1				
30.						13.	*forgive*	*3*
31.		27.	give	1				
32.		28.	have	9		14.	have	9
33.		29.	*leave*	*1*				
34.		30.	*let (fall)*	*2*				
35.		31.	*remove*	*1*				

4   Categories within parentheses are subsets of those immediately above and do not affect the total.

Table 4. Continued

	Slot/construction	ANGER			Total Slot/constr.	TĒNE			
36.		32.	*restrain*	*4*					
37.		33.	send	1					
38.		34.	*show*	*1*					
39.		35.	suffer	9		15.	suffer, sustain	11	
40.						16.	tell	9	
41.						17.	temper	1	
42.						18.	*timber*	*4*	
43.	**(Total oj.)**	36.	'work'	2	**43**	19.	*work*	*5*	**85**
44.	**sj**	37.	achieve	1					
45.		38.	be	9		20.	be	22	
46.		39.	befall	2					
47.		40.	begin	2					
48.						21.	betide	8	
49.		41.	cause	2					
50.		42.	cleanse	1					
51.						22.	come	1	
52.		43.	dwell	1					
53.		44.	enter	1		23.	enter	1	
54.		45.	gain	1					
55.		46.	go	1					
56.		47.	grieve	1		24.	grieve	1	
57.		48.	harm	1					
58.		49.	hit	1					
59.		50.	kindle	1					
60.		51.	overcome	2					
61.		52.	pass over	1					
62.		53.	show	1					
63.						25.	suffice	1	
64.		54.	tear (one's heart)	1					
65.		55.	terrify	1					
66.						26.	touch	1	
67.						27.	turn	3	
68.	**(Total sj)**	56.	wear out	1	**32**				**38**
69.	**Total**	57.		**284**	**284**			**351**	**351**

The most characteristic co-texts of *TĒNE* are printed in bold. Perhaps most significantly, *TĒNE* is twice as frequent in object position as *ANGER*, whereas in subject position the two nouns are about equal (cf. ll. 43 and 68). There is, however, a largish group of semantically related verbs which take only *anger* as an object. They are printed in italics in ll. 22ff.: *cease, destroy, endure, expel, feel, forget, leave, let* or *let fall, remove, restrain,* perhaps also *show.*

All these findings, I submit, point in the same direction: *TĒNE* is usually caused directly and often intentionally: if you inflict it on someone, that person will suffer it. In that respect it is like wounding or hurting. When the *MED* staff posited 'injury' as the first sense of *TĒNE*, they were probably aware of this.

With *ANGER* things are a little more complex: the Experiencers of anger are conceived of as intermediaries who have the freedom to choose their own reaction. As we have just seen, they can endure, restrain, or even expel their anger.

This leads us back to Table 1, which showed the distribution of both words in prose and verse. The home ground of *ANGER* is the field of religious instruction, which was largely written in prose, especially in its more ambitious parts.

TĒNE, after 1300, is virtually restricted to poetry especially narrative poetry.

1.3. Conclusion and interpretation

There is one aspect of the meanings of both word families which was briefly mentioned and which is amply documented in the lemmas of the *MED*, but which looks somewhat strange from the point of view of modern psychology. Both *TĒNE* and *ANGER* mean sadness or distress, as well as fear or anxiety – and anger in the modern sense. Nearly all the taxonomies which psychologists have derived from their experiments make a firm distinction between these three (Schwarz and Ziegler 1996: esp. Tabelle 1). Were our medieval ancestors less aware of these differences which seem so obvious to us?

The differences between them and us may be more apparent than real. First of all, we must remember that modern psychological experiments reflect intro-spective accounts, while narrative and instructive texts will reflect outsiders' observations. Secondly, there is also experimental evidence of a considerable overlap between fear, sadness, and anger (Shaver et al. 1987: 1069 and 1071, Figures 2 and 3). There is also linguistic evidence of a 'fuzzy' borderline between sadness and anger (Gevaert 2007: 27, 253 n.7): "I was saddened by your behaviour." is a common euphemism for "You've made me angry."

And Anna Wierzbicka has applied her "Natural Semantic Metalanguage" to an impressive array of "cognitive emotion scenarios". Her scenarios for *Sad* and *Angry* (1999: 62, 88–89) differ basically in only two respects: *angry* implies that "Someone has done something bad" and "I want to do something because of this", while *sad* implies only that "Something bad has happened" and "I know I can't do anything". In terms of semantic primes, the difference is thus not as great as it feels. Wierzbicka finds support in an earlier and even more distinguished witness: in the *Summa Theologica* of Thomas Aquinas.

> Causatur enim ira ex malo difficili jam injacente; ad cujus praesentiam necesse est quod aut appetitus succumbat, et sic non exit terminos **tristitiae** ...: aut habet motum ad invadendum malum læsivum, quod pertinet ad **iram**.
>
> [... what causes anger is some evil which will be hard to avert and which is already at hand. Then the orexis either capitulates, and the only emotion experienced is that of **sadness**, ...; or there is an impulse to attack the evil that threatens, and this is **anger**]. (Thomas [1265–1274] 1967. 26/27 (1a.2æ. 23,3))

Anger seems to presuppose a stronger, more powerful individual than sadness.

2. *JOY* and *BLISS*

2.1. Parts of speech and word formation

Trying to compare the parts of speech and the word formation patterns of *BLISS* and *JOY* (Figure 2) with those of *TĒNE* and *ANGER* (Figure 1), we are immediately faced with one of the vagaries of the form / meaning nexus. The sequence of *b, l, i/y, s, s* reappears in two verbs which the *MED* rightly treats as two different lemmas: *bliss(i)en* 'to be in bliss'(<OE *blissian*) and *blessen* 'to bless' (<OE *blētsian*). The latter was found about 2200 times in the *MED* quotations; nearly 1300 instances are spelt with *e*, almost 1000 with *i* or *y*. It is clear that *BLESSEN* does not belong in our topic, but it must also be clear that it is not always easy to decide under which lemma the string *b, l, i/y, s, s* should be subsumed when it occurs in a quotation outside these lemmas. The semantic similarity of the two verbs is evident from the *MED*'s definitions of the senses of *blessen*: two of them (1b, 3a) explicitly contain the elements *bliss* or *happy*, others imply them. For texts existing in more than one version it is quite common to spell the same word-token with *e* in one version and with *i or y* in others. Clearly, for many scribes the boundary between the two lexemes was quite blurred.

Figure 2, which represents only forms with *i* or *y*, endeavours to give an accurate representation of the two lexemes and finds 937 instances of *blissen* 'to bless' against only 62 forms of *blissen* 'to be in bliss', *i.e.* a ratio of about 15:1. A similar picture of strong disparity emerges from a comparison of the two lemmas, which contain 136 and 21 records respectively. *i.e.* a ratio of about 6.5:1. There is strong evidence that a desire to avoid the connotations of blessing led to the early demise of *BLISS(I)EN* and its replacement by *JOYEN* and possibly other verbs. To reliably discriminate between the two lexemes would require more detailed analysis, but the fact that the last witnesses of the *MED* lemma *blissen* (<OE *blissian*) should be from the West and from the early 13th century (*Owl and Nightingale*, Layamon's *Brut*) points in the same direction.

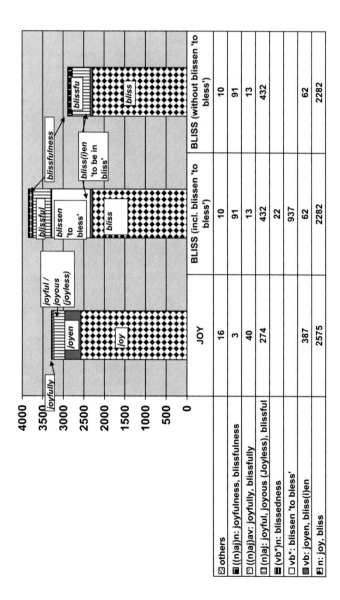

Figure 2. JOY and BLISS in MED quotations: POS and word formation patterns

In spite of the difficulties mentioned, there is one criterion which, whenever applicable, makes for a clear-cut distinction: *BLISSEN* 'to bless' is a transitive or reflexive verb whereas *BLISS(I)EN* 'to be in bliss', like *JOYEN*, is intransitive. In this respect the two verbs which genuinely designate positive emotions show an interesting difference from *ANGREN* and *TĒNEN*, which are both transitive. Angering someone else seems to be a more natural idea than to 'joy' someone. To make someone happy (especially one's husband or wife) is a common enough notion in the 18th and 19th century novel (Diller 2008b: 120–124). In the Middle Ages there seems to be little need for such an expression; perhaps to bestow happiness or bliss is the prerogative of God.

The blurring of *BLISS(I)EN* and *BLESSEN* is also shown by the fact that *blissedness* (in 22 *MED* quotations) is used synonymously with *blissfulness* (in 91). Both are often used to translate Latin *beatitudo*. *Blissful* and *joyful*, by contrast, are clearly distinct. An abstract noun derived from *joyful* or *joyous* was found only three times,[5] and while *blissful* colligates freely with nouns like *passion, body,* or *arms, joyful* and *joyous* do not. The difference is similar to one found in section 1: while the adjectives derived from *joy* designate only the experiencers of the emotion, *blissful* also designates its causes. The reality behind these syntactic peculiarities hardly needs to be spelt out: the blissful passion, body and arms are of course those of Christ, sometimes of his mother.

2.2. Syntactic contexts

When we look at the contexts of *JOY* and *BLISS* we find many commonalities, but also a few significant differences. The commonalities are unsurprising, most of them have already been noted by students of emotion metaphors, from Zoltán Kövecses to Małgorzata Fabiszak. I will begin with the verbs taking either of these nouns as objects, then turn to the prepositions.

---

5   c1450 *Spec.Chr.(2)* (Hrl 6580) 204/24 (*ioyfulnes*, s.v. 'hou'); ?c1450 *Knt.Tour-L.*(Hrl 1764) 128/29 (*Ioyeuseie*, s.v. 'Ioyeuseie'); a1475 *Cato(2)* (Rwl G.59) 77 (*ioyausnesse*, s.v. 'ioyausnesse').

2.2.1. Verbs taking *JOY* and/or *BLISS* as objects

Table 5. Verbs taking *JOY* and/or *BLISS* as objects[6]

oj. JOY		oj. BLISS	
have	272	*have*	143
make	128	*give*	39
give	34	*earn*	30
lose	26	*lose*	23
see	23	bring	19
kindle	19	*make*	18
betoken	13	*buy*	12
find	11	see	9
grant	9	*grant*	9
[send]	8	*find*	8
earn	7	*promise*	7
feel	7	*find*	7
forsake	7	*deserve*	7
promise	7	desire, covet, crave	9
send	7	*receive*	7
receive	6	announce	6
take	6	enjoy	6
tell	6	forsake	6
arrange	5	seek	6
increase	5	bear	5
		forego	5
		forfeit	5
		get	5
		leave	5
announce	2	show	5
buy	2	take	5
deserve	2	feel	4
		- 224 -	
		increase	4
...		...	
Total:	**771**		**493**

Among verbs taking *BLISS* and/or *JOY* as objects, *HAVE* leads by a long distance. Only *DO* with obj. *TĒNE* is comparable (cf. Table 4). This is remarkable in itself

---

6   The table lists only a selection, hence the sum of the verbs is less than the total in the bottom line.

and distinguishes these nouns from *TĒNE* and *ANGER*: *BLISS* and *JOY* are treated as properties that can be owned, as a "valuable object" or as a "commodity" (Fabiszak 2001: 91). Many of these colligations are stereotyped emphasizers taken from religious language: *as I have joy, so have I blisse*, etc. But these stereotypes are grounded in a soil of more differentiated ideas. Joy and bliss can also be "given", "granted", "bought", "earned", "deserved", "sought", "found", etc. The meanings of all these verbs share an element of POSSESSION, but they also reveal important theological nuances. When bliss or joy is given or granted, we are on safe theological ground; even a very strict Calvinist could not object: God gives or grants out of His goodness and mercy, a human part in the process is not implied. With *earn, deserve,* also with *seek* and *find* things are rather different: here, the human contribution is essential to the result. This is the grammatical expression of what a distinguished Roman Catholic theologian of my own university, Wilhelm Geerlings (1941–2008), used to call "the unacknowledged Semipelagianism" of the Catholic Church.[7] Pelagius, remember, was a British monk in the early 4th century who rejected the doctrine of Original Sin and taught that "salvation is effected by man's efforts" <http://en.wikipedia.org/wiki/ Semipelagianism, last visited 18 February, 2010>. Semipelagianism (or *reliquiæ Pelagianorum,* to use the medieval term) is a compromise between Pelagius and Augustine holding that "man and God could cooperate to a certain degree in [the] salvation effort: man can (unaided by grace) make the first move toward God, and God then increases and guards that faith, completing the work of salvation." (*ibid.*) Semipelagianism was condemned as a heresy at the Second Council of Orange in 529, but our verbs suggest that it continued to find expression, however unacknowledged.

The bliss and the joy we are discussing at the moment are not of this world. And the high frequency of our verbs indicates, clearly and unsurprisingly, the importance of otherworldly joy / bliss in Middle English texts. But there is a verb which does not colligate with otherworldly joy or bliss. That verb is *MAKE*. Clearly, when a human being "makes joy", it is literally of his or her "own making". They neither earn nor receive it.

2.2.2. Prepositions governing *JOY* and/or *BLISS*

The full significance of the frequency of *MAKE* with *JOY* (and its rarity with *BLISS*) will become apparent when we look at the preposition *for*, which is also much more frequent with *JOY* than with *BLISS*. To illustrate, I take the two earliest quotations which the *eMED* provides:

---

7   But compare a Protestant view: "Der Semipelagianismus entspricht noch heute der Position der Römisch-Katholischen Kirche." <http://www.efg-hohenstaufenstr.de/downloads/bibel/ pelagianismus.html> (last visited 18 February 2010) [efg=Evangelisch-Freikirchliche Gemeinde].

For þe **ioye** þat to was newe, leuedi, þov haue merci of me. [For the joy that then [at the Annunciation] was new, have mercy on me.] (*s.v.* 'thō (adv.)') (c1250 *Seinte marie leuedi* (Trin-C B.14.39) 11).

For **Ioye** huy stoden ase þei huy weren witlese and a-mad. [They stood as if they were senseless and beside themselves with joy] (*s.v.* 'amad (adj.)') (c1300 *SLeg.*(LdMisc 108) 328/206).

The first quotation is from a 13th-century "Prayer of the Five Joys" of Mary (Brown 1932: 27–29 [=No. 18]), the second is from the *South English Legendary*. We could call the first *for* the 'reasoning or argumentative *for*', the second one the 'causal *for*'. The first quotation could be paraphrased as "I invoke the joy that you (Mary) felt at the Annunciation as a reason that you may have mercy on me." The bodily reactions shown by St. Clement's brothers in the second quotation are caused by their joy at the miraculous reunion with their mother and brother. It is the second, the causal *for*, which deserves our interest above all, because it shows joy as an emotion in a very modern sense of the word: a sudden mental process which is expressed in and which causes involuntary physical symptoms. As we see in Table 6, more than 85% of all instances of *for* followed by *JOY* belong to the causal category. Only about 15% represent the 'reasoning' type. With *BLISS* it is almost the reverse: 20% 'causal' to 80% 'reasoning'.[8]

Table 6. Prepositions preceded by *BLISS* or *JOY*

	JOY	% of Total	*BLISS*	% of Total
for	157	4.93	36	1.30
('causal'	*137*		*6)*	
('reasoning'	*20*		*30)*	
in	202	6.34	377	13.66
to	176	5.52	296	10.73
Total occurrences	3187		2759[9]	

Table 7 gives a full list of the few 'causal *for*s' that do occur with *BLISS*. Note that all examples are either early or Western, or both. We can say perhaps that they are from a period and from a region which had not fully adopted the French import yet.

---

8   By way of postscript: we find the causal *for* also with *ANGER* and *TĒNE,* though not with *WRATH.*

9   Not counting forms of vt. *blessen* spelt *blissen.*

Table 7. 'Causal *for*' with *BLISS*

Lemma	Stencil	Quotations	Dialect
Kissen (v.)	c1300(c1250) *Floris* (Cmb Gg.4.27) 786:	Nu boþe togadere þes childre for blisse Falleþ to his fet, hem to kisse [vr. kis].	SW
lissen (v.)	c1300 *SLeg.*(LdMisc 108) 328/200:	Þis guode wyf bi-gan to weope sore, ake nathles for blisse Of hire sone..I-founde, hire seoruwe heo gan to lisse.	SW
wēpen (v.)	?a1300 *Jacob & J.*(Bod 652) 388:	He goþ into þe boure & wepeþ for blisse.	SW
hēp (n.)	c1330(?c1300) *Guy(1)* (Auch) 4072:	Amonges hem was gret gladnesse; þe most hepe [=the greater number] wepen for blis.	EML
lēpen (v.)	c1330 (?a1300) *Arth.& M.*(Auch) 1330:	For blis he ou3t to sing & lepe.	EML
abloi (ppl.)	c1400(?c1390) *Gawain* (Nero A.10) 1174:	Þe lorde for blys abloy [=carried away, reckless] Ful oft con launce & ly3t, & drof þat day wyth joy Thus to þe derk ny3t.	WML

3. Conclusion

At the end of this paper we should return to the original question: were *TĒNE* and *BLISS* not good enough? That question presupposes a need for new words, a lexical gap which had to be filled. Such gaps, such needs emerge in the terminologies of specialized discourses, not so much in the 'common language'. That common language is enriched by language contact. Words from the 'other' language are likely to be adopted for their stylistic 'feel' rather than for the newness of their content.

The stylistic 'feel' for *ANGER* and for *JOY* must have been very different. *ANGER* came from Old Norse but had powerful support in the Anglo-Saxon word family of *ang*-derivatives – cognates of German *Angst*. Its gradual development in the direction of irritation, vexation, frustration – in short of *anger* in the modern sense, is an English development which is to do with the growing need to denote goal frustration as distinct from status violation (which is the established province of *wrath*; cf. Diller forthcoming a). *JOY*, of French origin, entered English by way of the romances, a literary genre which is hospitable to sudden emotional experiences. Once adopted, they and their families became established as convenient lexical devices to distinguish the state of the experiencer from the nature of the cause. Both thus testify to the growing importance of the human subject.

References

Aquinas, Thomas
  1967   *Summa Theologiae. Volume XIX: The Emotions (1a2æ. 22-30).* (Latin text
  [1265-1274]   and English translation, Introduction and Notes, Appendices and
                  Glossaries [by] Eric D'Arcy). London and New York: Blackfriars, in
                  conjunction with Eyre & Spottiswoode, and McGraw-Hill Book
                  Company.
Brown, Charles (ed.)
  1932   *English lyrics of the 13th century.* Oxford: Clarendon Press.
Darwin, Charles
  1998   *The expression of emotions in man and animals.* (Third edition with intro-
  [1872]   duction, afterword and commentaries by Paul Ekman). Oxford: Oxford
                  University Press.
Diller, Hans-Jürgen
  2006   "The decline of the family of *mōd*: ICAMET and other corpora", in:
                  Mair, Christian and Reinhard Heuberger (eds.), 51–64.
  2007a   "From *mōd* to *emotion* (or almost): the medieval gestation of a modern
                  concept", in: Mazzon, Gabriella (ed.), 13–39.
  2007b   "Medieval 'with a mood' and modern 'in a mood': Changing a metaphor
                  we live by", *Poetica* [Tokyo] 66: 127–140. [Special Issue: *The Treatment
                  of Emotions, with an Emphasis on Old and Middle English*, ed. H. Sauer
                  and M. Ogura].
  2008a   "*Mood* in Middle English", in: Kruminiene, Jadvyga (gen. ed.), 46–57.
  2008b   "*Happy* in changing contexts: The history of word-use and the
                  metamorphoses of a concept", in: Pessi, Anne Birgitta – Mikko Salmeia –
                  Heli Tissari (eds.), 101–130.
  forthcoming a. "*Ssoong* on Ifaluk, *ANGER* and *WRATH* in Middle English: Historical
                  semantics as bridge-builder".
  forthcoming b. "*ANGER* and *TĒNE* in Middle English", in: Markus, Manfred – Yoko
                  Iyeiri – Reinhard Heuberger (eds.).
Duggan, Hoyt N. – Thorlac Turville-Petre (eds.)
  1989   *The Wars of Alexander.* (Early English Text Society, Supplementary
                  Series 10). Oxford: Oxford University Press.
Fabiszak, Małgorzata
  2001   *The concept of 'Joy' in Old and Middle English. A semantic analysis.*
                  Piła: Wyższa Szkoła Biznesu.

Kövecses, Zoltán
1990 *Emotion concepts.* New York: Springer.
2003 *Metaphor and emotion: Language, culture, and body in human feeling.* Cambridge: Cambridge University Press.
Kruminiene, Jadvyga (gen. ed.)
2008 *Texts and contexts: Spectrum of transformations.* Vol. 2. (Proceedings of the 2nd Kaunas Conference on Text and Context, 13-15 October, 2005). Vilnius: Vilnius University Press.
Mair, Christian – Reinhard Heuberger (eds.)
2006 *Corpora and the history of English. papers dedicated to Manfred Markus on the occasion of his sixty-fifth birthday.* (Anglistische Forschungen 363). Heidelberg: Winter.
Markus, Manfred – Yoko Iyeiri – Reinhard Heuberger (eds.)
forthcoming *Middle and Modern English corpus linguistics: A multi-dimensional approach.* Amsterdam/Philadelphia: John Benjamins.
Mazzon, Gabriella (ed.)
2007 *Studies in Middle English forms and meanings.* (Studies in English Medieval Language and Literature). Frankfurt: Peter Lang.
Pessi, Anne Birgitta – Mikko Salmeia – Heli Tissari (eds.)
2008 *Happiness: cognition, experience, language.* (COLLeGIUM. Studies across Disciplines in the Humanities and Social Sciences 3). Helsinki: Helsinki Collegium for Advanced Studies.
Schwarz, Manuela – Wolfram Ziegler
1996 "Emotionen in Neurolinguistik und Lexikologie. Ein Forschungsüber blick", *Lexikologie* 2: 34–62.
Shaver, Phillip R. – Judith Schwartz – Donald Kirson – Cary O'Connor
1987 "Emotion knowledge: further exploration of a prototype approach", *Journal of Personality and Social Psychology* 52 (6): 1061–1086.
Skeat, Walter W. (ed.)
1886 *The Wars of Alexander: An alliterative romance translated chiefly from 'the Historia Alexandri Magni de Preliis'.* (Early English Text Society, Extra Series 47). London: Early English Text Society.
Wars of Alexander
1886 see Skeat.
1989 see Duggan.
Wierzbicka, Anna
1999 *Emotions across languages and cultures.* Cambridge: Cambridge University Press.
Zoëga, Geir T.
2004 *Concise dictionary of Old Icelandic[10].* (Medieval Academy Reprints for
[1910] Teaching 41). Toronto: University of Toronto Press.

---

10 the individual pages of the dictionary can be assessed from: http://lexicon.ff.cuni.cz/png/oi_zoega/.

WEBSITES

Gevaert, Caroline
    2007   *The history of ANGER:. The lexical field of ANGER from Old to Early Modern English*. [Ph.D. dissertation]. Katholieke Universiteit Leuven. Available at: https://repository.libis.kuleuven.be/dspace/bitstream/1979/893/2/thesisgedrukt.pdf
MED online   <http://quod.lib.umich.edu/m/med/>
Semipelagianism
    <http://en.wikipedia.org/wiki/Semipelagianism> (last access: 18 February 2010).
    <http://www.efg-hohenstaufenstr.de/downloads/bibel/pelagianismus.html> (last access: 18 February 2010).

And this is a wonderful instrument...: Names of surgical instruments in Late Middle English medical texts

Marta Sylwanowicz, Academy of Management [SWSPiZ], Warsaw

ABSTRACT

The issue of language change, especially its mechanism, causes and regularities, has attracted various degrees of attention. While most works are concerned with semantic change, hardly any looks into a particular section of vocabulary. The present study aims to fill a gap which has long existed in English historical linguistic research.

The paper attempts at providing a general examination of the names of surgical instruments found in Late Middle English medical texts. Particular attention will be paid to the semantic development of the OF loan *instrument* and, subsequently, its various uses in medical compilations.

KEYWORDS: medieval medicine; medieval surgery; surgical instruments; Old and Middle English medical texts

1. Middle English surgery and practicioners

"Surgery is almost as old as humanity" (Porter 2001: 202). Archeology reveals that surgeons practised at least as early as 10 000 BC. Trepanation of a skull, bonesetting, amputations or minor operating abscesses or tumours and disorders of the ear, eye and teeth have been common procedures undertaken by people involved in healing (shamans, quacks, barbers or physicians) (Porter 2001: 203-204).

Although a medical division, surgery (Gk *cheirourgia* 'working with the hands, the practice of a handcraft or art'; hence ME *hand worchinge*) used to be viewed as an inferior practice, being a work of the hand rather than the head. Therefore neither Oxford nor Cambridge offered any surgical training, the only form of learning being experience and apprenticeship. This craft ideology allowed access for untrained artisans to enter the field of surgery, e.g., barbers, the third group of practitioners who undertook minor surgical operations such as bloodletting or cauterization (Norri 1992: 49-50).

Consequently, the Middle Ages established a hierarchy among medical practitioners. The doctor was to "speculate on the cases of illness, erect medical systems, and heal and cure the sick" (Bullough 1966: 109), usually with the help of medications derived from herbs. The surgeon, on the other hand, was expected to perform major operations in which he cut open the patient's body. As Guy de Chauliac states:

(1)

> The condiciouns þat beþ required in þe Cirurgien beeþ
> foure/ the ferste is þat// he be a lettred man/ þe
> secounde þat he be expert or cunnynge/ The þridde þat
> he be witty or wise/ þe fourþe þat he be wel þewed.
> It is firste þerfore required þat þe Cirurgien be a
> lettred man; nogt onliche in þe principles of
> Cirurgie, but also of phisiqg als wel in theoriqg as
> in practiqg

[1425 *Anatomy* 11-1]

Unlike doctors, who cured patients with medications derived from herbs and the treatment took time, surgeons were in an unfortunate position since surgery has a direct effect on the health of the patient. Surgeons performed major operations in which they cut open patient's body and the effects of the surgery were immediate – the patient either lived or died. Thus, a large portion of the documentation on surgeons comes from court records concerning malpractice suits.

2. Medieval medical texts

England is unique in having a vernacular medical tradition going as far back as the Anglo-Saxon period. Voigts and McVaugh (1984) propose a division of Middle English medical texts according to their origin into remedy books and academic textbooks.

With their long vernacular tradition remedy books represent the older and the larger category with conventions of writing established in Old English, which makes them less dependent on foreign models. Most Middle English medical compilations from before the latter half of the 14th century fall into this category (Norri 1992: 34).

Academic treatises constitute another category of Middle English medical texts. They are translations of ancient Latin medicine, Arabic writers, and medieval university masters. Especially common in this group are surgical books, occupying the intermediate position between academic writings and remedy books. Mostly originating in learned circles, they also belong to the academic tradition. Often illustrated, they usually include material on anatomy, remedies as well as some detailed instructions for surgery practices (Norri 1992: 35).

Most of Middle English surgeries remain unedited, the only elaborations on the surgeries being those by Lanfranc, Guy de Chauliac, Morstede, de Vigo, and the Englishman John Arderne. Of these, Guy de Chauliac was the most influential surgeon of the 14th-15th centuries. He became physician to three popes at Avignon (Clement VI, Innocent VI, and Urban V) and a leading surgeon at the school of Montpellier. His work, being the principal surgical text of this period, was copied and translated into French, English, Italian, Dutch, and even Hebrew. (Wallner, 1971: xiii) The English translations of Guy de Chauliac's *Anatomy* are found in the following manuscripts (cf. Wallner 1971: ix):

(i)   New York Academy of Medicine 12 (N.Y.) together with a number of
        related MSS; Bibl. Nat. Angl. (Paris) 25 (A.);
(ii)   Gonville and Caius College (Cambridge) 336/725 (C) and Univ. Libr.
        Cambridge Dd. 3 52 (D) in part;
(iii)   The Roger Marshall MS. (New York Acad. of Med.) Hunterian MS. 95
        (Glasgow), British Museum Sloane 3486, and Bodleian Ashmole 1468.

Although the majority of ME medical works (including surgical texts) are now
available in an electronic version (MEMT) published by Taavitsainen et al. (2005)
the present study is focusing on the first two versions of Chauliac's work
published by Wallner (1964). This choice is due the fact that the electronic corpus
includes only fragments whereas Wallner published full texts.

3. Surgical instruments

In the early medieval period English already possessed sufficient resources of its
own to represent various ideas without a need to have recourse to another
language for its medical terminology. Studies on the lexicon of medieval
medicine, cf. Norri (1992, 1998, 2004), Cameron (1993) or Sylwanowicz (2002,
2003, 2006, 2007a, 2007b) reveal that Middle English was not deficient in
scientific terminology and the Anglo-Saxon compilers of medical texts did not
merely copy from the classic originals without making any personal contribution
[cf. also examples from a *Thesaurus of Old English* (2000)]. This leads one to a
conclusion that the use of Latin/French forms (introduced after the Norman
Conquest) was not necessary to fill in linguistic or cultural gaps in English.
    This remark proves to be true in the case of names of body parts, sicknesses
or medicines that were numerous and that had laid solid foundations in the
development of English scientific vocabulary.
    However, a closer examination of medieval medical texts (in particular
surgical treatises) reveals that a part of the medical lexicon (i.e. names of surgical
instruments) seemed insufficient and needed to be filled in by a foreign element.

3.1 Old English surgical instruments

Old English medical compilations show that the main surgical operation was
phlebotomy (i.e. bloodletting). This practice was intimately associated with the
doctrine of the four humours and the belief that "blood carried the factors of
disease through the body" (Cameron 1993: 159). Apart from bloodletting there are
a few references to other operations, such as a plastic surgery of harelip,
amputation and a surgical treatment of the abscess of the liver.
    The main instrument used in these operations was a sharp knife or lancet,
hence the only OE names for surgical instruments (listed in *TOE* 2000: 132) are:

ædreseax, *blodseax*, *bor*, *ceorfseax*, *flytme*, *læceiren*, *læceseax* and *snidisen* – all referring to a sharp device used in surgical practices.

As seen in the examples, each term is composed of a lexical element whose prototypical meaning is that of 'a tool used for cutting, to cut', e.g., *bor*, *flytme*, *iren*, *seax* and *snid*. The remaining elements *ædre-*, *blod-* or *læce-* (modifiers of the nouns) are added to specify the character of the instrument, that is to use it in the practice of bloodletting or to be used by a specialist – here a healer, doctor (preferably having practice in surgery).

Interestingly, neither *TOE* nor other source available provides a general term for medical instruments. In the *TOE*, for instance, the terms for lancet are put under a general heading *lacnigendlic* (surgical terms) and not *tool*, *implements*, being productive OE terms, especially in the area of craft, agriculture, etc. Moreover, a close examination of OE medical texts reveals that the compiler(s) did not use the term *tool* when referring to surgical instruments. Rather, the scribe(s) preferred exact names (cf. terms for lancet – see examples above). In later texts (ME texts) also the term *tool* is not found in surgical compilations but rather a foreign element *instrument* is preferred.

3.2 Middle English surgical instruments

Unlike Old English, Middle English texts abound in various names of instruments. In Guy de Chauliac's *Anatomy* (version N.Y. and A.) the instruments are classified into two types: **common instruments** and **proper (specialised) instruments**, where the former are subdivided into **medicinal** and **iron instruments**. To **medicinal instruments** belong:

(2)
> N.Y.: gouernance & pocions & sanguinacions, vnguentes, emplasteres, and pulueres.
> A.: gouernaunces & drynkes, blood-latyng, oynmentes, Emplastres, and poudres.
>
> [Wallner 1964: 10 – 11]

The **iron instruments** are categorised according to surgical operations (Wallner 1964: 10-11):

(3a) instruments for cutting:

> N.Y.: some bene for to kutte as **sheres** or **cisours, rasours, & launcetes**.
> A.: some beeþ to kutte wiþ **scheres, rasoures**, and **launcetes**.

(3b) instruments for burning/cauterization:

> N.Y.: Som for to Cauterise as bene **oliuaria** and **cultellaria**.
> A.: and some to brenne wiþ as beeþ Instrumentis þat higte **oliuaria & cultellaria**.

(3c) instruments to "draw out" (retractors):

> N.Y.: Som for to drawen oute as **tonges** & **picecaroles** .i. **twitches**
> A.: and some to drawe out with as **tenacule** and **picecareole**.

(3d) instruments used in internal examination (surgical probes):

> N.Y.: Som for to proue as **probes** & **intromisse** .i. **serchers**.
> A.: and some to proue wiþ as **probe** and **intromissi**.

(3e) sewing/sealing instruments:

> N.Y.: Som for to sewe as **nedeles** and **canules**.
> A.: and some to sewe wiþ as a **nedel** and a **pype** or **penne**.

The next category of instruments – **proper (specialised) instruments** – includes for instance (Wallner 1964: 10-11):

(4)
> N.Y. Propre bene as **trepane** in þe heued, // **ffaux** in þe luer
> A.: proper Instrumentes beþ as **trepan** in þe hede, and **faux** in þe fundament.

The author of the surgical treatise advises also that a surgeon should always have with him (in his case) at least five instruments and needles, (Wallner 1964: 10-11):

(5)
> N.Y.: Also in his pennaculo .i. pennar or casse; he oweþ for to bere 5. Instruments .s. **sheres** or **cisours**, **picecaroles** .i. **tviches**, **Probe** .i. **serchour**, **Rasour**, & **launcet**, And **nedeles**.
> A.: Also he schulde bere in a case fyue Instrumentis, þat is to wete, **scheres**, **picecareola**, **proba** & a **rasoure**, and **launcetes** and a **nedel**.

The examples used for the presentation of the surgical instruments reveal two interesting aspects: (1) at least two different meanings of the term *instrument* (cf. medicinal instruments and iron instruments), and (2) how scribes/translators varied in their choice of words (vernacular or foreign element). These two aspects require a closer examination.

4. Middle English *instrument*

The term *instrument* has its source in the Latin verb *instruere* 'build, prepare, equip, teach' from which was derived the noun *instrumentum* 'tool, equipment'. When introduced to English (via Old French) at the end of the 13th century it was first used with reference to/for a musical instrument, cf.:

(6)

> c1290 *S. Eng. Leg.* I. 225/191 As a fiþele his wynges furde..Muriere **Instrument** neuere nas þan his wyngen were!

In time (i.e. in the 14^(th) c) a more general meaning 'implement, mechanical device, tool' and a metaphorical/figurative sense 'means' occurred, cf.:

(7)

> 1375 BARBOUR *Bruce* XVII. 342 The ynglis host..With **Instrumentis** on seir maneris, As scaffatis, ledderis, and coueryngis, Pykis, howis, and ek staff-slyngis.
> c1391 CHAUCER *Astrol.* Prol. 1 Conclusions apertenyng to the same **instrument** [Astrolabe].
> 1340 HAMPOLE *Pr. Consc.* 3139 Bot þat fire..es An **instrument** of Goddes ryghtwysnes.

The figurative meaning of the term developed yet another meaning – 'a person used by others, usually God/gods'. This might have led to the use of the term with reference to 'the part of the body', being an instrument of the human body in his earthly deeds, cf:

(8)

> a1340 HAMPOLE *Psalter* xliv. 2 *comm.*, His instrument, whaim he ledis as he will.
> c1386 CHAUCER *Man of Law's T.* 272 Thou madest Eua brynge vs in seruage..Thyn Instrument so..Makestow of wommen whan thou wolt bigile.

Middle English compilations used the OF term *instrument* instead of *tool*, although the latter was a general Anglo-Saxon term meaning 'any instrument of manual operation', cf. examples from the *OED*:

(9)

> c888 K. ÆLFRED *Boeth.* xiv. §1 þæt mete and drync & claðas, & tol to swelcum cræfte.
> c1000 ÆLFRIC *Exod.* xx. 25 Gif þu þin tol ahefst ofer hyt, hit biþ besmiten.
> a1100 *Gerefa* in *Anglia* (1886) IX. 262 He sceal fela tola to tune tilian.
> c1205 LAY. 29253 Nettes..and þa tolen þer to.
> 13.. *E.E. Allit. P.* B. 1342 Formed with handes Wyth tool out of harde tre, & telded on lofte.

The reasons for that choice of the term might be two-fold:

(i)   the term *tool* seems to have "disappeared" for about two centuries (according to the *OED* the term is recorded in the texts from the beginning of the 13^(th) century (1205) and later used in the 15^(th) century texts (having scarce occurrences in the end of the 14^(th) century);

(ii)   the term *tool* is not found in OE medical compilations with reference to any surgical instrument; the ME medical texts are mostly translations of Latin or French works, where *instrumentum* is in use; as the term *instrument* was already in English lexicon (cf. Example 6) the obvious choice of scribes was a Latin element – familiar and at the same time more learned.

5. Translations

As most Middle English scientific texts are translated from or derived from Latin or French treatises it is not unexpected to find a large number of foreign terms in vernacular writings.

The study of the medieval medical translations illustrates how compilers struggled with many problems to find adequate English words for the names of medical terms that represent various lexical fields, e.g.,: body parts, sicknesses, medicines or surgical instruments. The techniques employed in vernacularising learned medicine varied.

According to Pahta (2004: 81-82) there were two basic methods to deal with medical terminology: (1) to use the resources of the vernacular language, i.e. a technical source language term could be replaced by a more colloquial native word or a new equivalent could be coined; the (2) solution was to turn to the source language by (a) using the source language term or (b) turning the original term into an anglicised form.

A comparison of the two 15th century translations of Guy de Chauliac's *Anatomy* shows how translators varied in their choice of words.

The two texts, MS N.Y. (preserved in the Library of the New York Academy of Medicine, hence N.Y. in short) and MS A. (kept in the National Library in Paris) represent two different versions, one a close translation (N.Y.) and the other (A.) a free rendering of a Latin original. MS N.Y. generally makes use of words of Latin or French origin, while MS A. shows great freedom in translating into vernacular (cf. Table 1).

Although in many cases the choice of names of surgical instruments is the same (cf. Table 1, fragments in examples 3, 5, 6), there are instances where the manuscripts differ in the choice of the terms. For instance, where MS N.Y. chooses OE item *tonges* used as a general term denoting some 'forceps, pinces', the translator of MS A. uses the Lat. term *tenacule* (cf. example 4). In (7) the scribe of MS N.Y. uses a foreign term *canule* 'tube, pipe' whereas the author of MS A. uses an older/vernacularized (probably more familiar) term *pipe* (already in use in OE texts).

The material reveals also that the same compiler translated a given text with varying degrees of freedom, often being inconsistent in the choice of terms. For instance, in MS A. (see examples 2, 6, 10, 11, 12) the term *instrument* is used with various meanings: (1) general term for surgical instrument [example 6], (2) a term referring to types of medicines [example 2], and (3) a part of the body/organ [examples 10 and 11]. However, the scribe had an alternative term for a part of the body [cf. OF *membre* in example 12 or OE *lymes* in 9].

The study of terms representing the lexical field of surgical instruments shows that although occasional native terms are used copyists usually transferred Latin or French term into English. As a result, readers often encountered unfamiliar words or expressions. The writers, however, used various explicatory techniques to facilitate the understanding of foreign terms.

Interpolations and explanations, especially of the *that is* (*clepid/callid*) type, are common explicatory phrases, cf. examples: 6 in MS A. and 4, 5, 6, 12 in MS N.Y.

In such combinations usually the foreign technical term precedes the familiar word, whereas the opposite order, where the native element is placed first, occurs very seldom (cf. also Norri 1992).

Although Middle English was not deficient in scientific terms the study of surgical instruments reveals that the use of Latin/French forms was often necessary to fill the gaps in the English lexicon, as the terms in vernacular were not sufficient. Moreover, the compilers might have used the foreign element for reasons of style, prestige or to give the text the air of technicality (cf. also Pahta 2004).

Table 1. Translation strategies in the two ME versions of Guy de Chauliac's *Anatomy*.

	N.Y.	A.
1.	6/5-6 tvo **instruments** of medicyne, **videlicet of pocioun** & of diete	7/5-6 two **Instrumentis**, þat is to seie, of **drynkyng medecyne** & diet
2.	10/1-2 **Instruments medicinals** bene **gouernaunce** & **pocions** & **sanguinacions, vnguentes, emplasteres, and pulueres.**	11/1-2 The **medicynal instrumentes** beeþ **gouernaunces** & **drynkes, bloodlatyng, oynementes, Emplastres,** and **poudres.**
3.	10/3-4 for to kutte as **sheres** or **cisours, rasours,** & **launcetes**	11/3-4 to kutte wiþ **scheres, rasoures,** and **launcetes**
4.	10/5 to drawen oute as **tonges** & **picecaroles** .i. **twitches**	11/5 to drawe out with as **tenacule** and **picecareole**
5.	10/5-6 to proue as **probes** & **intromisse** .i. **serchers**	11/5-6 to proue wiþ as **probe** and **intromissi**
6.	10/13-15 5. Instruments .s. **sheres** or **cisours, picecaroles** .i. **tviches, Probe** .i. **serchour, Rasour,** & **launcet,** And **nedeles**	11/13-14 fyue Instrumentis, þat is to wete, **scheres, picecareola, proba** & a **rasoure,** and **launcetes** and a **nedel**

7.	10/6-7 to sewe as **nedeles** and **canules**	11/6-7 to sewe wiþ as a **nedel** and a **pype** or **penne**
8.	38/2-3 medecynes & instrumentes wyþ which is **made operacioun** in þe woundes of þe heued.	39/ 2-3 medicynes and Instrumentis wiþ þe whiche **wirkynge is I-made** in woundes of þe heed.
9.	62/17-18 **organica & instrumentales**, for þai bene instrumentes of þe soule, as hand, face, hert, lyuer.	63/14-15 **lymes & instrumentis**, ffor þai beeþ þe instrumentis of þe soule, as hand, þe face, þe herte, the lyuer…
10.	122/20-21 Ðe stomac or þe wombe is þe **organ** of þe first digestion generatif	123/23-24 The stomak or þe wombe is þe **instrument** of þe firste digestioun.
11.	124/27 Lyuer is **þe organe**	125/26 The lyuer is **þe instrument**
12.	136/22-23 Ðe matrix forsoþ (…) is an **organe** susceptiue .i. takyng	137/20-21 The matrice forsoþe (…) is a receyuynge **membre**

References

Bullough, Vern Leroy
    1966   *The development of medicine as a profession.* Basel: S. Karger.
Cameron, Malcolm Laurence
    1993   *Anglo-Saxon medicine.* Cambridge: Cambridge University Press.
Haubrich, William S.
    1997   *Medicinal meanings. A glossary of word origin.* Philadelphia, Pennsylvania: American College of Physicians.
Hunt, Tony
    1990   *Popular medicine in 13th century England. Introduction and texts.* Cambridge: Brewer.
Middle English dictionary. Available at: http://quod.lib.umich.edu/m/med/ (date of access: 3rd November 2009).
Norri, Juhani
    1992   *Names of sicknesses in English, 1400-1550. An exploration of the lexical field.* (Annales Academiae Scientiarum Fennicae, Dissertationes Humanarum Litterarum 63). Helsinki: Academia Scientiarum Fennicae.
    1998   *Names of body parts in English, 1400-1550.* (Annales Academiae Scientiarum Fennicae, Humaniora 291). Helsinki: Academia Scientiarum Fennicae.
    2004   "Entrances and exits in English medical vocabulary, 1400-1550", in: Taavitsainen, Irma and Paivi Pahta (eds.), 100-144.
Oxford English dictionary. Available at: http://www.oed.com/ (date of access: 9th November 2009).

Pahta, Paivi
    2004   "Code-switching in medieval medical writing", in: Taavitsainen, Irma and Paivi Pahta (eds.), 73-99.
Porter, Roy
    2001   *The Cambridge illustrated history of medicine.* Cambridge: Cambridge University Press.
Roberts, Jane – Christian Kay (eds.)
    2000   *A thesaurus of Old English.* 2 Vols. Amsterdam-Atlanta: Rodopi.
Sylwanowicz, Marta
    2002   "Remarks on Old English medical terminology", *Anglica* 12: 91-102.
    2003   "Leech, doctor, physician: on the loss of prototypical meanings", *Anglica* 13: 151-164.
    2006   "Medieval madness: the Anglo-Saxon terminology of mental diseases", *Anglica* 15: 117-128.
    2007a   *Old and Middle English sickness-nouns in historical perspective: A lexico-semantic analysis,* (Warsaw Studies in English Historical Linguistics 1). Warsaw: Institute of English Studies UW.
    2007b   "Madfolkes and Lunaticke persons...: the synonyms of *madness* in Middle English texts", *Anglica* 16: 173-184.
Taavitsainen, Irma – Paivi Pahta
    1998   "Vernacularization of medical writing in English. A corpus-based study of scholasticism", *Early Science and Medicine. A Journal for the Study of Science, Technology and Medicine in the Pre-modern Period* 3: 157-185.
Taavitsainen, Irma – Paivi Pahta (eds.)
    2004   *Medical and scientific writing in Late Medieval English.* Cambridge: Cambridge University Press.
Taavitsainen, Irma – Paivi Pahta – Matti Mäkinnen
    2005   *Middle English medical texts* (on CD-ROM). John Benjamins Publishing Company.
Voigts, Linda – Michael Rogers McVaugh
    1984   "A Latin technical phlebotomy and its Middle English translation", *Transactions of American Philosophical Society* 74/2: 1-69.
Wallner, Björn (ed.)
    1964   *The Middle English translation of Guy de Chauliac's Anatomy, with Guy's essay on the history of medicine.* (Lunds Universitets Arsskrift, N. F. Avd. 1, Bd. 56, Nr 5). Lund: Gleerup.
    1971   *A Middle English version of the introduction to Guy de Chauliac's "Chirurgia Magna"* (Acta Universitatis Lundensis, Sectio I. Theologica, juridica, humaniora, 12). Lund: Gleerup.

French influences on English surnames

Wolfgang Viereck, University of Bamberg

ABSTRACT

The publications dealing with the distributional patterns of English family names in the United Kingdom are anything but numerous and comprehensive. For this task researchers used either different data sets to differing degrees and from different periods in the past or from different current periods. A concerted action in onomastic research is still lacking. A project on English surname geography is being carried out at the University of Bamberg. The first volume appeared in 2007 and work on the second and final volume is nearing completion. The project's diachronic and synchronic databases and the mapping procedures are briefly described and some examples of surnames of French origin relating to the four major categories of English surnames are treated in this contribution. They often developed variants of various kinds that mirrored changes in the common language that either survived or died out there.

KEYWORDS: hereditary English surnames, diachronic and synchronic databases, mapping procedures, French influence on English surnames, surnames and dialects, doublets, folk etymology

1. Introductory remarks

In his dissertation from 1938, Gösta Tengvik discusses a most important aspect of Old English naming, namely the use of bynames. Already in the Old English period, the main types of additions to a name existed that gradually led to the hereditary family names in the course of the following centuries. At first they were used very rarely, becoming more frequent from the 10th century without, however, becoming the norm. These additions were descriptions of the individual person and, thus, not hereditary. The same person could be given two, sometimes even four bynames. Although Tengvik does not differentiate clearly between bynames found in genuine Old English sources and those found in the *Domesday Book* of 1086, it nevertheless becomes apparent that the bynames of the *Domesday Book* bear the stamp of the Norman Conquest, not only because for the first time many appear in French (see Hofmann 1934 on particular regions), because their number rose significantly, but also because the first rare cases of hereditary names, i.e. family names, are to be found there. Thus, two essential aspects in the development of the following centuries are already present in the *Domesday Book*: the general spread of the use of bynames and their gradual change into surnames.

The introduction of family names in England was, thus, due to an enormous cultural change that followed the Norman Conquest in 1066. There were, it is true, some pre-Conquest contacts between royalty and church on both sides of the

Channel, such as the Cluniac reform of the mid-10th century, but their linguistic impact remained insignificant. When exactly the bynames became hereditary is difficult to say, but it can safely be said that by 1350 very many people in the South and the Midlands of England of whatever social rank had a hereditary family name. This process took about one hundred years longer in the North of England, much longer in Scotland and several centuries longer in Wales (for more details on bynames becoming hereditary, see Barker et al. 2007: 4-11).

A family name could change over the course of a person's life or from generation to generation. Names could also change due to the practice of the scribes. To give an example: a man could first be called *Will Dickson*, later he could call himself *Will Potter* or *Will Feaver*, following his profession and later still, should he move away from home, he could, in his new surroundings, call himself after his place of birth, thus becoming *Will York* or *Will Chester*, for example. It, thus, becomes apparent that someone could have been called *Feaver* although he was no longer a smith or had never been one.

2. French influence

The French influence on English naming where one must differentiate between the giving of names and the word stock is of such dimensions that it cannot adequately be dealt with in a brief conference paper like this. I cannot do more than summarise this influence. While a uniform classification of English surnames does not exist, Reaney and Wilson (2005) suggest four major categories: local surnames, surnames of relationship, surnames of occupation or office/status and nicknames.

Local surnames are by far the largest group within which locative and topographical family names can be distinguished. A certain number of English formations of locative surnames are found already before the Norman Conquest, such as *Aelfstān on Lundene* (988) (cf. Tengvik 1938). In addition to *on* other prepositions were available back then, but after the Conquest the usual preposition was *de* which was often dropped later. In French surnames beginning with a vowel, this *de* has often coalesced with the place-name, as is the case with *Danvers* (from French Anvers [Flemish Antwerp]) or *Disney* (from Isigny in northern France). In *Danvers*, the final *-s* is retained. Generally, it is retained or dropped quite arbitrarily in surnames going back to French place-names. *De Vere* is an English surname going back as far as the *Domesday Book* (Alberic *de Ver*). The French place-name is *Ver* in northern France. A later namesake, Edward *de Vere* received recent recognition as "the man who invented Shakespeare" (Kreiler 2009). Today this surname (with variants) is extremely rare in England. Among the topographical surnames, e.g., *Castel* 'castle' is of (Old northern) French origin (see Kristensson 1969).

The following English surnames go back to

a) French place-names:
Callis (from Calais),
Chartres, Charters (from Chartres),
Bulleyn, B(o)ullin, Boullen(t), Bullon, Bollen, Bullan(t) (from Boulogne),
Boswall, Boswell (from Beuzeville-la-Giffard),
Semper, Samper, Simper, Symper, Sember, Samber (from Saint-Pierre des Préaux),
Sinclaire, Sinclair, St. Clair (from Saint-Claire-sur-Elle),
Seymour(e), Seymore, Seymer (from Saint-Maur-des-Fossés) (see Reaney 1978 : 69 for a map showing the distribution of further French place-names surviving as modern English surnames) and

b) to names of French provinces:
Angwin (from Anjou),
Bret(t), Britt(s), Bret(t)on, Le Breton, Brit(t)on, Brit(t)ain, Brittan, Britten, Brittin, Brittian, Brittney (from Breton, Brittany),
Gascoign(e), Gascoin(e), Gascoinge, Gascoyne, Gasquoine, Gaskain, Gasken, Gaskin(s), Gasking (from Gascogne),
Peto, Peyto, (Le) Poidevin, le Poideven, Podevin, Potvin(e), Potwin, Portwin(e), Putwain, Puddifin, Puddifant, Puttifent (from Poitou) (see Reaney 1978: 67 for a map showing further English surnames from French provinces).

Surnames of relationship are mainly patronymics, for instance *Williams*, the Norman form of French *Guillaume*. After the Conquest, *William* was the most popular Christian name in England. The final *-s* in *Williams* means 'son of William' versus *Gilliam(s)*, a loan from Central French. 'Son of' can also be expressed by prefixing Old French *fiz*. Often *Fitz* was assimilated to the following name. Thus *Fitzjohn* is also attested as *Fidgeon* as is *FitzRoy* as *Fillary*. Among the early bearers of *Fitz-* surnames is a *Matilda Fyznicole* (1312). She was named after her mother with the prefix meaning 'son of'. French diminutive suffixes are also often attached to shortened or pet-forms, e.g., *Willet(t), Willott* or *Dobbin*, partly with *-s* or *-son*. Sometimes two suffixes are added, e.g., *Robelett* (from *Rob* < *Robert* + suffixes *-el* and *-et*) or *Dabinett* (from *Dob* < *Robert* + suffixes *-in* and *-et*). With the last examples, substitutions operate on a consonantal and a vocalic level: *Rob* > *Dob* and *Dob* > *Dab*. This device occurs rather often with shortened or pet-forms (see McClure 1998). Such hypocoristic forms are often difficult to pinpoint to a specific origin. By taking onomastic and prosopographical evidence into account, McClure (1998) and Redmonds (1997) were able to correct the bias sometimes found in surname dictionaries towards the Old English and Old Norse name stocks in favour of Old French. A different type of relationship is expressed by *Cousen(s)* (from Old French *cusin, cosin* 'a kinsman or kinswoman', 'cousin'). Reaney and Wilson (2005) list a total of 18 different spellings of that surname. Among the occupational surnames, a well-known example is *Chaucer, Chauser* (from Old French *chaucier,* meaning also 'maker of shoes, boots and breeches'). Geoffrey Chaucer's grandfather was called *Robert le Chaucer,* but the article was already dropped in his father's name: *John Chaucer.* Sometimes the article remained, sometimes it was dropped, see, e.g., *Kew, Le Keux* and *Lequeux* (from Old French *queu, keu, kieu, cu* 'cook', 'probably one who sold cooked meat', 'keeper of an eating-house'). Diminutive suffixes could also be added to this group, as *Le Pastourel, Pasturel* (from Old northern French *pastour* 'shepherd' + suffix *-el*). Among the office/status examples, *Veck, Vick* can be mentioned. It goes back to Old French *le eveske* 'the bishop', which became *leveske,* which, in turn, was wrongly taken for *le vesk. Vesk* is an early loan as it retains the *-s-* before voiceless consonants. This was dropped in central French around 1200 so that *Veck* and *Vick* are later loans in English. The full form also survives as an English family name: *Levick* or *Leffek. Prentice, Prentis(s)* is among the examples of aphetic surnames. It goes back to Old French *aprentis* 'apprentice'.

Some nicknames are unintelligible and the meaning of many is doubtful. McClure quite rightly notes that "with regard to names employing metonymy or metaphor (or both), uncertainty of meaning is onomastic rather than lexical" (1981: 97). The nicknames are manifestations of social life where irony and sarcasm, ridicule and contempt play an important role. Many of these nicknames are more or less derogatory occupational names such as *Catchpole* (from Old northern French *cachepol* 'chase fowl', ' collector of poultry in default of money', 'a taxgatherer'). Reaney and Wilson (2005) list five different spellings of this surname. For Erlebach (1968) this is an example of an imperative compound, consisting of a verbal stem and a noun. Erlebach analyses many formation processes of English compound surnames of French origin. Clark notes that

> often a French term occurs far earlier as a nickname than it does as a loanword in the extant English literary and sub-literary records.... some of the French nicknames commonest in medieval England involve terms apparently not figuring at all as loanwords in the extant literary records...: thus *Basset* 'short-legged', *Blanchard* 'whitish', *Blund* and *Blundel* 'blond', *Corbeil* 'basket', *Gernoun* 'moustache', *Muissun* 'sparrow', *Picot* 'pick-axe', *Pinel* 'small pine-tree', *Poulleyn* 'colt', *Roussel* 'reddish'; others, like *Cheverell* 'kid(-leather)', *Cokin* 'rogue', *Cordel* 'rope', *Garegate* 'throat', *Sorel* 'reddish', involve terms rare in English, whose currency was either limited or specialised.

(Clark 1978: 38)

Moreover, Clark remarks that "byname-patterns... followed a common West-European tradition. This appears clearly in all modern work... the recorded nicknames, whether native formations or loans from French, likewise conform to these general semantic patterns – a consensus almost tempting one to theorize about 'the West-European view of human nature'." (1978: 39)

As to variant spellings of names, modern English family names reflect the situation before 1700, i.e. spelling variation remained, whereas words belonging to the general vocabulary became standardised in the 18th century. We, thus, find variant spellings also in surnames of French origin (*Painter, Paynter; Pointer, Poynter* or *Jolley, Jolly, Jollye, Jollie*). The scribal influence and the scribes' errors are not unimportant either. The following example of the place-name *Nuthall* (Nt) shows the progressive deterioration of its spelling. Extracts are from the Pipe Rolls. The spelling in 1194 is *Notehala*. In 1195 the scribe, confusing *t* and *c*, wrote *Nuchala*; this is followed in the next year by a misreading of *e* for *c*, thus giving *Nuehala*; then, in 1197, the scribe took the first element in the place-name as being the word "new", and so wrote *Niewehale* (Cameron 1961: 65). *Nuthall* also survived as a family name. As *Th-* did not occur in Anglo-Norman, it was substituted by *T-* in a number of English place-names and family names, as, e.g., in *Turstan* vs. *Thurstan(s)*. In the *Domesday Book*, only the *T-* forms occur, of course (see Reaney and Wilson 2005, s.v. 'Thurstan'). Moreover, *J-* was substituted for Old English *G-* before <y/e/i> as in modern English *Jarrow* (Old English *Gyrwe*). According to Wyld, "Norman scribes are very erratic in their use of *h-* in copying English manuscripts, and we therefore cannot attach much importance to thirteenth- or even to early fourteenth-century omissions of the letter which occur here and there" (1936: 295). It is, moreover, debateable whether /s/ was also sporadically substituted for /tʃ/ in, e.g., *Leicester, Gloucester* vs. *Colchester*. In any case, this was the theory favoured previously. Clark, however, demonstrated not only that /tʃ/ was current in Anglo-Norman and continental French in the period in question, but also that the distribution of names with /-tʃest-/ and /-st-/ makes little sense in terms of the socio-cultural history of the towns and cities concerned: "Socially, it is hardly obvious why Bicester or Towcester should seem to have been more of a hotbed of 'Anglo-Norman influence' than, of all places, Winchester" (Clark 1995: 152). What makes more sense is an explanation of these name forms as showing a sound change which sometimes occurred in a position of low stress, an observation supported also by the fact that a number of these names vary between forms with *-chester* and forms with *-cester* until late in the Middle English period. There are, for example, pairs of the type *Colchester/Colcester*, *Leichester/Leicester* and *Glouchester/Gloucester*, attested in England both as place-names and as surnames. It thus appears that *Leicester, Gloucester* etc. show a sporadic sound change which happens to be exemplified only by proper names and not by the general vocabulary.

The following surnames of French origin provide ample evidence of special phonological developments: *Servant(e)* – *Sarvent* (<Old French *serv(i)ant* 'serviteur'); *Service, Servis* – *Sarvis* (<Old French *cervoise* 'ale', for a seller of ale, a taverner); *Sertin* – *Sart(a)in* (<Old French *certeyn* 'self-assured, determined') etc. In family names, we find both Old northern French and Old central French variants

today, such as the doublets *Caplan, Caplin* (<Old northern French *capelain*) – *Chapl(a)in* (<Old central French *chapelain* 'priest, clergyman, chantry-priest'); *Cancellor* (<Old northern French *canceler*) – *Chancellor* (<Old central French *chanceler* 'usher of a lawcourt', 'custodian of records', 'secretary') or *Waite* (<Old northern French *waite*) – *Gait(e)s* (<Old central French *g(u)aite* 'watchman').

Many English family names go back to originally Latin or French words, such as *Butcher, Judge, Joiner* and *Taylor, Tailor*. They also obtained loanword status in English and won out against the English terms in the general language (e.g., *Butcher* instead of *Flesher*). The following words continued their existence in English only as family names: *Petcher, Peacher* 'fisherman' or *Venner, Venour* 'huntsman'. Here the opposite occurred: the English words won out against the foreign 'intruders': see *Fisher* instead of *Petcher* or *Peacher*, *Hunter* instead of *Venner* or *Venour* or *Smith* instead of *Faber* or *(Le)Fe(a)ver*.

The following tables provide a number of examples of Latin/French family names together with their English equivalents from various fields:

Occupations

French/Latin Family Name	English Equivalent
Bullinger, Pullinger, Pillinger (< OF *bolonger, boulengier* 'baker')	*Ba(c)ker, Baxter, Bagster*
Pester, Pistor (< Anglo-Norman *pestour*, OF *pestor, pesteur* < Lat. *Pistōr* 'baker')	"
Furner, Fournier (< OF *fornier, furnier* 'baker')	"
Venour, Venner, Fenner (< OF *veneor, veneur* < Lat. *Venator* 'hunter')	*Hunter, Huntsman*
Petcher, Peacher (< OF *pescheor, peche(o)r* < Lat. *Piscator* 'fisherman')	*Fisher*
Tiss(i)er (< OF *tisseur* 'weaver')	*Wheaver, Webb(e), Webster, Webber*
Verrier, Verriour (< OF *verrier, verrieur* 'worker in glass')	*Glazier, Glayzer, Glaysher, Glaisher, Glazyer*
Fe(a)ver(s), Lefe(a)ver, Faber (< OF *fev(e)re* < Lat. *Faber* 'smith')	*Smith(e)(r)(s)*
Scriven(s), Scrivin(g)(s) (< OF *escrivain, escrivein* 'writer')	*Writer*

Offices

French Family Name	English Equivalent
Ray(e), Rey, Roy	*King(e), Kings*
(< OF *rei* > *roi* 'king')	
Rain(e), Rayn(e)	–
(< OF *reine, raine* 'queen')	
Levick, Leffek, Veck, Vick	*Bishop(p), Bisshopp*
(< *OF eveske* 'bishop')	

Words for parts of the body

French Family Name	English Equivalent
Bouch, Buche, Budge	*Mouth*
(< OF *bouche* 'mouth')	
Gordge, Gorch	*Neck, Halse, Rake, Raikes*
(< OF *gorge* 'throat')	

Animal names

French Family Name	English Equivalent
Lever(s), Leaver	*Hare(s)*
(< OF *levre* 'hare')	
Low(e), Lowes	*Woolf(e), Wolf(e), Wolfes, Wulff, Woof, Wooff*
(< OF *lou* 'wolf')	
Che(e)ver(s), Chivers	*Goate*
(Anglo-Norman *chivere, chevre*; < OF *chievre* 'she-goat')	
Agnew	*Lamb(e), Lamm, Lomb, Loombe Loom(es), Lum(b)*
(< F *agneau, agnelle* 'lamb')	

Adjectives

French Family Name	English Equivalent
Douce, Dowse, Duce	*Sweet(t)*
(< OF *dolz, dous* 'sweet')	
Dowcett, Dowsett, Doucet	"
(< OF *doucet*, a diminutive of *dolz, dous*)	
Bell, Beal(e), Beal(e)s, Beall, Beel(s)	*Fair(s), Faire(s), Faiers, Faers, Fayer(s), Fayre, Feyer, Fyers, Phair, Phayre*

(<OF *bel, belle,* 'beautiful')

Bone, Bonn(e), Bunn	Good(e), Goude, Gudd, Gude, Le Good, Le(e)good

(< OF *bon, bonne* 'good')

Fort(e), Foort, Lefort (< OF *fort* 'strong')	Strong(e), Strang, Starks
Rous(e), Rowse, Ruse, Russ	Red(d), Read(e), Reed, Reid
(< OF *rous(e)* 'red')	
Russel(l), Russill, Roussel(l), Rousel(l)	"
(< OF *rousel,* a diminutive of *rous* 'red')	
Rudge (< OF *rug(g)e* 'red')	"
Main(e), Mayne(s), Mains	Greet; Mi(t)chel(l), Mutchell; Muckle; Mich, Mu(t)ch

(< OF *magne, maine* 'great')

J(e)une, Lejeune; Jevon(s), Jeavons	Yo(u)ng(e),Youngs
(< OF *jovene, jone* 'young')	
Veal(e), Veall, Veel	Old(s), Ould(s)
(< Anglo-Norman *viel;* OF *vieil* 'old')	
Court(s), Corte, Curt	Short(t)
(< OF *co(u)rt* 'short, small')	

Other nouns

French Family Name	English Equivalent
Pray	Mead(e), Meads, Meadow(s), Medewe
(< OF *pray* 'meadow')	
Boice, Boyce, Boy(e)s, Boyse	Wood(s), Woode, Woodd, Wod(e), Wald(e), Weald, Wolde, Waud, We(i)ld, Would(s)
(< OF *bo(i)s* 'wood')	
Pont(e), Punt	Bridge (and from Old Norse Brigg[s].)
(< OF *pont* 'bridge')	
Stoyle(s)	Starr
(< OF *estoile* 'star')	

The origin of a name is sometimes greatly disputed. One such example is *Arundel*. In England, it is attested both as a place-name and as a family name. As a surname, it occurs in the southwestern parts of England and in Yorkshire in the north (see also Reaney and Wilson 2005, *s.v.* 'Arundale ' and variants). Firstly, *Arundel* may be of Norman-French origin and a nickname for someone thought to resemble a swallow, from Old French *arondele,* a diminutive of *aronde* 'swallow'. The surname from this source is first recorded in the *Domesday Book*. *Arundel* may also be of Old English origin and a locational name from a Sussex parish thus called, recorded as *Harundel* in the *Domesday Book*, and so named from Old English *hārhūn-dell* 'hoarhound valley' (< Old English *hārhūne*). Early locational surnames include Robert *de Arundell* (Sussex 1332). Vennemann remarks:

> This etymology is likely to be a learned folk-etymology: First, the initial *h* in the *Domesday Book* rendering *Harundel* is surely but a French spelling and not an organic part of the name, as is shown by the later and modern forms, and even with this *h* a reconstruction of *hārhūne* from *(h)arun* [a river name as postulated by Ekwall 1960] would not be cogent. Second, Ekwall does not make it plausible that the place is or was in any way marked by hoarhound, and without such evidence the reconstruction is unfounded. Thus the etymology fails on both phonological and semantic grounds.

(Vennemann 2003: 486)

Instead, Vennemann proposes an analysis of *Arundel* as part of his *Europa Vasconica* approach that starts with Vasconic **Arana* 'the valley' and proceeds on the model of the Gascon *Val d'Aran*. He adds that such an analysis is also supported by the description of the place in *The New Encyclopaedia Britannica* (1973).

> When the Vasconic language of the region disappeared, the name **Arana* was no longer understood as a descriptive term meaning 'the valley', but since it did refer to a valley, namely the valley of the river Arun through the South Downs, the name, by this time shortened to **Aran* and with a reduced second syllable, [arən], was given new descriptive reference in Old English by adding a head, *dell* 'vale', yielding *Arundell* (a. 1087). The settlement was named for the valley.

(Vennemann 2003: 486-487)

This, no doubt, is an interesting alternative whose greatest weakness, however, is the lack of attestation for Arun prior to the mid-16th century. The greater age of this river name may be proved one day if earlier attestations are found.

So much for a brief survey of the French influence on English naming.

I would now like to present our project of an atlas of English surnames carried out at the University of Bamberg/Germany. The first volume was published two years ago (Barker et al. 2007). The second and final volume will go to press in two years' time. But first some general remarks.

3. Earlier research

The publications dealing with the distributional patterns of selected family names in the United Kingdom – and this overview is restricted to these – are anything but numerous and comprehensive. An early book was published by Guppy already in

1890 under the title *Homes of family names in Great Britain*. His distributional data are based on counting surnames of peasants in late Victorian county address books. Unfortunately, his book does not contain any maps. The first person who studied the geography of a name, his own, was Leeson (1964) who started from 16th century Parish Register Records over General Register Office Indexes of 1841 – 1850 down to an analysis of a telephone directory of 1961. Leeson was well ahead of his time. Only twenty years later did such surname geographic publications become a little more numerous. Brett (1985), Porteous (1987), Ecclestone (1989) and Titterton (1990) derserve to be mentioned in this regard. Their contributions contain a few distributional surname maps. A first peak in this kind of research was reached with Colin Rogers' *The Surname Detective* (1995). Worth mentioning from the surname-geographic point of view are, finally, Steve Archer's *The British 19th century surname atlas* (2003), mapping the 1881 Census results; Hey (1997) and (2000) who, for one thing, used the telephone directories of the late 1980s and, for another, the Parish Death Registers of 1842 and 1846; and, again, Hey (1999) and (2003) who apart from providing a general overview also mapped the distribution of some rarer family names on the basis of the Census results of 1881[1]. In the contributions mentioned, a welcome methodological diversity becomes noticeable, as does the fact that quite different data records from quite different periods of time were drawn upon. What is lacking, is a concerted action. Hopefully, this will come about one day. This concerted action should also include the Bamberg surname project that I would now like to present briefly. In compiling our atlas, we have done what the available databases permitted us to do. Of course, we could not investigate the origin of the single surnames in Parish Registers or tax lists that are hidden in English county archives. This task must be left to researchers in England. One such study is Porteous (1988) who traced the origin of the *Mells* family.

4. Databases used in the Bamberg project

We rely on the following databases:

1. *The International Genealogical Index* (IGI) for the period between 1538 and 1850 and *The British Isles Vital Records Index* (VRI) for the period between 1538 and 1906. It was in 1538 when Henry VIII introduced obligatory Parish Register Records shortly after the separation of the Church of England from Rome. The IGI is a compilation of Parish Register Records (consisting of birth, baptism, marriage and death or burial records) made available by the Church of Jesus Christ of Latter-Day Saints, better known as Mormons. The

---

1   The publications of the human biologists are not mentioned here since they pursued a different aim insofar as they selected some names whose bearers married in England and Wales during the first three months of 1975. For population geneticists the adult breeding population is of greater interest than the birth or death announcements.

Mormons' great interest in genealogy goes back to their belief that families stay together in the other world. Therefore members of this church seek their ancestors in order to prepare them for a "sealing of their families" that can only take place after all the ancestors have been discovered[2]. The IGI, of course, has weaknesses, such as the fact that the same persons were mentioned several times, or that a specific part of the population was not registered in most of the Parish Registers, namely those persons who did not belong to the Anglican Church. Records could also have been lost through fire and other catastrophes. The double listing of names in the IGI was largely removed in the VRI. This database was also made available by the Mormons; it consists of about 12.3 million records and is obtainable on two CD-ROMs, one of records of births and baptisms and the other of marriage records.

2. In Great Britain censuses have been carried out since 1801. Only since 1841 have they become more valuable, as since then they have contained statistical data. The Mormons published the census results of 1881 on CD-ROM. They are more exact than the IGI, but they are not flawless either. Occasionally one encounters orthographic mistakes. In those years about half the British population could either not read or write at all or only to a certain degree. The weaknesses of the database have, however, largely been corrected by genealogy experts. As the maps of the aforementioned *British 19th century surname atlas* by Steve Archer are in colour, we had to do without them as their publication would have been too costly. A conversion into black and white maps was only possible in exceptional cases, namely when the occurrences of the names were low, but normally it proved to be senseless as the various gradations were no longer distinguishable. As a consequence the census results of 1881 were usually presented in the form of tables.

3. With regard to the present-day geography of family names, telephone directories were used, the *UK-Info Disk 2004* to be more precise. Altogether 11.5 million entries were searched. People who did not want to be listed were disregarded, of course. However, there were also those who were listed twice – with a private and a business number.

5. Mapping procedures

Several possibilities existed in mapping the data. They were either presented on area fill maps using the county level, on point maps or on pie charts whenever several names or variants were to be compared with each other. The circles vary

---

2   The Mormons, of course, also made such records available for other countries, not just for the British Isles.

in size thus indicating a greater versus a lower concentration of the surname and its variants.

Maps based on the IGI or the VRI data were first cleared of double listings with the program *LDS Companion* and then generated with the software *GenMap UK*. The telephone directory data were first converted into Excel data lists which were then generated into maps with the software *PCMap*. These maps show, in addition, the absolute number of occurrences of the surnames per county.

6. Some results

For reasons of space only a few surnames can be presented here from each of the four main categories mentioned above.

6.1. *Disney*

The first example is a local surname, namely *Disney* (see Maps 1 and 2)[3], whose origin was already mentioned. Up to the 18th century, *Disney* occurred exclusivley in the east of the country. Yet from the 19th century onwards, the *Disneys* have moved to the west of England also, some even to Scotland. They have always been few in number. According to Reaney and Wilson (2005) the first bearers of the surname *Disney* were all from Lincolnshire (William *de Ysini*, ca. 1150; *de Yseigni*, 1177 and *Adam Dyseni*, 1202). This situation did not change from the 12th to the 18th century. Also the London area, East Anglia and Essex and Nottinghamshire have had their share of *Disneys* for centuries. The bearers of this name showed and still show a strong attachment to the soil where their ancestors had settled – a picture that we find rather often with other surnames also. The only difference here is that the southwesterly movement of the *Disneys*, already noticeable in the 19th century, increased during the following century. But the numbers are too low to draw any conclusions.

6.2. *Fitzgerald, Fitzpatrick* and *Fitzsimmons*

Among the surnames of relationship, patronymics were chosen, namely forenames with the prefix *Fitz-* 'son of' (<Old French *fiz*). These surnames are quite interesting. The *Fitz-* surnames were used first among the upper layers of the society that owned land in many parts of England and Ireland in the 11th and the 12th century. But in England the fashion of *Fitz-* surnames dropped out of use in the course of time both among the higher and the lower classes. In contrast to the decline in England, *Fitz-* surnames became very popular in Ireland. *Fitzgerald* and

---

3   Map A provides a list of the county abbreviations, Map B is used for the historical maps and
     Map C for the present-day maps.

Fitzpatrick occurred very often there. The surname *Fitzgerald* (in Irish *Mac Gerailt*) came to Ireland as a result of the Anglo-Norman invasion and *Fitzpatrick* (*Mac Giolla Phádraig* 'devotee of Saint Patrick') is the only *Fitz-* surname of Irish Gaelic origin (MacLysaght 1991). *Fitzsim(m)on(s)* came from England to Leinster in 1323 (MacLysaght 1991); it is listed in Reaney and Wilson (2005) with a number of spelling variants, as is *Fitzgerald*, but only under *Gerald*, *Jarrod* etc. There is no trace of *Fitzpatrick* in Reaney and Wilson (2005). As Maps 3, 5 and 7 reveal, these surnames were quite rare in England in earlier centuries. The picture changed, however, in the second half of the 19th century when the Irish emigrated in great numbers to England during the time of the potato famine. They reintroduced, so to speak, many of these *Fitz-* surnames to England on a large scale. The distribution of the three *Fitz-* surnames chosen in England today is strikingly similar. Their greatest density is in the historical Lancashire area, an area that with the county reform of 1974 was divided into several smaller units, and in London (see Maps 4, 6 and 8). Map 9 reveals an especially strong correlation of both areas with Irish immigration. The same tendency is borne out for the three surnames already in the 19th century (see Maps 3, 5 and 7). The third strongest concentration of these three *Fitz-* surnames today is to be found in Lanarkshire in Scotland. As in the other regions, the industrialized area in and around the third largest city in Great Britain, Glasgow, attracted many Irish looking for work, which they apparently found there. (On *Fitzhugh* and variants cf. Viereck 2008b.) A strikingly similar distribution is revealed by a surname with a rather short history in England, namely *Murphy* (cf. Viereck 2009).

6.3. *Wait* and *Gait*

Occupational surnames come next, namely first the doublets *Wait* and *Gait*. The person so named was originally a watchman either in a fortified place or a town. The town waits combined the functions of watchman and musician. *Wait* ultimately goes back to Old northern French *waite* 'watchman'. In the general vocabulary, the *OED* (1989), *s.v.* 'wait', *sb.*, provides many different spellings of which only *wait* survived, a spelling attested since the 14th century. *Waite* and *wayte* had existed between the 13th and the 17th century and *waight* and *weight* only in the 17th century. With the exception of *wait* the other variants are, thus, examples of English words fossilized in English family names. Reaney and Wilson (2005) list quite a number of variants of *Wait*, namely *Waite*, *Waites*, *Waits*, *Wates*, *Wayt*, *Wayte*, *Waytes*, *Waight*, *Waighte*, *Weight*, *Weait*, *Whait*, *Whaite*, *Whaites*, *Whaits* and *Whate* (the forms with *-s* mean 'son of W.'). According to this dictionary, the first bearers of this name were Ailward *Waite* 1170-87 (London), Roger *la Waite* 1197 (Warwickshire), Ralph *laweite* 12th century (Nottinghamshire), Roger *le Wayte* 1221 (Suffolk), John *la Wayte* 1243 (Somerset), Hugh *le Weyt* 1251 (Staffordshire), Roger *le Wate* 1296 (Sussex),

Adam *le Whaite* 1349 (Gloucestershire) and Richard *Waight, Weight* 1595, 1610 (no region mentioned). As the list makes clear the supposition, often heard, that the absence of the article points to a hereditary surname cannot be upheld, for as early as in the 12th century the article is already frequently omitted. The most frequently occurring variants from the 16th to the 19th century were *Wait, Waite, Wayte, Waight* and *Weight* (for their development also in map form, see Viereck 2008a). None of them ever occurred in Wales. Instead, the five variants often co-existed side by side in the same areas of England. All originated in the South and in the Midlands, as the above list of first bearers already suggested. Maps 10 and 11 feature the absolute distribution of *Wait* and *Waite* according to the UK-Info Disk 2004. The highest density of the surnames *Wait* and *Waite* is to be found in West Yorkshire, next comes the London area. Both regions witnessed a remarkable population increase due to important industrial developments providing work for thousands of people.

   Gait is a doublet of *Wait*. It ultimately goes back to Old central French *gaite, guaite* 'watchman'. According to Reaney and Wilson (2005), the first bearers of the name were Reginald *Gayt* 1139 (Oxfordshire), Robert *le Gayt* 1205 (Oxfordshire), William *le Guaite* 1208 (Staffordshire), Stephen, Thomas *Gayt(e)* 1297 and 1331 (Yorkshire), John *Gaytt, Gate* 1390 and 1416 (Yorkshire), Richard *Gaites* 1561 (Yorkshire). Reaney and Wilson (2005) assume that the Yorkshire forms are probably from Old Norse *geit* 'goat'. With the meaning 'watchman' *Gait* is neither attested in the *OED* (1989) nor in the *MED* (1954-1999). As was the case with *Waite*, the article is omitted already as early as in the 12th century. From the 16th to the 19th century, the occurrence of *Gait* is extremely low (see Map 12), much lower than the rarest of the *Wait* forms. In the 19th century, *Gait* was attested a little more often in Wiltshire, where it, surprisingly, occurred side by side with *Wait, Waite, Wayte, Waight* and *Weight*. In the 20th and early 21st centuries, the largest concentration of *Gait* – still in rather low numbers – is in south-western England in the area around Bristol, as well as in southern Wales (Newport and Cardiff) (see Map 13). This move from neighbouring Wiltshire certainly had economic reasons. (On the development of Bristol, see Hall 1976: 439f.). Interestingly, the *Gaits'* doublet relatives moved in the same direction.

6.4. *Chandler* and *Candler*

Another occupational surname doublet is *Chandler* and *Candler*, meaning 'maker or seller of candles'. While a medieval chandler no doubt made and sold other articles besides candles, the extended sense of modern English *chandler* does not occur until the 16th century. More rarely, the name denoted someone who was responsible for the lighting arrangements in a larger household (Hanks and Hodges 1988). *Chandler* goes back to Old central French *chandelier* and *Candler* to Old northern French *candelier*. According to Reaney and Wilson (2005), the first bearers of the surname were Matthew *le Candeler* (London 1274) and William le

Chandeler (Essex 1285). Black 1993: 146 informs us about a John the "Candelar" who was appointed to bring certain Scottish jewels and writings from Berwick to London in September 1296 and, thus, gives an early example of a northern British bearer of this name. McKinley 1988 notes that in many topographical surnames as well as in some occupational ones, the suffix *-er* is interchangeable with *-man*. He provides the doublets *Candeler* and *Candelman* (McKinley 1988). However, only four *Candelman* are registered in Surrey in the 1881 Census and none in the UK-Info Disk 2004 of the early 21st century. The VRI provides data for *Chandler* from the 16th century onwards. The distribution of this name is concentrated in the south of England except the extreme southwest (Map 14). Already in the 1881 Census, *Chandler* outnumbered *Candler* by far. The ratio is 9,619 *Chandlers* versus only 576 *Candlers*. In the late 19th century, the *Candlers* occurred mainly in the Southeast of England, but also in the North of the country, whereas the *Chandlers* were restricted almost exclusively to the South, mainly the Southeast. Today the predominance of *Chandler* has strengthened enormously. While only 808 *Candlers* can be found in the UK-Info Disk 2004, 22,195 *Chandlers* are registered in this data base. Their distribution patterns have not changed much throughout the centuries; the highest concentrations of *Chandler*, but now also of *Candler*, are in the southeast of England (see Maps 15 and 16).

6.5. *Cat(t)*

The next example is a nickname, namely *Cat(t)*. This name ultimately goes back to Old English *cat(t)* and Old northern French *cat* whose origins are unknown. The word is Common European, found in Latin and Greek and in the modern languages generally, as far back as their records go. History points to Egypt as the earliest home of the domestic cat; and the name is generally sought in the same area (*OED* 1989). For English, the *OED*, *s.v.* 'cat', *sb.*1, lists the following forms: *cat*, *catt*, *catte* (before 1100), *catt* (from the 12th to the 17th century), *catte* (from the 14th to the 16th century), *kat* (from the 13th to the 17th century) and *katte* (attested in the 16th century). An additional form *katt* is listed separately in this dictionary and marked as an obsolete form of *cat*. As family names, Reaney and Wilson (2005) provide the following main orthographic variants: *Catt*, *Katte* and *Chatt*. The latter form derived from Old French *chat*, which was the central French form as opposed to the Old northern French form *cat*. As first bearers of the surname Reaney and Wilson (2005) attest the following: Lufman*cat* (1066 Hampshire), Robert *le Cat* (1167 Norfolk), Geoffrey *Chat* (1190-1200 Suffolk), Margaret *Kat* (1202 London) and Adam *le Chat* (1203 Wiltshire). In addition *Catte* and *Katt* show up in the databases. *Catte* can be found in the 16th century. Its frequency as a surname decreased during the following centuries, but it still survives, as does *Katt*, if only sparingly. As only the spelling *cat* remained in the general language, the other variants mentioned – on *Chat(t)* see below – are spellings fossilized in English surnames.

With the exception of *Chatt* and *Catt*, none of the remaining variants appeared to be numerous. *Cat, Catte, Kat* and *Katte* are attested within the same areas as *Catt*. Most of the VRI entries of *Cat* and *Catte* can be found in Sussex and Kent. *Kat* is also located in Kent, while *Katt* appears twice in Suffolk and *Katte* once in Hampshire. In the data of the VRI and the 1881 Census, *Chatt* and *Chat* occurred most often in the northern English counties of Northumberland (*Chatt*), Durham (*Chatt, Chat*) and the North Riding of Yorkshire (*Chat*). Further, *Chat* is located in Norfolk and Surrey and *Chatt* in Hampshire. In the general language, *chat*, of course, exists but with an onomatopoetic origin and, consequently, with different meanings. From a dialectological point of view, Wright's *EDD* (1898-1905), *s.v.* 'chat', *sb*.3 and *v*.3, attests *chat* in the sense of 'kitten' only in southern England. The *Chat(t)s* in the north most probably go back to a different root, but only Barber (1968: 113) states that *Chatt* is likely to be a variant of *Chadd* (from Old English *ceadda* 'battle'). *Ceadda* was a 7th - century English saint whose name was possibly based on Welsh *cad* with the meaning already mentioned. Moreover, Reaney and Wilson (2005) assume that *Catt* probably sometimes refers to a pet-form of *Catelin*. So we have here a surname that goes back to more than one origin, a situation we find rather often in onomastics. The main origin is, of course, *cat*. Scholars are silent as to why a person was named after that animal. Probably a person was so named when he showed cat-like behaviour, either physically or referring to one's mental or moral characteristics. The latter could very well be rather negative (cf. Güntert 1987).

Map 17 shows the historical diffusion of *Catt, Catte, Cat* and *Chatt* from the 16th century and of *Catt* and *Chatt* in the early 21st century (Map 18). In contrast to the earlier point maps, Map 17 is a so-called area fill map, while Map 18 is a pie-chart map on which the points vary in size – as they do on the non-historical point maps – in order to display areas of higher versus lower concentration of the name. All maps show quite clearly that *Catt* is a south-eastern English family name with the highest number of entries in Sussex and Kent. The *Catts* have stayed in this area for centuries (see Map 17); only rather few have travelled to the Southwest, the Midlands and the north of England and very few to Scotland during the 19th and 20th centuries. This is a picture we find rather often: People tend to cluster near their onomastic origin. This is also true of other countries, such as Germany (cf. Wolff 2007).

6.6. *Flowerdew*

Anglicisation of English family names of French origin could even lead to folk etymology, insinuating English compounds, as is the case with *Flowerdew*. It goes back to Old French *flor-dieu* 'God's flower' and originated as an oath-name like *Debney* ('God bless [him]') – the first bearer of this name was a Robert *Deulebeneie* (1162), *Dugard* (<French *Dieu (te) garde* 'God guard (you)', the

modern French surname is *Dieutegard* - the first English bearer of that name was a Richard *Deugard* (1322), or *Pardew, Pardey, Pardy, Pardoe* and *Perdue* (<French *par Dieu* < *de par Dieu* 'in God's name'), first attested as an English surname in 1228 with a Richard *Parde*. Some of these names may also have been nicknames. In the case of *Flowerdew*, the term may have been given to someone who was greatly concerned with the smartness of dress. This surname is first recorded in England rather late, namely in the mid 15th century. The first bearers of this family name were a William *Flowerdew* and a Thomas *Flowerdew*. Map 19 shows that, according to the 1881 Census results, this unusual surname was found particularly often in Norfolk; of the 160 occurrences half of them were attested in that county. Since the late 19th century the surname *Flowerdew* has decreased more and more.

6.7. *Sartin* and *Sertain*

The final examples exhibit special phonological developments in English. Both *Sertain* and *Sartin* go back to Old French *certeyn* 'self-assured, determined'. The first bearers of this nickname were, according to Reaney and Wilson (2005), William *Certayn* (1394) and Richard *Sartin* (1693). A person with the spelling *Sertain* is not attested in this dictionary. During the 15th century /ɛ/ before /r/ of the same syllable was lowered to /a/ (for instance in *sterten, sterre, herte, hervest* > *start, star, heart, harvest*). At first, also Latin and French loanwords were covered by this change. But in Early Modern English, the pronunciation in most of the loanwords was changed back under the humanistic influence of the retained etymological spelling. This led to the present pronunciation in, for instance, *certain, servant, service* and *version*, whereas the sound change remained in only a few words, such as *clerk, parson* and *sergeant* (in British English). Yet in the family names we repeatedly find both pronunciations and both spellings, as in the surnames under discussion. Map 20 shows the historical development of *Sertain* and Map 21 the historical development of *Sartin*. Both surnames are quite rare: The VRI total (from the 16th to the 19th century) of *Sertain* is only 28, that of *Sartin* 108. The occurrences of the 1881 Census are 15 for *Sertain* and 156 for *Sartin*. The UK-Info Disk 2004 no longer lists *Sertain*, whereas *Sartin* shows 342 entries (see Map 22 for their distribution). In this case, the earlier pronunciation is retained more often than the later one.

 That surnames do not always follow the same pattern is shown by *Service/Sarvice* and *Servant/Sarvant*. In the first-mentioned surname pair the earlier pronunciation hardly ever occurs (only twice in the 1881 Census), whereas *Service* shows 901 entries in the UK-Info Disk 2004. The last-mentioned surname pair reveals the same picture. The numbers of UK-Info Disk 2004 entries for *Servant* amount to 65 and for *Sarvant* only to 7.

References

DATABASES

The British 19th century surname atlas v.1.04. Display and Print Maps for any Surname or Forename. *CD-ROM. Archer Software. April 2003.*
The British census 1881. CD-ROM. 24 disks. Intellectual Reserve. June 1998.
The British Isles Vital Records Index. Sec. ed. CD-ROM. 16 disks. Intellectual Reserve. March 2002.
International Genealogical Index v.5.0. 12 October 2001. Family Search Internet Genealogical Service. 01 May 2004. <http://www.familysearch.org>
UK-Info Professional V9 2004. CD-ROM. I-CD Publishing. London. October 2003.

SOFTWARE

GenMap UK v. 2.10. CD-ROM. Archer Software. November 2003.
LDS Companion v2.12. CD-ROM. Archer Software. March 2003.
PCMap 10.0. CD-ROM. GISCAD Institute Germany. 1998.

SECONDARY LITERATURE

Barber, Henry
    1968   *British family names: Their origin and meaning.* (2nd ed.). Detroit: Gale Research Comp.
Barker, Stephanie – Stefankai Spoerlein – Tobias Vetter – Wolfgang Viereck
    2007   *An atlas of English surnames.* Frankfurt: Lang.
Bächtold-Stäubli, Hanns – Eduard Hoffmann-Krayer (eds.)
    1987   *Handwörterbuch des deutschen Aberglaubens.* Berlin: de Gruyter.
Black, George F.
    1993   *The surnames of Scotland: Their origin, meaning and history.* New York: New York Public Library.
Brett, Donald
    1985   "The use of telephone directories in surname studies", *The Local Historian* 16: 392-404.
Cameron, Kenneth
    1961   *English place-names.* London: B. T. Batsford.
Clark, Cecily
    1995   *Words, names and history. Selected papers*, ed. by Peter Jackson. Cambridge: D. S. Brewer.
Darby, Henry C. (ed.)
    1976   *A new historical geography of England after 1600.* Cambridge: Cambridge University Press.
Ecclestone, Martin
    1989   "The diffusion of English surnames", *The Local Historian* 19: 63-70.

Ekwall, Eilert
1960   *Concise Oxford dictionary of English place-names*. Oxford: Clarendon Press.

Erlebach, Peter
1968   *Bildungstypen englischer Zunamen französischer Herkunft*. [Ph.D. dissertation]. University of Mainz.

Güntert, Hermann
1987   "Katze", in: Bächtold-Stäubli, Hanns – Eduard Hoffmann-Krayer (eds.), cols. 1107-1124.

Guppy, Henry Brougham
1968 [1890] *Homes of family names in Great Britain*. Baltimore: Genealogical Publishing Company.

Hall, Peter
1976   "England *circa* 1900", in: Darby, Henry C. (ed.), 374-446.

Hanks, Patrick – Flavia Hodges
1988   *A dictionary of surnames*. Oxford: Oxford University Press.

Harris, Alan
1976   "Changes in the early railway age: 1800-1850", in: Darby, Henry C. (ed.), 165-226.

Hey, David
1997   "Locating the home of a family name", in: Reaney, P.H. – R.M. Wilson (eds.), 511-520.
1999   "The local history of family names", *The Local Historian* 27 (4): I-XX.
2000   *Family names and family history*. London: Hambledon.
2003   "Recent advances in the study of surnames", *The Historian* 80: 13-17.

Hofmann, Matthias
1934   *Die Französisierung des Personennamenschatzes im Domesday Book der Grafschaften Hampshire und Sussex*. [Ph.D. dissertation]. University of Munich.

Kreiler, Kurt
2009   *Der Mann, der Shakespeare erfand – Edward de Vere, Earl of Oxford*. Frankfurt: Insel Verlag.

Kristensson, Gillis
1969   "Studies on Middle English local surnames containing elements of French origin", *English Studies* 50: 465-486.

Kurath, Hans et al.
1954-1999 *Middle English dictionary*. Ann Arbor: The University of Michigan Press.

Leeson, Francis
1964   "The study of single surnames and their distribution", *The Genealogists' Magazine* 14.2. Repr. in *The Journal of One-Name Studies* 3.6, 1989: 174-180.

MacLysaght, Edward
1991   *The surnames of Ireland*. (6th ed.). Dublin: Irish Academic Press.

McClure, Peter
    1981   "The interpretation of Middle English nicknames", *Nomina* 5: 95-104.
    1998   "The interpretation of hypocoristic forms of Middle English baptismal
                 names", *Nomina* 21: 101-132.
McKinley, Richard A.
    1988   *The surnames of Sussex*. (English Surnames Series 5). Oxford: Leopard's
                 Head.
The New Encyclopaedia Britannica. 1973. (15th ed.). Chicago: Encyclopaedia Britannica.
Porteous, J. Douglas
    1987   "Locating the place of origin of a surname", *The Local Historian* 18:
                 391-395.
    1988   *The Mells: surname geography, family history*. Saturnalia, B.C., Canada:
                 The Saturna Island Thinktank Press.
Reaney, P. H.
    1978   *The origin of English surnames*. (4th impr.). London: Routledge & Kegan
                 Paul.
Reaney, P.H. – R.M. Wilson
    2005   *A dictionary of English surnames*. (Rev. 3rd ed.). Oxford: Oxford Univer-
    [1997]   sity Press.
Redmonds, George
    1997   *Surnames and genealogy: A new approach*. Boston: New England
                 Historic Genealogical Society.
Rogers, Colin D.
    1995   *The surname detective. Investigating surname distribution in England,
                 1086 – present day*. Manchester: Manchester University Press.
Saramandu, Nicolae – Manuela Nevaci – Carmen Iona Radu (eds.)
    2009   *Lucrările Celui de al Doilea Simpozion Internaţional de Lingvistică.
                 Bucureşti, 28/29 noiembrie, 2008*. Bucharest: editura universităţii din
                 bucureşti.
Simpson, John A. – Edmund S. C. Weiner (comps.)
    1989   *The Oxford English dictionary*. (2nd ed.). Oxford: Clarendon Press.
Tengvik, Gösta
    1938   *Old English bynames*. (Nomina Germanica 4). University of Uppsala
                 dissertation.
Titterton, John
    1990   "Pinpointing the origin of a surname", *The Local Historian* 20: 3-8.
Vennemann, Theo
    2003   *Europa Vasconica – Europa Semitica*. Berlin: de Gruyter.
Viereck, Wolfgang
    2008a   "English family names", *Studia Anglica Posnaniensia* 44: 155-191.
    2008b   "Language on the map. On the historical and geographic diffusion of
                 English family names", *Revue Roumaine de Linguistique* 53 : 47-77.
    2009   "English surname geography", in: Saramandu, Nicolae – Manuela Nevaci
                 – Carmen Iona Radu (eds.), 21-48.

Wolff, Philip
    2007   "Hier wohnen Hinz und Kunz: Globalisierung hin oder her – die Deutschen bleiben gern am selben Flecken. Ihre Familiennamen verraten es". Available at: http://www.sueddeutsche.de/wissen/artikel/575/111464/print.html.

Wright, Joseph (ed.)
    1898-1905   *The English dialect dictionary.* (6 vols.). London: Henry Frowde.

Wyld, Henry Cecil
    1936   *A history of modern colloquial English.* (3rd ed.). Oxford: Blackwell.

Table of County Abbreviations (based on "Chapman Codes")

Abbreviation	County	Abbreviation	County
ABD	Aberdeenshire	SYK	South Yorkshire
ANS	Angus	STS	Staffordshire
ARL	Argylishire	STI	Stirlingshire
AVN	Avon	SFK	Suffolk
AYR	Ayrshire	SRY	Surrey
BAN	Banffshire	SUT	Sutherland
BDF	Bedfordshire	TWR	Tine and Wear
BRK	Berkshire	WAR	Warwickshire
BEW	Berwickshire	WGM	West Glamorgan
BKM	Buckinghamshire	WMD	West Midland
CAI	Caithness	SXW	West Sussex
CAM	Cambridgeshire	WYK	West Yorkshire
CHS	Cheshire	WLN	Westlothian
CLK	Clackmannanshire	WIG	Wigtownshire
CLE	Cleveland	WIL	Wiltshire
CLW	Clwyd*		
CON	Cornwall	**VRI and Census maps only**	
CUM	Cumbria	AGY	Anglesey
DBY	Derbyshire	BRE	Brecknockshire
DEV	Devon	BUT	Buteshire
DOR	Dorset	CAE	Caernarfonshire
DFS	Dumfriesshire	CGN	Cardiganshire
DNB	Dumbarton	CMN	Carmarthenshire
DUR	County Durham	CUL	Cumberland
DFD	Dyfed	DEN	Denbighshire
ELN	East Lothian	ERY	East Riding Yorkshire
SXE	East Sussex	FLN	Flintshire
ESS	Essex	GLA	Glamorgan
FIF	Fife	HEF	Herefordshire
GLS	Gloucestershire	HUN	Huntingdonshire
LND	Greater London	IOM	Isle of Man
GTM	Greater Manchester	IOW	Isle of Wight
GNT	Gwent	MDX	Middlesex
GWY	Gwynedd	MER	Merioneth
HAM	Hampshire	MGY	Montgomeryshire
HWR	Hereford and Worcester	MON	Monmouthshire
HRT	Hertfordshire	NRY	North Riding Yorkshire
HUM	Humberside	PEM	Pembrokeshire
INV	Inverness-shire	RAD	Radnorshire
KEN	Kent	RUT	Rutland
KCD	Kincardineshire	SSX	Sussex
KRS	Kinross-shire	WES	Westmorland
KKD	Kirkcudbrightshire	WOR	Worcestershire
LKS	Lanarkshire	WRY	West Riding Yorkshire
LAN	Lancashire	YOR	York
LEI	Leicestershire		
LIN	Lincolnshire	**Conversion Table**	
MSY	Merseyside	VRI and Census counties into UK-Info Disk counties	
MGY	Mid Glamorgan	Abbreviation	County
MLN	Midlothian	AGY	Not included
MOR	Morayshire	BRE+MGY+RAD	POW
NAI	Nairnshire	BUT	Not included
NFK	Norfolk	CAE+MER	GWY
NYK	North Yorkshire	CGN+CMN+PEM	DFD
NTH	Northamptonshire	CUL+WES	CUM
NBL	Northumberland	DEN+FLN	CLW
NTT	Nottinghamshire	ERY	HUM (Part of)
OKI	Orkney	GLA	MGM+SGM+WGM
OXF	Oxfordshire	HEF+WOR	HWR
PEE	Peeblesshire	HUN	CAM (Part of)
PER	Perthshire	IOM	Not included
POW	Powys	IOW	Not included
RFW	Renfrewshire	LAN	LAN+GTM+MSY
ROC	Ross-shire and Cromartyshire	MDX	LND
ROX	Roxburghshire	MON	GNT
SAL	Shropshire	NRY+YOR	NYK
SEL	Selkirkshire	RUT	LEI (Part of)
SHI	Shetland Islands	DUR	DUR+CLE+TWR
SOM	Somerset	SSX	SXE+SXW
SGM	South Glamorgan	WRY	WYK+SYK

*County Clwyd resembles the UK-Info data for Flintshire County. This seems to disregard the fact that the no longer existing county Clwyd consisted of Denbighshire and Wrexham as well as of Flintshire County. Yet, Denbigshire and Wrexham are searchable in a subfolder of Flintshire County and thus part of the data received for Flintshire County, i.e. Clwyd.

Map A

IGI, VRI and Census 1881 Map

The IGI, VRI and Census maps are generated directly with the software GenMap UK
and display the pre-1974 county borders. They very closely resemble the borders
used in the UK-Info maps generated with PCMap.

Map B

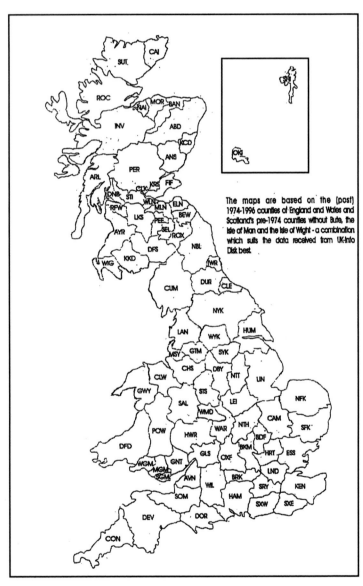

The maps are based on the (post) 1974-1996 counties of England and Wales and Scotland's pre-1974 counties without Bute, the Isle of Man and the Isle of Wight - a combination which suits the data received from UK-Info Disk best.

UK-Info 2004: County Codes Reference Map

Map C

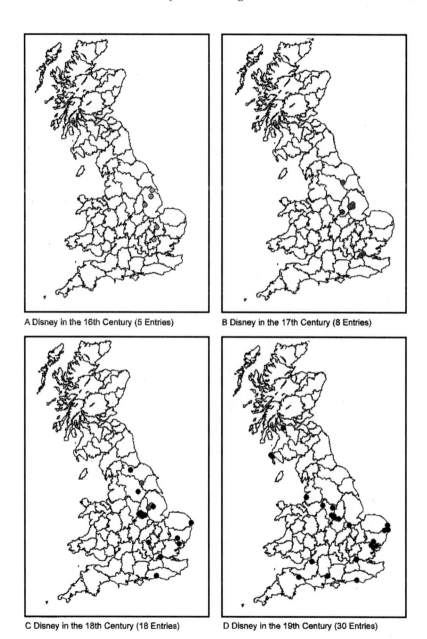

A Disney in the 16th Century (5 Entries)

B Disney in the 17th Century (8 Entries)

C Disney in the 18th Century (18 Entries)

D Disney in the 19th Century (30 Entries)

Map 1

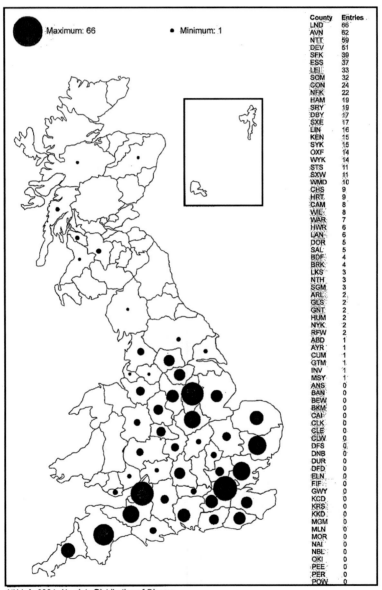

County	Entries
LND	66
AVN	62
NTT	59
DEV	51
SFK	39
ESS	37
LEI	33
SOM	32
CON	24
NFK	22
HAM	19
SRY	19
DBY	17
SXE	17
LIN	16
KEN	15
SYK	15
OXF	14
WYK	14
STS	11
SXW	11
WMD	10
CHS	9
HRT	9
CAM	8
WIL	8
WAR	7
HWR	6
LAN	6
DOR	5
SAL	5
BDF	4
BRK	4
LKS	3
NTH	3
SGM	3
ARL	2
GLS	2
GNT	2
HUM	2
NYK	2
RFW	2
ABD	1
AYR	1
CUM	1
GTM	1
INV	1
MSY	1
ANS	0
BAN	0
BEW	0
BKM	0
CAI	0
CLK	0
CLE	0
CLW	0
DFS	0
DNB	0
DUR	0
DFD	0
ELN	0
FIF	0
GWY	0
KCD	0
KRS	0
KKD	0
MGM	0
MLN	0
MOR	0
NAI	0
NBL	0
OKI	0
PEE	0
PER	0
POW	0

Maximum: 66   Minimum: 1

UK-Info 2004: Absolute Distribution of *Disney*

Map 2

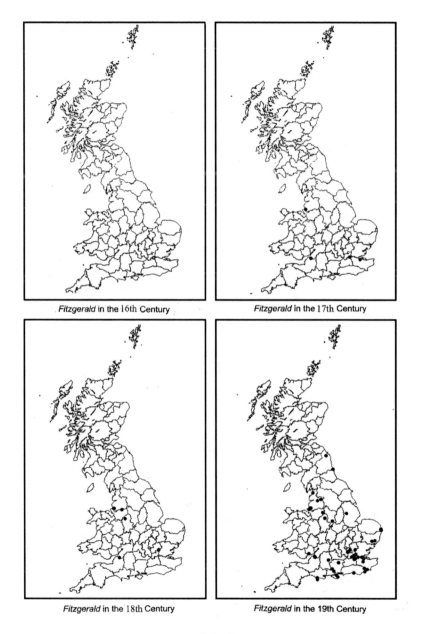

Fitzgerald in the 16th Century

Fitzgerald in the 17th Century

Fitzgerald in the 18th Century

Fitzgerald in the 19th Century

Map 3

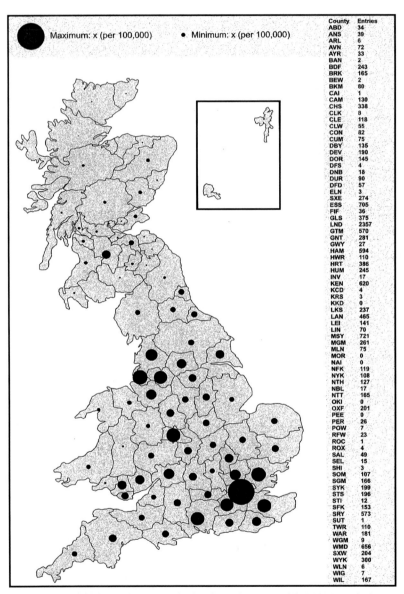

County	Entries
ABD	34
ANS	39
ARL	6
AVN	72
AYR	33
BAN	2
BDF	243
BRK	165
BEW	2
BKM	80
CAI	1
CAM	130
CHS	338
CLK	8
CLE	118
CLW	55
CON	82
CUM	75
DBY	135
DEV	190
DOR	145
DFS	4
DNB	18
DUR	90
DFD	57
ELN	3
SXE	274
ESS	705
FIF	36
GLS	375
LND	2357
GTM	570
GNT	281
GWY	27
HAM	594
HWR	110
HRT	386
HUM	245
INV	17
KEN	620
KCD	4
KRS	3
KKD	0
LKS	237
LAN	465
LEI	141
LIN	70
MSY	721
MGM	261
MLN	75
MOR	0
NAI	0
NFK	119
NYK	108
NTH	127
NBL	17
NTT	165
OKI	0
OXF	201
PEE	0
PER	26
POW	7
RFW	23
ROC	1
ROX	4
SAL	49
SEL	15
SHI	3
SOM	107
SGM	166
SYK	199
STS	196
STI	12
SFK	153
SRY	573
SUT	1
TWR	110
WAR	181
WGM	9
WMD	656
SXW	204
WYK	300
WLN	6
WIG	7
WIL	167

UK-Info 2004: Absolute Distribution of *Fitzgerald* (14611 entries)

Map 4

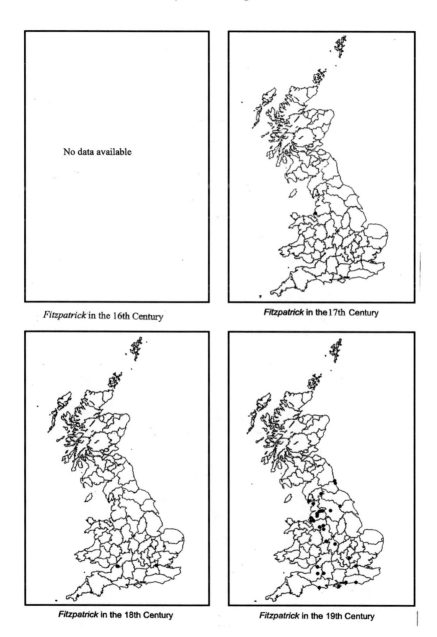

Map 5

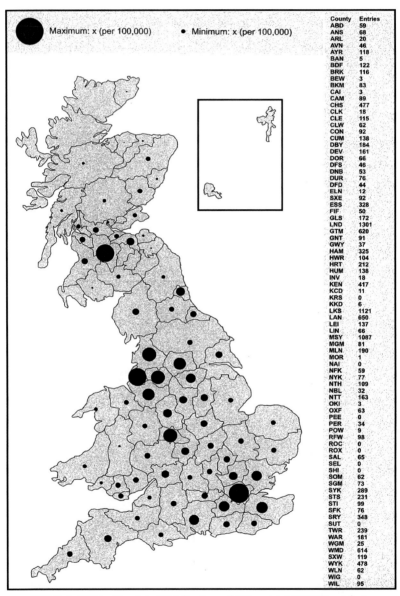

County	Entries
ABD	59
ANS	68
ARL	20
AVN	46
AYR	118
BAN	5
BDF	122
BRK	116
BEW	3
BKM	83
CAI	3
CAM	89
CHS	477
CLK	18
CLE	115
CLW	62
CON	92
CUM	138
DBY	184
DEV	161
DOR	66
DFS	46
DNB	53
DUR	76
DFD	44
ELN	12
SXE	92
ESS	328
FIF	50
GLS	172
LND	1301
GTM	620
GNT	91
GWY	37
HAM	325
HWR	104
HRT	212
HUM	138
INV	18
KEN	417
KCD	11
KRS	0
KKD	6
LKS	1121
LAN	650
LEI	137
LIN	66
MSY	1087
MGM	81
MLN	190
MOR	1
NAI	0
NFK	59
NYK	77
NTH	109
NBL	32
NTT	163
OKI	3
OXF	63
PEE	0
PER	34
POW	9
RFW	98
ROC	0
ROX	0
SAL	65
SEL	0
SHI	0
SOM	62
SGM	73
SYK	289
STS	231
STI	99
SFK	76
SRY	348
SUT	0
TWR	239
WAR	181
WGM	25
WMD	614
SXW	119
WYK	478
WLN	62
WIG	0
WIL	95

Maximum: x (per 100,000)   • Minimum: x (per 100,000)

UK-Info 2004: Absolute Distribution of *Fitzpatrick* (13240 entries)

Map 6

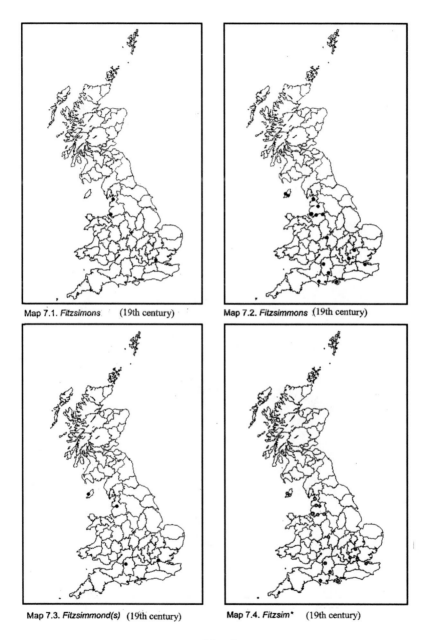

Map 7.1. *Fitzsimons* (19th century)

Map 7.2. *Fitzsimmons* (19th century)

Map 7.3. *Fitzsimmond(s)* (19th century)

Map 7.4. *Fitzsim** (19th century)

Map 7

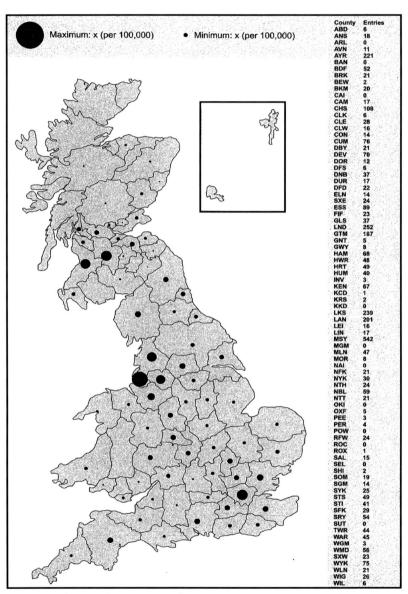

County	Entries
ABD	6
ANS	18
ARL	0
AVN	11
AYR	221
BAN	0
BDF	52
BRK	21
BEW	2
BKM	20
CAI	0
CAM	17
CHS	108
CLK	6
CLE	28
CLW	16
CON	14
CUM	76
DBY	21
DEV	70
DOR	12
DFS	6
DNB	37
DUR	17
DFD	22
ELN	14
SXE	24
ESS	89
FIF	23
GLS	37
LND	252
GTM	187
GNT	5
GWY	8
HAM	68
HWR	48
HRT	49
HUM	40
INV	3
KEN	67
KCD	1
KRS	2
KKD	0
LKS	239
LAN	201
LEI	16
LIN	17
MSY	542
MGM	0
MLN	47
MOR	8
NAI	0
NFK	21
NYK	30
NTH	24
NBL	59
NTT	21
OKI	0
OXF	5
PEE	3
PER	4
POW	0
RFW	24
ROC	0
ROX	1
SAL	15
SEL	0
SHI	2
SOM	19
SGM	14
SYK	25
STS	49
STI	41
SFK	29
SRY	54
SUT	0
TWR	44
WAR	45
WGM	3
WMD	56
SXW	23
WYK	75
WLN	21
WIG	26
WIL	6

Maximum: x (per 100,000)   • Minimum: x (per 100,000)

Uk-Info 2004: Absolute Distribution of *Fitzsimmon(s)/** (3527 entries)

Map 8

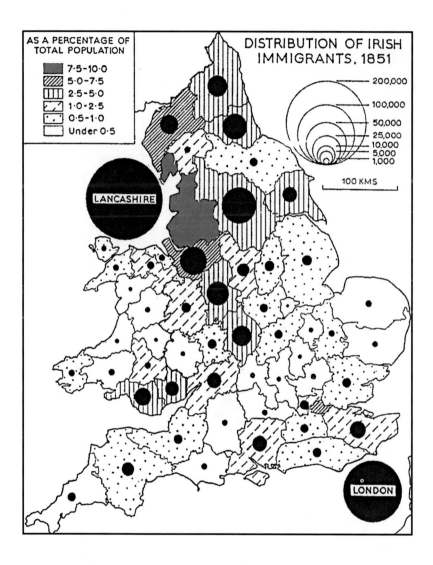

Distribution of Irish immigrants, 1851
Based on *Census of 1851: Population Tables, II*, vol. 1, pp. ccxc-ccxcvi (P.P. 1852-3, lxxxviii, pt 10.

Map 9

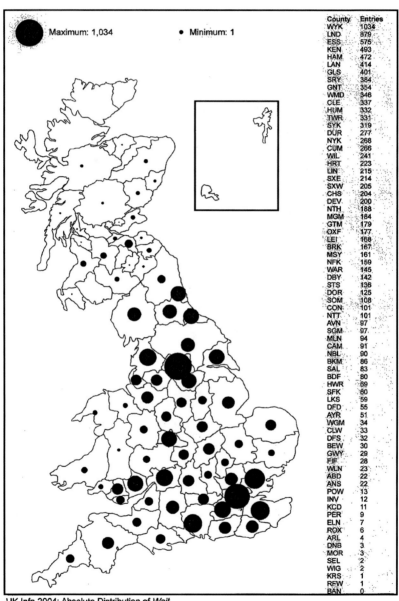

County	Entries
WYK	1034
LND	879
ESS	575
KEN	493
HAM	472
LAN	414
GLS	401
SRY	384
GNT	354
WMD	346
CLE	337
HUM	332
TWR	331
SYK	319
DUR	277
NYK	268
CUM	266
WIL	241
HRT	223
LIN	215
SXE	214
SXW	205
CHS	204
DEV	200
NTH	188
MGM	184
GTM	179
OXF	177
LEI	168
BRK	167
MSY	161
NFK	159
WAR	145
DBY	142
STS	136
DOR	125
SOM	108
CON	101
NTT	101
AVN	97
SGM	97
MLN	94
CAM	91
NBL	90
BKM	86
SAL	83
BDF	80
HWR	69
SFK	60
LKS	59
DFD	55
AYR	51
WGM	34
CLW	33
DFS	32
BEW	30
GWY	29
FIF	28
WLN	23
ABD	22
ANS	22
POW	13
INV	12
KCD	11
PER	9
ELN	7
ROX	6
ARL	4
DNB	3
MOR	3
SEL	2
WIG	2
KRS	1
RFW	1
BAN	0

Maximum: 1,034 • Minimum: 1

UK-Info 2004: Absolute Distribution of *Wait*

Map 10

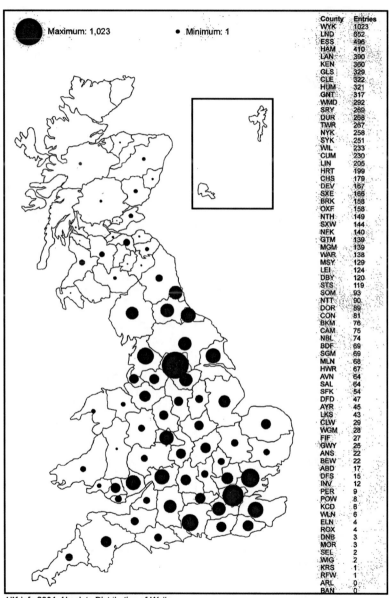

County	Entries
WYK	1023
LND	652
ESS	496
HAM	410
LAN	390
KEN	360
GLS	329
CLE	322
HUM	321
GNT	317
WMD	292
SRY	269
DUR	268
TWR	267
NYK	258
SYK	251
WIL	233
CUM	230
LIN	205
HRT	199
CHS	179
DEV	167
SXE	166
BRK	158
OXF	158
NTH	149
SXW	144
NFK	140
GTM	139
MGM	139
WAR	138
MSY	129
LEI	124
DBY	120
STS	119
SOM	93
NTT	90
DOR	89
CON	81
BKM	76
CAM	75
NBL	74
BDF	69
SGM	69
MLN	68
HWR	67
AVN	64
SAL	64
SFK	54
DFD	47
AYR	45
LKS	43
CLW	29
WGM	28
FIF	27
GWY	25
ANS	22
BEW	22
ABD	17
DFS	15
INV	12
PER	9
POW	8
KCD	6
WLN	6
ELN	4
ROX	4
DNB	3
MOR	3
SEL	2
WIG	2
KRS	1
RFW	1
ARL	0
BAN	0

Maximum: 1,023   Minimum: 1

UK-Info 2004: Absolute Distribution of *Waite*

Map 11

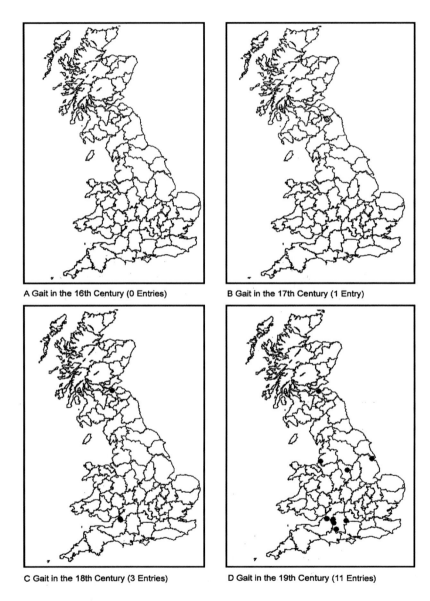

A Gait in the 16th Century (0 Entries)   B Gait in the 17th Century (1 Entry)

C Gait in the 18th Century (3 Entries)   D Gait in the 19th Century (11 Entries)

A black circle may stand for more than one entry.

Map 12

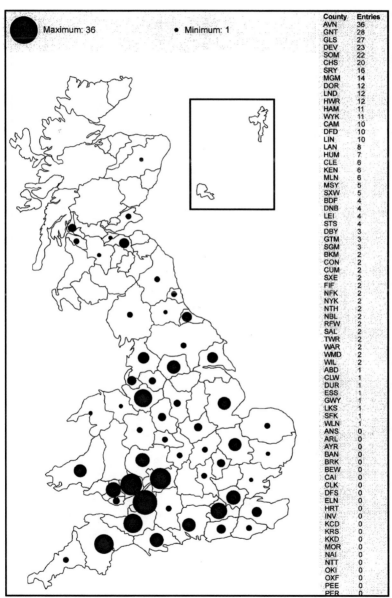

County	Entries
AVN	36
GNT	28
GLS	27
DEV	23
SOM	22
CHS	20
SRY	16
MGM	14
DOR	12
LND	12
HWR	12
HAM	11
WYK	11
CAM	10
DFD	10
LIN	10
LAN	8
HUM	7
CLE	6
KEN	6
MLN	6
MSY	5
SXW	5
BDF	4
DNB	4
LEI	4
STS	4
DBY	3
GTM	3
SGM	3
BKM	2
CON	2
CUM	2
SXE	2
FIF	2
NFK	2
NYK	2
NTH	2
NBL	2
RFW	2
SAL	2
TWR	2
WAR	2
WMD	2
WIL	2
ABD	1
CLW	1
DUR	1
ESS	1
GWY	1
LKS	1
SFK	1
WLN	1
ANS	0
ARL	0
AYR	0
BAN	0
BRK	0
BEW	0
CAI	0
CLK	0
DFS	0
ELN	0
HRT	0
INV	0
KCD	0
KRS	0
KKD	0
MOR	0
NAI	0
NTT	0
OKI	0
OXF	0
PEE	0
PER	0

Maximum: 36   Minimum: 1

UK-Info 2004: Absolute Distribution of *Gait*

Map 13

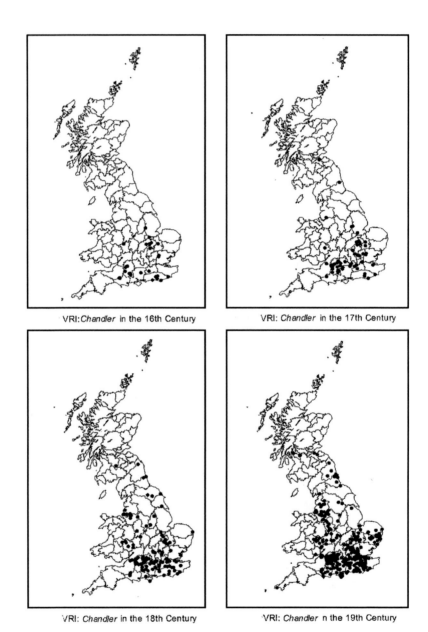

VRI:*Chandler* in the 16th Century   VRI: *Chandler* in the 17th Century

VRI: *Chandler* in the 18th Century   VRI: *Chandler* n the 19th Century

Map 14

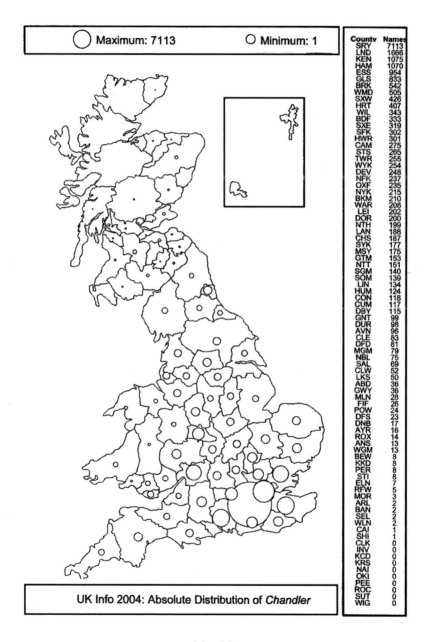

County	Names
SRY	7113
LND	1666
KEN	1075
HAM	1070
ESS	954
GLS	833
BRK	542
WMD	505
SXW	426
HRT	407
WIL	343
BDF	333
SXE	319
SFK	302
HWR	301
CAM	275
STS	265
TWR	255
WYK	254
DEV	248
NFK	237
OXF	235
NYK	215
BKM	210
WAR	208
LEI	202
DOR	200
NTH	199
LAN	188
CHS	187
SYK	177
MSY	175
GTM	153
NTT	151
SGM	140
SOM	139
LIN	134
HUM	124
CON	118
CUM	117
DBY	115
GNT	99
DUR	98
AVN	96
CLE	83
DFD	81
MGM	79
NBL	75
SAL	69
CLW	52
LKS	50
ABD	36
GWY	36
MLN	28
FIF	26
POW	24
DFS	23
DNB	17
AYR	16
ROX	14
ANS	13
WGM	13
BEW	8
KKD	8
PER	8
STI	8
ELN	7
RFW	5
MOR	3
ARL	2
BAN	2
SEL	2
WLN	2
CAI	1
SHI	1
CLK	0
INV	0
KCD	0
KRS	0
NAI	0
OKI	0
PEE	0
ROC	0
SUT	0
WIG	0

Maximum: 7113   **Minimum: 1**

UK Info 2004: Absolute Distribution of *Chandler*

Map 15

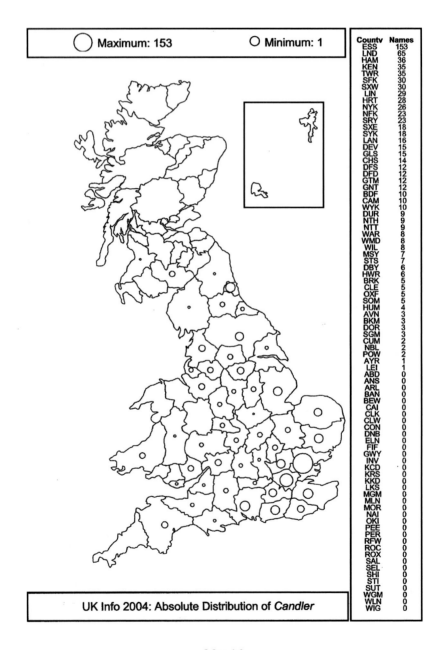

County	Names
ESS	153
LND	65
HAM	36
KEN	35
TWR	35
SFK	30
SXW	30
LIN	29
HRT	28
NYK	26
NFK	23
SRY	23
SXE	18
SYK	18
LAN	16
DEV	15
GLS	15
CHS	14
DFS	12
DFD	12
GTM	12
GNT	12
BDF	10
CAM	10
WYK	10
DUR	9
NTH	9
NTT	9
WAR	8
WMD	8
WIL	8
MSY	7
STS	7
DBY	6
HWR	6
BRK	5
CLE	5
OXF	5
SOM	5
HUM	4
AVN	3
BKM	3
DOR	3
SGM	3
CUM	2
NBL	2
POW	2
AYR	1
LEI	1
ABD	0
ANS	0
ARL	0
BAN	0
BEW	0
CAI	0
CLK	0
CLW	0
CON	0
DNB	0
ELN	0
FIF	0
GWY	0
INV	0
KCD	0
KRS	0
KKD	0
LKS	0
MGM	0
MLN	0
MOR	0
NAI	0
OKI	0
PEE	0
PER	0
RFW	0
ROC	0
ROX	0
SAL	0
SEL	0
SHI	0
STI	0
SUT	0
WGM	0
WLN	0
WIG	0

Maximum: 153   Minimum: 1

UK Info 2004: Absolute Distribution of *Candler*

Map 16

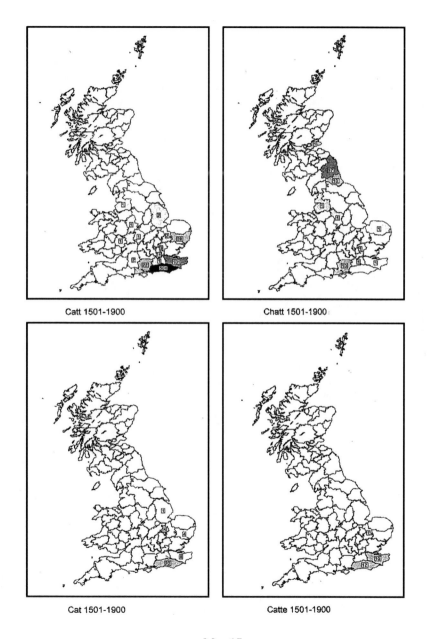

Catt 1501-1900

Chatt 1501-1900

Cat 1501-1900

Catte 1501-1900

Map 17

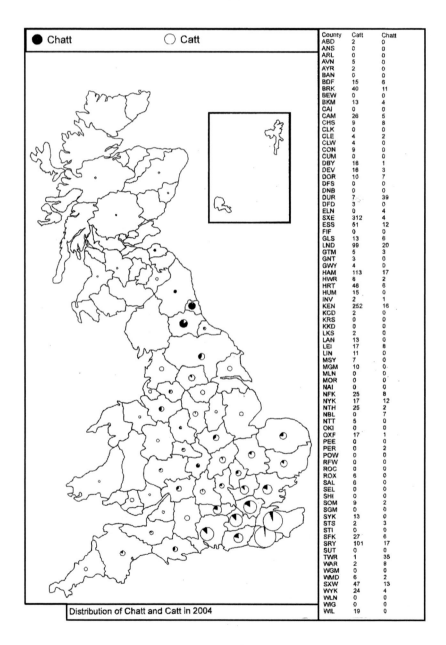

Distribution of Chatt and Catt in 2004

Map 18

Flowerdew

Based on actual numbers in each
County (Source: 1881 Census)

Map 19

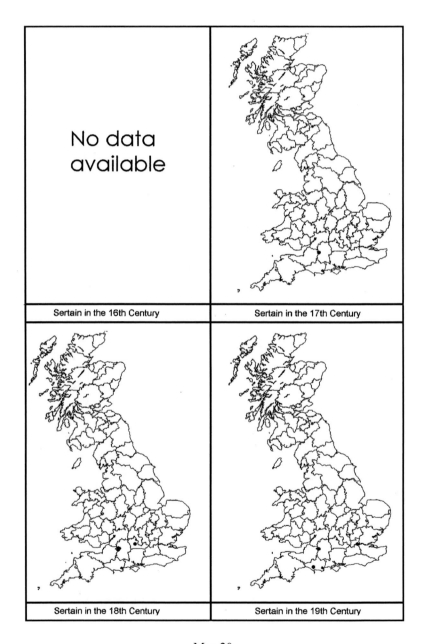

Map 20

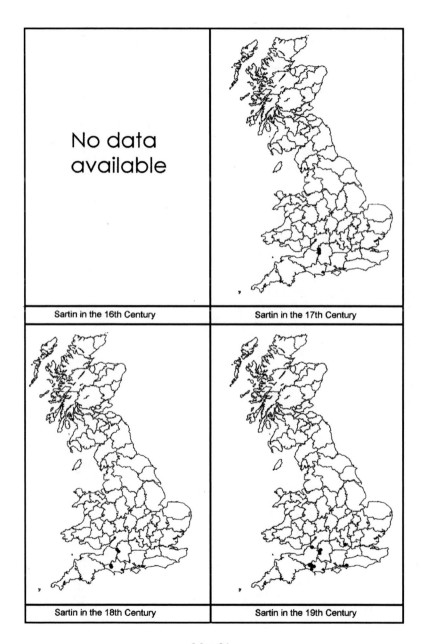

Map 21

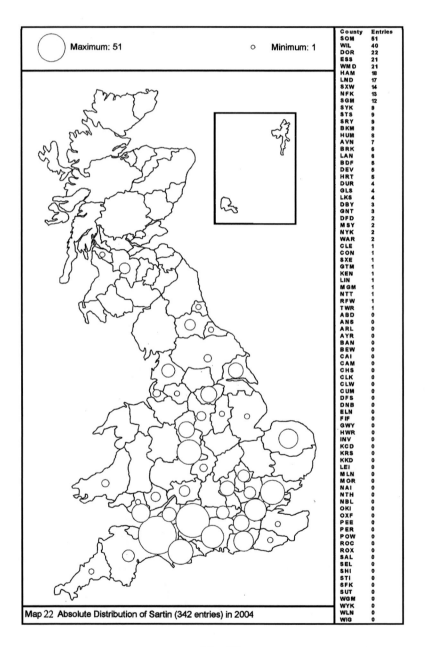

County	Entries
SOM	51
WIL	40
DOR	22
ESS	21
WMD	21
HAM	18
LND	17
SXW	14
NFK	13
SGM	12
SYK	9
STS	9
SRY	9
BKM	8
HUM	8
AVN	7
BRK	6
LAN	6
BDF	5
DEV	5
HRT	5
DUR	4
GLS	4
LKS	4
DBY	3
GNT	3
DFD	2
MSY	2
NYK	2
WAR	2
CLE	1
CON	1
SXE	1
GTM	1
KEN	1
LIN	1
MGM	1
NTT	1
RFW	1
TWR	1
ABD	0
ANS	0
ARL	0
AYR	0
BAN	0
BEW	0
CAI	0
CAM	0
CHS	0
CLK	0
CLW	0
CUM	0
DFS	0
DNB	0
ELN	0
FIF	0
GWY	0
HWR	0
INV	0
KCD	0
KRS	0
KKD	0
LEI	0
MLN	0
MOR	0
NAI	0
NTH	0
NBL	0
OKI	0
OXF	0
PEE	0
PER	0
POW	0
ROC	0
ROX	0
SAL	0
SEL	0
SHI	0
STI	0
SFK	0
SUT	0
WGM	0
WYK	0
WLN	0
WIG	0

Maximum: 51   o   Minimum: 1

Map 22 Absolute Distribution of Sartin (342 entries) in 2004

Map 22

French culinary vocabulary in the 14th-century English

Magdalena Bator, Academy of Management [SWSPiZ], Warsaw

ABSTRACT

After the Norman Conquest, the French influence on Middle English increased. Various studies show estimated percentage of the French borrowings present in English. However, all of these studies were based on a small sample of language, e.g., Jespersen (1978 [1905]) drew his conclusions from a sample of one thousand words; Mossé (1943) analysed only the letter 'A' in the *OED*.

The present research is a pilot study aiming at the analysis of the extent to which vocabulary of French origin was present in Middle English, with respect to various semantic fields. In the paper we will concentrate on the semantic field FOOD in the 14th c. The study will be based on *Curye on Inglysch (English culinary manuscripts of the 14th century)*, edited by Hieatt and Butler (1985).

We would like to examine both the nature of the borrowed words and their relation to the native vocabulary.

KEYWORDS: food; French influence; loanword; rivalry

1. Introduction

The Norman Conquest initiated the process of significant influx of French loanwords into the English lexicon. Scholars, however, agree with Jespersen (1978: 87) that "the linguistic influence did not begin immediately after the conquest." The early scholars estimated that the percentage of the French element in English in particular periods was small (see Table 1):

Table 1. The number of French loanword in English at various periods (see Jespersen 1978 [1905]).

	Jespersen	Koszal	Baugh	Herdan	Dekeyser
before 1050	2	–	2	2	–
1051-1100	2	1	–	–	–
1101-1150	1	2	2	1	–
1151-1200	15	11	7	14	8

The figures seem to be similar in proportion and they do not contradict Jespersen's (1978 [1905]) statement that significant French influence started not earlier than in the second half of the 13th c. After analyzing one thousand French words from the *New English dictionary* (the first one hundred French words for the first nine letters of the alphabet and 50 for each of the letters 'j' and 'l'), he found 64 loans in the period 1201-1250, 127 in 1251-1300, 120 in 1301-1350, 180 in 1351-1400, and only 70 in 1401-1450. For the later periods, the numbers do not exceed one hundred.

The more recent statistics, e.g., Scheler (1977) show that it was the 14th c. when the number of French loans recorded in English was greatest. According to Scheler (1977: 52), almost 32% of all French loans entered English in the 14th c., almost 16% in the 15th c. and 15% in the 16th c., compared to 13.5% in the 13th c.

However, the studies mentioned so far were based on a small sample of language, e.g., Jespersen (1978) drew his conclusions from a sample of one thousand words; Mossé (1943) analysed only the letter 'A' in the *OED*.

We are aiming at the analysis of the extent to which vocabulary of French origin was present in Middle English, with respect to various semantic fields, using the available dictionaries as well as books representative for a particular semantic field. The analysis will be based on selected texts, representative of particular semantic fields. In the present paper we will investigate the semantic field FOOD in the 14th c. English.

In earlier studies Mettig (1910) revealed the following (French) loans within the semantic field FOOD: *diete* 'diet', †*glutenerie* 'gluttonry', *licur* 'liquor', †*piment* and *potage* 'pottage'. Jespersen included (1978 [1905]): *beef, mutton, veal, pork, bacon, brawn, venison, cuisine, sauce, pasty, pastry, soup, sausage, jelly, dainty, dinner, supper, feast, fruits* and verbs: *boil, fry, roast* and *toast*. More numerous examples have been presented by Serjeantson (1962 [1935]). The earliest loans in her analysis come from the 11th c., e.g., *capun* 'capon', *gingifer* 'ginger', and *bacun* 'bacon'. Later she has not found any food vocabulary until the first half of the 13th c., when the following loans were recorded:

- *diet, pittance,* and *potage*; *Ancrene Riwle* (prob. WM);
- *feste* 'feast'; *King Horn* (SEM romance);
- *feast*; *Genesis and Exodus* (1250, EM);
- *capun*; *Bestiary* (1250, EM);
- *broys* 'broth', *clare* 'claret', *feast, flaun* 'pancake', *pastees, piment* 'sweet spiced wine', *simenels* 'bread of fine flour', *super* 'supper', *ueneysun* 'venison', *wastel* 'bread of the finest flour'; *Havelok the Dane* (1250-1300, NEM);
- *soper* 'supper'; *Floris and Blauncheflur* (1250-1300, NEM);
- *festys*; *Cursor Mundi* (1300, N);
- *brochen* 'broach', *diner, dinen, piment, sause, sopere, spisorie, vitaile*; *Sir Beues of Hamton* (14th c. romance).

Additionally, Scheler (1977: 56) records: beef, mutton, veel, pork, sausage, bacon, loin, haunch, poultry, orange, grape, confection, salmon, sardine, sturgeon, mackerel, oyster, vinegar, mustard, spice, nutmeg, roast, boil, fry, grate, mince, feast, dinner and supper.

2. The corpus

The present paper has been based on *Curye on Inglysch (English culinary manuscripts of the 14th-century)*, edited by Hieatt and Butler (1985). It is a collection of 14th-century recipes taken from more than 20 manuscripts. All the recipes date from the 14th c., which is the earliest period when such a collection can be found, however, they represent culinary traditions of the upper classes from the 12th-16th c. (cf. Hieatt and Butler 1985: 2). The book consists of 5 parts, containing altogether over 400 recipes: I. 'Diuersa cibaria' (63 recipes), II. 'Diuersa servisa' (92 recipes), III. 'Utilis coquinario' (37 recipes), IV. 'The forme of cury' (205 recipes), and V. 'Goud kokery' (25 recipes).

The five parts are preceded by 9 recipes taken from 'Historical documents', based on MS C (Durham, University Library Cosin v iii 11). Part I is based on MS He (London, BL Add. 46919); Part II is based on MS D (Oxford, Bodleian Douce 257); Part III on MS S (London, BL Sloane 468); Part IV, *The forme of cury*, is the most famous collection. It was first edited by Samuel Pegge in 1780 (based on MS A), and later by Richard Warner in 1791 (no reference to the manuscript was given). Following the note on the vellum scroll, *The forme of cury*

> techiþ a man for to make commune potages and commune meetis for howshold as þey shold be made craftly and holsomly. Aftirward it techiþ for to make curious potages & meetes and sotiltees for alle maner of States bothe hye and lowe. And the techyng of the forme of making of potages & of meetes bothe of flessh and of fissh.
>
> (after Pegge 1780: 14)

In the Hieatt and Butler's edition, the majority of recipes of Part IV were based on MS A (London, BL Add. 5016), those recipes which were not included in MS A were taken from MS C (Durham, University of Cosin v iii 11) – 3 recipes, and MS H (London, BL Harl. 1605) – 7 recipes. And finally, Part V is a collection of recipes, current in the 14th c., taken from various sources.

3. Collected loanwords

The analysis of the 431 recipes has yielded over 500 words of French origin[1]. They referred mostly to individual food products (46%) and names of dishes (21%). 14% of words were verbs denoting various ways of cooking, cutting or serving food. The remaining items are terms of measure and shape (5%), names of vessels and kitchen utensils (8.5%) and terms referring to the decoration of food or table (4%).

---

1   The etymology was based on the etymological notes found in the *OED*.

3.1 DISHES

The words grouped under DISHES consist only of the terms found within the body of the recipes, the titles preceding each recipe have not been included in the corpus, due to the fact that a great number of them were French and, not having been found in any other source, they seem not to have entered English. The loans denote either (i) particular dishes, e.g., *blankdesore* 'a fish-day dish (…) it is yellow, with egg yolks, cheese, and saffron, and contains cow's milk', *porrey* 'a soup or broth, usually made of leeks or peas and flavoured with a range of ingredients, such as almond milk and mussels'; *pommedorry* '(a dish made of) a meat ball or rissole, esp. one with a glazing of egg yolk', or (ii) types of meals in general, e.g., *paste, potage, tart, cream, omelette, sauce* and *soup*. Moreover, names of sauces and desserts have also been included in the section DISHES, e.g., *bruet* 'a broth or sauce for meat, fish, etc.', *cive* 'a spicy sauce containing chives or onions', *concy* 'a sauce for garnishing capons', *egredouce* 'a sauce made of sour and sweet ingredients, also meat or fish served with such a sauce'; *comfit* 'a sweetmeat made of some fruit, root, etc. preserved with sugar; now usu. a small, round or oval mass of sugar enclosing a caraway seed, almond, etc.; a sugar-plum', *cream, flan, fritter* 'a portion of batter, sometimes containing slices of apple, meat, etc. fried on oil, lard, etc.', *pommys* 'crushed apples'.

It is interesting to note that the *OED* postdates some of the general terms found in the corpus. For instance, according to the *OED*, *soup* $(2)^2$ entered English only in the 2nd half of the 17th c.; *omelette* (2) appears not earlier than in the 17th c.; *flan* (1) – occurs in the 19th c.

3.2 FOOD PRODUCTS

Names of various food products constitute the largest group of loans found in the analysed material. This group contains foods of both plant and animal origin, as well as spices, liquids and cereal products:

> animal products: 25%
> fish: 16%
> plant products: 35%
> spices: 7.5%
> cereal products: 7.5%
> liquids: 9%

Most of the terms were first recorded in English in the 14th c., e.g., *grease* (95), *pork* (44), *brawn* (42), *numbles* (13), *veel* (14), *mallard* (7), etc. Relatively few terms entered English before the 14th c., e.g., *cony* (22) – 1292, *fig* (19) – 1225, *grape* (9) –

---

2   The number of records of particular words found in the analysed material, has been given in brackets.

1290, *seam* (4) – 1200, *saffroun* (158) – 1200, *spices* (79) – 1225, *canel* (73) – 1205, *herb* (18) – 1290, etc. As has already been mentioned, a number of items recorded in the analysed material contradicts the dating presented in the *OED*. Some of the items found in the 14th c. material, according to the *OED*, were borrowed later, e.g., in the 15th c.: *lard* (6), *lardon* (3), *pestel* (5), *cabbage* (4), *egret* (1).

3.2.1 MEAT and FISH

The recipes were very rich in various kinds of animal meat and fish. Majority of the terms for animal meat were borrowed from French. This has been explained by Jespersen (1978: 82), who writes that:

> the names of several animals in their lifetime are English (ox, cow, calf, sheep, swine, boar, deer), they appear on the table with French names (beef, veal, mutton, pork, bacon, brawn, venison). This is generally explained from the masters leaving the care of the living animals to the lower classes, while they did not leave much of the meat to be eaten by them.
>
> (Jespersen 1978: 82)

The corpus contains also a number of parts of animal's body or animal products, such as: *loin* (2), *grease* (95), *numbles* (13), *fillet* (7); names of birds, e.g., *heron* (5), *pheasant* (8), *partridge* (17); and names of fish and mollusks, e.g., *salmon* (9), *pike* (13), *oyster* (13), etc.

3.2.2 PLANT PRODUCTS

Within the selected loanwords referring to plant products, we can distinguish 'fruit', 'vegetables', 'cereal products' and 'spices'.

Despite the fact that horticultural products were perceived as difficult to digest and rather unhealthy (Scully 1995: 70-1), and were associated with the diet of the poor, a considerable number of loans referring to names of fruit and vegetables were found, e.g., *almond* (182), *cabbage* (4), *onion* (60), *fig* (19), *cubeb* (17), *gourd* (2), *dittany* (2), *date* (14), *olive* (11), etc.

Following Stone (2009 [2006]: 11), grain provided the greatest caloric intake of vast majority of people at the beginning of the 14th c. Murphy (1998: 120) states that "[g]rain accounted for up to 80 per cent of a harvest worker's calories and 78 per cent of a soldier's; even among the lay nobility of medieval England, grain provided 65-70 per cent of their energy intake." Thus, loans such as *amidoun* (41) 'crushed hulled wheat', *flour* (104), *rice* (79), *grain* (16), *furmynte* (12) 'grain such as wheat, barley, etc.; also: potage made of boiled hulled grain mixed with milk and sweetened', *oble* (1) 'a small cake or wafer', *payndemayn* (5) 'a white bread', *rice* (79) and *wafer* (1) 'a small cake or flatbread' are of no surprise in the analysed recipes.

Finally, the analysed material suggests popularity of various herbs and spices, such as: *canel* (73) 'cinnamon', *galingale* (35), *mace* (22) 'the outer covering of the nutmeg used as a spice', *saffroun* (158), *gilofre* (21), etc. It should also be noted that the general terms *herb* (18) and *spice* (79) were borrowed from French.[3]

A great majority of these loans have remained in use until Present Day English.

3.2.3 LIQUIDS

Only 4% of the French loans referred to 'liquids'. The most numerous are: *oil* (62) and *vinegar* (58). However, terms such as *juice* (8), *liquor* (5) and †*claret* (3)/†*clary* (2) should also be noted.

3.3 VESSELS and KITCHEN UTENSILS

Only 8.5% of the selected loans referred to vocabulary denoting vessels and kitchen utensils. The most frequent ones were: *mortar* (78), *vessel* (29), *coffin* (22) 'a basket, a chest', *straynour* (16) 'strainer', *trap* (14) 'a kind of dish or pan', *platter* (12), *towel* (7), *griddle* (6) 'a circular iron plate upon which cakes are baked', *possynet* (5) 'a small metal pot or vessel for boiling', *fourneys* (5) 'a small oven', *spatur* (5) 'spatula', *mould* (4) 'a form used for baking, etc.', *pipe* (4) 'a large container of definite capacity for storing solids or liquids', *roller* (4), etc.

3.4 MEASURE and SHAPE

Among the loans referring to measure and shapes are: *party* (38) 'portion', *piece* (36), *goboun* (28) 'a piece, slice', *quarter* (21), *quantity* (17), *foil* (15) 'a leaf, a flat and thin piece of something', *plenty* (11), *portion* (10), *morsel* (8) 'a small piece of food', *leche* (6) 'a slice, a strip', *dice* (4), *gallon* (3), *purveyance* (2) 'a supply esp. of food', *slice* (2) and single occurrences of *bale* 'a large bundle or package', *poyne* 'a handful', *pint* and *roche* 'a rock (of sugar)'.

It is interesting to note that the French terms denoting 'plentitude' were usually accompanied by a native term, as if the author wanted to emphasize or make sure that enough of a particular ingredient will be added, e.g.,

> muche plente of ayren (I.17)
> sucre gret plente (I.17)
> gyngeer itried gret plente (I.18)
> poudre of gyngere gret plente (I.22)

---

3   According to the *OED* both nouns entered English in the 13th c. Hoad's dictionary dates the borrowing of *spice* to the 14th c. However, taking into account the number of occurrences of *spice* in the analysed material (79), the dating suggested in the *OED* seems more plausible.

god plente of poudre of gynger (II.59)
a god quantite of powder of pepir (II.50)
a gode quantite of vyneger (IV.15)
a grete quantite of sugur cypre (IV.43)
a god perty of applys (II.83)

3.5 DECORATION

The aim of the anlysed recipes was not only to present tasty but also good looking and well served meals. This has been reflected by numerous words (almost half of which are verbs) suggesting how to ornament either the food or the plate and table on which it would be served, e.g., *dress* (53) 'to arrange' (and related *dressur* and *dressing*), *enarme* 'to garnish (a dish)', *florisshe* (21) 'to ornament or garnish (a dish)', *array*, etc.

The most frequent word referring to the process of decorating food was *colour* (127). It occurred both as a verb and a noun, the former being over twice as frequently used as the latter. The most frequent ingredient used for dying food was saffron (43). The other food colourings were: saundres (9), alkenet (6), but also blood, fether, yolkes of eggs, etc. 6 of the occurrences of the verb were used without any specified dying ingredient. The noun was often followed by the specific colour which food was supposed to gain, e.g., the colour shall be red (10) / yellow (9) / green (3) / white (3) / inde (1) / black (1) / vernis (1).

3.6 VERBS

The verbs of French origin found in the analysed material constitute 14% of all the collected loans. They can be divided into 4 main lexical groups:

- verbs referring to various ways of cutting, e.g., *mince* (53), *bray* (65), *grate* (13), *press* (10), *dice* (9), *crush* (1);
- verbs referring to various ways of cooking, e.g., *boil* (201), *roast* (111), *fry* (90), *parboil* (36), *scald* (24), *toast* (9), *stew* (5);
- verbs referring to the process of food preparation and serving, e.g., *blanch* (40), *meddle* (32), *charge* (21), *clarify* (15); *serve* (176) and *messen* (67).

The analysis of verbs in particular, shows the presence of both French and native element throughout the recipes. On the one hand a certain degree of interchangeability can be observed, e.g., *boil* vs. *seethe*. However, on the other hand, the foreign element usually carries a more specific reference, e.g., *carve* 'to cut' vs. *dice* 'to cut into dice or cubes', *mince* 'to cut up or grind into very small pieces', *grate* 'to reduce to small particles by rubbing against a rough surface', etc. For a more detailed analysis of the native vs. borrowed element, see section 4.

4. Native vs. French vocabulary

Even though the French element predominates in the analysed material, one can observe a number of native English synonyms, which seem to have been used interchangeably throughout the recipes. Majority of the coexisting – synonymous – items are verbs, e.g., *boil* and *seethe* (see 4.1). However, more often some differences in the usage of words of various origins can be observed, e.g., 'verbs of cutting' (see 4.2).

4.1 'verbs for cooking'

The analysed recipes contained a number of verbs referring to various ways of preparing food. The most frequent native words referring to ways of cooking were as follows:
(i) *seethe* – 'to boil; to make or keep boiling hot; to subject to the action of boiling liquid; esp. to cook (food) by boiling or stewing; to make an infusion or decoction of (a substance) by boiling or stewing';
(ii) *bake* – 'to cook by dry heat acting by conduction, and not by radiation, hence either in a closed place (oven, ashes, etc.), or on a heated surface (bakestone, griddle, live coals); primarily used for preparing bread, then of potatoes, apples, the flesh of animals'.

French 'verbs for cooking' found in the analysed material are much more widely represented. Table 2 shows the borrowed verbs together with their meaning(s) and number of occurrences in the analysed recipes.

Table 2. 'Verbs for cooking' of French origin found in the analysed recipes.

verbs	sense (*OED*)	freq.
boil	(i) to reach the boiling point, to turn from the liquid into the gaseous state (ii) to move with an agitation like that of boiling water; to bubble, to seethe (iii) to cause (a liquid) to bubble with heat; to bring to the boiling point, esp. said of food, wholly or partly liquid in the process of cooking	201
decoct	to boil, cook, to prepare as food by the agency of fire	8
fry	to cook (food) with fat in a shallow pan over the fire	90
parboil	to cook partially by boiling	36
roast	to make (flesh or other food) ready for eating by prolonged exposure to heat at or before a fire	111
scald	(i) to heat liquid to a point just short of boiling point (ii) to scorch	24
scorch[4]	to heat to such a degree as to shiver	1

---

4   According to the *OED*, the verb was first recorded in English in the 15th c.

stew[5]	to boil slowly in a close vessel; to cook (meat, fruit, etc.) in a liquid kept at the simmering point	5
toast	(i) to heat thoroughly	9
	(ii) to brown (bread, cheese, etc.) by exposure to the heat of a fire, etc.[6]	

(1) Fr. *boil* vs. E. *seethe*

From among the verbs presented in Table 2, *boil* was most frequent. According to the *OED*, it was borrowed from OF *boillir* in the early 13ᵗʰ c., denoting (i) 'to reach the boiling point, to turn from the liquid into the gaseous state'. By the end of the 13ᵗʰ c. it gained the sense (ii) 'to move with an agitation like that of boiling water; to bubble, to seethe', and at the beginning of the 15ᵗʰ c. (iii) 'to cause (a liquid) to bubble with heat; to bring to the boiling point, esp. said of food, wholly or partly liquid in the process of cooking'.

Throughout the book, *boil* was used 201 times and the action of boiling could have been "performed" 'in water', 'wine', 'broth' or 'ale', however, in majority of its occurrences the liquid was not specified. When the manner of 'boiling' was specified, it was either 'soft', 'tender', 'thick' or 'well' (for examples of contexts in which boil occurs, see Table 3).

Additionally, 36 occurrences of *perboil* 'to boil partially by boiling' were found.

The native *seethe* was first recorded in 1000 with the sense (i) 'to boil, to make or keep boiling hot; to subject to the action of boiling liquid, esp. to cook (food) by boiling or stewing'. By the Middle English period it gained the sense (ii) 'to be boiled; to be subjected to boiling or stewing; to become boiling hot. Said of liquid, or a substance boiled in a liquid' (1300-).

It was recorded only 48 times, however, it occurred in similar contexts as the the verb *boil* (see Table 3), i.e. the action of 'seething' could take place 'in water', 'in wine', 'broth', but also 'in grease' and 'almond milk' (which were not used to specify *boil*).

Table 3. The contexts of occurrence of seethe and boil.

seethe	boil
seþ hem <u>togedere</u> (II.5)	boyle þam <u>togedere</u> (II.36)
–	mak it <u>softe</u> boillen (I.51)
seeþ it <u>tendre</u>, and lye with ʒolkes of eyren (IV.14)	and boile it <u>tendre</u> in fine broth oþer in water (IV.121)
… & seoþ it <u>wel</u> (I.56)	… and boyle it <u>wele</u> and serue it fort. (IV.15)
… & seþ hem <u>a god wyle</u> (II.2)	–

---

5 The *OED* does not record any occurrence of the verb before the 15ᵗʰ c.
6 This sense, according to the *OED*, was first recorded in the 15ᵗʰ c.

seeþ it <u>in a possynet</u> with faire broth (IV.54)	vchon of þoes schulen boillen <u>in a clene possenet</u> (I.1)
seeþ hem <u>in gode broth</u> (IV.36)	boile hem <u>in gode broth</u> (IV.35)
and seeþ it wel <u>in water</u> (IV.128)	& soþþen boill am <u>in watre</u> (I.49)
seeþ it wel half <u>in water</u> and half in wyne (IV.16)	... & boille heam <u>in god wyn</u> (I.42)
–	boile hem tendre <u>in</u> smale <u>ale</u> (IV.116)
seeþ hem <u>with þe blode</u> vnwaisshed in broth (IV.25)	–
... & seoþ it <u>in god milke of alemauns</u> (I.60)	–
and seeþ hem <u>in oile</u> (IV.76)	–

After anylysing the contexts in which both verbs were used it may seem they were used interchangeably. Sometimes the two verbs were used next to each other, probably to avoid repetitions, e.g.,

> <u>seeþ</u> it & salt it: <u>boile</u> it not to stondyng (IV.130)
> <u>seeþ</u> in <u>boillyng</u> water (IV.182)

However, some of the occurrences of *boil* and *seethe* seem to have carried slightly different meanings. E.g.,

> <u>seoþen</u> in water þou make hit <u>boillen</u>
> ... & <u>seþe</u> hem wel togidere til it <u>boile</u>

The examples given above may suggest that *seethe* was used with the sense 'to simmer' rather than 'to boil'.

(2) *bake* vs. *roast/fry*/etc.

These verbs were applied to various ways of cooking, only slightly differing semantically. The native *bake* originally was used with the sense 'to cook by dry heat acting by conduction, and not by radiation, hence either in a closed place (oven, ashes, etc.), or on a heated surface (bakestone, griddle, live coals); primarily used for preparing bread, then of potatoes, apples, the flesh of animals'. In the analysed material it occurred 37 times, majority of the records applied to the preparation of various kinds of animal meat and fish, but also to vegetables and flour products.

Roast was much more numerous. It was recorded 111 times, almost exclusively with reference to meat. Two of the occurrences referred to milk and gelofre.

The following citation may suggest that *bake* and *roast* did not carry the same meaning, although it does not specify the senses of the two verbs:

& set it in þe ouene til it bake, & if it be rosted diȝte hym in þe same manere but þat þou sethe þe galentyn with oynounes. (III.24)

Additionally, semantically similar *fry* was found 90 times. It seems that all of the verbs were used with slightly different meanings, depending on the manner of cooking, thus:

roast – implied 'cooking' on a griddle
bake – implied 'cooking' in a trap/pan
fry – was used when talking about cooking in oil or other grease.

4.2 'verbs for cutting'

The corpus contains three native general terms for cutting: *carve* (37 records) 'to cut: formerly the ordinary word for that action in all its varieties', *cut*[7] (13 records) 'to divide into two or more parts with a sharp-edged instrument' and *hew* (55 records) 'to divide with cutting blows; to chop into pieces'. All of them form phrases together with French nouns specifying the manner of cutting, e.g., 'in pecis', 'in gobetes', 'to dyce', 'in quarters', 'in mossels'. Additionally, such phrases are also formed with the native verbs 'do' and 'make' and one of the borrowed nouns defining the way in which something is cut.

The French 'verbs for cutting' found in the analysed material are more numerous (see Table 4):

Table 4. 'Verbs for cutting' borrowed from French.

verbs	sense (*OED*)	freq.
bray	'to beat small; to bruise, pound, crush to powder; usu. in a morter'	65
bruise[8]	to beat small, pound, crush, bray, grind down	1
crush	(i) to dash together with the sound of violent percussion, to clash, crash; to make the harsh grating noise of things forcibly smashed or pounded to fragments (obs) (ii) to bruise, bray, break down into small pieces; (1588–)	1
dice	to cut into dice or cubes, esp. in cookery	9
†gobbon[9]	to cut into gobbets (= slices)	1
grate	to reduce to small particles by rasping or rubbing against a rough or indented surface; to pulverize by means of a grater	13
leach	to cut in slices	9
mince	to cut up or grind into very small pieces	53

<hr>

7   The etymology is not certain. Hoad (1993) states: "The earlier dial. vars. *cutte, kitte, kette* point to an OE **cyttan*, f. **kut-*."
8   Its etymology may be ambiguous. According to the *OED*, the OE forms are of native origin, while the ME ones "must be from the OFr. forms".
9   *gobbon* as a noun occured 4 times.

†mye	to crumble or grate	13
powder	to reduce to powder; pulverize	1
quarter	to cut into quarters	6
quest	(H&B): to crush[10]	1

The most frequently used verbal loan, *bray*, was recorded 65 times, 25 of them do not specify the utensil used for the action, all the other verbal forms are accompanied by the phrase 'in a mortar'. Majority of ingredients being 'brayed' are spices: canel, gelofre, galingale; but also: wheat, bread and rice; almonds, parsley, and fruit; additionally, various kinds of meat could be brayed, e.g., poultry, pork or salmon. Only twice was it explained that ingredients should be 'brayed to dust/powder', which may suggest that the verb was rather used with reference to 'cutting to small pieces' than 'pulverizing'.

A number of its synonyms, also borrowed from French, were found, i.e. *bruise, crush, powder* and *quest*, however, each of them was found only once. *Bruise* was recorded with reference to wheat. *Crush* referred to 'crushing between teeth' and not to any culinary activity, whilst *quest* applied to cutting grapes. Although *powder* as a verb had a single occurrence, as a noun it appeared 248 times. The noun joined native verbs and formed verbal phrases synonymous with the verb *powder*, e.g., 'do powder', 'grind powder', 'make powder', 'beat to powder', etc. (similarly, the verb *quarter*, with only 6 records, occurs as a noun which together with native verbs forms phrases synonymous with the borrowed verb, e.g., 'hew in quarters').

All these loans have been outnumbered by the native *grind*, which occurred 164 times, with the sense 'to reduce to small particles or powder by crushing between two hard surfaces'. *Grind* was used in the same contexts as the borrowed *bray*, it referred to various spices, bread, fruit, vegetables and meat. *Grind* unlike the borrowed verbs referred to the action of 'reducing some ingredients with the addition of some liquid', e.g.,

take brede and grynde with the broth (IV.15)
take persel, and grynde with a litul cowe mylke (IV.69)

The other verbs describing ways of cutting denoted the action of cutting food in particular shapes, e.g., *dice, leach, gobbon*. However, the analysis has shown that certain verbs were used with reference to particular products. Thus:

- *grate* was used either with bread or cheese;
- *mince* referred to onions (70%), leek (10%), and parsley, dates, fruit;

---

10   The *OED* has no entry for this verb, the sense has been taken from Hieatt & Butler's glossary.

- every record of *mie* was used with reference to bread, except once when it referred to eggs.

Moreover, over half of the occurrences of *dice* revealed that the ingredients to be 'diced' were first to be parboiled. Similarly, dicing and leashing were preceded by carving, which may suggest that for the speakers the native term *carve* was too general and the activity had to be specified by the use of a loanword.

(3) Nouns

Nominal synonymy has not been as well represented as the verbal one. This may be accounted for by the fact that majority of the borrowed nouns found in the analysed material referred to products or ingredients introduced by the French or at least not recorded before the 14th c. when the analysed recipes were written down.

One of examples of nominal synonymy is the pair: *dust* ≈ *powder*. The former, native form occurred only 8 times, whilst the latter, borrowed from French had 248 records. Both were used with the sense 'solid matter in the form of dry particles'. Each but one of the occurrences of *dust* were accompanied by the native verb *grind* (one occurrence with *bray*), whilst *powder* was used in a wide variety of phrases, e.g., 'to do to powder', 'to beat to powder', 'to grind to powder', 'to bray powder', etc.

5. Conclusions

The analysis of the material described above, leads to several conclusions:

(i)   The number of French loans found in the corpus proves that the estimated number of French loans in English by earlier authors was far from available facts.

(ii) The lack of native synonyms denoting particular ingredients leads to the conclusion that a significant number of those ingredients were introduced by the French.

(iii) Numerous verbs borrowed from French, describing various ways of performing the same activity (i.e. various ways of cooking, cutting, preparing food) give evidence that together with the French linguistic influence more variety was added to the process of cooking and serving food – in the native stock of verbs found in the corpus, a great majority carried general senses.
It should be noted, though, that the recipes are very general, giving rather non-specific instructions how to prepare a particular dish and being more a list of ingredients required to prepare the dish (often without specifying the exact amount), e.g.,

and lat it seeþ til it be ynowh3 (IV.66)

See, e.g., the whole recipe for the preparation of 'sanc dragon':

> Milke of alemauns & flour of rys & god poudre of gyngere & sucre, & hit schal beon icolored wiþ sanc dragon. (I.30)

(iv) In some cases it turned out that words found in the 14th c. recipes were postdated in the *OED*, thus, a closer examination of the available textual sources may throw a new light on the dating of loanwords.

References

Baugh, Albert
    1935   "The chronology of loan-words in English", *Modern Language Notes* 50: 90-93.
Carlin, Martha – Joel Thomas Rosenthal (eds.)
    1998   *Food and eating in Medieval Europe*. London: Hambledon Press.
Dekeyser, Xavier
    1986   "Romance loans in Middle English: a re-assessment", in: Kastovsky, Dieter – Aleksander Szwedek (eds.), 253-266.
Herdan, Joseph
    1966   *The advanced theory of language as choice and chance*. Berlin: Springer.
Hieatt, Constance – Sharon Butler (eds.)
    1985   *Curye on Inglysch. English culinary manuscripts of the 14th century*. (EETS). London: Oxford University Press.
Hoad, Terry F.
    1993   *The concise Oxford dictionary of English etymology*. Oxford: Oxford University Press.
Jespersen, Otto
    1978 [1905] *Growth and structure of the English language*. [9th edition]. Oxford: Basil Blackwell.
Kastovsky, Dieter – Aleksander Szwedek (eds.)
    1986   *Linguistics across historical and geographical boundaries*. Berlin: Mouton de Gruyter.
Koszal, A.
    1937   *Bulletin de la Faculté des Lettres de Strasbourg*. [No indication of the publisher].
Mettig, Robert
    1910   *Die französischen Elemente im Alt- und Mittelenglischen (800-1258). Ein Beitrag zur Geschichte des englischen Wortschatzes*. Marburg: Lahn.

Middle English dictionary online. Available at: http://ets.umdl.umich.edu/m/mec. (date of access: November 2009 – January 2010).

Mossé, Ferdinand
    1943   "On the chronology of French loan-words in English", *English Studies* 25: 33-40.

Murphy, M.
    1998   "Feeding Medieval cities: some historical approaches", in: Carlin, Martha – Joel Thomas Rosenthal (eds.), 117-131.

Oxford English dictionary online. Available at: http://oed.com. (date of access: November 2009 – January 2010).

Pegge, Samuel (ed.)
    1780   *The forme of cury.* London: Nichols.

Scheler, Manfred
    1977   *Der englische Wortschatz.* Berlin: Erich Schmidt Verlag.

Scully, Terence
    1995   *The art of cookery in the Middle Ages.* Woodbridge: Boydell Press.

Serjeantson, Mary
    1962 [1935]   *A history of foreign words in English.* London: Kegan Paul and Routledge.

Stone, D.J.
    2006   "The consumption of field crops in late Medieval England", in: Woolgar, Christopher M. (et al.), pp. 11-26.

Sykes, N.J.
    1998   "From *cu* and *sceap* to *beffe* and *motton*", in Woolgar, Christopher M. (et al.), pp. 56-71.

Woolgar, Christopher M. – Dale Serjeantson – Tony Waldron (eds.)
    2009   *Food in Medieval England. Diet and nutrition.* Oxford: Oxford University Press.

Leal/real/viage or loyal/royal/voyage. On the distribution of the forms of loanwords from Norman and Parisian French in Middle English

Jerzy Wełna, University of Warsaw

ABSTRACT

Middle English borrowed extensively from both Central (Parisian) French and Norman French. The significant phonological differences between the two dialects of French were as a rule mirrored in the forms of English loanwords. The earliest borrowings represent the Norman type, while loanwords from the Parisian dialect began to come in larger numbers only in the 14th century. The present study is concerned with the distinction between Parisian [oi] and Norman [ei] and its variants as reflected in Middle English dialects. Special attention is paid to the phonological variation of forms reflecting Anglo-Norman *le(i)al, re(i)al, viage* vs. Parisian *loyal, royal, voyage*. It is essential to emphasise that some instances of variation in the Anglo-Norman forms (*leial, lial, leal, leel/reial, rial, real* etc.) originated on the French soil (cf. Pope 1952). The standard historical grammars (Luick 1940, Jordan-Crook 1974) devote little attention to this change. A more comprehensive account can be found in Diensberg (1985: 195-199), who confirms that the survival of *leal*-forms etc. was conditioned dialectally. The present study is an attempt to offer a more precise account of the regional conditioning of the variants of the three loanwords in question. The study is based on the *Innsbruck corpus of Middle English prose* of 2009, but *the Oxford English dictionary* and the *Middle English dictionary* are also consulted.

KEYWORDS: Norman French; Central French. dialect; Anglo-Norman; prose; *Innsbruck corpus*

1. Parisian French vs. Norman French

Following the Norman Conquest a wave of words from French entered English and contributed to a quick replacement of a large part of the native vocabulary by the foreign element. Middle English borrowed extensively from both Central (Parisian) French and Norman French. The significant phonological differences between the two dialects of French were as a rule mirrored in the spellings of English loanwords. The earliest borrowings represent the dialectal, Norman type, while loanwords from the Central, or Parisian French, began to come in larger numbers only in the 14th century. (Fisiak 1968: 40) The phonological contrast between the two dialects characterised both consonants and vowels, especially diphthongs. It is to the language of the conquerors that English owes the emergence of the new diphthongs [oi] from Central French and [ui] from Norman French, of which the first survives, while the other became displaced by the Parisian form. Also the members of another such pair with CF [oi] and NF [ei] have left their imprint on the evolution of English pronunciation.

The present study is an effort to reveal the distribution of forms from the two variants of French in Middle English dialects. The discussion has a rather limited scope as it is confined to only three Central French forms (*loyal, royal, voyage*) and their three Anglo-Norman replicas (*leal*, *real*, *viage*) as well as their variants. Thus it aims at presenting a more or less precise account of the temporal and regional conditioning of the variants of the three loanwords as supported by the data from the medieval prose. The study, originally planned to be based on the *Innsbruck corpus of Middle English prose* and the *Corpus of English letters*, had to be confined practically to only the former source since the *Innsbruck Corpus of English letters* supplied mere seven instances of the Middle English forms of the three words under scrutiny (these examples are listed as Appendix after the conclusions). The other sources consulted were standard, and included *the Oxford English dictionary* as well as the *Middle English dictionary*. As regards the two latter data bases an attempt was made to determine to what extent the *Innsbruck corpus* can be used as a single source of information when solving various problems of Middle English, without resorting to the aid of these two dictionaries or other data bases. As regards the utility of the *Innsbruck corpus* the reader may also be referred to Diller's recent paper (2006) on the ICAMET and other corpora.

2. Phonological dimension

In French, the diphthong [ei] developed from the vowel [é] finally and before palatals (Mincoff 1972: 236). In the 12th century Central French the diphthong [ei] became [oi] (>MoF [wa]), while in Norman French it remained unaffected, though sometimes it monophthongised to long open [ɛ:], hence the variation between CF *loial*, *proie*, *voile* and NF *le(i)al*, *prey*, *veil*, etc. Pope (1952: 451) calls attention to the displacement in Anglo-Norman of the dialectal forms with [ei] by those with [oi] of Central French, so that, for instance, *loial* 'loyal' was substituted for earlier *lęal/lęęl* 'leal' and *roial* 'royal' for *ręal/ręęl* 'real'. In general the subsequent contractions in English are determined by the effort to eliminate a hiatus. The effects of such variations are also reflected in Middle English phonology. Apart from these three the list of words with a reduction of the hiatus is longer as here also belong words such as *dean* (contraction of *doyen*, from Lat. *decanus*), *mean(s)* (contraction of *moien*. Lat. *medianus*). The last two, however, as less typical instances are not discussed in this presentation.

The examination of Middle English texts in the *Innsbruck corpus* reveals a lot of variation of the forms corresponding to ModE *loyal*, *royal* and *voyage*, although these words appear with variable frequencies in the particular segments of the *corpus*, the highest incidence belonging to the lemmas REAL/ROYAL, the lowest to LEAL/LOYAL, while the lemmas VIAGE/VOYAGE take an intermediate position as regards the statistics of their occurrence. With reference to the variation of forms of the six lemmas, under item (1) are listed variants of both types of forms of the six words, arranged in alphabetical order. The list also includes several related words, i.e. adverbs, derived nouns and one superlative form of the adjective *royal*:

(1)	Lemma	Variants	Related words
(a)	LEAL	leal, lel(l) lele	lelely, lelly
	LOYAL	loyal	loyally
(b)	REAL	real(l), realle, rial(l)e, rial(l), ryal(l), ryal(l)e	realli, rially, realte, rialte
	ROYAL	roiale, roial(l), roialle, royal(l), royal(l)e	royalest, royalte
(c)	VIAGE	viage (viagis, -es), vyage	
	VOYAGE	voyage	

It should be emphasised here that texts from the *Innsbruck corpus* fail to supply a complete list of the potential variants. The scrutiny of the *OED* and *MED* entries, chiefly referring to poetical texts, will reveal 14th-15th century forms such as:

(2) Scottish **leill(e)** (Barbour's *Bruce* iv. 576, *Sc. Leg. Saints* xxx. Theodera, 154), West Midland **leel(l)** (Langland *Piers Plowman* C. i. 146, *Destruction of Troy* 8800), **uyage** (*Gaw. & Gr. Knt.* 535), or Northern **vaiage** (*Ywaine & Gaw.* 532).

The phonological aspects of the above spelling variability are not completely clear. Of the two classic accounts of English sound change, Luick (1940) and Jordan (1974), neither supplies a satisfactory description of the fates of the words under examination. In Jordan, apart from a brief comment on the form *lel* [ε:] (Jordan 1974: 214), one fails to find any statement concerning the variation. Luick's (1940: 461) account is only a little more substantial because he explains the contracted form *lel* as reflecting the simplification of [ei] in hiatus (cf. OF *leiel* > ME [ε:]), while the forms *rēal*, *rīal* are interpreted there as by-forms.

The most satisfactory account, though scattered throughout the book, is Diensberg's (1985) study on the reception of Romance loanwords in Middle and Early New English, where each of the lemmas is treated separately. On the basis of the material adduced there one can reconstruct the following course of changes in the three words from Latin through French and Anglo-Norman to Middle English:

(3) Lat. legal-is > OF leial > CF loial > ME loial > ModE **loyal**
NF leial > AN/ME lele, lelle, leale, leial(e), lial(e) > ModSc. **leal**

Lat. regal-is > OF reial > CF roial > ME roial > ModE **royal**
NF reial > AN/ME real, rial, ryal //

Lat. [viatic-um] > OF veiage vaiage > CF voiage > ME voiage > ModE **voyage**
NF veiage, vaiage > AN/ME veage, viage //

As seen in (3), only the Parisian forms containing the diphthong [oi] survive in
Standard English. Of the contracted forms it is only *leal* which continues to be
used in Scottish English.

3. Temporal dimension

According to the chronology of the standard historical dictionaries of English
(*OED*, *MED*) the Norman French forms appeared in Middle English around or
after 1300, if reference is made to the manuscript and not to the date when the text
originated. A search among the *OED* entries will give the following results (dates
refer to the original, not to the manuscript):

(4)   LEAL 1300+ *Cursor Mundi* 27847 **Lele** of hert and fre of gyft.
        LOYAL 1531 Elyot *Gov. Proheme* (...) my **loyall** harte and diligent
        endeauour.
              but: > 1400 **loyaltee** (*Rom. Rose* > 1400)

        REAL 1399 Langl. *Rich. Redeles* i. 91 Reffusynge the reule of **realles**
        kynde.
              but > 1350 *Will. Palerne* 1426 **realy**

        ROYAL c1374 Chaucer *Troylus* 435 Myn estat **royal** here I resigne In-to
        hire hond.

        VIAGE c1297 R. Glouc. (*Rolls*) 4920 + 85 toward þys lond þe **veage**
        nome.

        VOYAGE 1477 Caxton *Jason* 26 ...like a **voyager** that had alle the day to
        fore haue **voiaged**.

A more reliable dating is offered in the *MED* where reference is made to both the
manuscript and the date of the origin of a text. As compared with the *OED*, here
the dating is much earlier. It should be noted that the *MED* fails to supply the *oi*-
forms of LOYAL and VOYAGE:

(5)   LEAL a1325 (c1300) *Songs Langtoft* (Cmb Gg.1.1) p. 303: he wende he
        were **liale**, but cf. 1200 *Pipe R.Cum.Wm.Dur.* in *SANT* (1847) 185: Johes.
        Lealeman (surname)

REAL c1330 (?c1300) *Guy*(1) (Auch) 3879: A **real** pauiloun; *Amis* (Auch) 1519: A **real** fest þai gan to hold; *Bevis* (Auch) 164/3480: Þe bredale.. was **riale**, but cf. 1289 *EPNSoc.* 23 (Oxf.) 22: Rewley (place name)

ROYAL c1375 Chaucer *CT.Mk* (Manly-Rickert) B.3341: of the blood roial

VIAGE c1325 (c1300) *Glo. Chron.A* (Clg.A.11) 4112: Euerichone to bar besflet & bes **veiage** nome.

In purely chronological terms, the dating in the two dictionaries is compatible as regards the lemma LEAL since both sources indicate the year 1300 when the word first appeared in English (as said earlier, the *OED* refers to the date of origin, not to that of the manuscript). But the dating of the surname *Lealeman* to 1200 is drastically earlier than the first form of LEAL listed in the *OED*.

Also the *MED* dating of the emergence of the form REAL is much earlier than that in the *OED*, owing to its reference to a place name, *Rewley* (1289), while non-proper nouns in the *MED* are dated to around 50 years later (c1300, date of origin) than those in the *OED* (the adverb *realy* 1350, in *William of Palerne*).

The situation is different with *viage*, as its forms in the *OED* and the *MED*, although they differ in spelling, come from the same author, Robert of Gloucester, and his *Chronicle*, which originated. around 1300. There is also agreement as regards the Parisian forms of REAL which are in both cases adduced from Chaucer (*The Canterbury tales*, *Troilus*), c. 1374/75.

As the next step the *Innsbruck corpus* data are compared with those in the *OED* and the *MED* with the focus on the first occurrences of the above set of words. The relevant dating in the *Corpus* is shown under (6):

(6)   LEAL c1440 *lele The Mirror of St. Edmund* N Lincoln Cath. Libr. Thornton Ms., lf. 197, Northern32/26-27 whils mane will duelle in His **lele** lufe als His awen childyre. Bot als tyte als we twyn fra þat **lele** lufe

a1450 Richard Rolle of Hampole, Yorkshire Writers, ed. Horstmann 153/31 Demesters þat **leal** men dampnid: & delyuerid starke theues

LOYAL 1485 *Paris and Viene* (Caxton); ed. Leach, MacEdward, London 16/13 that geffroy was vaynquysshed **loyally** & wel

REAL c1350+ Mandeville's *Travels*: Bodley Version, < N Oxford Bodl. E Musaeo 116>M ><O 58/22 but it were ayen the **real** dignete of the Soudon EM
ROYAL a1400 *Lollard Sermons*, ed. Cigman. EETS OS 294 (1989)><N

BL Add. 41321; 215/29 in the moost **royallest** wyse

VIAGE c1350+ Mandeville's *Travels*: Bodley Version, <N Oxford Bodl. E
Musaeo 116 and tok myn **viage** thedirward EM

VOYAGE 1420-1500 *The Paston Letters* 60/40 ... for the spede and help
of a **voyage**

This listing of the earliest forms of the six lemmas in question makes it clear that
the use of the *Innsbruck corpus* must be supported by consulting at least the *OED*
and the *MED* and possibly other corpora if our desired goal, i.e. an account of a
history of phonological or lexical processes is to be correct. The relevant
examples in the dictionaries, especially in the *MED*, come from much earlier
periods. Perhaps examining the distribution in the *Innsbruck corpus* texts of items
with higher frequency would bring more positive results.

4. Regional dimension

The tokens of the six lemmas LEAL/LOYAL, REAL/ROYAL and
VIAGE/VOYAGE discussed in the present paper were found in only 32 texts with
confirmed localisation out of the total number of 159 files, this being a rather
modest corpus, especially when we take into account the relatively peripheral
character of these items. It should not come therefore as a surprise that the number
of tokens extracted from the *Innsbruck corpus* was rather small.

In the last section of the paper the texts will be discussed with reference to the
five dialects which these texts represented: East Midland, London, which has a
separate regional specification in the *Innsbruck corpus*, further, West Midland,
South Midland/Southwestern (one text in each), and Northern.

Examples adduced after titles listed were selected from texts containing
contrasting forms coming from Norman French (vowel) and Parisian French
(diphthong [oi]) sources.

4.1 East Midland

(7)

MS date	LEAL	REAL	VIAGE	LOYAL	ROYAL	VOYAGE
Mandeville's *Travels* (1350-1400)	5	1				
Lantern of Life (a1415)	1					
Julian of Norwich's *Revelations* (c1420?)					1	
The *Paston Letters* (1420-1500)	11	7			10	4
Speculum Christiani (c1450)	1					
Lavynham, *A Litil Tretys* (c1450)	4					
The *English Register of Oseney Abbey* (1460)	5					

Capgraves's *Abbrev. of Chronicles* (c1462-63)	5	12
Cely Letters (1472-1488)	6	
Agnus Castus. A Middle Eng. Herbal (1500-99)	1	

Examples:

The Paston Letters v.2 121/6 and horrible treasons ayenst your most **roiale** persone; v. 3 26/5 lyke his Mageste **Ryall**
v. 2 5/3 that the [King did] gete in his secund **viage**;
v. 3 60/40 for the spede and help of a **voyage**

With the exception of the *Paston letters* texts from the East Midland do not confuse the Norman forms and Parisian forms, their majority retaining the chronologically earlier type, i.e. the non-diphthongal variant. Curiously, no instances of either LEAL or LOYAL type are found in the texts examined, which reflects the low frequency of the synonyms of the adjective *legal* in that dialect. The *Corpus* does not supply any evidence of the acceptance of forms with [oi] in the texts from the late 15th century, i.e. shortly before Parisian forms began to dominate in the post-1500 period. The evidence from the London dialect may shed more light on the problem whether acceptance of Parisian forms was correlated with the time transition.

4.2 London

(8)

MS date	LEAL	REAL	VIAGE	LOYAL	ROYAL	VOYAGE
Book of the Foundation of St. *Bartholomew's Church* (c1400)					3	
Chaucer, Boethius, *De Consolatione* *Philosophie* (a1425)		2				
Dicts and Saying of the Philosophers (1450-1500)			3		1	
Four Sons of Aymon (1489/1498)			1		4	2
Dialogues in French and English (c1483)			1			
The Book of the Knight of La Tour-Landry (1483)			2			
Paris and Viene (Caxton) (1485)				1		
Caxton, *Blanchardyn and Eglantine* (c1489)					1	
Le Doctrinal de Sapience (1489)					1	
Caxton's *Eneydos* (1490)			2		4	1
The Tretyse of Loue (1493/94)	3					
Prologues and Epilogues of *William Caxton* (c1500?)	5				1	

Examples:

Dicts and Saying of the Philosophers 177/28 And than come Alexaundre a-yen from his **viage**; 179/r13 he made him to sitt in the sege **roialle**

Four Sons of Aymon I/II II: 493/5 to make his **viage** beyonde see; 396/4 to kepe sege **royall** afore the castell I: 13/31 to accomplyshe hys **voyage**

Paris and Viene (Caxton) 16/13 that geffroy was vaynquysshed **loyally** & wel

Caxton's *Eneydos* 104/31 in the grete **viage**, 29/13 happy of their fleeynge and **voyage**; 125/29 a cepter **royall**

Prologues and Epilogues of William Caxton 102/24 le liure **Royal** that is to say the **ryal** book

The distribution of the older and the new forms in London reflects better the tendencies dominating in 15th century English which extensively borrowed words from Parisian French, simultaneously replacing the older forms from Anglo-Norman. Although Chaucer's *Boethius* contains only the conservative form *real*, in his poetical works the poet employed extensively the form with the diphthong [oi]. The slight prevalence of the Parisian *oi*-forms over the older non-diphthongal ones in Caxton confirms his preference for employing words of Central French origin. However, forms with the diphthong were not yet domesticated well in the language, which is confirmed by Caxton's explaining the sense of the adjective *royal* by adducing the form *ryal*, evidently better known to the public (see examples under 7). It is worth emphasising that the little known text *Paris and Viene*, attributed to Caxton, contains the only occurrence in the *Innsbruck corpus* of the form with [oi] for LOYAL, i.e. the adverb *loyally* (no adjective is found in the *Corpus*). In sum, London appears to have been much more advanced than the rest of the region in promoting the new diphthongal forms, especially by Caxton.

4.3 West Midland, South Midland (9a) and the Southwest (9b)

(9a)

MS date	LEAL	REAL	VIAGE	LOYAL	ROYAL	VOYAGE
3 ME Sermons, the Worcester Chapter						
MS F. 10 (c1400)		5				
E. English Versions of the Gesta Romanorum						
(c1440)		6	1			
Saint Nicholas (c1450)			1			
Three Kings of Cologne (c1450-1500)		2				
Saint George (c1460)		2				

(b)

Lollard Sermons (a1400) [SM]	19	1
A Myrour to Lewde Men and Wymmen (c1400)	1	

Examples:

Royal Sermons 60/268, 270 in so **rial** placis of halles, chaumbris, panteries, boteries, kechenes, and stables, and alle oþere housses of office **real** ynow for kyng

The tokens of the six lemmas in the texts from the westerly areas of England (West Midland, South Midland, Southwest) are here subsumed under one heading as the *Innsbruck corpus* offers only instances of the conservative Norman variant. In the material the only diphthongal form (*royal*) is found in *Lollard sermons* (c1400), a relatively early text. The absence in the Southwest of Parisian French words is not surprising, because Southwestern texts are rather early (c1400), but their absence after 1450 is difficult to explain.

4.4 North

(10)

MS date	LEAL	REAL	VIAGE	LOYAL	ROYAL	VOYAGE
Liber de Diversis Medicinis (c1422-1454)	8					
The English Conquest of Ireland (c1425)						
[Irish]		1				
The Mirror of St. Edmund (c1440)	6					
R.Rolle of Hampole and his						
Followers (a1450)	2				2	
Wisdom of Solomon (a1500) [Sc.]	2					

Examples:

Richard Rolle of Hampole, Yorkshire Writers 153/31 Demesters þat **leal** men dampnid: & delyuerid starke theues; 391/49 and a **royale** crowne scho had one hir hede of gold

It does not come as a surprise that a substantial number of examples of the surviving Anglo-Norman form *leal* can be found in the Northern areas of the British Isles, where this adjective has survived in Scottish English to our times. The Central French forms are only found in Richard Rolle, where one encounters the two tokens of *royal*. In this respect the North must be viewed as a conservative area.

5. Conclusions

The material adduced above (lemmas LEAL, REAL, VIAGE; LOYAL, ROYAL, VOYAGE), though statistically modest in terms of the number of tokens found in the *Innsbruck corpus of Middle English prose*, may nevertheless be helpful in formulating several concluding remarks:

1. With the exception of London and the *Paston letters* in the East Midland no trend is observed for the forms with the diphthong to displace the forms of Norman French (or Anglo-Norman) origin even at the close of the 15th century. The examination of texts from the later period would prove that the process gathered speed only in Early Modern English.

2. From among London writers it was Caxton who introduced forms with [oi] into his language. We should not however disregard Chaucer's early contribution in his poetical works (not part of the *Innsbruck corpus*).

3. The adjectives descending from Lat. *legalis*, i.e. LEAL/LOYAL, are hardly found in the texts from the *Innsbruck corpus*. Only Northern (now Scottish) texts testify to the survival of LEAL at the end of the 15th century and later in Modern Scottish.

4. The few texts from the Western and Southern region contain only the dialectal forms (note the single occurrence of the former Central French adjective *royal*). Equally conservative spellings are found in the North.

5. To obtain reliable diachronic materials, it is advisable that evidence from the *Innsbruck corpus* must be supplemented by the data from other corpora, especially the *Middle English dictionary*.

References

Diensberg, Bernhard
  1985   *Untersuchungen zur phonologischen Rezeption romanischen Lehnguts im Mittel- und Frühneuenglischen. Die Lehnwörter mit mittelenglisch oi/ui und ihre phonologische Rezeption.* (Tübingen Beiträge zur Linguistik 268). Tübingen: Gunter Narr Verlag.
Diller, Hans-Jürgen
  2006   "The decline of the family of *mōd*: ICAMET and other corpora", in: Mair, Christian – Reinhard Heuberger (eds.), 51-64.
Fisiak, Jacek
  1968   *A short grammar of Middle English.* Warszawa: Państwowe Wydawnictwo Naukowe.

Jordan, Richard
  1974   *Handbook of Middle English grammar*. Translated and revised by Eugene J. Crook. The Hague: Mouton.

Luick, Karl
  1940   *Historische Grammatik der englischen Sprache*. Vols. 1-2. Stuttgart: Tauchnitz.

Mair, Christian – Reinhard Heuberger (eds.)
  2006   *Corpora and the history of English: Papers dedicated to Manfred Markus on the occasion of his sixty-fifth birthday*. (Anglistische Forschungen 363). (Heidelberg: Universitätsverlag Winter).

Markus, Manfred (ed.)
  2008   *Innsbruck corpus of Middle English prose*. Innsbruck Computer Archive of Machine-Readable English Texts. University of Innsbruck.

Mincoff, Marco
  1972   *English historical grammar*. Sofia: Naouka i izkustvo.

Murray, James et al. (eds.)
  2002   *Oxford English dictionary*. (2nd ed.). CD-Rom. Oxford: Oxford University Press.

McSparren, Frances (ed.)
  2001   *Middle English dictionary*. Available at: http://ets.umdl.umich.edu/m/mec/

Pope, M. K.
  1952   *From Latin to Modern French with especial consideration of Anglo-Norman. Phonology and morphology*. (Revised ed.). Manchester: Manchester University Press.

Appendix

Additional data from the *Innsbruck corpus of English letters* 2.1 (2009):

L7/14 so faire begynnyng in our present **voiage** (1417)
L3/3 vnto your soueraign highnesse and **riall** power (1418)
L26/6 unto your **roial** mageste doo or devise (1442)
L28/33 Also please it your **roial** Ma_geste (1442)
L26/187/32 on the feld in all this **voyage** (1442)
L73/6 that ys, ij **ryallys** for a li. (1478)
L107/p.233/22 he was a noble man and woldbe a **ryall** ruler.(1503)

On the incorporation of *river* into English

Kinga Sądej-Sobolewska, Academy of Management, [SWSPiZ], Warsaw

ABSTRACT

As a result of a large influx of French borrowings in Middle English, lexical doublets appeared: many loanwords which entered English conveyed meanings already expressed by native words. The rivalry of synonyms led to either a complete loss of one of the two words or a differentiation in their meanings: in most cases it was the Old English word that was displaced.

The paper discusses the semantic development in English of the French loanword *river*, which displaced several Old English words referring to a flowing body of water. *The historical thesaurus of English* lists the following Old English nouns meaning 'river': *wæter, lacu, lagus-tream, ēa, ēastream, flōd, stream,* and *wæterstream*. It seems that the Old English key words denoting a river were *ēa* and *flōd,* which lost their central position in Middle English. The aim of the present paper is to account for the sense changes of the Old English synonyms of *river* after the introduction of this French word.

KEYWORDS: river; Old English; Middle English; lexical rivalry

1. Introduction

Following the Norman Invasion, a large number of words were borrowed from French. The domains of lexicon affected by the foreign influence included religion, government, social hierarchy, army, law, science, art, cooking and fashion, which "mirrored the dominant position held by the Norman élite and their descendants in the religious and secular life of England." (Nielsen 2005: 100-103) Yet, a large proportion of basic word stock, naming everyday concepts and objects, was incorporated into English. As Nielsen (2005: 104) explains, it was the result of linguistic coexistence, the English-French bilingualism of the 13th and 14th centuries. Many foreign words which entered English conveyed meanings already expressed by native words (cf. Baugh and Cable 1978: 179-180), e.g., OE *beorg* (>ModE *barrow*) vs. F *mountaine*, OE *blom(a)* (>ModE *bloom*) and *blostm* (>ModE *blossom*) vs. F *flour* 'flower', OE *denu* vs. F *vāle* 'valley', OE *deor* (>ModE *deer*) vs. F *beste* 'beast', OE *burg* (<ModE *borough*) vs. F *cite* 'city', OE *bliss* vs. F *joie* 'joy', OE *lyft* vs. F *air*, OE *stede* vs. F *place*, OE *deman* (<ModE *deem*) vs. F *jugier* 'judge', OE *miht* (>ModE *might*) vs. F *power*, etc. The rivalry of such lexical doublets led to either a complete loss of one of the two words or a differentiation in their meanings. In most cases it was the Old English word that was displaced. The lexico-semantic rivalry of native and foreign words in Middle English has been discussed in a number of studies, for example, Rynell (1948), Dekeyser and Pauwels (1990), Dekeyser (1996), Wełna (2005), Sądej (2007).

The aim of the present paper is to analyse the lexico-semantic situation which preceded the incorporation of *river* into English. An attempt is made to determine the possible reasons leading to the displacement of the native word. The data for the paper come from the *Oxford English dictionary*, *The dictionary of Old English*, *The dictionary of Old English corpus* and the *Middle English dictionary*.

2. Old English synonyms of *river*

The body of the Old English synonyms of *river* is characterised by a considerable variation with a number of words denoting the running water, i.e. a river. According to *A thesuarus of Old English* and *The historical thesaurus of English*, the meaning 'river' was expressed by such lexical items as *ēa, flōd, lacu, wæter, stream*, as well as by the compounds *lagustream, ēastream wæterstream*. Although classified as near-synonyms, the words enumerated above could not have occupied the same systemic position. In other words, their semantic and contextual value must have revealed at least some diversity to avoid redundancy.

Taking into consideration the frequency of the occurrence provided in *The dictionary of Old English* (*DOE*), the items *flōd* (ca. 600 occurrences) and *ēa* (ca. 500 occurrences) seem to be the main names for a river in Old English. In addition, the high morphological productivity of the two lexemes in question (*DOE* enumerates 24 derivatives of *flōd* and 19 derivatives of *ēa*) indicates their central position among other "*river*-nouns". The remaining items *lacu, wæter, strēam, lagustrēam, ēastrēam wæterstrēam* had a relatively weaker systemic role due to (1) their meaning 'river' being the marginal one, (2) their lower frequency of occurrence, and (3) the limited number of contexts in which they could appear (e.g., only in poetry).

With the biggest number of attestations in *The dictionary of Old English corpus*, *flōd* was a polysemous noun which could assume meanings such as 'the flowing in of the tide' (1a), 'a body of (flowing) water', synonymous with *wæter*, (1b), 'a river, a stream' (1cd), 'water (as opposed to land and other elements)' (1e) and 'flood, deluge' (1f). The translations provided aim to reflect the most probable readings of the discussed item. Consider the examples:

(1a)   …þær com flowende **flod** æfter ebban, lucon lagustreamas.
        '(…) there the flowing in of the tide came after the ebb, the waters formed one mass.'
                                                            (*The battle of Maldon*, l. 65)

(1b)   (...) **flod** wæs adæled under heahrodore (…), wæter of wætrum (…)
        '(…) water was divided under the lofty sky (…), water of waters (…)'
                                        (*Genesis* A, l. 150, Oxford, Bodleian Library, MS Junius 11)

(1c)   (...) lede þæt cyld þæron, & asette hine on anum hreodbedde be þæs
flodes ofre
[cf. Ex: *posuitque intus infantulum et exposuit eum in carecto ripae
fluminis*].
'(...) led the child there and placed him on a reed-bed beside the bank of
the river (...)'
                                        (*Exodus* 2.3, London, BL, MS. Cotton Claudius B.IV)

(1d)   He ofer sæs gesteaðelade hie & ofer **flodas** gearwað ða.
[cf. *Ipse super maria fundauit eam, et super flumina praeparauit illam.*]
'He over the seas established them and over the rivers prepared them.'
                                        (*Vespasian psalter*, Cotton MS Vespasian A.I)

(1e)   (...) we þuruh fyr farað and þuruh **floda** þrym (...)
[cf. *transiuimus per ignem & aquam*].
'(...) we passed through the fire and through the torrent of waters (...)'
                                        (*The Paris psalter*, 65.11)

(1f)   (...) on ðes ilces geares wearð swa micel **flod** on sancte Laurenties
messedæig þæt feola tunes & men weorðan adrencte (...)
'(...) on the same year there was such a great flood on St Lawrence mass
day that many towns and people were submerged (...)'
                                        (*The Anglo-Saxon chronicle*, Oxford, BL, MS. Laud Misc. 636, 1125.32)

OE *flōd* derives from Gmc **flôþu(z* and goes back to the PIE stem **plo-/*pleu-*
"flow, float". Thus, the primary sense of *flōd* was, according to the *OED*, 'the
action of flowing'. In Old English the original meaning underwent the following
semantic changes: (1) specialisation to designate the flowing of a tide (cf. 1a), (2)
metonymy to refer to the body of (flowing) water (cf. 1b) which, in turn, was
restricted to refer to a stream or a river (cf. 1cd), (3) specialisation to 'an
overflowing of a great body of water over land, a deluge' (cf. 1f) resulting in the
development of the meaning which has survived into Modern English. The
meaning 'river' survived until the beginning of the 19th century and the *OED*
provides a citation from Wordsworth as its latest attestation, cf.:

(2)   She will to her peaceful woods Return, and to her murmuring **floods**.
                                        (Wordsworth *The white doe of Rylstone*. II. 225)

As has already been mentioned, the noun *ēa* (cognate with L *aqua*) is the second
most frequently attested name for a river in Old English. Taking into
consideration the fact that 'river' was its sole meaning, a suggestion may be put
forward that *ēa* rather than *flōd* was the key word designating rivers in Old

English. The opinion that *ēa* was the standard word for a major river is voiced in
Gelling and Cole (2000: 14). Consider, for example, the following quotations:

(3a)   Ða sume dæge rad se cyng up be þære **eæ**, & gehawade hwær mon mehte
        þa **ea** forwyrcan, þæt hie ne mehton þa scipu ut brengan. & hie þa swa
        dydon. worhton þa tu geweorc. on twa healfe þære **eas**.
        'Then one day the king rode up by the river and observed where the river
        might be obstructed, that they might not bring out the ship and they did so,
        constructed a fortress on both sides of the river.'
        (*The Anglo-Saxon chronicle* [The Parker chronicle], Cambridge, Corpus
        Christi College, MS 173)

(3b)   (…) swa swa of þære sæ cymð þæt wæter innon ða eorðan (…) cymð
        þonne up æt þæm æwelme, wyrð þonne to broce, þonne to **ea**, þonne
        andlang **ea**, oð hit wyrð eft to sæ.
        '(…) so as the water comes of the sea to the earth (…) then comes up at
        the spring, becomes then a brook, then a river and then along the river, it
        goes again to the sea.'
        (Boethius, *The consolation of philosophy* 34.86.18)

(3c)   Seo Wisle is swyðe mycel **ea**, & hio toliað Witland & Weonodland;
        'The Vistula is a great river and it lies between Witland and Weonodland;'
        (*The Old English Orosius*, 1.16.29)

(3d)   (…) **ea** yðum stronge, and ðer inne wunað feola fisca kyn on floda
        gemonge.
        '(…) strong waves of the river, and many kinds of fish live in the waters.'
        (*The Durham ritual* 3)

The quotations above show that OE *ēa* possessed the meaning 'river'. Example
(3a) indicates that it has two sides ("on twa healfe þære eas"), example (3b)
highlights its "running" character, i.e. the movement of water from the spring
(*æwelme*) to a brook (*broce*) and then to a river (*ēa*) and from a river to the sea
(*sæ*). Example (3c) from Orosius shows that *ēa* was frequently used with
reference to some particular rivers such as the Vistula. Example (3d) contains
both *ēa* and *flōd* and it is clear from the context that the lexemes are not
synonymous as *ēa* means 'a river' while *flōd* is more general and stands for
'water'.

OE *ēa* continued in Middle English as *ē* or *æ*, but few instances of this form
can be found beyond the 12th century, e.g.,

(4a)   & tær iss i þatt illke land An **æ** Saba ʒehatenn.
        (*Ormulum,* line 7091, Oxford, Bodleian Library, MS Junius 1)

(4b)　In are swiðe feire **æ** þer Læire falleð i þa sæ..Brutus i þare hauene læi.
　　　　(Layamon *Brut* line1400, London, BL, MS Cotton Caligula A.9)

The *MED* does not adduce any other attestation of *æ* beyond the 13th century so it seems that it was the time when it was ousted from English. In addition, the type of texts in which this lexical item was used may indicate that it was felt to be obsolete.

　　　Other words that possessed the meaning 'river' in Old English included *lacu*, *wæter*, *strēam*, *lagustrēam*, *ēastrēam wæterstrēam*. Yet, they seem to have occupied a peripheral position with respect to *ēa* and *flōd* due to their limited distribution and the modification of the sense 'river'.

　　　As regards OE *lacu*, the *OED* shows that it is not the ancestor of ME *lac* (<OF *lac* < L *lacus* 'basin, tub, tank, lake, pond'), but it is a separate lexeme deriving from the Proto-Germanic root **lak-* denoting moisture (cf. OE *leccan* 'to water, to moisten', ModE *leach*, *leak*). As shown in the example below, it possessed the meaning 'a small stream of running water' so it appears to have been a hyponym of OE *ēa*, i.e. a type of a river:

(5)　　(…) ondlong ofres þ on Stanford of Stanforda ondlonges þære lace of þære lace suþ be þam heafdon þ on rahweg (…)
　　　　'along the border to Stanford, from Stanford along the stream, of the stream south beside the top to the roe way(…)'
　　　　　　　　(Charter of Eanberht, Uhtred and Ealdred, charter 55)

Thus, as indicated by the *OED* and *A concise Anglo-Saxon dictionary*, OE *lacu* possessed the meaning 'stream'. However, Bosworth and Toller's *An Anglo-Saxon dictionary* (*A-SD*) does not mention this meaning at all, glossing it as 'a pool, pond, piece of water, lake', which links OE *lacu* with ModE *lake*. Quotations from charters and bounds seem to illustrate the meaning 'lake', though in many cases it is difficult to decide on the actual meaning of the word in question with absolute certainty, e.g.,

(6a)　Ðonne gæþ sio mearc forþ andlang bliþan west oþ þæt seo **lacu** utscyt on bliþan wiþ ufan stan bricgge.
　　　　'Then this border goes forth along … west to the stream runs out on … with the stone bridge above.'
　　　　　　　　(Charter of King Edmund, charter 495)

(6b)　Andlang broces ut on temese þ forþ mid streme oþ geafling **lace** andlang **lace**.
　　　　'Along the brook out on the Thames forwards with the stream up to *geafling* lake, along the lake.'
　　　　　　　　(Charter of King Eadwig, charter 657)

In the example (6a) *lacu* is followed by the verb *utscyt* 'runs out' and thus it seems to designate running water. In addition, the charter mentions the stone bridge over *lacu*, which indicates the reading 'stream, river' rather than 'lake'. However, the meaning of *lace* in (6b) is doubtful as it can stand for a stream as well as a lake. Gelling and Cole (2000: 19) indicate that OE *lacu* meant 'small, slow-moving stream, side-channel'. Due to the homonymy with ME *lac*, OE *lacu* was ousted from Standard English and survived only dialectally (southern English), often with a slightly modified meaning 'a channel for water'. One of its last records in English dates back to the late 19th century and can be found in the *Glossary of words in use in Cornwall*:

(7)   *Lake*, a small stream of running water.

(Courtney and Couch: 91)

Another Old English word with the potential meaning 'river' was *wæter*. Incidentally, its primary meaning was that of 'the liquid of which seas, lakes, and rivers are composed, and which falls as rain and issues from springs', glossing L *aqua*, which is the sense found in Modern English. However, there are some attestations of the metonymic extension of OE *wæter* in which it was used with reference to the bodies of water such as lakes or rivers, but deciding about its actual meaning is in many cases impossible, cf.:

(8a)   Of blaca lace andlang **wætres** on costices mylne.
        'Of the black stream/lake along to the *costices* mill.'
                          (Charter of King Edgar, charter 695)

(8b)   (…) þa fixas, þe synd on þam flode, acwelað & þa **wæteru** forrotiað (…)
        [cf. Ex: *pisces quoque qui sunt in fluvio morientur*]
        '(…) the fish which are in the river, die and pollute the water (…)'
                          (*Exodus* 7.18 London, BL, MS. Cotton Claudius B.IV)

(8c)   (…) ne geseah ic nænne man buton þe oððe wildeor oþþe æniges cynnes nyten, siððan ic Iordanen þæt **wæter** oferferde.
        '(…) I did not see any man, only the wild beast or small animals of any kind, when I passed Jordan the river.'
                          (Ælfric's *Lives of saints* 23 (Mary of Egypt) 591)

The meaning 'river' of OE *wæter* seems to have been peripheral and in many cases doubtful, for example in (8a). If the Old English text is a translation from Latin (8b), we can see that *wæter* glosses L *fluvius* 'current, water, stream, river', but the conclusion that in this example it acutally means 'a river' would be far-fetched. In quotations such as (8c), the meaning 'river' is doubtless because *wæter* is in apposition to the Jordan and it proves that the item in question could be used with reference to rivers.

The onomastic evidence also does not provide us with a clear answer, for example Ekwall (1960: 501) explains that *Waterden* (<ME *Waterdenna*) means 'valley with stream or lake'. However, Jacobsson (1997: 32-33) explains that *wæter* was most frequently used with reference to the substances or bodies of water collectively, but it could also denote streams and rivers, e.g., *Freshwater*. A similar hypothesis is put forward in Gelling and Cole (2000: 30) who explain that *wæter* was "(...) an alternative to *mere* ('pond, lake, pool') in the names of some of the lakes of the Lake District" and that it was sometimes used with reference to some ancient river-names.

As regards OE *strēam*, most of the citations from Old English texts highlight the meaning 'stream, current, flowing water', but some of its uses exemplify the sense 'river' as well, e.g.,

(9a)   Ofer **iordanen ðone stream** (L. *trans. Jordanem*)
        'Over Jordan the river'
        (*Lindisfarne gospels* John i. 28, British Library, MS Cotton Nero D.IV)

(9b)   (...) hit gelumpe on Romebyrig, þæt **Tifrestream** wæs upp gangende & swa swiðe weaxende ofer þa weallas & in ðære byrig þa mæstan land abysgodon.
        '(...) it happened in Rome the Tiber river went up and grew so much over the walls and filled up the most land in the town.'
        (Gregory the Great dialogues, *Dialogue* 3 19.220.8)

(9c)   (...) ða wæs on þa tid Æðelbyrht cyning haten on Centrice, & mihtig: he hæfde rice oð gemæro **Humbre streames**, se tosceadeð suðfolc angelþeode & norðfolc (...)
        '(...) it was in the time when King Æthelbyrht ruled in Kent, and mighty: he had his kingdon from the boundaries of the river Humber, which divides the English people into southern and northern (...)'
        (Bede *The Old English version of Bede's ecclesiastical history of the English people*, 1 14.56.25)

The quotations (9abc) indicate that *stream* could designate a river in Old English as it appears in some river names (the *Jordan*, the *Tiber*, the *Humber*). Yet, the frequency of occurrence of the sense 'river' is too low to level it with *ēa* or *flōd*.

The three compound words *ēastrēam*, *lagustrēam*, *wæterstrēam* occupied a much weaker position within the stock of Old English synonyms of *river* due to their low frequency of occurrence and a limited distribution in Old English texts. OE *ēastrēam* (10ab) possessed the meaning 'a stream, river, current' and, according to the *DOE*, is attested only 5 times, 3 times in poetry and 2 in charters. The lexical item *lagustrēam* could assume such meanings as 'a sea, stream, river, water', according to the *A-SD*. It was recorded 7 times in *The dictionary of Old English corpus*, mainly in poetry (e.g., *The pheonix, The battle of Maldon*, Riddle 3). The quotation (10c), the fragment describing the Noah's Ark, illustrates the meaning 'water', which seems to have been the primary sense of *lagustrēam*, while (10d) shows that it could also designate a river (the Danube). The lexeme *wæterstrēam* is glossed in the *A-SD* as 'a stream of water' and such meaning appears to be recorded in the quotation (10e). Consider the examples:

(10a)   Land wæron freorig cealdum cylegicelum, clang wæteres þrym ofer eastreamas, is brycgade blæce brimrade.
        'The lands were frozen with cold icicles, the power of waters clung together in the river-currents, ice bridged over the black sea.'
                    (*Andreas* line1259-1261, Vercelli, Cathedral Library, MS CXVII)

(10b)   (…) of þan healan on hastinges lace, andlang lace on þone **eastream**.
        '(…) from the stone to the Hastings stream, along the stream to the river.'
                                      (Charter of King Edgar, charter 678)

(10c)   (…) he gelædde ofer **lagustreamas** maðmhorda mæst, mine <gefræge>;
        on feorhgebeorh foldan hæfde eallum eorðcynne ece lafe (…)
        '(…) he led the treasure-hoard, all creatures of the earth, everlasting legacy over the waters, as I have heard, to the refuge of the earth (…)'
                          (*Exodus*, line 367, London, BL, MS. Cotton Claudius B.IV)

(10d)   Sume healfcwice flugon on fæsten ond feore burgon æfter stanclifum, stede weardedon ymb Danubie. Sume drenc fornam on **lagostreame** lifes æt ende.
        'Some half-dead fled to the fortress and distant towns in the rocks, the place protected by the Danube. Some drowned in the water.'
                        (*Elene*, lines 133-137, Vercelli, Cathedral Library, MS CXVII)

(10e)   He **wæterstreamas** wende to blode (…) [cf. L *convertit in sanguinem flumina*]
        'He changed rivers into blood (…)'
                                    (*The Paris psalter*, psalm 77, line 123)

The brief discussion of the body of the Old English synonyms of *river* shows that they were rather vague. The major word designating a river was *ēa*, but its phonological shape made it a likely candidate for replacement. The monophthongisation taking place in Late Old English would change it into *ē* or *æ* which would constitute a form which is too weak phonetically to belong to the basic word stock. Other Old English words referring to a river were polysemous, the sense 'river' being the peripheral one and thus subject to deletion.

3. Incorporation of *river* into Middle English

The noun *river* was borrowed from Anglo-French (<OF *riviere* > pop.L **rīparia* 'a riverbank, seashore, river' < L *rīpa* 'a bank'). Thus, etymologically it was the name of the land bordering upon a body of water, which later, by metonymic extension, came to be used with reference to water flowing in a channel demarcated by this land. This word is also found in Dutch (*rivier*), ?German (*Revier*) and Danish (*revier, rever*), but only in English it managed to become the major word for 'a copious stream of water flowing in a channel towards the sea, a lake, or another stream' (*OED*).

As indicated in the *OED* and the *MED*, the first attestations of *river* in English date back to the turn of the 14th century, e.g.,

(11a)   Gret plente hii founde of fiss,...
Of wodes & of **riuers**, as is in e contreie.
(Robert of Gloucester *Metrical chronicle* (Rolls) 487)

(11b)   Huy wenden forth to þe **Riuer**, þare huy founden þat watur cler.
(*South English legendary, Infancy of Christ* (LdMisc 108) 307)

(11c)   Þe leuedi was sett onland To play bi þe **riuere**.
(*Sir Tristrem* (Auchinleck MS) 1884)

(11d)   Faile shul þe flodis, and thynned & dried shul ben þe **ryueres** of water..nakened shal ben..þe **ryueres** fro þer welle.
(*Wycliffite Bible* (1) (Bod 959) Is.19.6,7)

The quotations above show that ME *river* was used with reference not only to rivers (11abc), but also to the body of water in general (11d). Yet, this meaning seems to be the result of fluctuations at the periphery of the semantic spectrum of the word, rather than any stable development.

In order to attempt at answering the question of possible reasons for the incorporation of *river* in English, it is necessary to realise that in fact Middle English lacked any good name for a river. The main word *ēa* acquired a monophthongal pronunciation *ē/æ* and it is obvious that a single sound could not be used as a meaningful item too long (cf. OE **ǣ** 'law'). Another important word, *flōd*, still possessed the meaning 'river' in Middle English, but it was never its primary sense, which only precipitated the loss of this meaning. The rest of the historical synonyms of *river* (*lacu, wæter, strēam, lagustrēam, ēastrēam wæterstrēam*) were never salient representatives of their category due to their limited distribution, so they could not compete with a foreign element. If we confront such a linguistic situation with the continuous pressure of French on English, the replacement of native words by one loanword seems to be justified.

4. Conclusions

On the basis of data from the *DOE*, the *OED* and the *MED*, the following tentative conclusions can be drawn as regards the incorporation if *river* into English:

(1)   The Old English body of the synonyms of *river* was characterised by a relative vagueness, with a number of words possessing the meaning 'river'. Such lack of transparency could have facilitated and accelerated the introduction of a foreign lexeme into English.

(2)   The phonological weakening of OE *ēa* and the polysemy of *flōd*, the primary nouns designating a river, contributed to the necessity of finding a new word. Since there are hardly any attestations of *ēa* beyond Old English it must be assumed that English lacked a satisfactory name for a river and that this semantic gap was filled by the loanword.

(3)   The first attestation of *river* in English dates back to the late 13th century (Robert of Gloucester's *Chronicle*), which roughly corresponds with the last recorded instances of OE *ēa*. The process of substitution of loanwords for native elements was gradual, but as Nielsen (2005: 9) estimates "the strongest adoption was in the years 1251-1400".

References

INTERNET SOURCES

Bosworth, Joseph – T. Northcote Toller (eds.)
    An Anglo-Saxon dictionary. Available at: http://lexicon.ff.cuni. cz/texts/oe_bosworthtoller_about.html (date of access: 12th September 2009).
Courtney, Margaret – Thomas Couch
    A glossary of words in use in Cornwall. Available at: http://www. archive.org/details/glossarywordsin00quilgoog (date of access: 28th February 2010).
Kay, Christian (ed.)
    The historical thesaurus of English. Available at: http://libra.englang. arts.gla.ac.uk/historicalthesaurus/ (date of access: 5th September 2009).
McSparran, Frances (ed.)
    Middle English dictionary (part of the *Middle English compendium*). Available at: http://ets.umdl.umich.edu/m/med (date of access: 12th September 2009).

A thesaurus of Old English. University of Glasgow. Available at : http://libra.englang. arts.gla.ac.uk/oethesaurus/ (date of access: 5th September 2009).

ELECTRONIC SOURCES

Cameron, Angus (et al.)
    2003   *The dictionary of Old English on CD-ROM.* (A-F). Toronto: University of Toronto.
Healey, Antonette diPaolo (ed.)
    1998   *The dictionary of Old English corpus.* Toronto: University of Toronto.

DICTIONARIES

Clark Hall, John R.
    1960   *A concise Anglo-Saxon dictionary.* (4th edition). Toronto, Buffalo, London: University of Toronto Press.
Ekwall, Eilert
    1960   *The concise Oxford dictionary of English place-names.* (4th edition). Oxford: Clarendon Press.
Simpson, John – Edmund Weiner (eds.)
    1989   *The Oxford English dictionary online.* Available at: www.oed.com (date of access: November 2009 – February 2010)

SECONDARY SOURCES

Baugh, Albert C. – Thomas Cable
    1978   *A history of English.* Englewood Cliffs, NJ: Prentice Hall, Inc.
Dekeyser, Xavier
    1996   "Loss of prototypical meanings in the history of English semantics or semantic redeployment", *Leuvense Bijdragen* 85: 283-291.
Dekeyser, Xavier – Luc Pauwels
    1990   "The demise of the Old English heritage and lexical innovation in Middle English. Two intertwined developments", *Leuvense Bijdragen* 79: 1-23.
Jacobsson, Mattias
    1997   *Welles, meres, and pools. Hydronymic terms in Anglo-Saxon landscape.* (Acta Universitatis Upsaliensis. Studia Anglica Upsaliensia 98). Uppsala: Upsaliensis S. Academiae.
Gelling, Margaret – Ann Cole
    2000   *The landscape of place names.* Stamford: Shaun Tyas.

Nielsen, Hans Frede
    2005   *A journey through the history of English language in England and America.* Vol. 2. *From dialect to standard: English in England 1154-1776.* Odense: University Press of Southern Denmark.

Rynell, Alarik
    1948   *The rivarly of Scandinavian and native synonyms in Middle English, especially* taken *and* niman, *with an excursus on* nema *and* taka *in Old Scandinavian.* (Lund Studies in English 13). Lund: Gleerup.

Sądej, Kinga
    2007   "The rivalry of native words and their French synonyms in Middle English: OE *beorg* and F *mountaine*", in: Stalmaszczyk, Piotr – Iwona Witczak-Plisiecka (eds.), 263-275.

Stalmaszczyk Piotr – Iwona Witczak-Plisiecka (eds.)
    2007   *PASE studies in linguistics.* Łódź: Wydawnictwo Uniwersytetu Łódzkiego.

Wełna, Jerzy
    2005   "*Nim* or *take*? A competition between two high frequency verbs in Middle English", *Studia Anglica Posnaniensia* 41: 53-69.

Studies in English Medieval Language and Literature

Edited by Jacek Fisiak

Vol.   22 Masachiyo Amano / Michiko Ogura / Masayuki Ohkado (eds.): Historical Englishes in Va-
            rieties of Texts and Contexts. The Global COE Program, International Conference 2007.
            2008.

Vol.   23 Ewa Ciszek: Word Derivation in Early Middle English. 2008.

Vol.   24 Andrzej M. Łęcki: Grammaticalisation Paths of *Have* in English. 2010.

Vol.   25 Osamu Imahayashi / Yoshiyuki Nakao / Michiko Ogura (eds.): Aspects of the History of
            English Language and Literature. Selected Papers Read at SHELL 2009, Hiroshima. 2010.

Vol.   26 Magdalena Bator: Obsolete Scandinavian Loanwords in English. 2010.

Vol.   27 Anna Cichosz: The Influence of Text Type on Word Order of Old Germanic Languages.
            A Corpus-Based Contrastive Study of Old English and Old High German. 2010.

Vol.   28 Jacek Fisiak / Magdalena Bator (eds.): Foreign Influences on Medieval English. 2011.

www.peterlang.de